Practical Haskell

A Real-World Guide to Functional Programming

Third Edition

Alejandro Serrano Mena

Apress®

Practical Haskell: A Real-World Guide to Functional Programming

Alejandro Serrano Mena
Utrecht, The Netherlands

ISBN-13 (pbk): 978-1-4842-8580-0   ISBN-13 (electronic): 978-1-4842-8581-7
https://doi.org/10.1007/978-1-4842-8581-7

Managing Director, Apress Media LLC: Welmoed Spahr
Acquisitions Editor: Steve Anglin
Development Editor: James Markham
Coordinating Editor: Gryffin Winkler

Cover designed by eStudioCalamar

Cover image by Shubham Dhage on Unsplash (www.unsplash.com)

Distributed to the book trade worldwide by Apress Media, LLC, 1 New York Plaza, New York, NY 10004, U.S.A. Phone 1-800-SPRINGER, fax (201) 348-4505, e-mail orders-ny@springer-sbm.com, or visit www.springeronline.com. Apress Media, LLC is a California LLC and the sole member (owner) is Springer Science + Business Media Finance Inc (SSBM Finance Inc). SSBM Finance Inc is a **Delaware** corporation.

For information on translations, please e-mail booktranslations@springernature.com; for reprint, paperback, or audio rights, please e-mail bookpermissions@springernature.com.

Apress titles may be purchased in bulk for academic, corporate, or promotional use. eBook versions and licenses are also available for most titles. For more information, reference our Print and eBook Bulk Sales web page at http://www.apress.com/bulk-sales.

Any source code or other supplementary material referenced by the author in this book is available to readers on GitHub (https://github.com/Apress). For more detailed information, please visit http://www.apress.com/source-code.

Printed on acid-free paper

To Elena, and my two boys Quique and Julio,
who bring me joy every single day.

Table of Contents

About the Author

 **Alejandro Serrano Mena** has more than a decade of experience as a developer, trainer, and researcher in functional programming, with an emphasis in Haskell and related languages. He holds a PhD from Utrecht University on the topic of error message customization in compilers. Most of his work relates to tools helping programmers to write more correct and reliable code, including static analyzers and formal verification tools.

Alejandro is an active member of the community. He maintains several open source projects, has written three books on different levels about Haskell, and co-hosts a podcast on the same topics. He also gives talks and conducts workshops at different conferences, spreading the love and the techniques of functional programming.

About the Technical Reviewer

Germán González-Morris is a polyglot software architect/engineer with more than 20 years in the field, with knowledge in Java(EE), Spring, Haskell, C, Python, and JavaScript, among others. He works with web-distributed applications. Germán loves math puzzles (including reading Knuth) and swimming. He has tech-reviewed several books, including an application container book (Weblogic), as well as titles covering various programming languages (Haskell, TypeScript, WebAssembly, Math for coders, and regexp). You can find more details about him at his blog site (`https://devwebcl.blogspot.com/`) or Twitter account (`@devwebcl`).

Acknowledgments

These acknowledgments have been transported almost unchanged from the first to the second and now the third edition of the book. It is great to see how the people that supported you on your first writing adventure are still around and even more supportive than the first time.

First of all, I would like to acknowledge the great work of the technical reviewer and the editorial board. Their comments and suggestions have been extremely valuable for making the book better and more helpful. Jean-Philippe Moresmau did a great job in the first edition; this time, Germán has taken his witness, and the result is even better.

Writing a book is a very rewarding task, but it's also quite a consuming one. For those times where the mood goes sour, there has not been anything better than the support that Elena brought to me. She was there while I was thinking, refining the examples, and reviewing the text one more time.

My family and my friends have also encouraged me the entire time, so a bit of thanks to all of them too. My parents Carmen and Julián deserve a very special mention: they've supported me during every single project and, as crazy as it may sound, throughout my whole life. They bought me the first computer I worked with, which was the computer I started programming in an old Visual Basic environment. It's fair to say that without their help, you wouldn't be reading this book.

Being surrounded by people who share your passion is the best way to stay motivated to learn and communicate what you know; the colleagues I've worked with at Utrecht University and 47 Degrees are a prime example. Many ideas in this book have their roots on those days as a PhD student.

The entire Haskell community is wonderful. Having great mailing lists and IRC rooms full of (quite clever!) people always willing to help encourages you to be curious and to learn more. Every single library and compiler discussed in this book has been carefully crafted by this community: they are the reason why Haskell is such a great language.

Introduction

Functional programming is gathering momentum. Mainstream languages such as Java and C# are adopting features from this paradigm; and languages such as Haskell, Scala, Rust, Clojure, or OCaml, which embody functional programming from the very beginning, are being used in the industry. Haskell is a noise-free, pure functional language with a long history, having a huge number of library contributors and an active community. This makes Haskell a great tool for both learning and applying functional programming.

Why You Should Learn Functional Programming

The rise in functional programming comes from two fronts. Nowadays, most applications are heavily concurrent or need to be parallelized to perform better. Think of any web server that needs to handle thousands of connections at the same time. The way you express the intent of your code using Haskell makes it easier to move from a single-threaded application to a multithreaded one at a negligible cost.

Apart from becoming more concurrent, applications are becoming much larger. You would like your development environment to help you catch bugs and ensure interoperation between all modules of your system. Haskell has a very strong type system, which means that you can express a wide range of invariants in your code, which are checked at compile time. Many of the bugs, which previously would be caught using tests, are now completely forbidden by the compiler. Refactoring becomes easier, as you can ensure that changes in your code do not affect those invariants.

Learning functional programming will put you in a much better position as a developer. Functional thinking will continue permeating through mainstream programming in the near future. You'll be prepared to develop larger and faster applications that bring satisfaction to your customers.

Why You Should Read This Book

This book focuses both on the ideas underlying and on the practicalities of Haskell programming. The chapters show you how to apply functional programming concepts in real-world scenarios. They also teach you about the tools and libraries that Haskell provides for each specific task. Newcomers to functional programming will not be the only ones who will benefit from reading this book. Developers of Scala, Clojure, Lisp, or ML will also be able to see what sets Haskell apart from other languages.

The book revolves around the project of building a web-based storefront. In each of the five parts, the focus is on a subsystem of this store: representing clients and products in memory, data mining (including parallelization and concurrency), persistent storage, discounts and offers, and the general architecture of the application. The topics have been carefully selected for you to get a glimpse of the whole Haskell ecosystem.

Source Code

You can download the source code used in this book from `github.com/apress/practical-haskell-3e`.

PART I

First Steps

CHAPTER 1

Going Functional

Welcome to the world of Haskell! Before looking too deeply at the language itself, you will learn about what makes Haskell different from other languages and what benefits come with those differences. Haskell belongs to the family of functional languages, a broad set that includes ML, Lisp, Scala, and Clojure. If you have a background mostly in imperative or object-oriented languages, such as C, C++, or Java, you will see which of the ideas present in those languages can be transported into the functional world. If you already have experience with functional languages, you will see how other features in Haskell, such as lazy evaluation and type classes, make this language different from any other.

This book assumes some previous experience with the functional paradigm, regardless of the language, but not with Haskell. Also, some minimal practice with the shell or console is required.

After introducing Haskell, I will review how to use GHCUp to manage your Haskell installations. Finally, you will take your first steps with the language in the Glasgow Haskell Compiler (GHC) interpreter, a powerful tool that executes expressions in an interactive way. Throughout the book, you will develop parts of a time machine web store; as with many things in life, the best way to learn Haskell is by writing Haskell programs!

Why Haskell?

If you are reading this book, it means you are interested in learning Haskell. But what makes this language special? Its approach to programming can be summarized as follows:

- Haskell belongs to the family of *functional* languages.

- It embodies in its core the concept of *purity*, separating the code with side effects from the rest of the application.

© Alejandro Serrano Mena 2022
A. Serrano Mena, *Practical Haskell*, https://doi.org/10.1007/978-1-4842-8581-7_1

- The evaluation model is based on *laziness*.

- *Types* are *statically checked* by the compiler. Also, Haskell features a type system that is much stronger and expressive than usual.

- Its approach to polymorphism is based on *parametricity* (similar to generics in Java and C#) and *type classes*.

In the rest of this section, you will understand what the terms in this list mean and their implications when using Haskell. Also, you will get a broad view of the entire Haskell ecosystem in a typical distribution: the compiler, the libraries, and the available tools.

Why Pure Functional Programming?

Functional programming is one of the styles, or paradigms, of programming. A programming paradigm is a set of concepts shared by different programming languages. For example, Pascal and C are part of the imperative paradigm, and Java and C++ mix the imperative paradigm with the object-oriented one. The fundamental emphasis of functional programming is the empowerment of *functions* as *first-class citizens*. This means functions can be manipulated like any other type of data in a program. A function can be passed as an argument to another function, returned as a result, or assigned to a variable. This ability to treat functions as data allows a higher level of abstraction and therefore more opportunities for reuse.

For example, consider the task of iterating through a data structure, performing some action on each element. In an object-oriented language, the implementer of the structure would have surely followed the iterator pattern, and you as a consumer would write code similar to the following Java code:

```
Iterator it = listOfThings.iterator();
while (it.hasNext()) {
    Element e = it.next();
    action(e); // perform the action
}
```

As you can see, there is a lot of boilerplate code in the example. In Haskell, you would use the map function, which takes as its argument the action to perform on each element. The corresponding code is as follows:

```
map action listOfThings
```

The code now is much more concise, and the actual intention of the programmer is explicit from the use of the map function. Furthermore, you prevent any possible issue related to applying the iterator pattern poorly because all the details have been abstracted in a function. Actually, a function such as map is common in functional code, which gives you confidence that any bug in its implementation will be found quickly.

Performing the same task in Java (up to version 7) requires, on the provider side, you to create an interface that contains the function that will perform the operation. Then, on the user side, you need to implement that interface through a class or use an anonymous class. This code will be much longer than the one-line version you saw earlier. In fact, new languages like Scala or Kotlin and updated versions of Java (from version 8 on), C++, and C# are embracing functional concepts and allow you to write code similar to the previous line.

In Haskell, a piece of code consists of *expressions*, which are evaluated in a similar fashion to mathematical expressions. In an imperative language, methods consist of statements that change a global state. This is an important distinction because in an imperative program the same piece of code may have different results depending on the initial state when it is executed. It's important to notice here that elements outside of the program control (known as *side effects*), such as input and output, network communication, and randomness, are also part of this global state that may change between executions of the same function.

Expressions in Haskell cannot have side effects by default; these expressions are called *pure*. A common misunderstanding about functional programming is that it disallows any kind of change to the outer state. This is not true; side effects are possible in Haskell, but the language forces the programmer to separate the pure, side effect–free parts from the "impure" ones.

The main benefits of purity are the improved ability to reason about the code and an easier approach for testing the code. You can be sure that the outcome of a pure function depends only on its parameters and that every run with the same inputs will give the same result. This property is called *referential transparency*, and it's the foundation for applying formal verification techniques, as you will see in Chapter 15.

Pure functions are easier to compose because no interference comes to life in their execution. Actually, the evaluation of pure expressions is not dependent on the order in which it is done, so it opens the door to different *execution strategies* for the same piece of code. This is taken advantage of by the Haskell libraries providing parallel and concurrent execution and has even been used for scheduling code in a GPU in the Accelerate library.

By default, Haskell uses an execution strategy called *lazy evaluation*. Under laziness, an expression is never evaluated until it is needed for the evaluation of a larger one. Once it has been evaluated, the result is saved for further computation, or it's discarded if it's not needed in any other running code. This has an obvious benefit because only the minimal amount of computation is performed during program execution, but it also has drawbacks because all the suspended expressions that have not yet been evaluated must be saved in memory. Lazy evaluation is powerful but can become tricky, as you will see in Chapter 5.

Why Strong Static Typing?

Type systems come in various formats in almost all programming languages. A *type system* is an abstraction that categorizes the values that could appear during execution, tagging them with a so-called type. These types are normally used to restrict the possible set of actions that could be applied to a value. For example, it may allow concatenating two strings but forbid using the division operator between them.

This tagging can be checked, broadly speaking, at two times: at execution time (*dynamic* typing), which usually comes in languages with looser typing and allows implicit conversions between things such as integers and strings, or at the moment of compilation (*static* typing), in which case programs must be validated to be completely well typed in terms of the language rules before generating the target output code (usually machine code or bytecode) and being allowed to run. Haskell falls into this second category: all your programs will be type checked before they are executed. Within statically typed languages, some of them, such as Java or C#, need to perform extra type checking at runtime. In contrast, once a Haskell program has been compiled, no more type checks have to be done, so performance is vastly increased.

Haskell's type system is very *strong*. Strength here means the number of invariants that can be caught at compile time before an error materializes while the application is running. This increases the confidence in code that is type checked, and it's common to hear the following in Haskell circles: "Once it compiles, it works." This strong typing gives rise to a way of programming dubbed *type-oriented programming*. Basically, programmers know the type of the function they are developing and have a broad idea of the structure of the code. Then, they "fill in the holes" with expressions from the surrounding environment that fit into it. This approach has actually been formalized, and there is another language similar to Haskell, called Agda, which comes with an interactive programming environment that helps in filling in the holes and even does so automatically if only one option is available at one place.

In Chapters 13 and 15, I will move a bit from Haskell to Idris, a language with a similar syntax that features *dependent typing*. Dependent typing is an even stronger form of type checking, where you can actually express invariants such as "If I concatenate a list of n elements to a list with m elements, I get back a list with n+m elements" or "I cannot get the first element of an empty list." Then, you will see how some of these techniques can be transferred as patterns into Haskell.

The last difference in Haskell with respect to typing comes from polymorphism. The problem is twofold. First, you want to write functions on lists without caring about the type of the elements contained in them. This is known as *parametric polymorphism*, and you will explore it in Chapter 3. In other cases, you want to express the fact that some types allow some specific operations on their values. For example, the idea of applying a function to all elements in a list, as you did before with map, can be generalized into the concept of having an operation that applies a function to all elements in some data structure, such as a tree or a graph. The solution here is called *type classes*, which groups different types with a common interface. You will look at it in Chapter 4, where you will also realize that this concept is a very high-level one that allows for expressing several abstract ideas (functors, monads) and that gives an interesting flavor to Haskell code.

The Haskell Ecosystem

Until now, I have spoken only about Haskell the language. But the benefits of Haskell come not only from the language but also from the large and growing set of tools and libraries that can be used with the language.

Several compilers for Haskell are available, which usually take the name of a city: GHC (from Glasgow), UHC (from Utrecht), and so on. Of those, GHC is usually taken as the standard, and it's the one with the largest number of features. At the moment of writing, only GHC is actively maintained. You will follow this path and will work with GHC throughout the book.

Like any other popular programming language, Haskell has an online repository of libraries. It is called Hackage, and it's available at `http://hackage.haskell.org/`. A stable subset of Hackage, known as Stackage, is available at `www.stackage.org/`. Both repositories integrate seamlessly with Cabal and Stack, the two alternative building tools for Haskell projects. In Hackage, you can find libraries ranging from bioinformatics to game programming, window managers, and much more.

Apart from GHC and Cabal, in the book you will look at some tools that aim to help developers write better code faster. The first one will be the GHC profiler; you will learn about it in Chapter 5 to detect space and time leaks. You will also look at Hoogle and Haddock, which are used to browse and create documentation. In Chapter 14, you will use the UU Attribute Grammar System to help you build domain-specific languages.

The History of Haskell

Haskell is usually considered the successor of the Miranda programming language, which was one of the most important lazy functional programming languages in the 1980s. However, at that time, lots of other languages of the same kind existed in the wild. That made it difficult for researchers to have a common base in which to perform experiments in this paradigm. So, by the end of that decade, they decided to build a completely new language that would become the groundwork for that research.

During the 1990s, several versions of the language were produced. During this time, Haskell evolved and incorporated some of the features that give the language its particular taste, such as type classes and monads for managing input and output. In 1998, a report defined Haskell 98, which was taken as the standard for any compliant Haskell compiler. This is the version targeted by most library developers.

However, new ideas from researchers and compiler writers were integrated into Haskell compilers, mostly in GHC. Some of these extensions became widely used, which made the case for a revised Haskell standard, which came out in 2010.

As the language has become more popular, more extensions have been added to GHC and other compilers, and these features usually can be switched on or off at the developer's will. As a result, a more disciplined schedule has been created for issuing revised standards on a timely basis. In 2022, a new GHC-specific version of the language came to light, giving a standard name to the most commonly used set of extensions in the language by that time.

Your Working Environment

At this point, you are probably feeling the urge to try Haskell on your own computer. The first step for this is, of course, to have a working Haskell installation in your system. Following the lead of other communities like Rust or Common Lisp, the Haskell community has created a specific tool, *GHCUp*, to manage your Haskell environment.

Regardless of your operating system, the first step is to go to `www.haskell.org/ghcup/`. You should see a big box with a command you should type into your terminal. This command is different depending on your system, but the web page tries to figure out which is yours based on the information provided by your browser. Once the installation is over, you have a working compiler, which is enough to follow the next few sections.

Note   Be sure to install the developer tools for your system before installing GHCUp. In Ubuntu or Debian, you can install the `build-essential package`; in Mac, the *Xcode Command Line Tools* should be enough for our purposes.

Shortly, you're going to need some additional tools to build projects, either Cabal or Stack. You can get them using GHCUp by running

```
$ ghcup install cabal
$ ghcup install stack
```

At any point in time, you can ask GHCUp which is the status of your Haskell environment by running `ghcup list`. The output shows all available versions of every tool, with a single check for those which are installed and a double check for those marked as default. The tool itself comes with a list of recommended versions, which are marked with a `recommended` tag in that list. If a new recommended version is released, the tool tells you how to perform the upgrade (usually by simply running `ghcup install tool-name` again).

To get the better development experience, it's highly recommended that you also integrate the *Haskell Language Server* (HLS for short) with your editor of choice. HLS provides IDE-oriented features, like suggestions, completion of imports, or live compile error reporting, for all those editors supporting the Language Server Protocol. You can install the tool with GHCUp using `ghcup install hls`. The next step is to configure the editor; a non-exhaustive list follows:

- The *Haskell* plug-in for Visual Studio Code automatically sets up your system. In fact, it downloads HLS automatically if it's not detected in the running system.

- In Emacs, the integration is provided by the `lsp-mode`, `lsp-ui`, and `lsp-haskell` packages. Depending on your Emacs configuration, the way you get the packages may differ. Both Doom Emacs and Spacemacs contain specific integrations for Haskell which set up those packages for you.

- With Vim, you need to install an LSP integration, like CoC, and then point it to the HLS executable. Please consult the HLS documentation for an example of configuration.

GHCUp is a really flexible tool for managing Haskell installations. For example, if the moment ever comes for you to compile your own version of the provided tools, you can use `ghcup compile tool-name`, point to the source code, and GHCUp takes care of not only building it but also setting up the surrounding environment.

First Steps with GHCi

It's now time to see whether your Haskell Platform is correctly installed. To do so, open a console, type `ghci -e 5+3`, and press Enter. You should see 8 as output. This application is one instance of a *read-eval-print loop* (REPL), or, more succinctly, an *interpreter*. In GHCi, you input an expression and press Enter. The expression gets evaluated, and the result is shown on the screen. This allows for a programming methodology where you navigate into and discover the functionality of a library by issuing commands in the interpreter and also test your code interactively.

To open an interpreter in a console, just run `ghci`. A prompt with `Prelude>` at the beginning should appear. This line tells you that the interpreter is ready to accept commands and that the only loaded module at this moment is the Prelude, which contains the most basic functions and data types in Haskell. As a first approximation, GHCi can work as a fancy calculator, as shown here:

```
Prelude> 5 * 3
15
Prelude> 1/2 + 1/3
0.8333333333333333
```

If you now type s and press the Tab key, you will see a list of all possible functions beginning with that letter. If you then type q and press Tab again, only one possibility is left, sqrt, which is automatically written for you. One distinguishing choice made by Haskell creators was that parentheses are not used when applying a function. This means that if you want to find the square root of 7, you just write this:

```
Prelude> sqrt 7
2.6457513110645907
```

There are many other arithmetic operations you can perform in the interpreter: sin, cos, log, exp, and so forth. In the next chapter, you will learn how to use strings and lists and how to define functions, which will make your experience with the interpreter much more rewarding.

GHCi does not by default allow you to input several lines of code. For example, if you want to break the previous addition of two rational numbers into two lines, you cannot do it easily. Try entering the expression again, but press Enter after inputting the plus sign. If you press Enter, this error message will be produced:

```
Prelude> 1/2 +
<interactive>:2:6:
    parse error (possibly incorrect indentation or mismatched brackets)
```

The solution is to start a multiline block. A multiline block is an expression that is allowed to span more than one line. To do so, enter :{ and then press Enter. The prompt will change into Prelude|, showing that the input is expected to fill several lines. To end the block, enter the opposite of the beginning symbol, :}. Here's an example:

```
Prelude> :{
Prelude| 1/2 +
Prelude| 1/3
Prelude| :}
0.8333333333333333
```

Caution   To start a multiline block, :{ must be the only text entered in the first line.

All the internal actions of the interpreter (i.e., those that are not functions on any library) start with a colon. For example, typing :? and pressing Enter lists all the available commands. Other possibilities are looking at the language standard version you are using, in this case Haskell 2010 with some customizations. Here's an example:

```
Prelude> :show language
base language is: Haskell2010
with the following modifiers:
  -XNoDatatypeContexts
  -XNondecreasingIndentation
```

I stated before that Haskell has a strong static type system. You can check that it forbids dividing two strings (which are written between double quotes), producing an error when input in the interpreter, like so:

```
Prelude> "hello" / "world"
<interactive>:2:9:
    No instance for (Fractional [Char]) arising from a use of `/'
    Possible fix: add an instance declaration for (Fractional [Char])
    In the expression: "hello" / "world"
    In an equation for `it': it = "hello" / "world"
```

Fractional is the name of the type class that provides support for the / operator. The error message is saying that in order to be able to divide two strings, you should tell the compiler how to do so, by adding a declaration with the code for the Fractional type class in the case of strings.

To close the interpreter and go back to the console, you can issue the command :quit or just press the key combination Ctrl+D. In both cases, the result is the same.

```
Prelude> :quit
Leaving GHCi.
```

Note   GHCi is a powerful and customizable tool. You can find lots of tips and tricks on the Haskell wiki page devoted to the interpreter, https://wiki.haskell.org/GHC/GHCi.

The Time Machine Store

If you have already taken a look at the table of contents of this book, you will have noticed that it is divided into five parts. Each part is devoted to a different module of a small web store:

- In this first part, you will learn how to define the basic blocks of your application, representing clients, products, and orders, and how to manage them in memory.

- In Part 2, you will develop some data mining algorithms to get a better knowledge of the clients. In particular, you will develop a classification algorithm based on K-means and a recommendation algorithm.

- Part 3 will deal with saving data into a persistent store. For product data, you will use a custom file format, and for clients and orders, you will use a more traditional database solution. With all of this, you will be able to build the initial application by Chapter 12.

- Part 4 you will see how a domain-specific language can be used to model special offers in the system, such as "20 percent discount for all clients in Europe younger than 30."

- Finally, in Part 5 we will look at practical concerns that come along coding, like documentation, testing, and architecture.

What will you sell in this store? Time machines!

Welcome to the exciting world of time machines! These machines are quite special, and our clients come from all parts of the universe to get one. We would like to have a web store to handle all the orders. And we would also like to be developed in a language as special as our machines, like Haskell.

Sound exciting? Throughout this book, you'll be using Haskell to build your very own store for selling time machines. It's a fun example, and it should keep the book interesting.

Summary

In this chapter, you got familiar with Haskell.

- You learned about the distinguishing features of pure functional programming and how it helps to build code that is more concise, more maintainable, and *less error prone*.

- You looked at the benefits of having a strong, statically checked type system, like the one embodied in Haskell, and how dependent typing makes it possible to express invariants in a powerful way.

- The major tools in the Haskell ecosystem were introduced: the GHC compiler, the Cabal build tool, the Hackage library repository, and the GHC interpreter. You also took your first steps with the interpreter.

- You looked at the installation process of the Haskell Platform in the most common computer environments.

- You were presented with the main target in the book (apart from learning Haskell): building a web store focused on selling time machines, with modules for simple data mining and offer descriptions.

CHAPTER 2

Declaring the Data Model

You already know how to get a working installation of the Haskell Platform. The next step toward your Time Machine Store is to create the initial set of values and functions that will represent the data in the system: clients, machines, and orders.

This chapter will give you the basic ingredients for creating these values and functions. In a first approximation, you will create functions operating on basic types. You already know numbers, and you will add lists and tuples to the mix. Afterward, you will see how to create your own *algebraic data types* (ADTs) to better represent the kind of values you are interested in here. As part of this, you will learn about *pattern matching*, a powerful idiom to write concise code that follows closely the shape of the types.

Sometimes, ADTs and pattern matching lead to code that's not clear enough. Records introduce some syntactic forms that make values easier to create and modify, and they are a well-known tool of Haskell programmers. In addition, you will look at two design patterns that are common in Haskell libraries, namely, smart constructors and default values.

This chapter will also introduce how to manage projects using Cabal and Stack. In particular, you will see how to create a new project using both systems, along with the usual structure in folders, and how to load the code into the GHC interpreter to interactively test it.

Characters, Numbers, and Lists

Characters and numbers are universally accepted as the most basic kind of values that a language should provide to programmers. Haskell follows this tradition and offers dedicated character and number types that will be introduced in this section. Afterward, you will see how to put together several of these values to create strings or lists of numbers, as well as the basic operations you can perform on any kind of list.

© Alejandro Serrano Mena 2022
A. Serrano Mena, *Practical Haskell*, https://doi.org/10.1007/978-1-4842-8581-7_2

Characters

In some programming languages, numbers are also used to represent characters, usually in some encoding such as ASCII or Unicode. But following its tradition of clearly separating different concerns of a value, Haskell has a special type called Char for representing character data. To prevent problems with locales and languages, a Char value contains one Unicode character. These values can be created in two ways:

- Writing the character itself between single quotes, like 'a'.

- Writing the code point, that is, the numeric value which represents the character as defined in the Unicode standard, in decimal between '\ and ' or in hexadecimal between '\x and '. For example, the same 'a' character can be written as '\97' or '\x61'.

Using GHCi, you can check the actual type of each expression you introduce in the system. To do so, you use the :t command, followed by the expression. Let's check that characters indeed are characters.

```
Prelude> :t 'a'
'a' :: Char
```

Let's now explore some of the functionality that Haskell provides for Chars. Only a few functions are loaded by default, so let's import a module with a lot more functions, in this case Data.Char.

```
Prelude> import Data.Char
Prelude Data.Char>
```

The prompt of the interpreter changes to reflect the fact that now two different modules are loaded. Furthermore, if you now write to and press Tab, you will see a greater number of functions than before. In Haskell, everything has its own type, so let's try to find out toUpper's type.

```
Prelude Data.Char> :t toUpper
toUpper :: Char -> Char
```

The *arrow syntax* (shown as ->) is used to specify types of functions. In this case, toUpper is a function taking a character (the Char on the left side) and returning another one (because of the Char on the right side). Of course, types don't have to be equal. For example, chr takes an integer and gives the character corresponding to that code point.

```
Prelude Data.Char> chr 97
'a'
Prelude Data.Char> :t chr
chr :: Int -> Char
```

For functions with more than one parameter, each argument type is separated from the next with a single arrow. For example, if you had a min function taking two integers and returning the smallest one, the type would be as follows:

```
min :: Integer -> Integer -> Integer
```

I mentioned in the previous chapter that Haskell is very strict at checking types. You can indeed verify this: if you try to apply the chr function to a character, the interpreter refuses to continue.

```
Prelude Data.Char> chr 'a'
<interactive>:7:5:
    Couldn't match expected type `Int' with actual type `Char'
    In the first argument of `chr', namely 'a'
    In the expression: chr 'a'
    In an equation for `it': it = chr 'a'
```

Numbers

In Chapter 1, you may have noticed that several kinds of numeric constants were used. Like most programming languages, Haskell supports a great variety of number types, depending on the width, precision, and support for decimal parts:

- Int is the bounded integer type. It supports values between at least ±536870911, which corresponds to $2^{29}-1$ (even though GHC uses a much wider range). Usually, values of the Int type have the native width of the architecture, which makes them the fastest.

- Integer is an unbounded integral type. It can represent any value without a decimal part without underflow or overflow. This property makes it useful for writing code without caring about bounds, but it comes at the price of speed.

- The Haskell base library also bundles exact rational numbers using the Ratio type. Rational values are created using n % m.

- Float and Double are floating-point types of single and double precision, respectively.

Haskell is strict with the types. If you need to convert between different numeric representations, the functions fromInteger, toInteger, fromRational, and toRational will help you deal with conversions. For example, you can switch between rational and floating-point representations of values. The toRational function tries to create a Ratio not far from the original value (this depends on its width), and you can move from rational to floating-point by dividing the numerator by the denominator of the ratio. Be aware that many of these functions are found in the Data.Ratio module, so you should import it first.

```
Prelude> import Data.Ratio
Prelude Data.Ratio> 1 % 2 + 1 % 3
5 % 6
Prelude Data.Ratio> toRational 1.3
5854679515581645 % 4503599627370496
Prelude Data.Ratio> toRational (fromRational (13 % 10))
5854679515581645 % 4503599627370496
```

As you can see from the examples, perfect round-tripping between rational and floating-point values is not always possible. You may also get a puzzling result if you try to find the type of numeric constants.

```
Prelude> :t 5
5 :: Num a => a
Prelude> :t 3.4
3.4 :: Fractional a => a
```

Instead of making a numeric constant of a specific type, Haskell has a clever solution for supporting constants for different types: they are called *polymorphic*. For example, 5 is a constant that can be used for creating values of every type supporting the Num type class (which includes all types introduced before). On the other hand, 3.4 can be used for creating values of any type that is Fractional (which includes Float and Double but not Int or Integer). You will read in detail about type classes in Chapter 4, but right now you can think of a type class as a way to group sets of types that support the same operations. They share many commonalities with interfaces commonly found in object-oriented languages and are close relatives of Scala's traits and Swift's protocols.

Caution   Since Haskell doesn't use parentheses in function invocations, that is, you write `f a b` instead of `f(a,b)`, you must be a bit more careful than usual when using negative numbers. For example, if you write `atan -4` in GHCi, you will get an error indicating

```
Non type-variable argument in the constraint (Num (a -> a))
```

This means it has interpreted that you are trying to compute the subtraction of `atan` and 4. To get the arctangent of -4, you should instead write `atan (-4)`.

Strings

After playing for some time with characters, you may wonder whether you can have a bunch of them together, forming what is commonly known as a string. The syntax for strings in Haskell is similar to C: you wrap letters in double quotes. The following code creates a string. If you ask the interpreter its type, what do you expect to get back?

```
Prelude Data.Char> :t "Hello world!"
"Hello world!" :: [Char]
```

Instead of some new type, like String, you see your old friend Char but wrapped in square brackets. Those brackets indicate that "Hello world!" is not a character but a list of characters. In general, given a type T, the notation [T] refers to the type of all lists whose elements are of that type T. Lists are the most used data structure in functional programming. The fact that a type like a list depends on other types is known as parametric polymorphism, and you will delve into the details of it in the next chapter. Right now, let's focus on the practical side.

Lists

List *literals* (i.e., lists whose values are explicitly set into the program code) are written with commas separating each of the elements while wrapping everything between square brackets. As I have said, there's also special string syntax for a list of characters. Let's look at the types of some of these literals and the functions reverse, which gives a list in reverse order, and (++), which concatenates two lists.

```
Prelude> :t [1,2,3]
[1, 2, 3] :: Num t => [t]
Prelude> :t reverse
reverse :: [a] -> [a]
Prelude> :t (++)
(++) :: [a] -> [a] -> [a]
Prelude> reverse [1,2,3]
[3,2,1]
Prelude> reverse "abc"
"cba"
Prelude> [1,2,3] ++ [4,5,6]
[1,2,3,4,5,6]
```

Notice from this example that there are functions, such as reverse and (++), that can operate on any kind of list. This means once you know them, you can apply your knowledge of them to any list (including strings of characters). To tell this fact, these functions show in its type a type variable. It is a variable because it can be replaced by any type because regular variables can take different values. Type variables must be written in code starting with lowercase letters, and they consist usually of one or two letters. Here, the type variable is shown as a.

Note   Functions whose names are built entirely by symbols, like ++, must be called using the so-called *infix syntax*. That is, they should be written between the arguments instead of in front of them. So, you write a ++ b, not ++ a b. In the case where you want to use the function in the normal fashion, you must use parentheses around its name. So, you can write (++) a b, meaning the same as a ++ b.

Lists in Haskell are *homogeneous*: each list can handle elements of only a single type. Because of that, you are forbidden to create a list containing integers and characters and also to concatenate two lists with different kinds of elements.

```
Prelude> [1,2,3,'a','b','c']
<interactive>:13:2:
    No instance for (Num Char) arising from the literal `1'
Prelude> "abc" ++ [1,2,3]
<interactive>:11:11:
    No instance for (Num Char) arising from the literal `1'
```

Like in most functional languages, lists in Haskell are linked lists. Such lists are composed of a series of cells that hold the values in a list and a reference to the next cell and a special marker for the end of the list. The basic operations to construct lists are [ ] (pronounced "nil") to create an empty list and (:) (pronounced "cons") to append an element to an already existing list. That is, elt:lst is the list resulting from putting the value elt in front of the list lst. So, list literals can also be written as follows:

```
Prelude> 1 : 2 : 3 : []
[1,2,3]
Prelude> 'a' : 'b' : 'c' : []
"abc"
```

Note how GHCi writes back the lists using the most common representation using brackets. In the case of lists of characters, it uses string notation.

The functions that get information about the shape and the contents of the list are null, to check whether a list is empty; head, to get the first element; and tail, to get the list without that first element, also known as the rest of the list. Here are some examples of applying these functions:

```
Prelude> null [1,2,3]
False
Prelude> null []
True
Prelude> head [1,2,3]
1
Prelude> tail [1,2,3]
```

```
[2,3]
Prelude> head []
*** Exception: Prelude.head: empty list
```

Figure 2-1 shows a graphical representation of the operators and functions on lists I have talked about. The (:) operator is used to bind together an element with the rest of the list, and you can split those elements apart again using head and tail. You can also see how a list is a series of cons operations that always end with the empty list constructor, [].

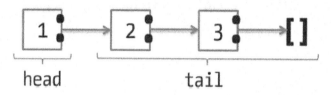

Figure 2-1. *Graphical representation of list constructors and destructors*

If you try to get the head or the tail of an empty list, you get an error, as you may expect. Be aware that exceptions are not the preferred way to handle errors in Haskell (you will see why in more detail in subsequent chapters) and by default make the entire program crash when found. To prevent errors from operations on empty lists, just be sure to check for nonemptiness before applying functions such as head and tail (or even better, use pattern matching, which will be introduced shortly).

In fact, looking at the output of null, you may have noticed two new values I talked about before: True and False. These are the only two elements of the Bool type, which represent Boolean values. Several standard functions for combining these two values (and (&&), or (||), and not) are provided in the Prelude. Most programming languages originating from C, such as C++ and Java, inherit from the former two kinds of Boolean operators. You'll find long-circuiting (& and |) operators, which always evaluate both sides of the expression, and short-circuiting (&& and ||) operators, which may stop after evaluating only one side. In Haskell, because of its lazy evaluation model, these operators always perform their job in the short-circuiting manner. Apart from that, there exist and and or functions that take a list of Booleans and perform the operations.

```
Prelude> (True && False) || (False && not False)
False
Prelude> or [True, False, and [False, True, True]]
```

```
True
Prelude> (2 == 2.1) || (2 < 2.1) || (2 > 2.1)
True
```

Caution   The usual warnings about comparing floating-point values apply here. Computers are not able to represent with exact precision all the values, so you may find that equalities that you expect not to hold actually do. For example, in my system the expression (4.00000000000000003 - 4) == 0 evaluates to True.

Along with these functions, another important construction related to Booleans is if-then-else. An expression with the form if b then t else f evaluates to t if the value of b is True, and it evaluates to f otherwise. This structure looks similar to the one found in imperative languages but has these important differences:

- Both then and else branches must be present along with the if. If this were not the case, then the expression wouldn't be evaluable for some of the values of b. Other languages opt to return a default value for the nonexistent else, but Haskell makes no commitment.

- The entire expression must have a defined type. The way Haskell manages to ensure that is by forcing both t and f expressions to have the same type. Thus, an expression such as if True then 1 else "hello" won't be accepted by either the compiler or the interpreter.

To make real use of if expressions, you need functions that return type Bool. This includes the comparison functions between numbers: == (equality), /= (inequality, but be aware that this function has a different name than in C and Java, where it's called !=), >= (greater than or equal to), > (greater than), <= (less than or equal to), and < (less than). The following is an example of an if expression:

```
Prelude> if 3 < 4.5 then "3 is less than 4.5" else "3 is not less than 4.5"
"3 is less than 4.5"
```

Let's make the interpreter return the head of a list of strings if it is not empty or return "empty" otherwise.

```
Prelude> :{
Prelude| if not (null ["hello","hola"])
```

```
Prelude|   then (head ["hello","hola"]) else "empty"
Prelude|   :}
"hello"
Prelude>   if not (null []) then (head []) else "empty"
"empty"
```

Lists can contain other lists as elements (or to any level of nesting). As [T] are lists of type T, lists of lists would be [[T]]. The inner lists inside the outer lists need not be of the same length (so they are not equivalent to arrays of multiple dimensions). One important thing to remember is that an empty list can be a member of a larger list of lists, so [] and [[]] are not equivalent. The first is a completely empty list of lists, whereas the second is a list that contains only one element, which is an empty list.

```
Prelude>   :t [['a','b','c'],['d','e']]
[['a','b','c'],['d','e']] :: [[Char]]
Prelude>   head [['a','b','c'],['d','e']]
"abc"
Prelude>   head (head [['a','b','c'],['d','e']])
'a'
Prelude>   head [[]]
[]
```

For sure, you have become bored while typing more than once the same constant list in the interpreter. To overcome this, you will learn about the essential ways to reuse functionality across all programming languages: defining functions that work on different input values and creating temporal bindings. But before that, Exercise 2-1 includes some tasks to see whether you have understood the concepts up to this point.

EXERCISE 2-1. LISTS OF LISTS

I have covered a lot of material about the most basic types and expressions in Haskell. The following tasks exercise the knowledge you have gained so far. In all cases, the solutions are expressions that can be typed in the interpreter to check whether they work.

- Rewrite the previous list literals using only (:) and the empty list constructor, [].

- Write an expression that checks whether a list is empty, [ ], or its first element is empty, like [[ ],['a', 'b']].

- Write an expression that checks whether a list has only one element. It should return True for ['a'] and False for [ ] or ['a', 'b'].

- Write an expression that concatenates two lists given inside another list. For example, it should return "abcde" for ["abc", "de"].

Use GHCi to check that those expressions work as required.

Creating a New Project

You can create a new project through *Cabal* and *Stack*, the main tools for packaging and building systems for Haskell projects. The advantage of using those tools is that they have been especially tailored for Haskell and its package repository, Hackage. In addition, the Cabal description file saves interesting metadata about the project, such as its name, maintainer, and license. In this section, you will see how to use both Cabal and Stack from the command line. Feel free to change between them because the project structures are fully compatible.

Creating a Project with Cabal

If you want to create a project using the command line, the first thing to do is to create the folder where the files will reside, usually named the same as the package name. Then move inside the folder in the shell (usually by issuing a series of cd commands) and run cabal init. You will need to answer some questions, as shown here:

```
$ cd path/to/my/haskell/projects
$ mkdir chapter2
$ cd chapter2
$ cabal init --interactive
Should I generate a simple project with sensible defaults? [default: y] n
What does the package build:
   1) Library
   2) Executable
   3) Library and Executable
```

Your choice? **1**
What is the main module of the executable:
 * 1) Main.hs (does not yet exist, but will be created)
   2) Main.lhs (does not yet exist, but will be created)
   3) Other (specify)
Your choice? [default: Main.hs (does not yet exist, but will be created)]
Please choose version of the Cabal specification to use:
    ...
Your choice? [default: 2.4   (+ support for '**' globbing)
Package name? [default: chapter2]
Package version? [default: 0.1.0.0] **0.0.1**
Please choose a license:
    ...
Your choice? [default: (none)]
Author name? **Alejandro Serrano**
Maintainer email? **my@email-address.com**
Project homepage URL? **http://my-web-page.com**
Project synopsis? **Project example for Chapter 2**
Project category:
 * 1) (none)
    ...
Your choice? [default: (none)]
Application (Main.hs) directory:
 * 1) app
   2) src-exe
   3) (none)
   4) Other (specify)
Your choice? [default: app] **1**
What base language is the package written in:
 * 1) Haskell2010
   2) Haskell98
   3) Other (specify)
Your choice? [default: Haskell2010]
Include documentation on what each field means (y/n)? [default: n] **n**

Note   You might receive a warning about cabal update. Don't worry, we will download a list of packages shortly, after I introduce how to add dependencies to a Cabal project.

The most important answers to give are the package name and whether you want to create a library or an executable, because what you create affects the name and structure of the project file. The essential difference between a library and an executable project is whether a final program will be produced (in the latter case) or the code is just for consuming other libraries or executables. Right now, it does not matter which one you choose because you will be testing the code using the GHC interpreter. Furthermore, you can refine the project later to add more library or executable descriptions.

Because having all the files in the root of the project makes them difficult to manage, it's customary to create a folder to hold all the source files of a project, as it is done in other build tools such as Maven for Java. I strongly recommend placing your files in a `src` folder, as shown in the project initialization earlier.

Creating a Project with Stack

The creation of a new project in Stack follows a very similar structure. In contrast to Cabal, you do not have to create the project folder before issuing the corresponding command, and instead of `init` you use `new`:

```
$ cd path/to/my/haskell/projects
$ stack new chapter2
Downloading template "new-template" to create project "chapter2" in
chapter2...
...
Looking for .cabal or package.yaml files to use to init the project.
Using cabal packages:
- chapter2/

Selecting the best among 21 snapshots...

* Matches https://raw.githubusercontent.com/commercialhaskell/stackage-
snapshots/master/lts/19/12.yaml
```

```
Selected resolver: https://raw.githubusercontent.com/commercialhaskell/
stackage-snapshots/master/lts/19/12.yaml
Initialising configuration using resolver: https://raw.githubusercontent.
com/commercialhaskell/stackage-snapshots/master/lts/19/12.yaml
Total number of user packages considered: 1
Writing configuration to file: chapter2/stack.yaml
All done.
```

Stack asks much fewer questions. It is your further responsibility to change the author name, maintainer email, and subsequent fields to the correct value.

There is another possibility to initialize a project using Stack. If you already have a Cabal file, maybe because you have created it previously, you can accommodate it for using Stack by running the command stack init. The only visible difference is the creation of a stack.yaml file in the root of the project.

EXERCISE 2-2. YOUR FIRST PROJECT

Create a new library project called chapter2 using either of the methods explained so far.

When doing Exercise 2-2, a pair of files named Setup.hs and chapter2.cabal will be created in the folder. The file Setup.hs is not useful, so you will focus on the .cabal file you have just created. The name of this file always coincides with the name of the package you are developing.

A Cabal project file is composed of a series of package properties followed by several blocks of code, called *stanzas* in Cabal terminology, that define the components (libraries and executables) to be built, the source files making each of them, and the options for compilation (such as flags or enabled extensions). If you are familiar with the JSON format or with Python code, you will find Cabal syntax comfortable to read and interpret. The following are the two important rules of interpretation:

- Each property is given a value in the form name: value. The name is case-insensitive (it doesn't matter whether you write name, Name, or nAmE), and the value is written without any kind of quotes or marks. If the value is a list, the elements are separated by commas.

- Stanzas begin with a header, usually `library` or `executable`, followed by an application name. Be aware that there is no colon (`:`) after the header. All properties within the stanza must be indented an equal number of spaces or tabs.

For example, here is an extract of a possible Cabal file created after initializing a project as required by Exercise 2-2:

```
name:           chapter2
version:        0.1
cabal-version:  >=1.2
build-type:     Simple
author:         John Doe
library
  hs-source-dirs:  src
  build-depends:   base >= 4
  ghc-options:     -Wall
```

Understanding Modules

You build Haskell projects by writing what are termed *modules*. Each module contains a set of definitions, such as functions and data types, and groups them under a common umbrella. The names of modules are nested in a hierarchical fashion. For example, inside `Data` there are a bunch of different modules, like `Data.Bool`, `Data.Ratio`, and so forth. This nesting makes modules similar to packages in Java or to namespaces in C#.

You define each module in its own file. The file name should be equal to the last component of the module name (the part after the last dot) and must be nested in folders named like the rest of the components. For example, you would create a module named `Chapter2.Section2.Example` in the path `Chapter2/Section2/Example.hs`. At the source directory of your project (which is `src` if you have followed the instructions earlier), create a folder named `Chapter2`. Inside it, create another folder named `Section2`. Finally, inside `Section2` create the `Example.hs` file.

CHANGING THE SOURCE DIRECTORY

You can always choose another source directory by adding a property

```
library
  hs-source-dirs:  src
```

to each of the stanzas in the Cabal file. In fact, you can use different source folders for each stanza, which helps us keep files from libraries, executables, and tests apart.

Always begin a module file with a module declaration giving its name. For example, you would begin the Example.hs module just mentioned by writing the following line:

```
module Chapter2.Section2.Example where
```

Then, you can start writing the definitions for that module.

To tell Cabal to compile a module file, you must include that module in some stanza. To do so, include a new property under the stanza adding the module either to the exposed-modules property or to the other-modules property (the difference is that when using your library from another project, only exposed modules will be available; the others remain as internal). Here's an example:

```
library
  exposed-modules: Chapter2.Section2.Example
  -- or
  other-modules:   Chapter2.Section2.Example
```

If you are using the command line, you can now compile the project by optionally running cabal configure and then cabal build, or stack setup and then stack build, depending on your choice of tool. At this point, you shouldn't encounter any compiling errors.

In summary, to add a new module to your project, you follow these steps:

1. Choose a name for the module, for example, A.B.C.

2. Create a folder for each component of its name but the last one, in this case a folder A inside a folder B.

3. Create a file with the same name of the last component ending in
   .hs (here C.hs) and write the module declaration you saw earlier.

4. Tell Cabal to include the file in your project.

Note   From now on, create a new project for each chapter in the book. Create a new module or set of modules for each section. This convention will help keep your work organized.

Cabal and Stack

The Haskell ecosystem has not one but two tools for building projects and managing their dependencies. A fair question to ask is what the differences between them are. In general, Stack is focused on having *reproducible* builds, whereas Cabal encompasses many more usage scenarios.

The first point of divergence between the two tools is that Stack manages your Haskell installation (including the compiler), whereas Cabal does not. Each Stack project comes with a stack.yaml file in addition to the .cabal one which declares which version of the compiler is targeted. If that specific version is not present in the system, Stack would download and install it in a local directory.

The other main difference is the source of the dependencies declared by each project. Cabal by default uses *Hackage*, the community-maintained repository of packages. This provides access to every single package in the Haskell ecosystem, but there is no guarantee that a specific combination of packages will work (or even compile) together.

Stack, on the other hand, targets *Stackage* by default. In Stackage, packages are grouped as resolvers, which specify not only an available set of packages but also their specific versions. Each of those sets is known to compile together in a specific version of the compiler. Thus, by declaring that your project uses a certain resolver, you are fixing the version of every tool and package, leading to reproducible builds. The downside is that Stackage provides a smaller set of packages than Hackage, although there are ways to declare that some dependency ought to be obtained from the bigger brother.

If you are in doubt of which tool to use, don't worry and start with any. As I discussed earlier, both share the same package description format, so changing from one to the other is fairly easy.

Defining Simple Functions

Now you are going to start creating *functions* in a module file. Function declarations include the following:

- A *name*, which in Haskell always starts with a *lowercase* letter

- The list of parameters, each of which must also begin with a lowercase letter, separated from the rest by spaces (not by commas, like in most languages) and not surrounded by parentheses

- An = sign and the body of the function

Creating a Simple Function

Let's abstract the functionality of, given a list of strings, return either the first string in the list or the string "empty" if there is nothing in the list. You can reuse most of the expression, replacing the constant lists by the parameter name.

```
firstOrEmpty lst = if not (null lst) then head lst else "empty"
```

To test the function, first create a new module Chapter2.SimpleFunctions for holding it. Then, load the file in the interpreter by issuing the command :l followed by the entire path to the file. Afterward, you can call firstOrEmpty directly.

```
Prelude> :l src/Chapter2/SimpleFunctions.hs
[1 of 1] Compiling Chapter2.SimpleFunctions ( src/Chapter2/SimpleFunctions.
hs, interpreted )
Warning: Top-level binding with no type signature:
     firstOrEmpty :: [[Char]] -> [Char]
Ok, modules loaded: Chapter2.SimpleFunctions.
*Chapter2.SimpleFunctions> firstOrEmpty []
"empty"
*Chapter2.SimpleFunctions> firstOrEmpty ["hello","hola"]
"hello"
```

You surely have noticed that loading the file has resulted in a warning. This warning tells you that you have given no type signature, that is, that you haven't specified the type of the function.

Specifying the Function's Type

I emphasized in Chapter 1 that Haskell is a strong, statically typed language, and now you are writing functions without any kind of type annotation. How is this possible? The answer is in the same warning message: you didn't tell anything to Haskell, and it inferred the correct type for the function. *Type inference* (i.e., the automatic determination of the type of each expression based on the functions and syntax construct being used) is a key point that makes a strong type system such as Haskell's still manageable to developers. This is a big contrast with other programming languages, such as Java and C#, which until their last revisions asked developers to write the types of all variables in the code.

However, it's not considered good practice to leave a function definition without an annotation about its type. That's the reason why a warning shows up even when the interpreter was able to realize the type of the function. The way to solve this is by adding a *type signature*: the name of the function being defined followed by :: and its type. Type signatures are conventionally added just before the definition of the element being typed. Being reminded that function types are written using ->, you can see that the type signature for firstOrEmpty is as follows:

```
firstOrEmpty :: [[Char]] -> [Char]
firstOrEmpty lst = if not (null lst) then head lst else "empty"
```

Developing a Robust Example

Now you'll try to define your own functions for concatenating and reversing a list, which you will call (+++) and reverse2, respectively. A general way to define functions over lists (and most of the other data structures) in Haskell is by using recursion. In this case, defining a function by recursion boils down to considering these two general cases:

- What to do when the list is empty

- What to do when the list has some initial element and some tail

The basic skeleton is the same in both cases:

```
if null list
then <case for empty list>
else <do something with (head list) and (tail list)>
```

Let's start with the concatenation function. First, because of its symbolic name of (+++), you have to write the name infix. So, in the definition, you will write the following:

```
lst1 +++ lst2
```

Remember the two general cases from the earlier list. Now that you are implementing a specific function, those cases can be stated in more specific terms:

- When concatenating an empty list with any other list, just return the second list because the first one adds no elements.

- When having a nonempty list and appending it to a second list, you have to think about what to do with the head and tail of the first list. Using recursion, you can call (+++) to append the tail of the first list and the second one. The return value from this call will be the list you need, but without the first element. To solve this problem, you can just plug the head of the first list using the (:) operator.

When this definition is translated into code, the result is as follows:

```
lst1 +++ lst2 = if null lst1   {- check emptyness -}
                then lst2      -- base case
                else (head lst1) : (tail lst1 +++ lst2)
```

This example also showcases for the first time the use of comments in Haskell code. Comments can include any kind of text and are completely ignored by both the interpreter and the compiler (although some tools like Haddock get information from the comments). As in many programming languages, there are two kinds of comments in Haskell. The first one is a multiline comment, which spans from {- to the nearest -}. Multiline comments are not affected by carriage returns like single-line comments are. Single-line comments span from -- to the first newline symbol found in the source code.

If you have problems understanding this recursive definition, I encourage you to try applying it to some small lists. For example, the following are the steps when evaluating [1, 2] +++ [3, 4]:

- The initial expression comes in as [1,2] +++ [3,4].

- It evaluates recursively to 1:([2] +++ [3,4]).

- That evaluates recursively to 1:(2:([] +++ [3,4])).

- The first list is now empty, so the recursion ends by returning lst2 with 1:(2:[3,4]).

- The colon operators simply append list items. Thus, 2:[3,4] evaluates to [2,3,4], and so forth.

- The final result is [1,2,3,4].

From now on, you will go through traces of execution often. To make the examples more concise, the book will use the convention of showing the steps separated by the => symbol. Here's what that looks like for the previous example:

```
[1,2] +++ [3,4] => 1:([2] +++ [3,4]) => 1:(2:([] +++ [3,4]))
                => 1:(2:[3,4]) = [1,2,3,4]
```

Now let's move on to the reverse2 function. Once again, you will follow the methodology of separating the work by the possible cases of a list to be passed as input. Reversing an empty list is quite easy: you simply return an empty list. To reverse a list with some number of elements, you could take the following approach:

1. Reverse the tail of the list.

2. Concatenate the head of the list to the end of the reversed tail.

The recursion occurs in step 1. Reversing the tail of a list means to reverse a list that is shorter by one element than the original input list. That shorter-by-one list is passed to the reversal function, creating yet another list, shorter by one more element. This process continues until the tail becomes empty.

Since you have no direct way to add elements at the end of a list, you will use the (+++) function just defined to concatenate a list with a single element. The result in this case is as follows:

```
reverse2 list = if null list
                then []
                else reverse2 (tail list) +++ [head list]
```

I mentioned in Chapter 1 that a useful feature of the Haskell ecosystem is the ability to interactively test functions. Exercise 2-3 describes the steps you should follow for the functions in this section.

EXERCISE 2-3. TESTING FUNCTIONS

Load the file where you defined the functions into GHCi and call them with different arguments to test them. Based on the warnings that appear, add type signatures to your code.

Returning More Than One Value

You are moving toward defining larger functions. The next one will compute the maximum and minimum of a list of numbers. The first question you may have is, how can I return more than one value in a function? In other programming languages, doing so would require defining some kind of structure or data type to hold the result. Doing this is a valid approach in Haskell, but for easy cases like this one, you can use a built-in type called the *tuple*. A tuple is just a type with a fixed number of components, each of them holding a value, not necessarily of the same type. Tuple values are written between parentheses and separated by commas, and the same notation is used for tuple types. For example, the following code creates a tuple with two elements; the first one is just the string "hello", and the second one is the result of evaluating a numeric condition:

```
Prelude> :t ("hello", True, if 2 > 3 then 'a' else 'b')
("hello", True, if 2 > 3 then 'a' else 'b') :: ([Char], Bool, Char)
```

Warning Tuple types of different lengths are completely different types. For example, a function working on tuples in the form (a,b) cannot be applied to tuples such as (a,b,c) that have some other number of values.

Right now, you will work only with *pairs*, that is, tuples of two components. For those tuples, there are two destructor functions: fst gives the first component, and snd gives the second one. Now you have all the ingredients to create a function computing both a maximum and a minimum of a list. If you forget for now the case of empty lists that

don't have a well-defined maximum or minimum, you can proceed again by cases. The
first case is the list with a single element, and that element should be returned as both
the maximum and the minimum and thus in both components of the tuple. If the list
has more than one element, you can get the maximum and minimum of the tail of the
list and then compare those values with the head. Thus, the recursive solution looks as
follows:

```
maxmin list = if null (tail list)
              then (head list, head list)
              else ( if (head list) > fst (maxmin (tail list))
                     then head list
                     else fst (maxmin (tail list))
                   , if (head list) < snd (maxmin (tail list))
                     then head list
                     else snd (maxmin (tail list))
                   )
```

Wow! Somehow, a function for such an easy task has become completely
incomprehensible and unmaintainable: the code is full of repetition, and even worse,
maxmin (tail list) is recomputed four times per recursive call, which is not very
performant. The solution is to use a *local binding*, which gives a name to an expression
to be used in a larger one. There are two kinds of binding constructs in Haskell: let and
where. In both cases, a binding is introduced by name = expression. The difference
lies in the position over the main expression: let introduces bindings before the main
expression and must end with the in keyword. On the other hand, where does so after
the expression. The following code rewrites the previous code by using local bindings to
refer to the head of the list and the return values of the recursive case:

```
maxmin list = let h = head list
              in if null (tail list)
                 then (h, h)
                 else ( if h > t_max then h else t_max
                      , if h < t_min then h else t_min )
                   where t = maxmin (tail list)
                         t_max = fst t
                         t_min = snd t
```

The special position of the code in all of these examples is not random or just aesthetic, as you have noticed if you've tried to copy the code by hand into an editor. A first guess about the reason may lead you to think about indentation-sensitive languages such as Python. However, Haskell uses a different solution, called *layout*. In a layout-based syntax, how a line is indented isn't as important as the fact that all elements in the same block start in the same column. Here's an example:

- In an if block, the lines for then and else must be indented the same way.

- In a let or a where block, all local bindings must start in the same position.

Note   When reading Haskell code, you will notice that Haskellers also tend to align other symbols, like the = signs in a local bindings block. The layout rule applies only to the beginning of expressions, so alignment is not enforced. However, it's a common convention that you should follow or at least get used to.

As a final remark, Haskell also allows you to group blocks with { and } and separate expressions with ;. For example, you can rewrite the last where clause in the example as follows:

```
where { t = maxmin (tail list) ; t_max = fst t ; t_min = snd t }
```

Be aware that this kind of syntax is highly discouraged when writing new code (it is typically used in cases where Haskell code is produced automatically by some other program).

Working with Data Types

Haskell provides tuples to group a fixed number of components of different types and lists to contain an unlimited number of elements of a homogeneous type. It seems that this is enough to start modeling the data for the web application. For example, a client named Paul, age 25 and buyer of two time machines, could be represented as follows:

```
("Paul", 25, ["Super Time Machine 2013", "Medieval Machine"])
```

There are two problems with using this approach. First, code is difficult to read because of nested calls to fst, snd, and head. Second, it defies strong typing because the compiler cannot distinguish a client from, say, the description of a fish with its common name, its length, and a list of seas where it is found. The solution is to introduce a new data type specific for representing clients. The most basic kind of data type that you can create in Haskell is called an *algebraic data type* (ADT) and will be the focus of this section. An ADT is defined by two pieces of data:

- A name for the type that will be used to represent its values.

- A set of constructors that will be used to create new values. These constructors may have arguments that hold values of the specified types.

In many languages, different constructors can be defined for a data type (or a class, if you are working on an object-oriented language). However, these constructors are somehow linked and tend to be more like shortcuts for default values. In most functional languages, such as Haskell, different constructors are used to represent completely different alternatives to construct values.

To make these ideas clear, let's begin modeling clients. There are three kinds of clients, listed here:

1. Government organizations, which are known by their name

2. Companies, for which you need to record a name, an identification number, a contact person, and that person's position within the company hierarchy

3. Individual clients, known by their name, surname, and whether they want to receive further information about offers and discounts

The way to represent these three client types in Haskell is as follows:

```
data Client = GovOrg     String
            | Company    String Integer String String
            | Individual String String Bool
```

As you can see, the syntax for declaring data types starts with the data keyword, followed by the type name. After that, constructors are listed, separated by |. Each of them starts with a constructor name and then the types of the arguments to that constructor.

CAPITALIZATION IN HASKELL

One of the special characteristics of Haskell syntax is that names given by the user must follow some capitalization rules. Here is a brief summary of the conventions:

- Functions, parameters, and bindings must start with a *lowercase* letter. In the case of an operator name, it must not start with :.

- Types, constructors, type classes, and kinds must start with an *uppercase* letter. If using an operator name, it must start with the : symbol.

These rules make it easier to determine the kind of element you are looking at.

Using constructors, you can create values of type Client by just writing the constructor name and the value for each of the parameters in the order in which they appear in the declaration.

```
*Chapter2.DataTypes> :t GovOrg "Nasa"
GovOrg "Nasa" :: Client
*Chapter2.DataTypes> :t Company "Pear Inc." 342 "Mr. Sparrow" "CEO"
Company "Pear Inc." 342 "Mr. Sparrow" "CEO" :: Client
```

But when you try to print the values, something goes wrong.

```
*Chapter2.DataTypes> Individual "Jack" "Smith" True
    No instance for (Show Client) arising from a use of `print'
    Possible fix: add an instance declaration for (Show Client)
    In a stmt of an interactive GHCi command: print it
```

To show the values on the screen, the interpreter internally calls a print function over them. However, you haven't written the corresponding code for this data type, so an error arises. To fix this problem, you can use a facility in Haskell called *automatic deriving* that allows you to add some functionality to an ADT without writing any code. In this case, you want to be able to get a string representation of the values, so you need to derive Show. Show is a type class: implementing it means that there's a way to get a string out of any value of this type. You can write the code yourself, or you can allow Haskell to write it for you. The following example specifies deriving Show, causing Haskell to generate it automatically:

```
data Client = GovOrg String
            | Company    String Integer String String
            | Individual String String Bool
            deriving Show
```

Now the interpreter can display the values on the screen.

```
*Chapter2.DataTypes> Individual "Jack" "Smith" True
Individual "Jack" "Smith" True
```

There's no impediment when using one ADT that you define inside another one. For example, in the previous code, there are some divergent options for representing a person as a member of a company and as an individual. One path you can take is to define a completely new data type called Person and use it inside Client.

```
data Client = GovOrg     String
            | Company    String Integer Person String
            | Individual Person Bool
            deriving Show

data Person = Person String String
            deriving Show
```

Here are some key points regarding this refactoring:

- If you tried to create a completely new ADT, for example, named Client2, but you used the same constructor names, you would get a build error. This is because inside a module all constructors must have different names. If you think about it, it's sensible to ask for that condition because otherwise the compiler wouldn't be able to distinguish which type you are trying to create.

- Data types and constructor names live in different worlds. That means it is possible to create a constructor with the same name as a data type. Indeed, it's a common convention for one-alternative types, such as Person, to have two names that coincide.

41

- To be able to use the default deriving functionality, all types used inside another one must be showable. For example, if you didn't include deriving Show in Person, a compilation error would be signaled.

Sometimes, you are just interested in the alternatives themselves, without saving any extra information apart from the constructors. For example, you could add gender information for people. Instead of using a raw Boolean value, for which you can forget which value corresponds to men and which to women, you can create a new Gender data type. This kind of data type with empty alternatives is similar to enumerations in other languages.

```
data Gender = Male | Female | Unknown
```

Exercise 2-4 provides a step-by-step recipe on how to integrate this new Gender data type in the existing code base and how to modify the existing functionality for covering it. In the following sections, I assume that the Gender type has been defined.

EXERCISE 2-4. MORE TYPES OF VALUES

You have just defined a new Gender data type. The reason you defined it was to include such information in a Person record, so you should add a new field in Person.

- Add a Gender argument to Person and make it Showable.

- Create new values of the new Client data type with the enhanced definition you worked with throughout this section.

You have learned how to define new data types, so it's time to look at other types that could be useful for the Time Machine Store. Time machines are defined by their manufacturer, their model (which is an integer), their name, whether they can travel to the past and to the future, and a price (which can be represented as a floating-point number). Define a TimeMachine data type holding that information. Try to use more than one ADT to structure the values.

Pattern Matching

Now it's time to define functions over your shiny new data types. The bad news is that I haven't taught you how to extract the information from the constructors because you have been taught to use head and tail for lists and to use fst and snd for tuples. The general solution for this task is *pattern matching*. Matching a value against a pattern allows you to discern the structure of the value, including the constructor that was used to create the value, and to create bindings to the values encoded inside it. When entering the body of the match, the *pattern variables* will hold the actual inner values, and you can work with them.

Simple Patterns

To see a first example, let's create a function giving the name of a client. In the case of a company or a government organization, the client name will be the first component of the constructor. In the case of an individual, you will have to look inside Person and concatenate the first and last names. As you can see, the patterns in this case look exactly like the ADT constructors but with the parameters replaced by bindings:

```
clientName :: Client -> String
clientName client = case client of
                  GovOrg   name                -> name
                  Company name id person resp -> name
                  Individual person ads        ->
                      case person of
                        Person fNm lNm gender -> fNm ++ " " ++ lNm
```

Let's see how the execution of a call to clientName (Individual [Person "Jack" "Smith" Male]) False proceeds. First, the system finds a case expression. So, it tries to match with the first and second patterns, but in both cases the constructor is not the same as the value. In the third case, the system finds the same constructor, and it binds the values: person now holds Person "Jack" "Smith" Male, and ads holds the value False. In the body of the match, there's again a case expression, from which a match is done to the Person constructor, binding fNm to "Jack", lNm to "Smith", and gender to Male. Finally, the system proceeds into the innermost body and executes the concatenation, giving "Jack Smith" as the result.

Note   When loading this definition into the interpreter, you will receive a collection of warnings that look like

```
Defined but not used: `id'
```

This tells you that you created a binding that was not used in the body of the match. The solution for this warning is telling the compiler that you won't use that binding in your code, and this is done by replacing its binding variable by a single underscore, _. For example, the nonwarning pattern for Company name id person resp would have been Company name _ _ _ because you are using only the first pattern variable in the subsequent matching code.

For this example, I have used the simplest kind of match, which just looks at the constructors and binds the values of the parameters. But you can specify more complex patterns, in which some inner parts of the value will have to match also against other patterns. Using this approach, you can rewrite the match in clientName to be shorter, as shown here:

```
clientName :: Client -> String
clientName client = case client of
                    GovOrg  name        -> name
                    Company name _ _ _  -> name
                    Individual (Person fNm lNm _) _ -> fNm ++ " " ++ lNm
```

One important question that arises here is, what happens if no pattern matches the value that is given? The best way to find this out is by an easy example. Let's consider a companyName function, as shown here:

```
companyName :: Client -> String
companyName client = case client of
                    Company name _ _ _ -> name
```

The interpreter already warns about the pattern not covering all the cases, that is, not being exhaustive.

```
Warning: Pattern match(es) are non-exhaustive
In a case alternative:
    Patterns not matched:
```

```
        GovOrg _
        Individual _ _
```

Applying the function to a value that is not expected yields an exception. This is similar to what happens if you try to get the head of an empty list.

```
*Chapter2.DataTypes> companyName (GovOrg "NATO")
"*** Exception: Non-exhaustive patterns in case
```

The functions that are not defined over the complete domain of their arguments are called *partial* (the other side of the coin are the *total* functions). In some cases, a default value can be returned when you don't get an applicable value (e.g., returning "unknown" in companyName if the input is not a Company). However, this problem is so common in practice that the Haskell Platform already bundles a special data type for this matter: Maybe T. As lists and tuples, the Maybe type is parameterized by the type of value it holds, so you have Maybe Integer, Maybe String, Maybe [Integer], and so on. There are only two kinds of values that this type can have: Nothing, with no arguments, usually signaling that the function has nothing sensible to return for that specific value; and Just v, which holds a single value v of the corresponding type. Let's rewrite companyName.

```
companyName :: Client -> Maybe String
companyName client = case client of
                       Company name _ _ _ -> Just name
                       _                  -> Nothing
```

One interesting fact is that you can pattern match directly on let and where bindings. In that case, you can handle only one pattern, but it is useful when you know that only one kind of value can happen in a specific place. Let's say you are sure at some point that the client you are working with is a company. Instead of this not very clear code

```
let name = case companyName client of
             Just n -> n
```

you can write the following much more concise version:

```
let Just name = companyName client
```

Constants are also patterns, which match the exact values written. Let's focus on an archetypical example for teaching programming languages: the Fibonacci numbers. The

nth Fibonacci number, $F(n)$, is defined as $F(0) = 0$, $F(1) = 1$, and $F(n) = F(n-1) + F(n-2)$ for a larger value of n. This is easily expressed in terms of patterns and recursion.

```
fibonacci :: Integer -> Integer
fibonacci n = case n of
                0 -> 0
                1 -> 1
                _ -> fibonacci (n-1) + fibonacci (n-2)
```

In this case, you have implicitly used the fact that patterns are checked in the same order they appear in the code. This order-dependent behavior can lead to subtle bugs and sometimes even to programs that don't terminate or run out of resources. As an exercise, rewrite the fibonacci function putting the last pattern in the first position. Now try to test the function in the interpreter. You will see that it never terminates.

Also, once a pattern has matched, it completely stops trying other alternatives, even if a further match raises an error. For example, the following two functions are not equivalent:

```
f :: Client -> String
f client = case client of
             Company _ _ (Person name _ _) "Boss" -> name ++ " is the boss"
             _                                    -> "There is no boss"
g :: Client -> String
g client = case client of
             Company _ _ (Person name _ _) pos ->
               case pos of "Boss" -> name ++ " is the boss"
             _                                  -> "There is no boss"
*Chapter2.DataTypes> f (Company "A" 5 (Person "John" "Do" Male) "Director")
"There is no boss"
*Chapter2.DataTypes> g (Company "A" 5 (Person "John" "Do" Male) "Director")
"*** Exception: Non-exhaustive patterns in case
```

When the value is given to f, the first pattern does not match because "Director" is not equal to "Boss". So, the system goes into the second black-hole match and sees that there is no boss. However, on g it first matches into being a Company, which the value satisfies, and in this point it enters the body of the match and forgets about other alternatives. Then, the inner match fails, raising the exception.

Note   I strongly emphasize the fact that pattern matching does not backtrack when something goes wrong in the body of a match. This is important to remember, especially if you are coming from a logic programming background in which unification with backtracking is the norm.

You may have noticed that most of the case expressions just pattern match on some parameter to a function. For these cases, Haskell allows you to encode the pattern directly in the definition. You include several lines for the function, each defining it for a pattern. This approach creates code that is similar to the way you write mathematical functions. For example, new versions of clientName and fibonacci look like this:

```
clientName (GovOrg name)                    = name
clientName (Company name _ _ _)             = name
clientName (Individual (Person fNm lNm _) _) = fNm ++ " " ++ lNm
fibonacci 0 = 0
fibonacci 1 = 1
fibonacci n = fibonacci (n-1) + fibonacci (n-2)
```

Try to use this new syntax when writing the solution for Exercise 2-5, which provides a set of tasks to practice pattern matching on different kinds of values, both clients and time machines.

EXERCISE 2-5. THE PERFECT MATCH FOR YOUR TIME MACHINES

These exercises focus on pattern matching on data types defined by you. For working with lists, follow the pattern of having different branches for the empty and general case. Also, think carefully about the order of the patterns. Afterward, test the functions in the interpreter.

For statistical purposes, write a function that returns the number of clients of each gender. You may need to define an auxiliary data type to hold the results of this function.

Every year, a time comes when time machines are sold with a big discount to encourage potential buyers. Write a function that, given a list of time machines, decreases their price by some percentage. Use the `TimeMachine` data type you defined in Exercise 2-4.

Lists and Tuples

One question that may have naturally arisen while doing the previous exercises is whether it's also possible to use pattern matching on lists and tuples because it seems that doing so will lead to more concise code. It's indeed possible because lists and tuples are no more special than any other user-defined data type. List constructors are [ ] and (:), and those are the ones you can use to pattern match. Furthermore, using pattern matching in lists allows you to get rid of all the `null` checks and calls to `head` and `tail`. For example, the function (+++) defined earlier could be rewritten as follows:

```
(+++) :: [a] -> [a] -> [a]
list1 +++ list2 = case list1 of
                    []   -> list2
                    x:xs -> x:(xs +++ list2)
```

Or directly matching in the function declaration would look like this:

```
[]      +++ list2 = list2
(x:xs) +++ list2 = x:(xs +++ list2)
```

Note   It's customary in Haskell to write pattern matching on lists using a letter or a small word followed by the same identifier in plural, like `x:xs`.

The `Prelude` function's `null`, `head`, and `tail` have no special magic inside them; they can be defined easily using pattern matching. Are you able to do so?

Sometimes, you need to match on lists of more than one element. A possible function where you would need these is one that checks whether a list of integers is sorted. To check for sorted data, three cases need to be considered. The first two are the empty or singleton cases, and those are always sorted. But if more than one element is contained in a list, you need to compare the first with the second and then see whether the list comprised of the second and subsequent elements is sorted. That check on the second and subsequent elements is done recursively. The implementation of such a sorted function is as follows:

```
sorted :: [Integer] -> Bool
sorted []        = True
sorted [_]       = True
sorted (x:y:zs) = x < y && sorted (y:zs)
```

There is still some repetition in this code; you are matching on y:zs just to later reconstruct it. This sequence of checking whether some value conforms to some pattern but later to use the value as a whole and not its components is quite common in Haskell code. For that reason, Haskell introduces a syntactic form referred to by the term *as pattern*. As pattern allows you to bind some value in the match while at the same time allowing you to match on inner components of that value. To use it, you have to wrap into parentheses the whole pattern you want to give a name to and prepend it by the variable that will be used to refer to the whole pattern and the @ symbol. A new definition of sorted that uses as patterns for y:zs looks like this:

```
sorted []              = True
sorted [_]             = True
sorted (x : r@(y:_)) = x < y && sorted r
```

One last remark about matching on lists: In many cases, you have a function that at first sight makes sense only on a nonempty list, such as when computing the sum of all elements in a list. In most cases, this function can be extended in a sensible way to empty lists. For example, you can assign the value 0 to the sum of an empty list because if you add that value to any number, it does not change. Values such as 0, which can be safely applied with respect to an operation, such as sum, are called the *neutral elements* of that operation. I will cover such neutral elements in more detail in Chapter 3 when discussing folds and again in Chapter 4 when discussing monoids.

Matching on tuples is also easy. Just use the syntax of a comma-separated list of components between parentheses. Rewriting the maxmin example from the previous section in this style makes the algorithm much more apparent to the reader or maintainer of that code.

```
maxmin [x]    = (x,x)
maxmin (x:xs) = ( if x > xs_max then x else xs_max
```

```
            , if x < xs_min then x else xs_min
            ) where (xs_max, xs_min) = maxmin xs
```

Guards

A *guard* is part of the pattern-matching syntax that allows you to refine a pattern using Boolean conditions that must be fulfilled by the bound values after a successful match. Guards are useful for writing clearer code and avoiding certain problems, helping you to obtain the full power of pattern matching.

Two examples can help make the need for guards clear. The first is an extension of the Fibonacci function to any integer value. You will wrap the value on a Just if you are asked to get the Fibonacci number of a nonnegative number and return Nothing otherwise. With the syntax introduced up to this point, you could write the following code:

```
ifibonacci :: Integer -> Maybe Integer
ifibonacci n = if n < 0
               then Nothing
               else case n of
                    0  -> Just 0
                    1  -> Just 1
                    n' -> let Just f1 = ifibonacci (n'-1)
                              Just f2 = ifibonacci (n'-2)
                          in Just (f1 + f2)
```

At this time, your developing sense of clear code signals you that the initial check for negativeness hides part of the algorithm, which is mostly expressed in a pattern match. And that is true. Apart from that, notice that the case statement has used a binding n'. You could have reused n, but the interpreter would complain about shadowing a previous definition. Even though the interpreter knows completely well which n the code refers to, the fact you have used the same name twice may create confusion for another developer. It's customary in Haskell code to use the same identifier, but with ' (pronounced *prime*) afterward, to refer to a highly related binding.

Another mathematical function I will cover is the binomial coefficient of n and k, usually written $\binom{n}{k}$. This coefficient gives the number of ways in which you can get k balls from a bag of n without repetition. Using the famous Pascal's triangle, you can give a closed definition of this coefficient as follows:

$$\binom{n}{k} = \begin{cases} 1, k = 0 \lor n = k \\ \binom{n-1}{k-1} + \binom{n-1}{k}, \textit{otherwise} \end{cases}$$

Your task is translating this mathematical definition into Haskell code. A first approximation could be as follows:

```
binom _ 0 = 1
binom x x = 1
binom n k = (binom (n-1) (k-1)) + (binom (n-1) k)
```

But sadly this approach doesn't make the interpreter happy, which shows the error `Conflicting definitions for `x'`. This error is because of the restriction imposed on patterns in which a variable can appear only once in each of them. A possible solution is to change the entire shape of the function. Once again, it seems that pattern matching is not giving you all the power you are asking from it.

The solution to the problems found in both functions is to use guards. A guard is itself part of a pattern, so it allows backtracking (choosing other alternatives) if it fails, in contrast to matching a pattern and later checking for a condition. The Boolean conditions in a guard are separated by a | sign from the rest of the pattern and allow the use of the variables bound during the match. The following is how you would rewrite the Fibonacci and binomial functions using guards:

```
ifibonacci n | n < 0      = Nothing
ifibonacci 0              = Just 0
ifibonacci 1              = Just 1
ifibonacci n | otherwise = let Just f1 = ifibonacci (n-1)
                               Just f2 = ifibonacci (n-2)
                           in Just (f1 + f2)
binom _ 0            = 1
binom x y | x == y = 1
binom n k           = (binom (n-1) (k-1)) + (binom (n-1) k)
```

Apart from the use of guards, you should notice another tidbit in the previous code. The use of otherwise in the last pattern when using guards is a common convention in Haskell. While using `otherwise` doesn't add anything to the code (using no guard is equivalent), it signals clearly that the remaining pattern takes care of all the cases not handled by other cases.

Any expression returning a Boolean value can be used in a guard. This means you can also call a function that you have defined. For example, the following code returns special strings when a number is a multiple of 2, 3, or 5, and a default string otherwise:

```
multipleOf :: Integer -> Integer -> Bool
multipleOf x y = (mod x y) == 0

specialMultiples :: Integer -> String
specialMultiples n | multipleOf n 2 = show n ++ " is multiple of 2"
specialMultiples n | multipleOf n 3 = show n ++ " is multiple of 3"
specialMultiples n | multipleOf n 5 = show n ++ " is multiple of 5"
specialMultiples n | otherwise      = show n ++ " is a beautiful number"
```

For this example where you are checking several conditions on the same argument, Haskell allows an even more compact declaration. You don't need to write specialMultiples n every time.

```
specialMultiples :: Integer -> String
specialMultiples n
  | multipleOf n 2 = show n ++ " is multiple of 2"
  | multipleOf n 3 = show n ++ " is multiple of 3"
  | multipleOf n 5 = show n ++ " is multiple of 5"
  | otherwise      = show n ++ " is a beautiful number"
```

Up to this point, I have introduced matching on user-defined data types, on lists, and on tuples and guards. The tasks in Exercise 2-6 will help ensure that you understand these concepts.

EXERCISE 2-6. MORE MATCHES AND GUARDS

Up to this point, I have introduced matching on lists and tuples and guards. The following tasks will help you ensure that you understand these concepts:

Define the famous Ackermann function. Try using guards:

$$A(m,n) \begin{cases} n+1, m=0 \\ A(m-1,1), m>0, n=0 \\ A(m-1, A \vdash (m,n-1)), m>0, n>0 \end{cases}$$

Define the `unzip` function, which takes a list of tuples and returns two lists, one with all the first components and other one with the seconds. Here's an example: `unzip [(1,2),(3,4)] = ([1,3],[2,4])`.

View Patterns

Sometimes, you want to look for patterns in a value, but in some way they are not directly encoded. So, you need to preprocess the value before matching. For those cases, you can use *view patterns*. These patterns extend all of those previously seen with a new syntax element, `(function -> pattern)`, which applies `function` to the value and then matches the result with the pattern. For example, remember the `clientName` function from the beginning of the chapter, and let's add a responsibility one:

```
responsibility :: Client -> String
responsibility (Company _ _ _ r) = r
responsibility _                 = "Unknown"
```

Now you can create a function returning whether a given client is special. Let's consider a client special if the client is the director of a company or the client's name is "Mr. Alejandro". View patterns allow very clear code.

```
specialClient :: Client -> Bool
specialClient (clientName -> "Mr. Alejandro") = True
specialClient (responsibility -> "Director")  = True
specialClient _                               = False
```

Oops! It seems that you rushed into making some sort of mistake. Notice the following interpreter error:

```
Illegal view pattern:  clientName -> "Mr. Alejandro"
Use ViewPatterns to enable view patterns
```

This problem arises because view patterns are not part of the Haskell 2010 specification but rather an extension made by GHC developers. For that reason, you are asked to explicitly enable compatibility with this extension. You can do so adding special options to the compiler or interpreter, but the suggested approach is to add a pragma to the file. A *pragma* is a special comment that is interpreted by the compiler and that is used to enable or disable some flags. In this case, you need to include the following at the *beginning* of the source:

```
{-# LANGUAGE ViewPatterns #-}
```

If you are working in the interpreter, you need to execute a :set command to enable an extension. Notice that the extension name must be prefixed by -X.

```
Prelude> :set -XViewPatterns
```

In the rest of the book, I shall remark that an extension needs to be enabled for a specific piece of code by including the corresponding pragma as you would do in the beginning of a source file.

Note   GHC includes a great many extensions (more than 100 at the moment of writing). They range from simple extensions to the syntax (like the view patterns discussed earlier) for complete overhauls of the type system. Being so different in power, some of them are accepted by the community, while others are controversial. All the GHC extensions that will be introduced in this book belong to the first set: they are seen as beneficial because they make code more elegant and easier to understand, without running into any problems. The main con of extensions, even with not-controversial ones, is that they are not part of the Haskell 2010 Report, so in theory they could make your code less interoperable between different Haskell compilers. However, this interoperability is almost never a problem.

Records

In most programming languages, you can find the idea of a field as something that holds a value in a larger structure. Furthermore, fields can be accessed or changed easily (e.g., in C or Java using structure.field). From what you have learned so far, you can see that pattern matching on big structures may get unwieldy quickly, because it forces to write long matches to retrieve just a single value and to re-create entire data structures merely to change just a single field.

Creation and Use

The concept of a data structure with fields that can be accessed by name does exist in Haskell. Records make accessing or updating part of a structure much easier than otherwise. Records are defined using data declarations, but instead of just using a type for each parameter, you write parameter name :: parameter type. These declarations are the only exception to the layout rule. You always need to write the set of fields between { and } and to separate them by commas.

Let's write the Client and Person definitions but now using record syntax. To leave all the previous functions from this chapter unchanged, you are going to encode the new records in new ClientR and PersonR types. Remember, constructor names should not clash; that's why you need to use new names for the record types. But field names can, so you are allowed to use clientRName for fields in different alternatives, given that they have the same type. Here are the new record definitions:

```haskell
data ClientR = GovOrgR  { clientRName :: String }
             | CompanyR { clientRName :: String
                        , companyId :: Integer
                        , person :: PersonR
                        , duty :: String }
             | IndividualR { person :: PersonR }
             deriving Show

data PersonR = PersonR { firstName :: String
                       , lastName :: String
                       } deriving Show
```

You can create values from these types using the same constructor syntax that you've been using. However, if the data is declared as a record, you can also use the constructor name followed by a list of each field name, followed by an = sign and the corresponding value. There are two benefits for doing this. First, constructing the new value this way results in better documentation because you can see directly to which field each value corresponds. Also, this syntax allows you to write the field names in any order, giving you more freedom. Here's an example showing this named notation:

```haskell
*Chapter2.DataTypes> IndividualR { person = PersonR { lastName = "Smith",
firstName = "John" } }
IndividualR {person = PersonR {firstName = "John", lastName = "Smith"}}
```

```
*Chapter2.DataTypes> GovOrgR "NATO"
GovOrgR {clientRName = "NATO"}
```

Field names are also used to create special functions that access those particular fields. Here's an example:

```
*Chapter2.DataTypes> clientRName (GovOrgR "NATO")
"NATO"
*Chapter2.DataTypes> :t duty
duty :: ClientR -> String
```

Because these functions will be automatically created, Haskell enforces two extra restrictions on field names:

- They must not clash with any other field or function name.

- As I mentioned earlier, you are allowed to use the same field name in more than one alternative of your data type. However, if you do so, all those fields must have the same type. If such is not the case, no correct type can be given to the corresponding function.

Records are useful when pattern matching. For a traditional constructor, you need to write a binding or another pattern for each field in it. Thus, in many cases the code ends up with a collection of _ bindings, which are difficult to maintain. With a record, you can use a new pattern that resembles the building one: the constructor, plus a list of `field name = pattern` elements enclosed in brackets. You don't need to include all the fields, just those for which you want to bind or match. You are even allowed to write an empty list of fields, as this example highlights:

```
greet :: ClientR -> String
greet IndividualR { person = PersonR { firstName = fn } } = "Hi, " ++ fn
greet CompanyR    { clientRName = c } = "Hi, " ++ c
greet GovOrgR     { }                 = "Welcome"
```

There are two interesting additions in GHC to record matching that encode very usual patterns, allowing for a lesser amount of boilerplate code. The first addition is *record puns*, which are enabled by the pragma `NamedFieldPuns`. When using record puns, you can replace all field patterns of the form `field name = field name`, which creates a binding for the corresponding field available with the same name in the body of the match, with a single field name. You can interleave this kind of matching with the more usual one. Here's an example:

```
{-# LANGUAGE NamedFieldPuns #-}

greet IndividualR { person = PersonR { firstName } } = "Hi, " ++ firstName
greet CompanyR    { clientRName } = "Hi, " ++ clientRName
greet GovOrgR     { }             = "Welcome"
```

Another common idiom is making some field obey a pattern and binding the rest of the fields to use them in the body of the match. Even with record puns, doing so can take a large amount of code. But GHC can take advantage of its knowledge of the field names and automatically generate all that code for you. In particular, the extension RecordWildCards allows the use of .. (two dots) to automatically create bindings for all variables that haven't been mentioned in the pattern up to that point. The previous example could get a minimal form such as the following:

```
{-# LANGUAGE RecordWildCards #-}

greet IndividualR { person = PersonR { .. } } = "Hi, " ++ firstName
greet CompanyR    { .. }                      = "Hi, " ++ clientRName
greet GovOrgR     { }                         = "Welcome"
```

Note Remember that to use these extensions, you need to include the {-# LANGUAGE Extension #-} declaration at the beginning of your source code.

I have spoken about facilities for record building and matching. The last step is using record syntax for updating a record. If r is a binding containing a value of a record type, you can use r { field name = new value } to create an exact copy of r where the corresponding field has been changed. For example, here is a function that ensures that PersonR's first name always starts with a capital letter:

```
import Data.Char (toUpper)

nameInCapitals :: PersonR -> PersonR
nameInCapitals p@(PersonR { firstName = initial:rest }) =
```

```
      let newName = (toUpper initial):rest
      in  p { firstName = newName }
nameInCapitals p@(PersonR { firstName = "" }) = p
```

Take the time to understand this last example because it shows a lot of features from this chapter. Record syntax is used to pattern match on PersonR. Inside it, x:xs is used to match a list. As you later want to refer to the entire value to update it, an as pattern is used to bind it to p. Finally, the new name is computed inside a let expression, which is used to update p using record-updating syntax.

As you have done for clients, you can also benefit from record syntax when describing time machines. That is the purpose of Exercise 2-7.

EXERCISE 2-7. TIME MACHINE RECORDS

Rewrite the TimeMachine data type defined earlier using records. You should find that updating the prices of time machines is now much more concise.

The Default Values Idiom

We are going to end this chapter by showing a particularly helpful convention the Haskell community has come up with to support a common use case. You will look at functions that can take a long list of parameters, but most of the time those parameters take on default values. Take as an example a network library. For creating a connection, you need information about the following:

- URL to connect to

- Connection type: TCP or UDP

- Connection speed

- Whether to use a proxy

- Whether to use caching

- Whether to use keep-alive

- Time-out lapse

These elements can be encoded as follows:

```
data ConnType = TCP | UDP
data UseProxy = NoProxy | Proxy String
data TimeOut = NoTimeOut | TimeOut Integer

data Connection = ...   -- Definition omitted
                deriving Show

connect :: String -> ConnType -> Integer -> UseProxy
        -> Bool -> Bool -> TimeOut -> Connection
```

Of course, most people simply want to connect to a target URL using TCP at the highest speed, with some sensible defaults for proxying, caching, keep-alive, and time-out lapse. A first solution is to create a special function for that case.

```
connectUrl :: String -> Connection
connectUrl u = connect u TCP 0 NoProxy False False NoTimeOut
```

This solution makes it easy to connect in the simple case but poses two problems:

1. Maintainability is harmed. If at some point you need to add a new connection parameter, all users of the function need to change their calls to connect. Or if the default value changes, all the uses must be reconsidered and rewritten.

2. Using the library is easy only for the simplest case. If you want to connect to a URL using a proxy, you need to step back and use the full connect function, passing all the parameters. In some cases, knowing which the sensible defaults are may be difficult.

Records come to the rescue. Instead of passing parameters one by one, you can group all or most of them into a record and use the record as a parameter. Here's how that would look for the connection example:

```
data ConnOptions = ConnOptions { connType     :: ConnType
                               , connSpeed    :: Integer
                               , connProxy    :: UseProxy
                               , connCaching  :: Bool
                               , connKeepAlive :: Bool
                               , connTimeOut  :: TimeOut
```

```
                                          }
connect' :: String -> ConnOptions -> Connection
connect' url options = ...
```

The second step is to create a constant, which encodes sensible defaults.

```
connDefault :: ConnOptions
connDefault = ConnOptions TCP 0 NoProxy False False NoTimeOut
```

Now creating a connection with the default parameters takes just a tad more code, but you gain in return the ability to change just one parameter (like the type to UDP) without having to write all the default values. The following examples show the simplest case and also the case of specifying UDP as the connection type:

```
*Chapter2.DefaultValues> connect' "https://apress.com" connDefault
*Chapter2.DefaultValues> :{
*Chapter2.DefaultValues> connect' "https://apress.com"
*Chapter2.DefaultValues>            connDefault { connType = UDP }
*Chapter2.DefaultValues> :}
```

There is only one problem left. If you add a new option and the developer has made direct use of the constructor for the record type, that use must be changed. The solution is to forbid calling the constructor directly, forcing the use of connDefault in some way or another. This can be done by *not exporting* the constructor. You will see how to do this in the next chapter, where you will also learn about smart constructors.

Summary

In this chapter, you learned the basics of first-order Haskell programming.

- Basic data types were introduced: characters, Booleans, lists, and tuples.

- You learned how to define new functions and how to use let and where to create temporary bindings that allow reusing expressions and thus writing better code. Afterward, you learned how to define a function by cases.

- You defined your first data types, learned about ADTs and constructors, and played with creating new values in the interpreter.

- Pattern matching is a fundamental tool for Haskell programming, which I touched upon in this chapter. You saw how to match both primitive and user-defined types and how guards, as patterns and view patterns, make matching more concise.

- Records were introduced as a better syntax for building, accessing, and updating fields in a Haskell value. You saw the default value design pattern, which uses records at its core.

CHAPTER 3

Increasing Code Reuse

Chapter 1 explained that a functional language like Haskell is characterized by its profuse use of functions as parameters or return values. However, Chapter 2 didn't mention anything about this topic. I'll rectify that here. In this chapter, you will focus on not one but three ways in which Haskell allows for a great amount of reuse.

One of the ways in which Haskell shines in the area of reusability is through the creation of functions that can work over values of any type that respects a certain form or design. List functions such as head can operate on any type of the form [T], whatever type T is. This concept is also applicable to data types that can store values on any possible type, which is known as *parametric polymorphism*.

Another way in which Haskell allows for reuse is this ability of using functions as any other value of the language. Functions that manipulate other functions are called *higher-order* functions. In contrast, the concepts in the previous chapter belong to *first-order* Haskell.

The third way in which code can be reused (and shared) is by taking functions or data types from one module and applying them in another. You will learn how to do that from both sides: *exporting* definitions to make them available and *importing* them later.

Most of the examples in this chapter focus on *lists* and the functions in the module Data.List. The intention is twofold: lists illustrate the new concepts to be introduced, and at the same time, they are practical tools in daily programming with Haskell. As proof of their importance, the language includes special syntax to create and manage them, namely, the syntax of *comprehensions*. I'll explain how to use the syntax before moving to the last stop of the list train: how to *fold* and *unfold* lists properly.

© Alejandro Serrano Mena 2022
A. Serrano Mena, *Practical Haskell*, https://doi.org/10.1007/978-1-4842-8581-7_3

Parametric Polymorphism

You may have noticed that in previous chapters all the functions defined operated on some particular data type. However, some built-in functions such as head or empty seem to be able to operate on any kind of list: [Integer], [Client], and so forth. A fair question is, are list functions somehow treated differently by the compiler and interpreter, or do I also have the power to create such functions that can operate on any type? The correct answer is the latter: you could have defined the list functions by yourself with no problem. You do have the power.

Let's look at the type of a function such as head:

```
*Chapter3.ParamPoly> :t head
head :: [a] -> a
```

In the previous chapter, you learned that type names must start with an uppercase letter. However, you can see a lowercase identifier in this particular signature. If you remember the conventions, you know lowercase identifiers are reserved for function definitions, bindings, and parameters. Indeed, that identifier refers to a type variable that can be bound to different types depending on each use.

For example, consider the application of head to the string "Hello". The type of the string is [Char]. At the moment of application, you need to find the value for the type parameter a in the type of head. The solution in this case is a = Char. So, the type that head gets when applied to "Hello" is [Char] -> Char (once a type parameter gets assigned to a value, it must be replaced throughout the type in its entirety). Figure 3-1 illustrates the logic I've just described, where a type variable and a concrete type are unified to be the same one.

Figure 3-1. *Inferring the type of head* "Hello"

Functions such as head are said to work for any value of the type parameter a: they don't care about the shape of the inner elements. This is parametric polymorphism, and it allows multiple ("poly") types (μορφή – *morphé* is Ancient Greek for "shape") as parameters. The etymology for the concept is actually a bit misleading because a polymorphic function must work for *all* types, not just for some. Haskell also allows functions to be applicable for just a subset of all types. That is referred to as ad hoc polymorphism and will be presented in the next chapter.

Note   Parametric polymorphism is available in many programming languages under different names; for example, *templates* in C++ and *generics* in Java or C# provide similar functionality.

Note that a function may have more than one type parameter, and each of them will take its value independently from the others. One example of this kind of function is fst, which gives the first component of a tuple of two elements.

```
*Chapter3.ParamPoly> :t fst
fst :: (a, b) -> a
```

When you supply a concrete tuple to fst, the type of (a, b) is inferred from the types within that tuple. For example, you can supply the tuple ([3,8], "Hello"), and the type (a, b) becomes ([Integer], [Char]).

There is no special syntax, apart from type parameters, for writing polymorphic functions. When you do not use a value in a way in which its type plays a role (e.g., pattern matching on its possible constructors), Haskell will infer a parametric type. For example, let's write a function that returns a different string depending on a Maybe value.

```
maybeString (Just _) = "Just"
maybeString Nothing  = "Nothing"
```

If you now load this function into the interpreter, and ask for its type, you will get the one inferred by GHC:

```
*Chapter3.ParamPoly> :t maybeString
maybeString :: Maybe a -> [Char]
```

Polymorphism is available not only in functions but also in data types. This assumption was implicit when you wrote [T] to refer to a list of any possible type T. As you can see from the examples, a polymorphic type is written with its name along with a list of all its type parameters, like Maybe Integer. The definition of polymorphic types is similar to that of basic types, but after the name of the type, you write the names of the type parameters for that declaration. Later, you can use those names in the constructors in the position of any other type. For example, you may decide to give a unique identifier to each client in your program, but it does not matter which kind of identifier you are using (integers or strings are usual choices) because you never manipulate the identifier directly.

The following is a good example of polymorphism:

```
data Client i = GovOrg  { clientId :: i, clientName :: String }
              | Company { clientId :: i, clientName :: String
                        , person :: Person, duty :: String }
              | Individual { clientId :: i, person :: Person }
              deriving (Show, Eq, Ord)
                        -- Eq and Ord will be introduced in Chapter 4
data Person = Person { firstName :: String, lastName  :: String }
              deriving (Show, Eq, Ord)
```

When you create a value, the type parameter will be instantiated to a specific type, in this case Char.

```
*Chapter3.ParamPoly> :t GovOrg 'n' "NTTF"   -- National Time Travel Fund
GovOrg 'n' "NTTF" :: Client Char
```

More than one type variable can be used in a data type. This is the case for tuples. For example, those with three components have type (a,b,c). If you were to define triples by yourself, the data declaration would look like this:

```
data Triple a b c = Triple a b c
```

Note that you can use the same type variable multiple times in the definition of your ADT. But that doesn't mean the values on the fields must be the same, just that they must have the same type. This is a typical source of confusion when learning Haskell, but a counterexample is easy to build: ('a','b') has type (Char,Char), with both type variables holding the same type Char, but the value 'a' is different from the value 'b'. Another tidbit to remember is that even though a type parameter may appear several times in a constructor, it is a single type variable. For example, let's declare a type for a pair of elements, with each element being of the same type. Here's how you would do that:

```
data SamePair a = SamePair a a
```

A value like SamePair 1 2 will have type SamePair Integer, not SamePair Integer Integer. Admittedly, the fact that the same identifier is usually reused for both the type name and its constructor adds more confusion to the mix, but it's something you must get used to. Exercise 3-1 will help you.

EXERCISE 3-1. A NEW LIFE AS TYPE CHECKER

Try to understand what the following functions do and which type will be inferred by the interpreter. Give the most polymorphic answer from all possible ones.

```
swapTriple (x,y,z) = (y,z,x)

duplicate x = (x,x)

nothing _ = Nothing

index []    = []
index [x]   = [(0,x)]
index (x:xs) = let indexed@((n,_):_) = index xs
                in  (n+1,x):indexed

maybeA [] = 'a'
```

Remember that you can use GHCi to check your answers. Refer to Chapter 2 if you need a reminder on how to do that.

Functions As Parameters

This is finally the point where we explain how to treat functions as any other value in Haskell. You may already be familiar with this idea, as the concept of "function as parameter" has permeated to many other languages, not necessarily functional. For example, Java or C# includes them as a language feature.

As mentioned at the beginning of the chapter, most of the examples relate to lists. Lists are one of the basic data structures in functional programming, especially while learning. Many more complex concepts, such as functor or fold, are generalizations of patterns that can be found when working with lists.

Higher-Order Functions

The first, most basic, function you will look at is map, which applies another function throughout an entire list. Consider the function succ, which adds 1 to a number.

```
*Chapter3.FnsParams> succ 1
2
```

Caution   It may be the case that the interpreter shows warning messages about Defaulting the following constraint(s) to type `Integer`. I mentioned in the previous chapter that a constant like 1 is polymorphic on the number type, so the interpreter makes a choice in order to run the code. The warning is telling you that Integer is its default choice. You can safely ignore these warnings, or you can disable them by running the interpreter using ghci -fno-warn-type-defaults. In the rest of the book, I will omit this kind of warning in the output.

You can now add 1 to all members of the list [1,2,3] using map in combination with the function succ:

```
*Chapter3.FnsParams> map succ [1,2,3]
[2,3,4]
```

How does it work? First, let's look at the type.

```
*Chapter3.FnsParams> :t map
map :: (a -> b) -> [a] -> [b]
```

You can see the notation for functions, a -> b, but now in the position of a parameter. This type signature encodes the fact that map takes a function from a to b and a list of a's, and it returns a list of b's. Functions such as map, which take other functions as parameters, are known as *higher-order functions*.

In the declaration of functions, other functions given as parameters follow the same naming conventions as any other argument to a function. You don't need any special marker to distinguish a parameter for having a functional type. But being a function, you can apply the parameter to any other parameter or value as if it were defined elsewhere. For example, the definition of map looks like this:

```
map _ []     = []
map f (x:xs) = (f x) : (map f xs)
```

This is also an example of parametric polymorphism. However, polymorphism and higher-order functions are completely separate concepts. You could define a function that applies another function but to an integer two units higher and then multiplies it by 3, that is, $3f(x+2)$. In this case, reasonable fs should take and return a number, so the function should have an Integer -> Integer type.

```
apply3f2 :: (Integer -> Integer) -> Integer -> Integer
apply3f2 f x = 3 * f (x + 2)
```

Let's follow the steps for a call to this function using succ as a value for f.

```
apply3f2 succ 7 => 3 * succ (7 + 2) => 3 * succ 9
                => 3 * (9 + 1) => 3 * 10 => 30
```

Now that you're in touch with higher-order functions, it's time to introduce a popular idiom in Haskell code. The idiom works around the ($) function, which performs function application.

```
($) :: (a -> b) -> a -> b
f $ a = f a
```

Why is this ($) function useful at all? At first glance, it seems like a rather cumbersome way to apply a function to some arguments, given that this is the main use of functions. But apart from this definition, Haskell gives a very low precedence to ($), so both sides of this operator will be evaluated before f is applied to a. Therefore, you can omit a lot of parentheses when using ($). Doing this is common in Haskell. For example, the following:

```
maximum (map succ [1, 2, 3])
```

would usually be written like so:

```
maximum $ map succ [1, 2, 3]
```

Anonymous Functions

Until now, you have always used as parameters other functions that were defined elsewhere. However, it may be the case that you want to create a small function just to be applied via map to a list. It wouldn't make sense to add an entire new declaration, polluting your module. You already know a solution, which is to define the function inside a let or where block. The following example demonstrates this solution by adding 2 to every number in a list:

```
*Chapter3.FnsParams> :{
*Chapter3.FnsParams| let f x = x + 2
*Chapter3.FnsParams| in  map f [1,2,3]
*Chapter3.FnsParams| :}
[3,4,5]
```

This solution is not completely satisfactory: Haskell encourages passing and returning functions, so with this design, the code would be full of let blocks. Instead, Haskell includes *anonymous functions*. These are function bodies that are not given a name and that can be written anywhere in the code where a function is expected. The function body syntax is as follows:

```
\param1 param2 ... -> body
```

The previous map operation can then be written as follows:

```
map (\x -> x + 2) [1,2,3]
```

Note   The notation \... -> ... comes from a mathematical theory of computation called *lambda calculus*. In that formalism, an expression like \x -> x + 2 is called an abstraction and is written $\lambda x.\ x + 2$ (Haskell designers chose the symbol \ because it resembles λ but it's easier to type). Because of these historical roots, anonymous functions are sometimes called *lambda abstractions*, or simply *abstractions*.

In anonymous functions, as in any other function, you can pattern match directly on the parameters. For example, you can build a function checking whether pairs of integers are equal.

```
equalTuples :: [(Integer,Integer)] -> [Bool]
equalTuples t = map (\(x,y) -> x == y) t
```

However, not all forms of regular function declarations are allowed when used anonymously. Anonymous functions don't have a name, so they cannot call themselves, thus forbidding recursion. Furthermore, only one pattern can be matched. So, if you want to match several patterns, you must resort to a case statement.

```
sayHello :: [String] -> [String]
sayHello names = map (\name -> case name of
                                "Alejandro" -> "Hello, writer"
                                _           -> "Welcome, " ++ name
                      ) names
```

This last restriction is lifted if you are using GHC and enable the LambdaCase extension. Then, you can use the special syntax \case to create an anonymous function with only one parameter to match on. Here's an example:

```
{-# LANGUAGE LambdaCase #-}
sayHello names = map (\case "Alejandro" -> "Hello, writer"
                            name        -> "Welcome, " ++ name
                      ) names
```

Abstractions are also useful for returning functional values. For example, say you want to define a function that takes a number n and returns another function that multiplies by n.

```
multiplyByN :: Integer -> (Integer -> Integer)
multiplyByN n = \x -> n*x
```

You can now use that returned function in places that take one, such as map.

```
*Chapter3.FnsParams> map (multiplyByN 5) [1,2,3]
[5,10,15]
```

As you can see, the function multiplyByN 5 "remembers" the value given to n when it is applied. You say that the function encloses the values from the surrounding environment (in this case, only n) along with the body. For that reason, these functions are usually known as *closures* in almost all languages supporting functional features.

filter is another function operating on lists. In this case, filter takes a function of type a -> Bool (i.e., a function returning a Boolean value) and applies it to each element, returning just those that fulfill the condition. For example, you can filter a list of numbers and keep only the even ones using the aforementioned function and giving as an argument the even function from the standard libraries.

```
*Chapter3.FnsParams> filter even [1,2,3,4,5]
[2,4]
```

EXERCISE 3-2. WORKING WITH FILTERS

Using the function filter as the basis for your solution, write the following functions:

- filterOnes, which returns only the elements equal to the constant 1.

- filterANumber, which returns only the elements equal to some number that is given via a parameter.

- filterNot, which performs the reverse duty of filter. It returns only those elements of the list that *do not* fulfill the condition.

- filterGovOrgs, which takes a list of Clients (as defined before) and returns only those that are government organizations. Write it using both an auxiliary function isGovOrg and a \case expression.

Hint: Search for documentation of the function not :: Bool -> Bool.[1]

Partial Application of a Function

Let's get back to map. You already know two ways to write a function that doubles all elements in a list.

```
double list = map (\x -> x * 2) list
double      = \list -> map (\x -> x * 2) list
```

---

[1] The easiest way is to point your browser to www.haskell.org/ghc/docs/latest/html/libraries/base/Prelude.html#v:not.

Haskell allows a third approach. The keyword `list` is at the end of both parameter lists, so you can just omit it.

```
double     = map (\x -> x * 2)
```

To better understand the reason why omitting `list` makes sense, let's look at the process in which the compiler infers the type of the `double` function. First, start with `map :: (a -> b) -> [a] -> [b]`. The function `(\x -> x * 2)` takes and returns a number; for example, it can be typed as `Integer -> Integer`. Now, if you apply the numeric function to `map`, you are first matching `a = b = Integer` and then removing the first parameter in the type because you already have provided a value for it. The result is the following:

```
map (\x -> x * 2) :: [Integer] -> [Integer]
```

That is, if given a list of integers, it will return a new list of integers.

Following this path of partial application, you can apply it also for the `\x -> x * 2` anonymous function. There is just one syntactic remark to be made: when the function has an operator name (only with symbols, like *), you cannot just use its name and arguments; you need to use a *section*. A section is just a specification of the operation to be done, enclosed in parentheses. The syntax resembles the application of the operator where the parameters have been wiped out. In this case, the new definition for `double` is as follows:

```
double     = map (*2)
```

Caution   The usual warnings about commutativity of operations apply here. You must be careful about where you are omitting the parameter because it may make a huge difference in the result.

Look carefully, for example, at the difference in the result from the following two examples:

```
*Chapter3.FnsParams> map (/2) [1,2,3]
[0.5,1.0,1.5]
*Chapter3.FnsParams> map (2/) [1,2,3]
[2.0,1.0,0.6666666666666666]
```

It should be noted that type constructors also behave as functions in any possible sense except for the distinction in capitalization (remember that function names must start with a lowercase letter and type constructors must start with an uppercase one). You can ask the type of a constructor or partially apply it as usual.

```
*Chapter3.FnsParams> :t Just
Just :: a -> Maybe a
*Chapter3.FnsParams> :t ('a' :)
('a' :) :: [Char] -> [Char]
```

Once you know about the possibility of partially applying functions, it's time to look more deeply into the meaning of the function types as they are written. First, the -> symbol binds to the right. That is, the type a -> b -> c -> d is a prettier, but equivalent, version of a -> (b -> (c -> d)). So, at its core, every function with more than one parameter is just a function that takes one parameter and returns a closure with one parameter less, which may indeed consume another parameter, and so on, until you reach a nonfunction type. At that moment, all the information to apply the function is there, and its body can be evaluated. So, now you have at least four interchangeable ways to declare the same two-argument function.

```
f x y = ...
f x   = \y -> ...
f     = \x y -> ...
f     = \x -> \y -> ...
```

Let's look at map with these new glasses. Previously, I spoke about map as taking a function and a list and applying the function to the list. But, if now the type is written as (a -> b) -> ([a] -> [b]), there's a new view: map takes a function and returns a version of that function that works over a list!

Partial application encourages a programming style where functions are combined without ever mentioning their parameters. This is called *point-free style* (because in mathematics, parameters to functions are called *points*). Without any doubt, the most important of these combinators is the period[2] (.), which composes two functions. By

---

[2] Since (.) could also be called a *point*, there's some risk of confusion about the name *point-free*. The point-free style encourages the use of (.) and discourages explicit parameters.

composes, I mean that the period applies one function after the other. For example, the following is how to write function f applied to the output from g:

f . g = \x -> f (g x)

As a reminder, functions are written backward in comparison to other notations: you write first the outermost function that will be applied to the result of the innermost. This comes again from the roots of the language in lambda calculus and mathematics, where composition is denoted this way.

For example, say you want to write a function that duplicates all the odd numbers in a list. The most natural way seems to be as follows:

```
duplicateOdds list = map (*2) $ filter odd list
```

Here, you want to first apply filter odd, which takes out the even numbers, and then double each of the elements of the resulting list using map (*2). This is exactly the composition of the two functions, so you can write the following in point-free style:

```
duplicateOdds = map (*2) . filter odd
```

In many cases, an expression can be written in point-free style as a sequence of transformations over some data, rendering the code clear once you become accustomed to the notation.

In the rest of the section, I'll introduce additional functions that create a point-free style. Since these functions have the task of combining other functions, they are sometimes called *combinators*. The two next combinators are used to convert multi-argument functions to single-argument functions which take a tuple of values.

```
uncurry :: (a -> b -> c) -> (a,b) -> c
uncurry f = \(x,y) -> f x y
curry :: ((a,b) -> c) -> a -> b -> c
curry f = \x y -> f (x,y)
```

Functions that take a sequence of arguments are called the *curried* versions of those that take a tuple. I'll stress the subtle difference: the not-curried version of a function takes only *one* argument, but it is a tuple, so in one value it holds more than one piece of information. For example, the max function, returning the maximum of two numbers, takes two arguments.

```
*Chapter3.FnsParams> max 3 2
3
```

But if you curry it, you must call it with only one argument, which is a tuple.

```
*Chapter3.FnsParams> (uncurry max) (3,2)
3
```

Usually, you will prefer these curried versions, because you can partially apply them. But sometimes an uncurried version is also interesting to consider. For example, say you are given a list of pairs of numbers, and you want to get the list of the maximums of pairs. You cannot directly use map max because max requires two arguments. The solution is to curry the function before application.

```
*Chapter3.FnsParams> map (uncurry max) [(1,2),(2,1),(3,4)]
[2,2,4]
```

You may need to define an extra combinator to reverse the order of parameters in a function. The most usual name for this combinator is flip, with the following type:

```
flip :: (a -> b -> c) -> (b -> a -> c)
flip f = \x y -> f y x
```

Note   Both the language Haskell and the term *curried function* take their names from the American logician Haskell Brooks Curry (1900–1982), who studied a field called *combinatory logic* that provided the groundwork for later developments in functional programming.

More on Modules

In the previous chapter, you learned how to create modules to organize your functions and data types. The next logical step is being able to get the definitions in one module to be used in another. This is called *importing* a module, and it's similar to importing packages in Java or namespaces in C#.

Module Imports

Module imports are listed after the module declaration but before any other definition. There are different ways to import a module. The most basic approach brings into scope all the functions from the module and makes them available for use as if they were defined in the importing module. In this chapter, you are learning about list functions, so you can import Data.List and use the permutations function, such as the function permutationsStartingWith, which returns all the permutations of a string that start with a specific letter.

```
module Chapter3.MoreModules
import Data.List
permutationsStartingWith :: Char -> String -> [String]
permutationsStartingWith letter
  = filter (\l -> head l == letter) . permutations
```

Note   Even though Haskell modules have a hierarchical structure, importing a module does not bring into scope any child modules. For example, importing Data won't provide any access to Data.List.permutations because permutations lives in module Data.List, and Data.List was not imported.

In some cases, names found in different modules clash. That is, you import definitions from two modules, and both include the same function or type, so the compiler doesn't know which one to use. The better solution is to control exactly which definitions to import. To do so, you must include a list of desired elements in a list surrounded by parentheses. For example, you can specify that you want to import only the permutations and subsequence functions, like so:

```
import Data.List (permutations, subsequence)
```

Sometimes, the case is just the opposite: you want to import an entire module except some specific elements (usually, those whose names clash). This usually happens when some names conflict between the imported module and the one being developed. For those cases, Haskell provides *hiding imports*. The declarations you don't want to bring into scope are written again as a list but preceded by the keyword hiding. For example, to import all but the head and tail functions, you use this:

```
import Data.List hiding (head, tail)
```

Data types need some extra syntax for being selected for import or hiding. This need comes from the fact that an ADT really encompasses two pieces of information: the type itself and its constructors. The Haskell committee decided to use Type(List of Constructors) for this matter. Here are several ways in which you can import the Client data type from the first section:

```
import Chapter3.ParamPoly (Client())    -- only type, no constructors
import Chapter3.ParamPoly (Client(GovOrg,Individual))
                                    -- a subset of constructors
import Chapter3.ParamPoly (Client(..)) -- .. imports all constructors
```

Until now, I have spoken about how to import modules *without qualification*. Once declarations are imported, you don't need any further syntax to use them. *Qualified imports* are the other side of the coin. A qualified import requires you to prefix a function with the name of the module it came from. In that way, you can use functions or types with the same name but from different modules without any problem. For example, you can import filter and permutations as qualified imports.

```
import qualified Data.List (filter, permutations)
permutationsStartingWith :: Char -> String -> [String]
permutationsStartingWith letter
  = Data.List.filter (\l -> head l == letter) . Data.List.permutations
```

As you can see, you can combine the selection of a subset of functions with the qualification of the module. Indeed, those concepts are orthogonal, and you can combine them freely.

In some cases, the name of a module is too long to be used as a prefix. To save endless typing, you can *rename* the module using an as clause. Afterward, you prefix the declarations with the new name.

```
import qualified Data.List as L
permutationsStartingWith :: Char -> String -> [String]
permutationsStartingWith letter
  = L.filter (\l -> head l == letter) . L.permutations
```

As in the previous case, you can mix qualified imports with renaming and explicit import lists. The module import that just includes `permutations` and `subsequences` is as follows:

```
import qualified Data.List as L(permutations, subsequences)
```

THE PRELUDE

By default, any Haskell module always imports without qualification the module named `Prelude`. This module contains the most basic and used functions in the Haskell Platform, such as `(+)` or `head`. This automatic import is essential to your being able to write Haskell code without worrying about importing every single function you invoke. You have actually been benefiting from `Prelude` throughout all the examples so far in this book.

In rare cases, you may need to disable this automatic import. You can do so in GHC by enabling the language extension `NoImplicitPrelude`. Remember that, in this case, if you need to use any function in `Prelude`, you need to import it explicitly.

Smart Constructors and Views

You not only can control imported declaration from a module but also can control which of the declarations in your own modules you want to make public for consumption elsewhere. That is, you can control which declarations you want to *export*. By default, every single declaration in a module is exported. To restrict the availability of your functions and data types, you need to build an explicit export list in which all the public declarations are written and write that list just after the module name. For example, the following module exports only the function `f`:

```
module M (f) where
f = ...
g = ...
```

Of course, you can also control which data types and type constructors will be exported. As with importing lists, you have several options for exporting a data type: merely exporting the type but no constructor (thus disallowing the creation of values by directly calling the constructors), exporting just some subset of constructors, or exporting all of them.

Remember that in the previous chapter, I talked about the default value design pattern but also stated that it was not completely finished because there was no way to restrict the creation of ConnOptions values. Now you have what is needed to finish the pattern. You can export only the ConnOptions data type, without any of its constructors, and also the connDefault constant that is refined by changes to the default values. Here's an example:

```
module Chapter2.DataTypes (ConnOptions(), connDefault) where
```

This idea of hiding the constructors of a given data type opens the door to a new design pattern, usually called *smart constructors*. The use case is as follows: sometimes, not all the values that can be obtained using a constructor are correct values for the concept you are modeling. In those cases, you want to make sure that the developer can only construct values in the correct space.

For example, you may need to represent a closed integer range, that is, the set of values between some integers a (the lower bound) and b (the upper bound). A sensible invariant is that $a \leq b$ in all cases. But the definition of the Range ADT looks like this:

```
data Range = Range Integer Integer deriving Show
```

This definition does not prevent incorrect values. Instead, the idea is to provide a function range that performs the check. If everything is OK and the check is passed, the function range proceeds with the construction. Otherwise, the function throws an error.

```
range :: Integer -> Integer -> Range
range a b = if a <= b then Range a b else error "a must be <= b"
```

Note   error is a built-in function that can be used anywhere to signal a point at which the program cannot continue and should be halted, showing the specified error message. This is one of several possibilities for dealing with errors in Haskell. You will explore other ways to signal errors throughout the book.

This range function is called a *smart constructor*. It works basically like a regular constructor but performs some extra checking on its parameters. You can enforce the use of this constructor in all cases by not exporting the Range constructor, but only the type. Here's an example:

```
module Chapter3.Ranges (Range(), range) where
```

But there is a problem! Since you have hidden the constructor, any pattern match of the following form outside the private code of the module won't even compile:

```
case ... of Range x y -> ...
```

Code in this form won't compile because the constructor is not available. The solution is to create a new data type that encodes the observed values of that type and then uses views when pattern matching. Of course, this doesn't stop users from creating wrong RangeObs values, but in case all functions work with Range and not RangeObs, there will be no choice but to use it correctly. In this case, the observation data type and the conversion function can be as follows:

```
data RangeObs = R Integer Integer deriving Show
r :: Range -> RangeObs
r (Range a b) = R a b
```

If you export the RangeObs constructor, you can now pattern match using a view. Remember to include the ViewPatterns extension in your source file.

```
{-# LANGUAGE ViewPatterns #-}
prettyRange :: Range -> String
prettyRange rng = case rng of
                (r -> R a b) -> "[" ++ show a ++ "," ++ show b ++ "]"
```

You can go one step further and create a *pattern synonym* which packages this specific form of building and deconstructing Range values. By doing so, the user of your type does not have to be aware of the implementation using several types. In this case, we need to use a *bidirectional pattern*, because we require different behavior for matching and constructing.

```
{-# LANGUAGE PatternSynonyms #-}
pattern R :: Integer -> Integer -> Range
pattern R a b <- Range a b
  where R a b = range a b
```

The syntax is a big cumbersome, though. A bidirectional pattern synonym is composed of three parts. The first one is a type signature, which coincides with the Range constructor. In general, the arguments refer to each of the positions in the pattern. The next element is the matcher: in this case, I declare that matching over R a b is equivalent to writing a pattern match of the form Range a b. The trick comes in the final element, after the where keyword, which declares that using R x y in a building position is equivalent to calling the range function. Note that this is not Range, the constructor, but the smart constructor which checks the invariant.

Finally, this is a solution to the problem of not exposing constructors for creating values, while at the same time not harming the ability to use pattern matching for working on it.

Diving into Lists

You have already learned about two of the most common list functions, namely, map and filter. In this section, you will see more examples of higher-order functions on lists and discover some patterns such as folds that are useful in Haskell code. Most of these functions live in the Prelude module, so you don't need to explicitly import them. The rest of them live in the Data.List module.

DIVING INTO LISTS CODE

While reading this section, try to write the definition of each list function once its description has been introduced. Doing so is a good exercise to cement the concepts of parametric polymorphism and higher-order functions in your mind. You can start by writing the filter function.

Folds

The first function you will look at is foldr, which introduces you to the world of folds. A *fold* over a data structure such as a list is a function that aggregates or combines all the values contained in that structure to produce a single result. Folds are an expressive and powerful tool, often underestimated. Examples of folds are summing all integers in a list and finding the maximum of the values in the nodes of a tree (I will speak more about trees later).

The definition of foldr includes three arguments: a binary function f that is used to combine elements step by step, the initial value for starting aggregation, and finally the list itself.

```
foldr :: (a -> b -> b) -> b -> [a] -> b
foldr f initial []     = initial
foldr f initial (x:xs) = f x (foldr f initial xs)
```

This initial value plus binary operation is a common pattern in Haskell code. Usually, the initial value is chosen in such a way that using it as an argument in the binary operation doesn't change the result. We call such a value a *neutral* or *identity element* of the operation. Take, for example, the task of summing all the elements in a list. The chosen operation should intuitively be addition, (+). Then, the initial value should be chosen so as not to affect that operation, and you should now ideally be thinking in terms of the value 0. Let's follow the evaluation of a call to foldr that exactly performs that task of summing all the elements in a list.

```
foldr (+) 0 [1,2,3] => 1 + foldr (+) 0 [2,3]
                    => 1 + (2 + foldr (+) [3])
                    => 1 + (2 + (3 + foldr (+) 0 []))
                    => 1 + (2 + (3 + 0))
                    => 1 + (2 + 3) => 1 + 5 => 6
```

As you can see, foldr traverses the list element by element until it reaches the end. At that moment, foldr uses the initial value to start evaluating the whole call stack that has been created, from the end up to the first application of the corresponding combining function, in this case (+). If you look at a list as a combination of (:) and [] constructors, you can rephrase the algorithm as follows: foldr replaces all instances of (:) by f and all occurrences of [] by the initial value. Figure 3-2 illustrates this thinking.

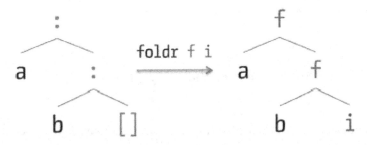

Figure 3-2. *Visual description of foldr*

Another example of fold is maximum, which finds the largest value from a list. In this case, the initial value is a bit more elusive because you must consider what the maximum of an empty list is. To help in answering that question, you need to recall the other property that is wanted for the initial value: it should not change the outcome of the binary operation, which in this case is max. This means you have to find a value z such that max(z,x) = max(x,z) = x any value x. You can check that the value that satisfies that property is negative infinity ($-\infty$).

By default, Haskell integers don't allow representing infinite values, so you need to define a custom data type for this matter. After some thought, you find that the concept of adding infinity values is not unique to integers. The concept also applies to ratios, floating-point values, and so forth. To make the new type more useful, you can define the InfNumber data type as being polymorphic.

```
data InfNumber a = MinusInfinity
                 | Number a
                 | PlusInfinity
                 deriving Show
```

By making the type polymorphic, you allow for the possibility of using the type for more than just integers. The immediate problem requires just infinite integer values, but future problems might require, say, infinite floating-point values. Polymorphism here is an investment in the future.

The next step is defining a new binary operation, infMax, to combine two of these numbers.

```
infMax MinusInfinity x        = x
infMax x MinusInfinity        = x
infMax PlusInfinity _         = PlusInfinity
infMax _ PlusInfinity         = PlusInfinity
infMax (Number a) (Number b) = Number (max a b)
```

Let's try to write the fold.

```
*Chapter3.Lists> foldr infMax MinusInfinity [1,2,3]
    No instance for (Ord t0) arising from a use of `infMax'
```

Clearly, it's not done yet. You are getting an error because the expression that has been written doesn't pass the type checker. The operation infMax combines elements of type InfNumber, but [1,2,3] is a list of integers. A first solution is to convert the list to InfNumbers by mapping the Number constructor over the list.

*Chapter3.Lists> **foldr infMax MinusInfinity $ map Number [1,2,3]**
Number 3

However, if you look carefully at the type of foldr, you will see that there's no need for the combining function (the f argument in foldr) to take values of the same type because it's not of type a -> a -> a. Rather, the type is a -> b -> b, which means that f should take as the first parameter a value of the type contained in the list, and the second should be the one of the type you are accumulating, which coincides with the type of the initial value (called initial in the definition of foldr shown here). In this case, this means the aggregation function should have type Integer -> InfNumber Integer -> InfNumber Integer since the initial value is MinusInfinity :: InfNumber Integer. You already know how to convert existing numbers into InfNumbers, which is the only special thing you need in the fold.

*Chapter3.Lists> **foldr (\x y -> infMax (Number x) y) MinusInfinity [1,2,3]**
Number 3

The name foldr is a reminder of the algorithm the function implements. It is a fold that *associates to the right*. That is, the innermost parentheses will be found on the right side of the expression. Similarly, you can build a fold that associates to the left, which is included in the Haskell Platform as foldl.

```
foldl :: (a -> b -> a) -> a -> [b] -> a
foldl _ initial [] = initial
foldl f initial (x:xs) = foldl f (f initial x) xs
```

The innermost parentheses are now at the left, as this evaluation trace shows:

```
foldl (+) 0 [1,2,3] => foldl (+) (0 + 1) [2,3]
                    => foldl (+) ((0 + 1) + 2) [3]
                    => foldl (+) (((0 + 1) + 2) + 3) []
                    => ((0 + 1) + 2) + 3
                    => (1 + 2) + 3
                    => 3 + 3 => 6
```

The result value of the fold in the examples so far does not depend on whether it is performed to the right or to the left. But for this to hold, the aggregation operator that is chosen must be commutative. In other words, the following must hold true: $f(x,y) = f(y,x)$ $f(x, y) = f(y, x)$. So long as the order in which parameters are input does not matter, you can make it so that folding left or right also does not matter.

Some operations cannot be made commutative. Subtraction, for example, is not commutative, so the result changes between folds.

```
*Chapter3.Lists> foldr (-) 0 [1,2,3]
2
*Chapter3.Lists> foldl (-) 0 [1,2,3]
-6
```

One last version of folds is the one composed of those that do not take an initial value, namely, foldr1 and foldl1. In those, the starting value is the last element (in foldr1) or the first element (in foldl1) of the list. If you know any language derived from Lisp, such as Common Lisp, Racket, or Clojure, you will know this folding operation as reduce. It is not used much in Haskell, but it may come in handy in cases where handling the empty list case is guaranteed not to happen and where handling it tangles the code. As an example, the previously defined maximum function is much easier using foldr1.

```
maximum' :: [Integer] -> Integer
maximum' = foldr1 max
```

EXERCISE 3-3. YOUR FIRST FOLDS

Consider the functions product, minimumClient, and all. The product function computes the product of a list of integers. The minimumClient function computes the Client with the shortest name. Finally, the all function computes the conjunction (&&) of a list of Boolean values. Given these functions, do the following:

- Write the functions using pattern matching, without resorting to any higher-order function.

- Write the functions as folds. In each case, first try to find the aggregation operation and from that derive a sensible initial value.

Can you find the structure that all these functions share when written in the first style? In which cases is it true that using `foldr` and `foldl` give the same results?

Extra: Try to write a `minimumBy` function such that the order is taken by first applying a function g on the result. For example, `minimumBy (\x -> -x) [1,2,3]` should return 3.

Lists and Predicates

Another big family of list functions comprise those that take Boolean predicates, that is, functions with the type `a -> Bool`. The `filter` function I've already talked about is a representative of this family. I have already asked you to write the dual version of `filter`, which only takes elements from a list that doesn't fulfill a condition. One often needs to group the members of a list depending on whether they satisfy a condition. A naïve way to do this would be as follows:

```
bothFilters :: (a -> Bool) -> [a] -> ([a],[a])
bothFilters p list = (filter p list, filter (not . p) list)
```

This definition is correct but has a problem: it will traverse the whole list twice. Intuitively, just one pass should suffice. Haskell defines a function `partition` inside the `Data.List` module just for that matter: splitting a list in just one go.

```
*Chapter3.Lists> import Data.List
*Chapter3.Lists Data.List> partition (> 0) [1,2,-3,4,-5,-6]
([1,2,4],[-3,-5,-6])
```

If you want to get only the first element in the list that satisfies the condition, you should use `find` instead of `filter`. There's the chance that the list contains no such element. For that reason, `find` returns a `Maybe` value.

```
*Chapter3.Lists Data.List> find (> 0) [1,2,-3,4,-5,-6]
Just 1
*Chapter3.Lists Data.List> find (> 7) [1,2,-3,4,-5,-6]
Nothing
```

Let's now move to the following use case: you have a processing system for the shop, with a queue for the clients, which is itself represented as a list where the head is the next client to be served. At high load times, you want to impose the following policy: skip all the clients that are not government organizations. The `Data.List` module provides a dropWhile function that returns some list from the point in which some predicate becomes false.

```
skipUntilGov :: [Client a] -> [Client a]
skipUntilGov = dropWhile (\case { GovOrg {} -> False ; _ -> True })
```

Note   Remember you need to enable the LambdaCase extension for the previous code to be accepted by GHC.

Its counterpart is takeWhile, which takes the initial elements until the predicate becomes false. You can use takeWhile to get a list of all the commands in a list until one equals "stop", at which point you quit processing. Here's the code to do that:

```
*Chapter3.Lists Data.List> let lst = ["hello", "send", "stop", "receive"]
*Chapter3.Lists Data.List> takeWhile (/= "stop") lst
["hello","send"]
```

The takeWhile and dropWhile functions are the two components of the function span, which returns both the taken list and the dropped list:

```
*Chapter3.Lists Data.List> span (/= "stop") lst
(["hello","send"],["stop","receive"])
```

A related function is break, which does the same work as span but negates the predicate before. Actually, break could be defined as span (not . p).

The last couple of functions that take unary predicates are any and all. As their names suggest, they check whether at least one or all the elements of the list, respectively, fulfill some condition. They are similar to the logical quantifiers "exists" (∃) and "for all" (∀). For example, in the monthly analytics you may want to be sure you have an individual registered in the web shop and that you have at least a company or government organization in the system, that is, some Client that is not an Individual. You may define an isIndividual function to start.

```
isIndividual :: Client a -> Bool
isIndividual (Individual {}) = True
isIndividual _               = False
checkAnalytics :: [Client a] -> (Bool, Bool)
checkAnalytics cs = (any isIndividual cs, not $ all isIndividual cs)
```

Now let's move to another kind of predicate: binary ones. These are functions that take two arguments and return some Boolean value by comparing them somehow. The first kind of comparison you can do is whether two elements are equivalent (or not): (==) and (/=) belong to that family. And those are the kind of predicates that the function nubBy expects: it takes out elements such that no two elements in the returned list are equivalent. In this example, you get only one representative of each parity.

```
*Chapter3.Lists Data.List> let p x y = (even x && even y)||(odd x && odd y)
*Chapter3.Lists Data.List> nubBy p [1,2,3,4,5]
[1,2]
```

If you use (==) in nubBy, you are essentially removing duplicates in the list.

```
*Chapter3.Lists Data.List> nubBy (==) [1,2,1,1,3,2,4,1]
[1,2,3,4]
```

In many cases, types come equipped with a default comparison. You will see how to add that default comparison to your own types in the next chapter, when I talk about type classes. If the values support it, like those of the Integer type, you can just use nub and drop the equivalence function.

```
*Chapter3.Lists Data.List> nub [1,2,1,1,3,2,4,1]
[1,2,3,4]
```

Note   nub and nubBy are not very performant functions because they must check for equality between all possible pairs of elements. This means the order of the function is quadratic. In the next chapter, you will learn a faster way to remove duplicates from a list.

Equality checks, or more broadly equivalence checks, can be used to maintain lists as sets: holding only a copy of each value. The main functions are union(By), which returns a new set with all the elements from the initial ones; intersect(By), which returns a set holding only the elements in both sets; insert(By), which adds only one element to a set; and (\\), which performs the difference between sets: x1 \\ x2 contains all elements in x1 that are not in x2. In each case, the version ending in By takes a parameter telling how to check elements for equivalence, whereas the other versions use the default comparison.

```
*Chapter3.Lists Data.List> :{
*Chapter3.Lists Data.List | let x1 = [1,2,3,4]
*Chapter3.Lists Data.List |     x2 = [2,3,5]
*Chapter3.Lists Data.List | in (x1 `union` x2, x1 `intersect` x2, x1 \\ x2)
*Chapter3.Lists Data.List | :}
([1,2,3,4,5],[2,3],[1,4])
```

This example also shows an interesting feature of Haskell syntax: *infix notation*. Each time you have a two-argument function that doesn't have a name made only of symbols (such as union or intersect), you can write the name between the arguments surrounding it by back quotes, `` ` ``.

Finally, elem just points out whether an element is a member of a list.

```
*Chapter3.Lists Data.List> 2 `elem` [1,2,3]
True
*Chapter3.Lists Data.List> 4 `elem` [1,2,3]
False
```

Mini-exercise   Write elem using find and pattern matching.

The other usual meaning for binary predicates is ordering: p x y means that in some way x precedes y. However, for both clarity and performance reasons, ordering in Haskell is not defined by returning a Bool but by returning an Ordering value, which can be LT (less than), EQ (equal), or GT (greater than). For example, you can define a function representing that companies and government organizations go first in an ordering of clients and individuals are next. In each level, draws are decided by the names of the clients. The following is the code to implement that function, and it is written knowing that the built-in compare function defines an Ordering for strings:

```
compareClient :: Client a -> Client a -> Ordering
compareClient (Individual{person = p1}) (Individual{person = p2})
                              = compare (firstName p1) (firstName p2)
compareClient (Individual {}) _ = GT
compareClient _ (Individual {}) = LT
compareClient c1 c2             = compare (clientName c1) (clientName c2)
```

In the following examples, the code will use part of my list of clients. As you may suspect, many of the popular scientists, writers, and adventurers of the time buy or read books in the store.

```
listOfClients
  = [ Individual 2 (Person "H. G." "Wells")
    , GovOrg 3 "NTTF"  -- National Time Travel Foundation
    , Company 4 "Wormhole Inc." (Person "Karl" "Schwarzschild") "Physicist"
    , Individual 5 (Person "Doctor" "")
    , Individual 6 (Person "Sarah" "Jane")
    ]
```

Using the auxiliary function named compareClient, you can sort a whole list of Clients using sortBy.

```
*Chapter3.Lists Data.List> sortBy compareClient listOfClients
[ GovOrg { clientId = 3, clientName = "NTTF" }
, Company { clientId = 4, clientName = "Wormhole Inc."
          , person = Person { firstName = "Karl"
                            , lastName = "Schwarzschild" }
          , duty = "Physicist"}
, Individual { clientId = 5, person = Person { firstName = "Doctor"
                                            , lastName = "" }}
, Individual { clientId = 2, person = Person { firstName = "H. G."
                                            , lastName = "Wells" }}
, Individual { clientId = 6, person = Person { firstName = "Sarah"
                                            , lastName = "Jane" }} ]
```

Some types already come defined with a default way in which to order values. Numbers and characters are examples of such types, which are readily compared. In those cases, you can invoke the function sort, which doesn't need a comparison function. Here's an example:

```
*Chapter3.Lists Data.List> sort [1,4,2,-3]
[-3,1,2,4]
```

It's interesting to see that orders are also defined for tuples and lists if their contained elements have a default comparison. In both cases, this order is lexicographic: values are compared element by element. Lexicographic comparison means that if the first component of the tuples is different, then the ordering of those two values decides the ordering of the tuple. If the leading values match, the second elements are compared, and so on. The same approach is taken for lists as with tuples. Also, for lists, a smaller list is considered previous in order to a longer list that contains the shorter list as a prefix. Let's look at same examples of comparison that clearly show this lexicographic comparison. In the first and third cases, tuples or lists are equal up to some point, whereas in the second case the first list is shorter than the second one.

```
*Chapter3.Lists> compare (1,2) (1,1)
GT
*Chapter3.Lists> compare "Hello" "Hello world
LT
*Chapter3.Lists> compare "This" "That"
GT
```

When a compare function is defined, Haskell also provides implementations of the (>), (<), (>=), and (<=) operators. These operators usually help clarify the code that you write because you don't need to call compare and then pattern match on the output. Furthermore, these operators are more familiar. The previous example could have been expressed also using (<=), as follows. Notice that this operator returns a simple Boolean instead of a value of the Ordering type.

```
*Chapter3.Lists> (1,2) <= (1,1)
False
*Chapter3.Lists> "Hello" <= "Hello world"
True
*Chapter3.Lists> "This" <= "That"
False
```

It may become handy when performing analytics to group clients depending on some characteristic. The function groupBy, with type (a -> a -> Bool) -> [a] -> [[a]], puts in a single list all those elements for which the equivalence predicate returns True; that is, they must be in the same group.

For example, you would like to find out which company duties are the most common in the database (which right now is just a list). To find this out, you can first filter out those elements that are not companies, using filter. Then, you can group the clients depending on their duty (the comparison function to groupBy). A third step would be sorting the lists depending on their length. While sorting, keep in mind that if you want to have the most common duty first, you need to sort the list lengths in reverse order; you need the longest list first. Finally, you retrieve the duty from each list by accessing the head element. You can do so safely because all lists will be nonempty. You also know that all elements in a given list will share the same duty, so any element that you access is as good as any other. The resulting function to do all this would be as follows:

```
companyDutiesAnalytics :: [Client a] -> [String]
companyDutiesAnalytics = map (duty . head) .
                   sortBy (\x y -> compare (length y) (length x)) .
                   groupBy (\x y -> duty x == duty y) .
                   filter isCompany
                 where isCompany (Company {}) = True
                       isCompany _             = False
```

There's a more elegant way to write this function. As you can see, there's a pattern in which two elements are compared but only after applying some operation to the values. The higher-order function on, in the module Data.Function, allows composing the comparison and the value-extracting functions as you want, as the following code illustrates. To reverse the ordering for list lengths, a useful trick is calling the comparison function with the arguments in the reverse order. There's a combinator specifically designed for calling a two-parameter function with the arguments reversed, which is called flip :: (a -> b -> c) -> (b -> a -> c). The following code is a point-free version of the previous one:

```
companyDutiesAnalytics :: [Client a] -> [String]
companyDutiesAnalytics = map (duty . head) .
                   sortBy (flip (compare `on` length)) .
                   groupBy ((==) `on` duty) .
                   filter isCompany
                 where isCompany (Company {}) = True
                       isCompany _             = False
```

HASKELL IS DECLARATIVE

You may wonder why Haskell provides so many different functions on lists, whereas other programming languages do fine with constructs such as iterators or `for` loops. The idea is that instead of explicitly transforming a list element by element, you declare transformations at a higher level of abstraction. Languages supporting this idea, such as Haskell, are called *declarative*.

A classical fear when programming in Haskell is that this higher level of abstraction hurts performance. However, compilers of declarative languages are able to apply a wider range of optimizations because they can change the code in many more ways while retaining the same behavior. A typical example takes the form `map f . map g`. This code performs multiple passes over the data but can safely be converted by the compiler to `map (f . g)`, which performs the same duty in just one pass over the data.

Lists Containing Tuples

Another family of list functions is the one that considers lists that have tuples inside. These list types will all ultimately be founded on some instance of the type `[(a,b)]`. I've already mentioned that default comparisons work on tuples lexicographically. Set functions such as `nub` and sorting functions such as `sort` work in that same way.

Previously in the book, you wrote a function converting two lists into a list of tuples. This function is known as `zip` because it interleaves elements like a zipper does. One use of `zip` is to include the position of each element next to the element itself. For example, applying `zip` to `['a', 'b', 'c']` would give you `[(1,'a'),(2,'b'),(3,'c')]`. This involves zipping the original list with a list from the number 1 to the length of the list itself. Picture two sides of a zipper, one corresponding to the list of numbers and the second to the list of characters. As you pull up the fastener, each number is associated to a character, one by one.

As an example, let's define a function `enum` that generates a list of numbers.

```
enum :: Int -> Int -> [Int]
enum a b | a > b = []
enum a b         = a : enum (a+1) b
```

The length function in Prelude returns the number of elements contained in a list. With these two ingredients, you can build the function you want.

```
withPositions :: [a] -> [(Int,a)]
withPositions list = zip (enum 1 $ length list) list
```

There is a special way to construct lists for types that have a default ordering, such as integers or characters. This is called a *range* and has the syntax [a .. b] to get a list with all elements in between and including a and b. For example, you can substitute the function enum as shown here:

```
withPositions list = zip [1 .. length list] list
```

There is an unzip function that does the reverse of zip and gets two lists back from a list of tuples. For example, let's split countries and their capitals from a list of pairs.

```
*Chapter3.Lists> unzip [("France","Paris"),("Spain","Madrid"),("Portugal","
Lisbon")]
(["France","Spain","Portugal"],["Paris","Madrid","Lisbon"])
```

This last example shows one possible use of a list of tuples: to implement a mapping between keys and values. A list of such characteristics is called an *association list* and is a well-known structure in functional programming. The function named lookup enables searching for the value associated with a particular key. Once again, the possibility of not finding the key implies that the returned value is wrapped on a Maybe.[3]

```
*Chapter3.Lists> lookup "Spain" [("France","Paris"),("Spain","Madrid"),
("Portugal","Lisbon")]
Just "Madrid"
*Chapter3.Lists> lookup "UK" [("France","Paris"),("Spain","Madrid"),
("Portugal","Lisbon")]
Nothing
```

---

[3] The expression "wrapped on Maybe" means that rather than a value of type T, you use Maybe T. In addition, it implies that in the regular case, the function will return a value constructed with Just.

Caution   You have seen how a list can be used to represent sets and maps. However, those implementations are inefficient because they require traversing a list for most operations. In the next chapter, you will look at other containers such as those found in the modules `Data.Set` and `Data.Map`. These other containers are especially suited for their particular uses and have highly performant implementations.

List Comprehensions

The fact that so many list functions are included in the standard library, and most of them even in `Prelude` (and hence available by default in any Haskell source), highlights the importance of lists in functional programming. You have seen how function composition allows for a very declarative programming style, where transformations are defined by steps. Remember the function `duplicateOdds` for computing the double of all odd numbers in `list` is written as follows:

```
duplicateOdds :: [Integer] -> [Integer]
duplicateOdds list = map (*2) $ filter odd list
```

However, if you remember your algebra classes, mathematicians have a terse but intuitive language for manipulating sets. The previous example can be written in set notation as $\{2x|\ x \in list.\ odd(x)\}$. The Haskell designers also like this syntax, so they included list comprehensions to mimic it. The example becomes the following:

```
duplicateOdds list = [ 2 * x | x <- list, odd x ]
```

List comprehensions have two parts, separated by | and wrapped by square brackets. The first part is the *expression*, which defines a transformation to apply to all the elements that will be returned. The second part consists a list of *qualifiers* and specifies from whence the elements will come and the constraints upon them.

The first kind of qualifiers are generators, which take the form `e <- list`. Generators indicate that elements from `list` will be acted upon, and each of the elements will be referred to as `e` in the rest of the comprehension. Optionally, the `e` part can be a pattern, stating that only values matching it will be included. For example, you can get the client names of all government organizations using this:

```
*Chapter3.Compr> [ clientName x | x@(GovOrg _ _) <- listOfClients ]
["NTTF"]
```

A list comprehension may have multiple generators. The simplest way to implement multiple generators is to iterate in two different lists without any relationship between them and get all possible combinations of elements coming from each list. This result of all possible combinations is called the *product* of those lists. As an example, the following code applies the product of two lists to the problem of generating the multiplication tables from 1 to 4:

```
*Chapter3.Compr> [(x,y,x*y) | x <- [1 .. 4], y <- [1 .. 10]]
[(1,1,1),(1,2,2),(1,3,3),(1,4,4),(1,5,5),(1,6,6),(1,7,7),(1,8,8),(1,9,9)
,(1,10,10),(2,1,2),(2,2,4),(2,3,6),(2,4,8),(2,5,10),(2,6,12),(2,7,14),(2,
8,16),(2,9,18),(2,10,20),(3,1,3),(3,2,6),(3,3,9),(3,4,12),(3,5,15),(3,6,18)
,(3,7,21),(3,8,24),(3,9,27),(3,10,30),(4,1,4),(4,2,8),(4,3,12),(4,4,16),(4,
5,20),(4,6,24),(4,7,28),(4,8,32),(4,9,36),(4,10,40)]
```

But a generator may also depend on other values in the comprehension, in particular on an element from another generator. For example, you may want to enumerate all possible dominoes. But you know that once you have (1,6), the piece (6,1) is exactly the same, so you shouldn't show that one. A way to get the correct result is, for each first component in the list of dominoes, get only values equal or greater than that in the second component. Thus, a result of (6,1) is excluded, because 1 is less than 6. Here's some code to implement that approach:

```
*Chapter3.Compr> [(x,y) | x <- [0 .. 6], y <- [x .. 6]] [(0,0),(0,1),(0,2)
,(0,3),(0,4),(0,5),(0,6), (1,1),(1,2),(1,3),(1,4),(1,5),(1,6),
(2,2),(2,3),(2,4),(2,5),(2,6),
(3,3),(3,4),(3,5),(3,6),
(4,4),(4,5),(4,6),
(5,5),(5,6),
(6,6)]
```

Finally, an element in a list may itself be a list, which allows it to appear on the right side of the generator. Given a list of words (remember that a string is itself a list of characters), you can concatenate all of them and show them in uppercase by iterating twice.

```
*Chapter3.Compr> import Data.Char
*Chapter3.Compr Data.Char> [ toUpper c | s <- "A","list"], c <- ' ':s ]
" A LIST"
```

Sometimes, you want to introduce local bindings inside a comprehension, usually to enhance the readability of the code. This second form of qualifiers has a syntax that is similar to that in expressions, and the form is let b = expression. For example, you may be interested in computing the norms of a list of vectors represented as tuples.[4]

```
*Chapter3.Compr> [ sqrt v | (x,y) <- [(1,2),(3,8)], let v = x*x+y*y ]
[2.23606797749979,8.54400374531753]
```

Finally, list comprehensions allow filtering out some elements using a *guard*. Guards are the third form of qualifiers and are syntactically just a call to a predicate. Only those elements satisfying the guard will go in the returned list. Guards allow expressing the invariant for dominoes in a different way.

```
*Chapter3.Compr> [(x,y) | x <- [1 .. 6], y <- [1 .. 6], x <= y]
[(1,1),(1,2),(1,3),(1,4),(1,5),(1,6),(2,2),(2,3),(2,4),(2,5),(2,6),
(3,3),(3,4),(3,5),(3,6),(4,4),(4,5),(4,6),(5,5),(5,6),(6,6)]
```

Note   If you know Scala, list comprehensions in Haskell will be familiar to you. The changes are merely syntactic: [e | q] becomes for (q) yield e;, and the generators are written the same. Local bindings are introduced without any keyword, whereas guards must be preceded by if.

---

[4] The norm of a vector (x, y) is the quantity $\sqrt{x^2 + y^2}$.

You have looked at comprehensions as coming from mathematical notation for sets. But if you look closer, they also look a bit like SQL. The notation [x | x <- list, b x] can be seen in SQL as select x from list where b=x. However, if you want to have a full-fledged query language, you need also grouping and sorting. The great news is that GHC already provides those operations; you need only to enable the TransformListComp extension.

The first qualifier that is provided by the TransformListComp extension is then. A qualifier then f transforms the input list by applying the function f to the result of the comprehension up to that point. The constraint is that f should have type [a] -> [a], so its applicability is a bit limited. Nevertheless, you can use it to reverse a list at the end.

```
*Chapter3.Compr> :set -XTransformListComp
*Chapter3.Compr> [x*y | x <- [-1,1,-2], y <- [1,2,3], then reverse]
[-6,-4,-2,3,2,1,-3,-2,-1]
```

A more powerful enhancement is then f by e, which must transform the list depending on some expression. The most common use is to sort a list. To do so, you first need to import the module GHC.Exts, which contains the function sortWith. Now, include the qualifier then sortWith by v to sort depending on the values in v. You may decide to return the previous list but now ordered by the values of x.

```
*Chapter3.Compr> import GHC.Exts
*Chapter3.Compr GHC.Exts> :{
*Chapter3.Compr GHC.Exts| [x*y | x <- [-1,1,-2], y <- [1,2,3]
*Chapter3.Compr GHC.Exts|      , then sortWith by x]
*Chapter3.Compr GHC.Exts| :}
[-2,-4,-6,-1,-2,-3,1,2,3]
```

The final extension concerns grouping. The syntax is then group by e using f, where f is a function of the type (a -> b) -> [a] -> [[a]]. In the most common case, you use as groupWith, also in GHC.Exts, which computes e for each element in the list and groups together those values for which e returns the same result. After a grouping qualifier, all the previous bindings are considered to be lists made up of the previous elements. This is important because all the transformations to the grouped elements should be done prior to that point. In many cases, all grouped elements will be equal, so GHC provides a the function that takes just one element from the list.

For example, you can group the numbers from the previous example according to whether they are positive.

```
*Chapter3.Compr GHC.Exts> :{
*Chapter3.Compr GHC.Exts| [ (the p, m) | x <- [-1,1,-2]
*Chapter3.Compr GHC.Exts|                , y <- [1,2,3]
*Chapter3.Compr GHC.Exts|                , let m = x*y
*Chapter3.Compr GHC.Exts|                , let p = m > 0
*Chapter3.Compr GHC.Exts|                , then group by p using groupWith ]
*Chapter3.Compr GHC.Exts| :}
 [(False,[-1,-2,-3,-2,-4,-6]),(True,[1,2,3])]
```

Notice how this code computes the product of the items before the grouping using let m = x*y. Then you group according to the value m > 0, and at this point you have the list [([False,False,False,False,False,False],[-1,-2,-3,-2,-4,-6]),([True, True,True],[1,2,3])]. Finally, you apply the to conflate the first components to a single element.

To help you understand these ideas about list comprehensions, let's try to build a comprehension to analyze your enterprise clients. As you may remember, you can have more than one person from each company in the database. The idea is to group all the records belonging to the same company sorted by duty and then to sort the companies by the number of records. The following code accomplishes those goals:

```
companyAnalytics :: [Client a] -> [(String, [(Person, String)])]
companyAnalytics clients = [ (the clientName, zip person duty)
                           | client@(Company { .. }) <- clients
                           , then sortWith by duty
                           , then group by clientName using groupWith
                           , then sortWith by length client
                           ]
```

Note   These comprehensions resemble the query expressions introduced in the C# language in version 3.0.

GHC supports another extension, *parallel comprehension*, which performs a duty that is not found in SQL queries: traversing several lists at the same time. The extension is enabled via the `ParallelListComp` pragma. Using this functionality, more than one branch of qualifiers can be stated in the comprehension, each of them separated by |. Instead of performing nested iterations, the result of all the branches will be zipped and available for the expression. Here's an example where you perform the multiplication of pairs of numbers, each component being given in a different list. Compare the result when using traditional nesting and when zipping.

```
*Chapter3.Compr> :set -XParallelListComp
*Chapter3.Compr> [ x*y | x <- [1,2,3], y <- [1,2,3] ]    -- nesting
[1,2,3,2,4,6,3,6,9]
*Chapter3.Compr> [ x*y | x <- [1,2,3] | y <- [1,2,3] ]    -- zipping
[1,4,9]
```

Haskell Origami

Origami is the Japanese art of folding and unfolding paper in order to create beautiful pieces of art. You have already looked at list folds. In this section, you will look at them and meet their colleagues, the unfolds. The goal is gaining some deeper understanding of the structure of list functions and how this huge set of functions I have described can be fit into a small family of schemas. Since these schemas are based on fold and unfold functions, they are known as Haskell *origami*. This section contains some optional and more advanced material. Don't worry if you don't understand this upon first read; just come try it again after some time.[5]

Let's start with an observation: folds are much more powerful than you imagine. You can write almost all list functions using `foldr`. For example, you can write `filter` as a fold by accumulating values on a list.

```
filterAsFold :: (a -> Bool) -> [a] -> [a]
filterAsFold p = foldr (\x l -> if p x then x : l else l) []
```

But, how to ensure that the definition of `filter` using regular pattern matching and recursion on lists and this definition using a fold are equivalent? The answer lies in *induction* and *equational reasoning*, a technique for formally verifying code that manipulates equations between functions. In this particular case, you need to prove that

---

[5] Most of these ideas are taken from the papers "A tutorial on the universality and expressiveness of fold" by Graham Hutton and "Origami programming" by Jeremy Gibbons.

both ways to define filtering work in the same way for the empty list (this is called the *base case*) and that by assuming that they are equal for a list xs you can prove that they are equal for a longer list x:xs (this is called the *inductive step*).

Remapping our landscape, we want to prove that filter p xs is equal to filterAsFold p xs for any list xs. We start by considering the base case, in which we make xs = []. By the definition of the function, filter p [] = []. For the other side, we can write the following set of equalities:

```
filterAsFold p [] = foldr (\x l -> if p x then x : l else l) [] []
                  = []   -- we get back the initial value
```

Since both expressions give us the same result, they must be equal among themselves. Now for the inductive step, we need to consider a list of the form x:xs.

```
filter p (x:xs) = if p x
                  then x : filter p xs
                  else     filter p xs
filterAsFold p (x:xs) = foldr (\x l -> if p x then x : l else l) [] (x:xs)
                      = (\x l -> if p x then x : l else l)
                          x (foldr (\x l -> if p x then x : l else l) [] xs)
                      = if p x
                        then x : (foldr (\x l -> if p x then x : l else l) [] xs)
                        else     (foldr (\x l -> if p x then x : l else l) [] xs)
```

We can see that the structure of the code is the same. Remember that we are allowed to assume that the equality foldr p xs = filterAsFold p xs holds; let us call this common expression ys. Thus, both expressions can be rewritten to

```
if p x then x : ys else ys
```

By induction, the equality between both ways to write the function is now proven, in the mathematical sense of the word.

You can also define map in terms of foldr. Exercise 3-4 asks you to prove that both definitions are equivalent:

```
mapAsFold :: (a -> b) -> [a] -> [b]
mapAsFold f = foldr (\x l -> f x : l) []
```

EXERCISE 3-4. PROOF FOR MAP

Using the same techniques as we used for `filter`, prove that the usual `map` definition and the one given in terms of `foldr` are equal.

The techniques of induction and equational reasoning are not limited to prove equivalence between different function definitions. We can also state *laws* which combine several operations. One such law is

```
foldr f v . map g = foldr (\x xs -> f (g x) xs) v
```

In that form, this law relates two functions. However, in order to prove their equality, we need to introduce explicit arguments. That is, what we want to hold is that for any input list `is`

```
foldr f v (map g is) = foldr (\x xs -> f (g x) xs) v is
```

At this point, we can start using our techniques. First, we have to prove that the equality holds for the case in which `is` is the empty list.

```
foldr f v (map g []) = foldr f v [] = v
foldr (\x xs -> f (g x) xs) v is    = v
```

Since both expressions rewrite to the initial value `v`, the base case is proven. The inductive step leads us to consider the case in which the list has the form `i:is`.

```
foldr f v (map g (i:is)) = foldr f v (g i : map g is)
                         = f (g i) (foldr f v (map g is))
foldr (\x xs -> f (g x) xs) v (i:is)
  = (\x xs -> f (g x) xs) i (foldr (\x xs -> f (g x) xs) v is)
  = f (g i) (foldr (\x xs -> f (g x) xs) v is)
```

As in the case of `filter`, we see that the final expressions have the same structure. Remember that we can assume that the equality already holds for `is` while proving the inductive step. If we call such common expression `js`, in both cases we obtain `f (g i) js`. The proof is finished.

If you don't feel completely confident about how I reasoned, try to go step by step with pencil and paper. Pay close attention in each step to how you apply the rules of the game. Once you are sure about the details, try to prove the so-called *fusion law* for maps:

```
map f . map g = map (f . g).
```

Note   Knowing these laws may seem like just a theoretical exercise. However, they have important applications for Haskell programs because the compiler uses them to transform the code into a more efficient one while ensuring the same behavior. For example, map (f . g) traverses a list only once, whereas map f . map g does it twice and needs an intermediate data structure in memory. So, the compiler aims to replace each instance of the latter with the former.

Up to now, I have talked about folds, which consume lists to provide a single value. However, there's a corresponding concept, *unfolds*, which create lists out of some seed. Like with folds, there are both right and left unfolds. Here, the focus will be on the right unfold function unfoldr, which is available in Data.List. Let's begin looking at its type.

```
*Chapter3.Origami Data.List> :t unfoldr
unfoldr :: (b -> Maybe (a, b)) -> b -> [a]
```

The algorithm for unfolding is the following: start with a seed of type b. Apply the function given as the first argument. You can get two kinds of output: Nothing signals that unfoldr should stop producing elements, whereas Just (x, s) attaches x to the new list and continues the process with a new seed, s. For example, let's create a list from n to m. The function should produce a number in each step and increase it for the next iteration, and it should stop when the seed is larger than m. Here's the code to do this:

```
enumUnfold :: Int -> Int -> [Int]
enumUnfold n m = unfoldr (\x -> if x > m then Nothing else Just (x, x+1)) n
```

Figure 3-3 illustrates the step-by-step execution of this code.

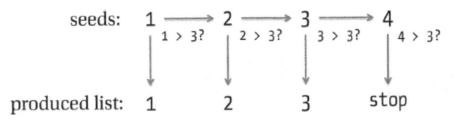

Figure 3-3. *Evaluation steps for enumUnfold 1 3*

Another algorithm that can be expressed as an unfold is minimum sort for lists. In minimum sort, you make a series of steps, and in each one you find the minimum element in the input list, take it out of this input list, and add it to the output list, which will end sorted. To implement it as an unfold, you will use a list as the seed, containing the elements that are yet to be ordered. In each step, take the minimum element from the list, making the new seed the previous list without that element. When you have an empty list as a seed, you should stop generating new elements. Here, it is in Haskell code:

```haskell
minSort :: [Integer] -> [Integer]
minSort = unfoldr (\case [] -> Nothing
                         xs -> Just (m, delete m xs) where m = minimum xs)
```

WHY ARE FOLDS AND UNFOLDS DUALS?

The two concepts of folding and unfolding are dual, but how do I back up that claim? The key point is that unfoldr returns either Nothing for stopping or Just for continuing, whereas foldr takes different arguments for the empty and general cases. You can group the initial value and combination function into a single function of type Maybe (a,b) -> b, which will return the initial value if given nothing or apply the combination for Just.

```haskell
{-# LANGUAGE LambdaCase #-}
foldr2 :: (Maybe (a,b) -> b) -> [a] -> b
foldr2 f []     = f Nothing
foldr2 f (x:xs) = f $ Just (x, foldr2 f xs)
mapAsFold2 :: (a -> b) -> [a] -> [b]
mapAsFold2 f = foldr2 (\case Nothing    -> []
                             Just (x,xs) -> f x : xs)
```

Now you can see how the two functions have reflected types.

```
foldr2  :: (Maybe (a,b) -> b) -> [a] -> b
unfoldr :: (b -> (Maybe (a,b)) -> b -> [a]
```

I find this duality elegant and an example of how higher-order functions allow you to find relations between different abstractions.

Summary

The chapter covered many concepts related to reusability and lists. It finished with a look at list origami.

- You got in touch with the idea of parametric polymorphism, which allows you to define functions operating on several types and also write data types that may contain values of different types.

- You learned how to use functions as parameters or return values, giving rise to higher-order functions, which greatly enhance the reusability of your code.

- Anonymous functions were introduced as a way to write some code directly in place instead of having to define a new function each time you want to pass it as an argument.

- You saw how the idea of functions returning functions permeates the Haskell language and saw the syntax for partially applying them.

- You looked at the point-free programming style, which encourages the use of combinators between functions to write more concise code. In particular, the focus was on the (.) composition operator.

- The chapter covered the import and export of definitions in other modules in a project. In particular, you saw how hiding definitions allows for the smart constructors pattern.

- You walked through the most important functions in the Data.List module, introducing the important concept of a fold.

- In many cases, list comprehensions provide an intuitive syntax for list transformations. You delved into its basic characteristics and the particular GHC extensions providing sorting and grouping à la SQL.

- Finally, you saw how folds and unfolds are at the core of most list functions, and you learned how to use them and reason with them.

CHAPTER 4

Using Containers and Type Classes

You have seen how parametric polymorphism and higher-order functions help in the process of abstraction. In this chapter, I'll introduce a new kind of polymorphism that sits in between parametric and the absence of polymorphism: *ad hoc polymorphism*. Using this feature, you can express that certain types exhibit a common behavior. Incidentally, you will also learn how Haskell makes it possible to use addition, (+), on different numeric types like Integer and Float while maintaining a strong type system.

Containers will be used in the examples throughout this chapter. A *container* is any data structure whose purpose is to hold elements of other types in it, such as lists or trees. In addition to writing your own implementation of binary trees with a caching mechanism, you will look at implementations that are available in *Hackage* and *Stackage*, the Haskell community's package repositories. This will lead you deeper into the features of Cabal and how you can use it to manage not only projects but also their dependencies. In addition to repositories or libraries, the Haskell community provides a lot of ways to search for code and documentation; I'll introduce the Hoogle tool in this chapter.

While using and implementing these containers, a lot of *patterns* will emerge. This will be the dominant situation from now on; after looking at some useful types, you will look at their commonalities. In particular, this chapter will introduce functors, foldables, and monoids.

Using Packages

Until this point, you have been using functions and data types from the base package. However, a lot of functionality is available in other packages. In this section, you will first learn how to manage packages and add them as dependencies to your projects.

© Alejandro Serrano Mena 2022
A. Serrano Mena, *Practical Haskell*, https://doi.org/10.1007/978-1-4842-8581-7_4

A *package* is the distribution unit of code understood by Cabal and Stack, the tools I have already introduced for building projects. Each package is identified by a name and a version number and includes a set of modules. Optionally, the package can include some metadata such as a description or how to contact the maintainer. In fact, the projects you created previously are all packages.

You can manipulate packages by hand, but there's an easier way to obtain and install them in your system: to make your own projects depend on them. If Cabal finds out that a package is not available in your system, it contacts the *Hackage* package database (which lives at `http://hackage.haskell.org`) and downloads, compiles, and installs the corresponding package. Hackage started as a mere repository for hosting packages, but now it provides some extra features such as the ability to generate documentation. Anyone with an account is allowed to upload new packages to Hackage. This ability, combined with the active Haskell community, means a wide range of libraries are available.

When you use Stack to build your projects, Hackage is not consulted by default. Instead, packages are looked for in Stackage (which lives at `www.stackage.org`). Stackage provides *snapshots* of Hackage (called *resolvers*) in which all packages are known to work well together. This provides a huge gain for reproducibility at the expense of not always containing the bleeding-edge version of the packages.

Tip   Go to the Hackage web page and click the *Packages* link. Take some time to browse the different categories and the packages available in each of them. Then, find the `containers` package in the *Data Structures* category and click it. Now go to the Stackage web page and click the link of the latest LTS corresponding to your version of GHC. Try to find `containers` in the list of packages. Compare the version of this package to the latest one available in Hackage.

In both cases, you will see the list of modules that are exported, along with its documentation. It's important that you become comfortable with these sites because they are the main entrance to the world of Haskell libraries.

Managing Dependencies

The most common way of getting a package is not by manually downloading it but rather by adding it as a dependency of another package. You just need to add it to the property `build-depends` of the corresponding stanza in your `.cabal` file. You can add a package dependency both in the library and in executable stanzas. For example, let's create a new project for this chapter and add the `containers` package as a dependency because you will use it throughout this chapter. The relevant parts of the package description file will look like this:

```
name:          chapter4
version:       0.1
library
  hs-source-dirs:  src
  build-depends:   base >= 4, containers
```

Dependencies may also specify constraints over the versions that are required. Versions are of the form `a.b.c.d`, with each of them being a number. The order is lexicographical; to compare two versions, the first component, `a`, is checked, and only if they are equal is the second is checked. If that also coincides, further components are checked in the same way. You can use any comparison operator (==, >=, >, <=, and <) and also combine them using && for conjunction and || for alternative constraints. Even though the constraint system is powerful, you should follow this rule of thumb: add a constraint requiring the minimum version where you know that your package compiles and runs (usually the version installed in your system), and another constraint to limit future versions to the next major one, that is, the next `a.b` in the lexicographical order. For example, at the moment of writing, the current `containers` version is 0.6.0.1, so the next major version would be 0.7. The suggested dependency declaration is thus as follows:

```
containers >= 0.6.0.1 && < 0.7
```

PACKAGE VERSIONING POLICY

The meaning of the version numbers for Haskell packages has been in flux for a long time. That made it difficult to decide the range to express for a particular dependency. In Hackage, package authors are expected to adhere to the following *policy:*[1]

- If any function, data type, type class, or instance has been changed or its type or behavior removed, the major version (i.e., the first two components) must be increased.

---

[1] You can read the full Package Versioning Policy at `pvp.haskell.org`.

- Otherwise, if only additions have been done, you can just increase the remaining components. This also holds for new modules, except in the case of a likely conflict with a module in another package.

In addition to these recommendations for package writers, the previously explained rule for specifying dependencies was introduced.

Note however that this versioning policy is a controversial issue within the Haskell community. You might find fierce arguments by defendants and opponents. But in practice, as a user of Haskell, tools work well enough even when not all packages in the repositories adhere to this practice.

As you can see, the package name and version are important parts of the project Cabal file. Furthermore, if your package is intended to be published in Hackage or publicly available in any other way, it's important to include precise metadata. The metadata is specified by top-level properties in the package description file. The only required ones are name and version, but it's also common to include the license, the author, the current maintainer, a small synopsis, and a larger description, the project home page, and a list of categories in which Hackage will include the package. For the chapter4 package, it might look like this:

```
name:          chapter4
version:       0.1
cabal-version: >=1.2
build-type:    Simple
author:        Alejandro Serrano
synopsis:      Package for chapter 4
maintainer:    Alejandro Serrano <my@email.com>
homepage:      http://haskell.great.is
```

Note   You may see some extra properties, such as cabal-version and build-type. Those are meant to be used when the developer needs to tweak the building system or maintain compatibility with older versions of Cabal. My suggestion is to leave those properties as they are initially created.

Building Packages

In Chapter 2, we looked very briefly at the steps required to build a package with either of the build tools of the Haskell ecosystem, namely, Cabal and Stack. In this section, we look at them in more detail and describe the underlying notions in their package systems.

Building Packages with Cabal

Cabal used to be one of the very few sources of mutability in a Haskell system. All packages, including dependencies, were installed in a global location. This made the state of a Haskell installation quite brittle, especially when different packages required different versions of the same package. Fortunately, this landscape changes with the introduction of *sandboxes*, which isolated the dependencies of each package being developed. For a long time, sandboxes have been opt-in, and global installation remained the default method. Not anymore: if you use the Cabal commands starting with new-, you use an enhanced form of sandboxes. This is now the recommended way of dealing with Haskell packaging, and it's the one we shall describe in this section.

Since the new- commands try to isolate the package being developed from the rest of the system state, they must be run in a folder in which a .cabal file exists. This is in contrast to the previous mode of operation, in which commands could be run anywhere since they affected the global environment.

As we have discussed earlier, Cabal uses Hackage by default as source for our dependencies. However, the Hackage index is not consulted every time you build a package. Instead, your local Cabal installation maintains a list of all the available packages in the remote Hackage repository. Alas, this mirror of the package list is not updated automatically. You must explicitly ask Cabal to download the new version, something you should do from time to time. When using the command line, you do this by executing the cabal update command, as shown here:

```
$ cabal update
Downloading the latest package list from hackage.haskell.org
```

Now you are ready to build a package along with its dependencies. You do so by simply running cabal build:

```
$ cabal build
Build profile: -w ghc-8.10.7 -O1
In order, the following will be built (use -v for more details):
 - exceptions-0.10.0 (lib) (requires build)
 - ...
Downloading exceptions-0.10.0...
Configuring exceptions-0.10.0 (lib)...
Configuring exceptions-0.10.0 (lib)...
...
Configuring library for chapter4-0.1...
Preprocessing library for chapter4-0.1..
Building library for chapter4-0.1..
```

If you get any error in this step, double-check that the src folder exists.

In a first step, all the dependencies (in this example output, package exceptions version 0.10.0) are downloaded and built. Then, the package itself (in this case, chapter4) is configured and built. Of course, dependencies are only compiled in the first run, or whenever they change.

A very common scenario when developing Haskell projects is to have several packages you are developing together. Cabal can help you in that situation; the only requirement is to put all the packages in a common folder. Then create a cabal.project file with the following line:

```
packages: chapter4 wonderful
```

Then you can build one specific package by issuing the new-build command followed by the name of the package. The great benefit of using a cabal.project file is that if one of the packages depends on any other, Cabal knows where to find it. This solves one of the problems of the older behavior of Cabal, in which global mutation of the environment was the only way to develop several interdependent packages in parallel.

Building Packages with Stack

In my initial description of building packages with Stack, I hinted to the idea of *resolvers*. This is in fact a central idea for Stack: a resolver describes a set of packages with a specific version and a specific compiler environment in which they work. In other words, a resolver is defined by giving a version of GHC and a version of all the packages belonging to that resolver. There are two types of resolvers: nightlies, which include newer versions but are less stable, and LTSs, which are guaranteed to work correctly. I recommend to always use an LTS for production environments.

In order to start using Stack with a Cabal project, you need to create a `stack.yaml` file. The main goal of that file is to specify which resolver to use. From that point on, Stack creates an isolated environment for your project, including a *local* version of GHC as specified by the resolver.

You don't need to create that file by hand, though. By running `stack init`, Stack infers which resolver to use from the current set of dependencies in your package. In particular, it tries to use the most recent LTS resolver in which all dependencies can be satisfied. Here's the output for the `chapter4` project; note how the `lts-13.7` resolver is chosen.

```
$ stack init
Looking for .cabal or package.yaml files to use to init the project.
...
Selecting the best among 21 snapshots...
* Matches lts-19.6
Selected resolver: https://raw.githubusercontent.com/commercialhaskell/
stackage-snapshots/master/lts/19/12.yaml
```

Afterward, you need to run `stack setup`. This downloads the corresponding version of GHC, if needed.

```
$ stack setup
Preparing to install GHC to an isolated location.
This will not interfere with any system-level installation.
...  - downloads and installs compilers and utilities
```

What a waste of space, I hear you muttering. GHC is not light, indeed, and having one copy per project would result in thousands of duplicated files. Fortunately, Stack tries to share as many compilation artifacts as possible, so the same compiler is used for all the packages using the same major LTS version.

Building a package is quite similar to Cabal. Just run `stack build`. The main difference is that Stack takes care of updating the information about its repositories before downloading any dependencies. Then the packages are built, starting with the dependencies and ending with the package being developed.

```
$ stack build
exceptions-0.10.0: download
exceptions-0.10.0: configure
exceptions-0.10.0: build
exceptions-0.10.0: copy/register
chapter4-0.1.0.0: configure (lib)
Configuring chapter4-0.1.0.0...
chapter4-0.1.0.0: build (lib)
Preprocessing library for chapter4-0.1.0.0..
Building library for chapter4-0.1.0.0..
chapter4-0.1.0.0: copy/register
Installing library in <somewhere>
Registering library for chapter4-0.1.0.0..
```

Let's have a look at the contents of the `stack.yaml` file. In your system, you might find many additional comments, which are lines starting with the # symbol.

```
resolver: lts-19.6
packages:
- .
# extra-deps: []
```

The first line specifies the resolver. The `packages` section defines which are the folders containing the packages. By default, this section points to the folder in which the `stack.yaml` file resides. You can use this option to create a project with more than one package, in the same fashion as I described for Cabal. For example, you can move the file one folder up and then indicate that your folder contains both a `chapter4` and a `wonderful` package using

```
packages:
- chapter4
- wonderful
```

The last section specifies *extra dependencies*, which are packages which are not available in Stackage, but are available in Hackage. Remember that Stackage provides a snapshot of Hackage, so this is a common scenario. You need to declare both the name of the package and the version. For example:

```
extra-deps:
- wonderful-0.2.1.0
```

The reason for mandating a version with every package is to keep the reproducibility guarantees of the Stack tool. Another nice ability of Stack is to point not to a package, but to a Git repository:

```
extra-deps:
- git: my.server/my.repo.git
  commit: a67bc8...
```

With all this information, you are ready to create the package for the store. Follow Exercise 4-1, and try looking carefully at all the steps needed to bring a new package to life.

EXERCISE 4-1. TIME MACHINE STORE PACKAGE

Create a new package that will be the origin of Time Machine Store, using either Cabal or Stack. Since it will become a web application, make it an executable. Add `containers` and `persistent` as dependencies (remember to use the version rule) and then configure and build the project. Experiment with the different metadata fields.

In addition, create both a `cabal.project` and a `stack.yaml` file. Ensure that your package builds with both tools.

Obtaining Help

I already mentioned that the Hackage and Stackage websites contain documentation about all the packages available in their databases, including module, function, type, and class descriptions. It's a great source of information for both when you want to find information about some specific function and when you want to get a broad overview of a module. Furthermore, all the packages in the Haskell Platform come with high-quality explanations and examples.

One really cool tool that helps in daily Haskell programming is Hoogle, available at www.haskell.org/hoogle/. The powerful Hoogle search engine allows you to search by name but also by type. Furthermore, it understands Haskell idioms. For example, if you look for a function with a specific type, it may find a more general function using a type class that the types in the signature implement, or the order of the arguments may be swapped in the found version. This tool is available also as the command-line program hoogle, which you can obtain by running cabal install hoogle in the command line. Note that this will take some time, since it needs to download and compile all dependencies in addition to the executable. Before being able to issue any query, you must run hoogle generate at the console.

Here is an example of the outcome of Hoogle for a map-like function:

```
$ hoogle '(a -> b) -> ([a] -> [b])'
Prelude map :: (a -> b) -> [a] -> [b]
Data.List map :: (a -> b) -> [a] -> [b]
GHC.Base map :: (a -> b) -> [a] -> [b]
GHC.List map :: (a -> b) -> [a] -> [b]
GHC.OldList map :: (a -> b) -> [a] -> [b]
...
-- plus more results not shown, pass --count=20 to see more
```

Containers: Maps, Sets, Trees, Graphs

In this section, you will look at some container types that are common in programming. As I introduced earlier, a *container* is a data type whose main purpose is to hold any number of elements of a homogeneous type. In particular, you will look at maps, trees, graphs, and sets. All these structures could be implemented by using lists and tuples (e.g., you have already seen how association lists can be used to represent maps). But using specialized data types has two advantages:

- They are much faster because they were specially developed for a particular pattern. For example, looking for the value associated to a key in a list involves searching the entire list, whereas in a map the time is almost constant.

- Libraries implementing these structures provide functions that were created for the specific use cases of each of them. For example, you have functions for visiting nodes or getting the strongly connected components of a graph. These functions could be implemented if using lists but are not already available in the Haskell Platform.

All the containers I will talk about are provided by the containers package, so to try the examples, you need to include that package as a dependency, as in the previous section.

Maps

Let's start with *maps*, which allow you to associate values with keys efficiently. No duplicate keys are allowed, so if you want to alter the value for a specific key, the new one will override the previous one. In contrast, with association lists, by implementing mappings as a list of tuples, you were responsible for maintaining such an invariant.

You'll find the implementation of maps in the Data.Map module. However, many functions in that module collide with names from the built-in Prelude module. For that reason, you will need to qualify the module when you import it. Here, you'll qualify Data.Map by the name M, so you'll prefix any declaration from the module with M instead of Data.Map. It's common practice to abbreviate the qualification to a small one-letter name to write less code. In the following examples, I'll assume that the module has been imported with this line:

```
import qualified Data.Map as M
```

The type itself is Map k a. It takes as parameters the type k of the keys that will index values of type a. For example, a mapping between clients and the list of products that each client has bought will have type Map Client [Product]. In the examples, you will work with simpler maps from strings to integers, which are much more concise.

In the previous chapters, I introduced the special syntax for creating lists: either using the constructor [ ] for an empty list or listing the elements between square brackets. Haskell has no special syntax for maps or for exporting any of its data constructors. Rather, you must create new maps either by using empty to create a map with no pairs or by using singleton, which takes a key and a value and generates a map with that single element.

```
*Chapter4.Containers M> M.empty
fromList []
*Chapter4.Containers M> M.singleton "hello" 3
fromList [("hello",3)]
```

Maps are by default shown as a list of pairs. You can convert between that style of lists and real maps by using the fromList function. If two pairs have the same key, only the last value is retained.

```
*Chapter4.Containers M> M.fromList [("hello",1),("bye",2),("hello",3)]
fromList [("bye",2),("hello",3)]
```

When inserting new values, you must remember that only one value can be associated with a specific key. This leads to two different ways in which you can proceed if a value is already associated with a key:

- You can completely ignore that old value and just replace it with the new one. This is achieved via the insert function, which takes just the new key and value, and the map where the association must be changed, in that order.

- You can combine the old value with the new one. To do so, use insertWith, of the following type:

  ```
  (a -> a -> a) -> k -> a -> Map k a -> Map k a
  ```

  The first parameter is the combining function that will be called with the old and new values whenever the corresponding key is already present. In some cases, you will also want to have the key as a parameter of the combining function; in that case, you should use insertWithKey, whose first parameter is of type k -> a -> a -> a. This is an instance of a common pattern in the Data.Map module; each time that a function will be called with a value of the map, there's an alternative function ending in WithKey that also gives the key to the function.

Here's an example of several chained insertions:

```
*Chapter4.Containers M> :{
*Chapter4.Containers M| let m1 = M.singleton "hello" 3
*Chapter4.Containers M|     m2 = M.insert "bye" 2 m1
*Chapter4.Containers M|     m3 = M.insert "hello" 5 m2
*Chapter4.Containers M|     m4 = M.insertWith (+) "hello" 7 m3
*Chapter4.Containers M|  in (m1,m2,m3,m4)
*Chapter4.Containers M| :}
( fromList [("hello",3)]
, fromList [("bye",2),("hello",3)]
, fromList [("bye",2),("hello",5)]
, fromList [("bye",2),("hello",12)] )
```

Notice how in the last step the pair ("hello",5) lived in the map and ("hello",7) was going to be inserted. You specified addition as the combinator, so you get ("hello",12) in the final map.

Note   If you come from an imperative language such as C or Java, you will be used to functions directly changing the contents of a container. By contrast, Haskell is pure, so all these functions return a new map with the corresponding change applied. However, the underlying implementation does not create a whole new copy of the data structure every time it's changed, due to laziness (which will be explained in the next chapter). That way, performance is not compromised.

In addition to holding elements, maps are used to query by key. The null function allows you to check whether the map is empty, whereas member tells whether a specific key is available in the map. To get the associated value of a key, you can either use lookup, which returns Just value if available, or use Nothing if the key is not present. Alternatively, findWithDefault takes a value to return if the key that you query is not present. In the following interpreter session, you can see examples of what these functions do in a range of cases:

```
*Chapter4.Containers M> M.null M.empty
True
*Chapter4.Containers M> let m = M.fromList [("hello",3),("bye",4)]
*Chapter4.Containers M> M.null m
False
*Chapter4.Containers M> M.member "hello" m
True
*Chapter4.Containers M> M.lookup "hello" m
Just 3
*Chapter4.Containers M> M.lookup "welcome" m
Nothing
*Chapter4.Containers M> M.findWithDefault 0 "welcome" m
0
```

You can also delete pairs from the map, using the delete function, as shown here:

```
*Chapter4.Containers M> M.delete "hello" m
fromList [("bye",4)]
```

In addition to inserting or deleting, you can also change the value of a specific key via adjust. It takes the function that will be applied to the old value to get the new value. If the key is not present, the map is not modified.

```
*Chapter4.Containers M> M.adjust (+7) "hello" m
fromList [("bye",4),("hello",10)]
```

insert, delete, and adjust are all instances of a general function called alter that subsumes all of them. The first argument is a function of type Maybe a -> Maybe a. The input will be Nothing if the key is not already present, or it will be the previous value wrapped in a Just. What to do with that key is specified by the return value of that function. If it is Nothing, the key will be dropped, and if it is Just v, that would be the new value for the key. The following code does the same work of the previous example:

```
*Chapter4.Containers M> M.alter (\(Just v) -> Just (v+7)) "hello" m
fromList [("bye",4),("hello",10)]
```

Exercise 4-2 asks you to check whether alter is a general form of the functions that were introduced earlier.

EXERCISE 4-2. ALTERING YOUR MAPS

It's common for Haskell libraries to contain a fully general function such as alter, which is later made more concrete in other functions. This makes it easier to work with the library. Put yourself for a moment in the place of a library designer and write the functions insert, delete, and adjust using alter.

You can also combine entire maps using union, intersection, and difference, which will produce a new map key from both maps (even if they appear in only one of them), appearing in both maps or in the first map but not the second, respectively. In the case of a key with different associated values in each map, the first map will take precedence, and its value will be used. You can have finer control by using unionWith, intersectionWith, and differenceWith, which take an extra argument that is the function that combines the elements with the same key.

```
*Chapter4.Containers M> :{
*Chapter4.Containers M| let m1 = M.fromList [("hello",3),("bye",4)]
*Chapter4.Containers M|     m2 = M.fromList [("hello",5),("welcome",6)]
*Chapter4.Containers M|  in (m1 `M.union` m2, M.intersectionWith (-) m1 m2)
*Chapter4.Containers M| :}
( fromList [("bye",4),("hello",3),("welcome",6)]
, fromList [("hello",-2)] )
```

Once you know how to operate on lists, you can usually transfer that knowledge to other data structures. In the case of maps, there are functions map, foldr, foldl, filter, and partition, among others, that have the same behavior as they have for lists but return a map. Again, for each function, there's a corresponding one suffixed by WithKey whose parameter functions also take the key that you are modifying, folding upon, or filtering. Let's duplicate all the values in a map and then return its sum.

```
*Chapter4.Containers M> (M.map (*2) m, M.foldr (+) 0 m)
( fromList [("bye",8),("hello",6)], 7 )
```

I have already talked about converting from a list of tuples into a map using fromList. You can do the inverse transformation using assocs. You may have noticed that maps are always shown with their keys ordered. The map itself maintains that invariant, so it can easily access the maximal and minimal elements in the map. Indeed, functions such as findMin/findMax, deleteMin/deleteMax, and updateMin/updateMax take advantage of this fact and allow for fast retrieving, deleting, or updating of the values associated to those keys.

Sets

Sets are found in the Data.Set module. They behave essentially like lists but do not allow duplicates. The set of functions for this data type is virtually identical to that of maps, but only taking the value as a parameter (elements in a set don't have a key). In the following examples, the module Data.Set will be imported qualified as S:

```
Prelude> import qualified Data.Set as S
```

You create sets with empty and singleton, much like their map counterparts. empty creates a set with no elements, and singleton creates a set with a single element. Later, you can add new elements via the insert function. The following example showcases a way to create a set with the elements "welcome" and "hello":

```
Prelude S> S.insert "welcome" $ S.singleton "hello"
fromList ["hello","welcome"]
```

Alternatively, you can create a set directly from a list of their elements using the fromList function. Duplicate elements in the list will be taken to just one, since sets can contain a sole appearance of each element.

```
Prelude S> S.fromList ["hello","bye","hello"]
fromList ["bye","hello"]
```

Similarly, there's a toList function to convert a set to a list of its elements. The behavior of these two functions provides a way to implement the functionality of removing duplicates from a list (and also sort it in ascending order), which is actually much more performant than the nub function.

```
Prelude S> S.toList $ S.fromList ["duplicate","boom","duplicate"]
["boom","duplicate"]
```

As mentioned, the interface for Data.Set is similar to that of Data.Map. The following code shows an example of using set operations (in this case, intersection, but also union and difference are available). You can see how to check for membership with the member function. Finally, like with lists and maps, you can apply a function to each element in the set using map (but be careful because duplicate results will be compressed into just one element, and order may not be respected).

```
Prelude S> :{
Prelude S| let set1 = S.insert "welcome" $ S.singleton "hello"
Prelude S|     set2 = S.fromList ["hello","bye"]
Prelude S|  in ( set1 `S.intersection` set2
Prelude S|     , "welcome" `S.member` set1
Prelude S|     , S.map length set2 )
Prelude S| :}
(fromList ["hello"], True, fromList [3,5])
```

INTMAP, INTSET, HASHMAP, AND HASHSET

Maps can be made much more efficient if you use only integers as keys. The same happens for sets holding only integer values. For that reason, the containers library provides specific data types for that purpose, namely, IntMap and IntSet.

Alternatively, the keys on a map or the values on a set might not be integers but could be mapped almost uniquely to one integer. This mapping is called a *hash* of the original value. The types HashMap and HashSet in the unordered-containers package provide implementations of maps and sets whose keys and elements, respectively, can be hashed; this is much more efficient than the Map and Set types discussed in this section, if the type can be hashed.

Like with any other value, the following containers can be nested one inside another: lists of sets, maps with string keys and values that are lists of numbers, and so on. In Exercise 4-3, you will use a map with sets as values to classify a list of clients in the store.

```
┌─────────────────────────────────────────────────────────────────┐
│                EXERCISE 4-3. CLASSIFYING CLIENTS                  │
└─────────────────────────────────────────────────────────────────┘
```

For analysis purposes, it is interesting to classify clients according to their type such as government organization, company, or individual. First, create a new data type to represent these kinds of clients:

```
data ClientKind = GovOrgKind | CompanyKind | IndividualKind
```

Now, create a function called classifyClients that traverses a list of clients (of type [Client Integer], with Client defined as in the previous chapter) and generates a value of type Map ClientKind (Set (Client Integer)). You should create two different implementations.

- The first should traverse the list element by element and perform on each element the classification, decide which map item to modify, and then add itself to the set.

- The second should first create lists corresponding to the three different kinds and at the end convert those lists to sets and generate the mentioned map from them.

You can create a large client list and run the two implementations to compare which one behaves better in speed.

Trees

Trees are composed of nodes, which hold a value and may have other trees as children. In the Data.Tree module, those children are represented as a bare list of trees, sometimes called a *forest*. Be aware that this representation is not specialized for any particular purpose. For some algorithms, you may want to use another kind of tree, such as AVL or red-black trees. For those cases, we have specialized packages supporting these data types, such as TreeStructures, AvlTree, and RBTree. Here's the code defining Data.Tree.Tree:

```
data Tree   a = Node { rootLabel :: a, subForest :: Forest a }
type Forest a = [Tree a]
```

The type keyword, which I haven't yet introduced, is used to create *type synonyms*, that is, to give an alternative name to a type. Usually, it's used to call a large type by a smaller or more expressive name. For example, you can introduce the following synonym for those functions returning a Boolean value:

```
type Predicate a = a -> Bool
```

The type synonym and its expansion are interchangeable in all circumstances. That is, you can also write the type of filter as Predicate a -> [a] -> [a], and the compiler would be fine with it. In contrast, the other way to define alternative names, using newtype, doesn't make the types equivalent. When should you use this second option will be covered later in the chapter.

As you may already know, there are several ways to visit a tree (such as traversing all of their elements), which are broadly divided into two families: depth-first traversal and breadth-first traversal. In depth-first traversal, each node of the tree recursively visits its subtrees. There's still a choice of when to visit the value in the node itself: before any subtree (pre-order) or after all subtrees are visited (post-order). Figure 4-1 illustrates both ways of traversing a tree's elements.

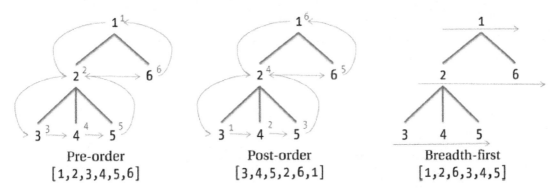

Figure 4-1. *Traversing in pre-order, post-order, and breadth-first fashions*

Let's try to implement a function that traverses the tree in pre-order, applying a function to each value and returning the result in a list.

```
import Data.Tree

preOrder :: (a -> b) -> Tree a -> [b]
preOrder f (Node v subtrees)
  = let subtreesTraversed = concat $ map (preOrder f) subtrees
    in f v : subtreesTraversed
```

Notice how the code uses the map function to run the partially evaluated preOrder f on each of the subtrees. Thus, you will obtain a list of elements for each subtree, and map will return a list of lists. So, you need to flatten it to get just a single list, which is achieved using concat. Indeed, this pattern of mapping against a list and then flattening the resulting list is so common that the Prelude includes a function concatMap f, which is exactly defined as concat . map f. You can check that the function works on the tree shown in Figure 4-1.

```
pictureTree :: Tree Int
pictureTree = Node 1 [ Node 2 [ Node 3 []
                              , Node 4 []
                              , Node 5 [] ]
                     , Node 6 [] ]

-- In GHCi
*Chapter4.Containers> preOrder show pictureTree
["1","2","3","4","5","6"]
```

This pre-order traversal can be achieved using the flatten function defined in the Data.Tree module. However, it does not apply any operation of the node values; it just returns them as they are. The breadth-first traversal is available via the levels function, where also each level is returned as a list.

```
*Chapter4.Containers> flatten pictureTree
[1,2,3,4,5,6]
*Chapter4.Containers> levels pictureTree
[[1],[2,6],[3,4,5]]
```

Like any other container, trees in Haskell support mapping and folding over them. However, instead of functions in the same module, these operations are available through the functions fmap in Prelude and foldr in Data.Foldable. In the rest of the chapter, I will discuss why this is the case.

```
*Chapter4.Containers> fmap (*2) pictureTree
Node { rootLabel = 2
     , subForest = [ Node { rootLabel = 4
                          , subForest = [ Node { rootLabel = 6
                                               , subForest = [] }
                                        , Node { rootLabel = 8
                                               , subForest = [] }
                                        , Node { rootLabel = 10
                                               , subForest = [] } ] }
```

```
                , Node { rootLabel = 12, subForest = [] } ] }
*Chapter4.Containers> Data.Foldable.foldr (+) 0 pictureTree
21
```

Graphs

Trees are just an instance of a more general data structure called a *graph*. A graph is composed of a set of vertices, joined via a set of edges. In the implementation in Data. Graph, nodes are always identified by an integer, and edges are directed (an edge from a to b does not imply an edge from b to a) and without weights.

There are two ways to create a graph:

- You use graphFromEdges when you have a list of nodes; each of them is identified by a key and holds a value, and for each node you also have its list of neighbors – that is, the list of any other nodes that receive an edge from the former. In such a case, you call graphFromEdges, which takes a list of triples, (value, key, [key]), the latest component being the aforementioned list of neighbors. In return, you get a graph but also two functions. The first one of type Vertex -> (node, key, [key]) maps a vertex identifier from the graph to the corresponding information of the node, whereas the second one, with type key -> Maybe Vertex, implements the inverse mapping: from keys to vertex identifiers.

- If you already have your graph in a form where you have integer identifiers, you can use buildG instead. This function takes as parameters a tuple with the minimal and maximum identifiers (its bounds) and a list of tuples corresponding to each directed edge in the graph.

There is a large set of functions for inspecting the graph itself, like vertices and edges, returning the sets corresponding to their names. However, the great power of this module is the complete set of functions for walking through the elements in graphs and working with them, which are usually quite tricky to implement by hand. For example, let's say you have a list of things to do for building a time machine. However, these tasks have some relative order. To create the door of the time machine, you first need to buy the aluminum from which it is made. This ordering can be represented using a graph, where there's an edge from a to b if a must precede b. The following code generates the first graph in Figure 4-2:

```
import Data.Graph

timeMachineGraph :: [(String, String, [String])]
timeMachineGraph =
  [("wood","wood",["walls"]), ("plastic","plastic",["walls","wheels"])
  ,("aluminum","aluminum",["wheels","door"]),("walls","walls",["done"])
  ,("wheels","wheels",["done"]),("door","door",["done"]),("done","done",[])]

timeMachinePrecedence
  :: (Graph, Vertex -> (String,String,[String]), String -> Maybe Vertex)
timeMachinePrecedence = graphFromEdges timeMachineGraph
```

You can build a plan for constructing the time machine by asking for a *topological sort* of the elements. In this sort scheme, each node n is always before any other node that receives an edge from n. Notice how in the example the mapping between vertices and keys has been used to write the results using the string representations, not the internal integer identifiers.

```
*Chapter4.Containers> :{
*Chapter4.Containers> let (g,v,_) = timeMachinePrecedence
*Chapter4.Containers>   in map (\x -> let (k,_,_) = v x in k) $ topSort g
*Chapter4.Containers> :}
["wood","plastic","walls","aluminum","door","wheels","done"]
```

One detail that most of the people don't know about time machines is that you cannot travel to any point in time with a machine. Instead, each machine has some points where you can travel, and it may be the case that you can travel to one point in only one direction. So, when performing time travel, you should be sure you are able to get to the time where you want to go or that you can go back to the initial point. You can model these constraints as a graph. From each year, you will have edges to each year to which you can arrive. The following code translates this idea applied to the second graph in Figure 4-2 to code:

```
timeMachineTravel :: Graph
timeMachineTravel = buildG (103,2013)
```

```
[(1302,1614),(1614,1302),(1302,2013),(2013,1302),(1614,2013)
,(2013,1408),(1408,1993),(1408,917),(1993,917),(917,103),(103,917)]
```

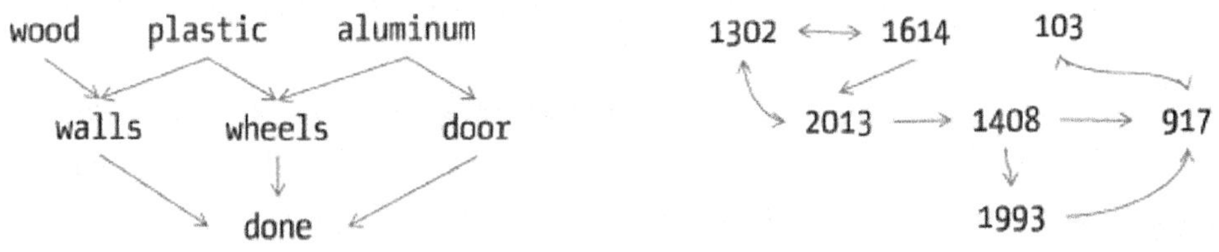

Figure 4-2. *Graphs about time machines*

You may ask whether you can travel from 1302 to 917; the path function will give the answer. Indeed, if you want to know every vertex that can be reached from that year, you can use reachable to find them. Let's look at some examples starting from 1302:

```
*Chapter4.Containers> path timeMachineTravel 1302 917
True
*Chapter4.Containers> reachable timeMachineTravel 1302
[1302,2013,1408,917,103,1993,1614]
```

How can you partition the vertices such that you can always travel between all years in each set? Each component of this partition is called a *strongly connected component*. You can get it using scc, which will return a set of trees, each of them specifying one of those components. But if you run this function directly, you will get some enormous output. This is because when creating a graph using buildG, the library creates vertices for all identifiers in between. For that reason, you are going to filter the trees with only one node. This filtering will eliminate those vertices that were not in the initial list but also the connected components with only one element. Here's the filtering code:

```
*Chapter4.Containers> filter (\(Node { subForest = s }) -> s /= []) $ scc
timeMachineTravel
[Node { rootLabel = 103
    , subForest = [
          Node { rootLabel = 917, subForest = []}]}
      , Node { rootLabel = 2013
              , subForest = [
                    Node { rootLabel = 1302
                          , subForest = [
```

```
                          Node { rootLabel = 1614
                               , subForest = [] } ] } ] } ]
```

The previous output is definitely not very manageable. If instead of using `buildG` your graph is represented as with `graphFromEdges`, the output is much better. You need only to use `stronglyConnComp`. A special type `SCC` is used for representing each component. You need to run `flattenSCC` to obtain a printable version, as shown in the following example:

```
*Chapter4.Containers> map flattenSCC $ stronglyConnComp timeMachineGraph
[["done"],["door"],["walls"],["wood"],["wheels"],["plastic"],["aluminum"]]
```

Ad Hoc Polymorphism: Type Classes

Up to this point in the book, you have seen the types of several functions in the Haskell Platform. However, if you look at some functions in the `Data.Map` or `Data.Set` module, you will find something that hasn't yet been explained.

```
*Chapter4.Containers> :t M.insert
M.insert :: Ord k => k -> a -> M.Map k a -> M.Map k a
```

Notice how `Ord k` is separated from the rest of the type by `=>` (not to be confused by the arrow `->` used in the type of functions). The purpose of `Ord k` is to constrain the set of possible types that the `k` type variable can take. This is different from the parametric polymorphism of the list functions in the previous chapters. Here, you ask the type to be accompanied by some functions. This kind of polymorphism is known as *ad hoc polymorphism*. In this case, the `Ord` type class is saying that the type must provide implementations of comparison operators such as `<` or `==`. Thus, it formalizes the notion of default order that I talked about previously.

Declaring Classes and Instances

A *type class* (usually abbreviated as simply *class*) is a declaration of a set of functions along with their types, and it receives a name (in the previous case, `Ord`). The declaration of a type class has this syntax:

```
class ClassName variable where
  oneFunction  :: oneType
```

```
...
otherFunction :: otherType
```

The variable introduced in the declaration can be used in the functions to refer to a type that supports the type class. For example, both clients and time machines have a name, so you can introduce a type class for expressing the concept "values of this type have a name" that you will call Nameable. Check how the type variable n is used in the type of the function name, as shown here:

```
class Nameable n where
  name :: n -> String
```

Now if you look at the type of name, it declares the constraint of being a Nameable.

```
*Chapter4.TypeClasses> :t name
name :: Nameable n => n -> String
```

From now on, using the name function also comes with the associated restriction, which must be specified in the corresponding type declaration. An example using Nameable could involve a function, declared outside the type class, which returns the initial of the name.

```
initial :: Nameable n => n -> Char
initial n = head (name n)
```

Of course, the main purpose of having a type class is to declare that some specific type supports the operations introduced by the class. Such a type is called an *instance* of a type class. The declaration of such a fact must include the implementation of the functions declared in the class.

```
instance ClassName Type where
  oneFunction  = ... -- implementation
  ...
  otherFunction = ... -- implementation
```

Following the example, the following is the instantiation of the Nameable type class by Client. Here's a reminder of how this type looked in Chapter 3:

```
data Person  = Person { firstName :: String, lastName :: String }
               deriving (Show, Eq, Ord)
```

131

```
data Client i = GovOrg  { clientId :: i, clientName :: String }
              | Company { clientId :: i, clientName :: String
                        , person :: Person, duty :: String }
              | Individual { clientId :: i, person :: Person }
              deriving (Show, Eq, Ord)
```

In the instance declaration, you need to include the whole type. This means you must also write the type parameters that should be applied in the declaration (in this case, the i parameter).

```
instance Nameable (Client i) where
  name Individual { person = Person { firstName = f, lastName = n } }
        = f ++ " " ++ n
  name c = clientName c
```

Caution   Type classes in Haskell should not be confused with classes in object-oriented (OO) programming. Actually, if you had to make a connection, you can think of type classes as interfaces in those languages, but they have many more applications, such as linking together several types in a contract (e.g., specifying that an IntSet holds elements of type Int). The word *instance* is also used in both worlds with very different meanings. In OO languages, it refers to a concrete value of a class, whereas in Haskell it refers to the implementation of a class by a type. This points to a third difference: in OO, the declaration of a class includes a list of all the interfaces it implements, whereas in Haskell the declaration of a type and its implementation of a type class are separated. Indeed, in some cases, they are even in different modules (these instances are referred to as *orphan* ones).

When you use a type that implements a class, the Haskell compiler must look for the corresponding instance declaration. It does so by looking in all the modules that are imported, independently of how they are imported. Currently, it's not possible to prevent an instance declaration from being imported. This means that if you see some source code like the following, it may not be an error (what's the point of having such a declaration if nothing is imported?) but rather an import of the instance declarations found in Module:

```
import Module ()
```

Exercise 4-4 shows you how to use type classes and instances. It does so in the direction of fulfilling the main target: creating a powerful time machine store.

EXERCISE 4-4. PRICES FOR THE STORE

Besides time machines, the web store will also sell travel guides and tools for maintaining the machines. All of them have something in common: a price. Create a type class called `Priceable` of types supporting a price, and make those data types implement it.

The next step is creating a `totalPrice` function, which, given a list of things with price, computes the total amount of money to pay. The type of this function will be as follows:

```
totalPrice :: Priceable p => [p] -> Double
```

Be aware that the meaning of this signature may not match your intuition, especially if you are coming from an object-oriented programming background. When the compiler processes this code, it will look for a concrete type for the type variable p. This means it can work only with homogeneous lists. You can compute the price of a list of time machines, [TimeMachine], or a list of books, [Book]. But there's no way to type or create a heterogeneous list containing both values of type TimeMachine and Book.

`Nameable` is similar to the `Show` type class, which provides a function called `show` to convert a value into a string. You have already met this type class in the definition of previous data types, but you haven't written any instance for those data types. The reason is that Haskell can automatically write instances of a set of type classes, deriving them from the shape of the data type. This is called the `deriving` mechanism because the instances to generate are specified after the `deriving` keyword at the end of the data type definition.

Note According to the standard, Haskell is able to derive instances for only some type classes, which are hard-coded in the compiler. However, there's a field of functional programming, called *generic programming*, that provides ways to write functions that depend on the structure of data types. Chapter 14 provides an introduction to that topic.

There's a dual class to Show, called Read, which performs the inverse function: converting a string representation into an actual value of a type, via the read function. The implementation of a Read instance is usually tricky since you must take care of spacing, proper handling of parentheses, different formats for numbers, and so forth. The good news is that Haskell also allows you to derive Read instances automatically, which are guaranteed to read back any value produced by the show function. If deriving both, you can be sure that read . show is the identity on the values of the data type; that is, the final value will be the same as the initial one.

Let's derive Read also for the Person data type.

```
data Person = Person { firstName :: String, lastName  :: String }
            deriving (Show, Eq, Ord, Read)
```

And now let's try to parse a string representing a person.

```
*Chapter4.TypeClasses> read "Person { firstName = \"A\", lastName =
\"S\" }"
*** Exception: Prelude.read: no parse
```

The problem is that GHC has no clue about which instance of Read should be used. You haven't specified any further operation on the result that Haskell could use to infer the final type. From the compiler point of view, the string may refer to any type. The solution is to explicitly tell what the type to be returned is. This is achieved by annotating the expression with :: followed by the type.

```
*Chapter4.TypeClasses> :{
*Chapter4.TypeClasses| read "Person { firstName = \"A\", lastName =
\"S\" }"
*Chapter4.TypeClasses>  :: Person
*Chapter4.TypeClasses| :}
Person {firstName = "A", lastName = "S"}
```

Once again, you can check that Haskell infers always the most general type based on the functions used in the expressions. For example, the function read . show would work on any data type supporting both Show and Read. But in general, it also works if some data type supports Show and another one supports Read, which is more general than a single type supporting both.

```
*Chapter4.TypeClasses> :t read . show
```

```
read . show :: (Read c, Show a) => a -> c
```

Built-In Type Classes

I have spoken in the previous chapters about some list functions involving types having "default comparisons" and "default equivalences." Now that you know about type classes, it is time to introduce the specific classes that encode those concepts, namely, Ord and Eq.

Eq is the type class declaring that a type supports checking equality (and inequality) between their values. Let's look at its definition from the GHC source code (you can access it by looking at the base package, surfing inside the Prelude module, and then clicking the *Source* link next to the class information).

```
class Eq a where
    (==), (/=) :: a -> a -> Bool
    x /= y = not (x == y)
    x == y = not (x /= y)
```

I mentioned that type classes include only the declaration of functions to be implemented, but here you find some code implementation. The reason is that those are *default definitions*: code for a function that works whenever some of the rest are implemented. For example, if you implement (==), there's a straightforward way to implement (/=), as shown earlier. When instantiating a type class, you are allowed to leave out those functions with a default implementation.

This means that when implementing Eq, you may do it without any actual implementation because all functions have default implementations. In that case, any comparison will loop forever because (/=) calls (==), which then calls (/=), and so on, indefinitely. This may lead to the program crashing out of memory or just staying unresponsive until you force its exit. For preventing such cases, type classes in Haskell usually specify a *minimal complete definition*; in other words, which set of functions should be implemented for the rest to work without problems? For Eq, the minimal complete definition is either (==) or (/=), so you need to implement at least one.

Caution   Knowing the minimal complete definitions for a type class is important since it's the only way to enforce that programs behave correctly. The GHC compiler is able to check that you have defined all necessary functions from version 7.8 on. However, because this feature was not present since the beginning in the compiler, some libraries do not explicitly mention the minimal complete definition in code. Thus, you should double-check by looking at the documentation of the type class.

Given (==), you can always write (/=) as not . (==), so you may be wondering why you would include both in the type class and then have to introduce the concept of minimal complete definition. Shouldn't (/=) be defined *outside* the type class? The reason for having everything in the same type class is twofold:

- *Ease of instantiation*: For some types, it may be more natural to write the Eq instance by defining (==), whereas in others the code for (/=) will be easier to write. Being able to do it in both ways makes it easy for consumers to instantiate the type class. This may not be so apparent for Eq, but for more complex type classes, it is important.

- *Performance*: Having both functions in the type classes allows you to implement the two of them if desired. This is usually done for performance reasons; maybe your type has a faster way of checking for nonequality than trying to check equality and failing.

The case of equality leads to other interesting features of Haskell's type class system: instantiation for a type with variables and restrictions for instantiating a type class. For example, you can implement an instance of Eq for any possible list type in a generic way. You only have to check the equality element by element. However, in order to be correct, you must require the inner elements to also implement the Eq class. Let's look at the code:

```
instance Eq a => Eq [a] where
  []     == []     = True
  (x:xs) == (y:ys) = x == y && xs == ys
  _      == _      = False
```

Let's focus on the highlighted parts. First, there is the restriction on the elements that have been introduced using the same syntax as in functions. Then, the declaration uses a parametric [a] in the type name, with a type variable. In sum, this instance is applicable to lists of any type a that also is an Eq. The Haskell Platform already includes these declarations for many common containers, not only lists. Instances of Eq are specified for tuples, maps, sets, trees, Maybe, and so on.

As usual, the power of instantiating type classes by parametric types is not exclusive of a special set of built-in types, but it's available for use in your own data types, as Exercise 4-5 shows.

EXERCISE 4-5. THE SAME CLIENT

Implement Eq for the Person and Client i types introduced in the previous chapters so that it checks the equality of all the fields. Notice that for Client you may need to add some restrictions over the type of the identifiers.

The good news is that in daily work you don't need to write those instances because Haskell can also derive Eq like it does with Show and Read.

In addition to equality, in some cases you need the notion of ordering. This is the duty of the Ord type class.

```
class Eq a => Ord a where
    compare              :: a -> a -> Ordering
    (<), (<=), (>), (>=) :: a -> a -> Bool
    max, min             :: a -> a -> a

    compare x y = if x == y then EQ
                  else if x <= y then LT
                  else GT
    x <  y = case compare x y of { LT -> True;  _ -> False }
    x <= y = case compare x y of { GT -> False; _ -> True }
    x >  y = case compare x y of { GT -> True;  _ -> False }
    x >= y = case compare x y of { LT -> False; _ -> True }
    max x y = if x <= y then y else x
    min x y = if x <= y then x else y
```

Once again, it has a lot of members, but thanks to default definitions, the minimal complete one is either implementing compare or implementing <=. However, if you look at the code in compare, you may notice that it's using (==), which is a member of Eq. Indeed, at the beginning of the definition of Ord, there's a prerequisite for its implementation. Every type belonging to the class Ord must also belong to the class Eq. The syntax is similar again to including restrictions in functions or in instance implementations: Eq a =>.

In this case, you say that Eq is a *superclass* of Ord. Once again, I must warn you against any possible confusion when comparing the concept with the one in object-oriented languages. A type class does not inherit anything from its superclass but the promise that some functions will be implemented in their instances. For all the rest, they are completely different type classes. In particular, type implementations will go in separate instance declarations.

Like with Eq, Haskell provides automatic derivation of Ord instances. When doing so, it will consider that different alternatives follow the same order as in the data declaration. For example, in the declaration of clients at the beginning of the section, government organizations will always precede companies, which will always precede individuals. Then, if two values have the same constructor, Haskell will continue looking along each field in declaration order. In this case, it means that after the kind of client, the next thing to compare is its identifier. However, this may not be the best behavior, as Exercise 4-6 points out.

EXERCISE 4-6. ORDERING CLIENTS

The automatically derived Ord instance for Clients doesn't make much sense. As discussed, it checks the kind of client and then its identifier. Instead of that, write a new instance with the following properties: first, the instance should compare the name of the client. Then, if they coincide, it should put individuals first and then companies and government organizations at the end. You may need to add further comparisons in the rest of the fields to make the order correct (e.g., for two companies whose responsibility fields are different, so you must decide which one to put first).

Think beforehand whether you need to include some restriction in the instance.

Other type classes you have been using are Num and its subclasses. As you may guess, Num is the class for all those types representing numbers, whether integers, rationals, or floating-point. Each subclass adds some refinement. For example, Num includes only addition, subtraction, and multiplication, but Integral adds to the mix integer division and remainders. The operations belonging to each class are summarized in Table 4-1, along with the superclass relations.

Table 4-1. *Number-Related Type Classes*

Type Class	Parent Class	Description
Num	n/a	Basic number type. Supports addition (+), subtraction (-), multiplication (*), unary negation (negate), absolute value (abs), sign (signum), and conversion from an Integer value (fromInteger).
Real	Num	Subclass supporting conversion to Rational values (using toRational). Integer is an instance of this class because integral values can be embedded as fractions with a denominator of 1.
Integral	Real	Subclass for integer values that support integer division and integer modulus. Related functions come in triples: quot, rem, and quotRem compute the division, modulus, or both (truncating toward 0), whereas div, mod, and divMod do the truncating toward negative infinity (-∞).
Fractional	Num	Subclass for fractional values. Supports division (/), taking the reciprocal (recip) and conversion from a Rational value (fromRational).
Floating	Fractional	Subclass for floating-point values. Supports common values such as pi and e. Allows for square roots (sqrt), natural logarithms (log), exponentiation (exp for natural base and (**) for general base), and circular and hyperbolic trigonometric functions.

One of the most interesting parts in Haskell's treatment of numbers is how it treats constants. For example, if you try to get the type of 1 in the interpreter, the result may be puzzling at first.

```
*Chapter4.TypeClasses> :t 1
1 :: Num a => a
```

As you can see, the constant itself is polymorphic. It may represent 1 in any type that instantiates Num. The reason for that is the fromInteger function, which allows you to extract a value from an integer constant.

As an example, you are going to create a data type for complex numbers and implement its Num instance.[2] You may remember from your algebra class that a complex number has the form $a+bi$, where a is the real part and b is the imaginary part. The laws that govern their operations can be derived from the fact that $i^2 = -1$. Finally, each complex number has the concept of absolute value, $|x|$, and argument θ_x, which satisfy the condition $|x|\theta_x = x$, which is exactly the one you need for abs and signum in a Num instance.

```
data Complex = C Double Double deriving (Show, Eq)

instance Num Complex where
  (C a1 b1) + (C a2 b2) = C (a1 + a2) (b1 + b2)
  (C a1 b1) - (C a2 b2) = C (a1 - a2) (b1 - b2)
  (C a1 b1) * (C a2 b2) = C (a1*a2-b1*b2) (a1*b2+b1*a2)
  negate (C a b)        = C (negate a) (negate b)
  fromInteger n         = C (fromInteger n) 0
  abs (C a b)           = C (sqrt $ a*a+b*b) 0
  signum c@(C a b)      = let C n _ = abs c in C (a / n) (b / n)
```

You have seen that type classes are a powerful tool for abstracting concepts and patterns. In the previous chapters, you looked at the default values idiom, so you may be wondering whether there's a type class for this matter. The answer is found in the Data. Default module, in the data-default package, which provides a Default class with just one member, def, which will return the default value. If you recall the discussion in Chapter 2 about connection options, a solution using a type class would use the following, instead of connDefault:

```
instance Default ConnOptions where
  def = ConnOptions TCP 0 NoProxy False False NoTimeOut
```

---

[2] The Haskell Platform is quite complete, so it also includes a type for complex numbers, which you can find in the Data.Complex module. This definition will be merely illustrative.

Binary Trees for the Minimum Price

Until now, you have saved all the information about clients in lists for this chapter. Even though you now know about where to look for already implemented types, this section is going to step back and look at the design of a custom container type that completely suits the needs of the application. In particular, the aim is to provide support for the discount module, which needs access to the cheapest elements in the container. In the process, you will see how type classes allow for a greater degree of generalization, thus increasing reusability.

In this section, the container will be holding travel guides. A travel guide consists of a title, a list of authors, and a price. You can model it using a record. As you will see later, you will need some notion of less and greater than, so you need an Ord instance and with it an Eq instance.

```
data TravelGuide = TravelGuide { title :: String
                               , authors :: [String]
                               , price :: Double }
               deriving (Show, Eq, Ord)
```

Step 1: Simple Binary Trees

A first solution is to use bare lists. The greatest problem with them is that querying for elements in them is costly because the only option you have is to traverse the list element by element. In the worst case, you may need to traverse the entire list until you find an answer. A solution for this is to use binary trees, which have a better complexity in this task (in particular, logarithmic vs. linear).

A *binary tree* is a data structure made up of nodes. Each node holds a value and two references to subtrees. To indicate that a node doesn't have some of the subtrees, you use a special *leaf* marker. The special property of binary trees is that any node in the left subtree will hold only those values smaller than the one in the node, whereas in the right subtree you will find values that are greater than that in the node itself. This is the reason why you need to derive Ord for the TravelGuide type. Figure 4-3 shows an example of a binary tree, with the constraints over the nodes specified in the edges.

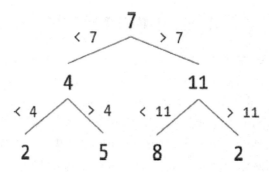

Figure 4-3. *Graphical example of binary tree*

Now you can create the data structure of travel guide binary trees.

```
data BinaryTree1 = Node1 TravelGuide BinaryTree1 BinaryTree1
                 | Leaf1
                 deriving Show
```

As explained, searching in a binary tree is much faster because by comparing the element to look for with the node you are currently exploring, you can decide in which subtree to look while being sure that it will never be in the other subtree.

```
treeFind1 :: TravelGuide -> BinaryTree1 -> Maybe TravelGuide
treeFind1 t (Node1 v l r) = case compare t v of
                              EQ -> Just v
                              LT -> treeFind1 t l
                              GT -> treeFind1 t r
treeFind1 _ Leaf1           = Nothing
```

You also need a way to initially create empty trees and to insert values in a tree while keeping the invariant. In the latter case, the algorithm is simple; you traverse the tree as if you were looking for the value to insert. If you reach a Leaf1, it means the value is not there and that the position for it is in the place of the leaf itself.

```
treeInsert1 :: TravelGuide -> BinaryTree1 -> BinaryTree1
treeInsert1 t n@(Node1 v l r) = case compare t v of
                                  EQ -> n
                                  LT -> Node1 v (treeInsert1 t l) r
                                  GT -> Node1 v l (treeInsert1 t r)
treeInsert1 t Leaf1            = Node1 t Leaf1 Leaf1
```

Step 2: Polymorphic Binary Trees

The basic data structure for binary trees cries out for generalization. You are not using any information inside TravelGuide for anything other than its order. This means you should work with Ord instances. The parametric version of the binary tree and its associated treeFind function now looks like this:

```
data BinaryTree2 a = Node2 a (BinaryTree2 a) (BinaryTree2 a)
                   | Leaf2
                   deriving Show
treeFind2 :: Ord a => a -> BinaryTree2 a -> Maybe a
treeFind2 t (Node2 v l r) = case compare t v of
                              EQ -> Just v
                              LT -> treeFind2 t l
                              GT -> treeFind2 t r
treeFind2 _ Leaf2         = Nothing
```

Note   You may wonder whether you can encode the restriction on the class of elements that the binary tree may hold directly in the declaration of BinaryTree2. It's indeed possible, but it's not recommended. The best way is to encode the restriction in each of the operations that work on that structure, as has been done in this example. Be aware that in order to impose this restriction, you must hide the Node2 and Leaf2 constructors from public consumption.

The treeFind function has been generalized, but you still need to make some changes to the treeInsert function to make it fully general. Exercise 4-7 dives into this problem.

EXERCISE 4-7. MORE OPERATIONS ON GENERIC TREES

Make the changes needed in treeInsert to work with the new BinaryTree2.

Also, try to implement concatenation of binary trees by repeatedly inserting all the elements in one of the binary trees.

At this point, notice that the automatically derived Ord instance for TravelGuides compares first the title, then the list of authors, and finally the price. But this is not what you need; the application needs to order the travel guides by price. A first attempt would be to write a new Ord instance, like so:

```
instance Ord TravelGuide where
  (TravelGuide t1 a1 p1) <= (TravelGuide t2 a2 p2) =
    p1 < p2 || (p1 == p2 && (t1 < t2 || (t1 == t2 && a1 <= a2)))
```

Of course, you get an error about duplicate instances, as shown here:

```
Duplicate instance declarations:
      instance Ord TravelGuide
        -- Defined at MinimumPrice.hs:4:38
      instance Ord TravelGuide
        -- Defined at MinimumPrice.hs:6:10
```

A first solution is to create a one-field data type to hold travel guides by price and then create the instance for it.

```
data TGByPrice = TGByPrice TravelGuide
instance Ord TGByPrice where ...
```

The problem is that you are creating a new constructor, which at execution time must be pattern matched and unwrapped, thus taking time and hurting performance. What you need is just a way to tag values with a new type so that the compiler is able to distinguish which instance must be applied. But you want to do it without having to rewrite the initial type or having performance problems. Haskell includes a solution for this problem: a newtype declaration declares another name for an already existing type. But, in contrast to type declarations, the new name is not a synonym, but it's viewed as a completely unrelated type. The good news is that newtype has no performance overhead because at compile time the compiler knows that values of that type will always be equal to a value of the original type, and it can delete all the constructor wrapping and pattern matching. The following code declares a newtype for TravelGuide and associates with it a new instance of the Ord type class, but now by comparing by price first:

```
newtype TGByPrice = TGByPrice TravelGuide deriving Eq
```

```
instance Ord TGByPrice where
  (TGByPrice (TravelGuide t1 a1 p1)) <= (TGByPrice (TravelGuide t2 a2 p2)) =
    p1 < p2 || (p1 == p2 && (t1 < t2 || (t1 == t2 && a1 <= a2)))
```

Let's assume now that ordering by price is used for the rest of the examples.

Step 3: Binary Trees with Monoidal Cache

Still, finding the smallest price in the tree takes some time because you have to go into the left subtree until you reach a leaf. However, in the web page, you need to show that element often. A solution is to include a cache in every node, which stores the price of the smallest element in the tree. Let's create a new version of binary trees, where the cache type has also been made parametric for greater generality.

```
data BinaryTree3 v c = Node3 v c (BinaryTree3 v c) (BinaryTree3 v c)
                     | Leaf3
                     deriving (Show, Eq, Ord)
```

And here's the corresponding implementation of treeInsert, where the cache is updated at every step:

```
treeInsert3 :: (Ord v, Ord c)
            => v -> c -> BinaryTree3 v c -> BinaryTree3 v c
treeInsert3 v c (Node3 v2 c2 l r)
  = case compare v v2 of
      EQ -> Node3 v2 c2 l r
      LT -> Node3 v2 (min c c2) (treeInsert3 v c l) r
      GT -> Node3 v2 (min c c2) l (treeInsert3 v c r)
treeInsert3 v c Leaf3 = Node3 v c Leaf3 Leaf3
```

At some point, you may be told that in addition to minimum prices, the marketing team wants to have information about the average price of travel guides to analyze what percentage of people are buying books under and over the average. To do this, you need to create a new insertion function, which instead of the minimum computes the sum of all the prices, so you can later divide by the total number of guides. But altogether, the structure of the function remains the same.

145

Let's try to untangle the structure in both cases. What you are doing is caching some information that comes from the cached values in the subtrees and the value in the node itself. In the case of the minimal price, the operation that creates the new cached value is min, and in the case of sum, it is +. Can the exact requirements for such a function be made more precise?

- For any two elements, you need to find another one of the same type. That is, you need a function f of type c -> c -> c.

- Also, depending on the way you have inserted elements in the tree, the structure may not be the same. But this should not matter for the final cached value. So, you need to be sure that the parenthesis structure does not matter. In other words, the operation must be associative.

- One last thing comes from the observation that when you concatenate two binary trees, you should be able to recover the new cached value for the root from the cached values from the initial roots. That means an empty tree, which contains no elements, should be assigned a value e such that f e x = f x e = x.

This structure, an associative binary operation with an element that does not affect the outcome (called a *neutral* element), is called a *monoid* and has its corresponding class in the module Data.Monoid.

```
class Monoid a where
  mempty  :: a              -- neutral element
  mappend :: a -> a -> a  -- associative binary operation
  mconcat :: [a] -> a
```

Since GHC version 8.4, Monoid is a subclass of a more general notion called Semigroup. A semigroup drops the neutral element requirement and just includes the associative binary operation.

```
class Semigroup a where
  (<>) :: a -> a -> a
class Semigroup a => Monoid a where ...   -- since GHC 8.4
```

This means that you usually won't write mappend; rather, you can use its synonym, (<>), coming from Semigroup.

Now you can write the most general treeInsert version. Notice how in this general version you need to apply the (<>) operator both to subtrees and to the information in each node. In the version computing the minimal elements, you could take advantage from the fact that values are ordered in the tree, but in general this cannot be used.

```
treeInsert4 :: (Ord v, Monoid c)
            => v -> c -> BinaryTree3 v c -> BinaryTree3 v c
treeInsert4 v c (Node3 v2 c2 l r)
  = case compare v v2 of
      EQ -> Node3 v2 c2 l r
      LT -> let newLeft = treeInsert4 v c l
                newCache = c2 <> cached newLeft <> cached r
            in Node3 v2 newCache newLeft r
      GT -> let newRight = treeInsert4 v c r
                newCache = c2 <> cached l <> cached newRight
            in Node3 v2 newCache l newRight
treeInsert4 v c Leaf3 = Node3 v c Leaf3 Leaf3

cached :: Monoid c => BinaryTree3 v c -> c
cached (Node3 _ c _ _) = c
cached Leaf3           = mempty
```

Monoid is one of the type classes that may have multiple implementations for just one type, which has led to the creation of newtypes for some common types. Some of the most important ones are All, which implements the monoid structure of Bool under the operation (&&) with neutral element True; and All, which does the same with (||) and neutral element False. Numbers also admit two monoidal structures: Sum uses addition as an operation and 0 as a neutral element, whereas Product uses multiplication and 1.

In fact, another monoidal structure for numbers should be provided if you want to use this general cache insertion algorithm. The code needed to declare the newtype along with the new instance follows. Notice how the code uses the infinity element for floating-point, which can be obtained through 1/0.

```
newtype Min = Min Double deriving Show

instance Semigroup Min where
  Min x <> Min y = Min $ min x y
```

```
instance Monoid Min where
  mempty  = Min infinity where infinity = 1/0
  mappend = (<>)  -- use the definition from Semigroup
```

Container-Related Type Classes

In many cases while developing an application, you need to change the container you are using to handle the values. So, it might be interesting to step back and think about the commonalities between them because it may be possible to abstract from them and discover some useful type class.

Functors

Let's try to write a function applying a discount to each travel guide in a list.

```
modifyTravelGuidePrice
  :: Double -> [TravelGuide] -> [TravelGuide]
modifyTravelGuidePrice m  = map (\tg -> tg { price = m * price tg })
```

And if you wanted to do it in a map or a tree, here's how you would do that:

```
modifyTravelGuidePriceMap
  :: Double -> M.Map a TravelGuide -> M.Map a TravelGuide
modifyTravelGuidePriceMap m = M.map (\tg -> tg { price = m * price tg })
```

```
modifyTravelGuidePriceTree
  :: Double -> T.Tree TravelGuide -> T.Tree TravelGuide
modifyTravelGuidePriceTree m = fmap (\tg -> tg { price = m * price tg })
```

You should start seeing a pattern here; all these containers allow you to apply a function inside the data structure.

```
map    :: (a -> b) -> ([a]        -> [b])
M.map  :: (a -> b) -> (M.Map k a -> M.Map k b)
fmap   :: (a -> b) -> (T.Tree a  -> T.Tree b)  -- version for trees
```

A data type supporting a function like map is called a *functor*. The corresponding class is defined as follows:

```
class Functor f where
  fmap :: (a -> b) -> f a -> f b
```

So, now you can write the most general function to modify the price of a travel guide.

```
modifyTravelGuidePrice'
  :: Functor f => Double -> f TravelGuide -> f TravelGuide
modifyTravelGuidePrice' m = fmap (\tg -> tg { price = m * price tg })
```

You may notice a strange fact about the Functor class; in the definition of fmap, the type variable corresponding to the instance is applied to another type variable, instead of being used raw. This means that those types that are to be functors should take one type parameter. For example, IntSet, which takes none, cannot have such an instance (even though conceptually it is a functor).

The way in which the Haskell compiler checks for the correct application of type parameters is by the *kind* system. Knowing it may help you make sense of some error messages. Until now, you know that values, functions, and constructors have an associated type, but types themselves are also categorized based on the level of application. To start with, all basic types such as Char or Integer have kind *. Types that need one parameter to be fully applied, such as Maybe, have kind * -> *. This syntax resembles the one used for functions on purpose. If you now have Maybe Integer, you have a type of kind * -> *, which is applied to a type of kind *. So, the final kind for Maybe Integer is indeed *.

Functor is one of the most ubiquitous type classes in Haskell. Exercise 4-8 guides you in writing the corresponding instances for one of the basic types in Haskell, Maybe, and also for the binary trees that have been introduced in the previous section.

EXERCISE 4-8. FUNCTOR FUN!

Write the corresponding Functor instances for both Maybe and the binary trees from the previous section. The functor instance of Maybe is quite interesting because it allows you to shorten code that just applies a function when the value is a Just (a pattern matching plus a creation of the new value is just replaced by a call to map). You will need to create a new type for Maybe values in order to make the compiler happy.

From all the binary tree types shown so far, choose BinaryTree2 as the type for instantiating Functor. In this last case, remember that you must respect the order invariant of the tree, so the best way to write the map function may involve repeatedly calling treeInsert2 on an empty tree.

Although the concept of functors came via containers, the concept is much broader. One instance of a functor that doesn't fit that box is (->) r. The elements of this type are those functions of the form r -> a, which are functions that take as input a value of a specific type, r. Haskell syntax doesn't help too much. In this case, just remember that a f b can also be written (f) a b if f is completely made of symbols, which is the case for ->. To begin with, let's try to write the type for the corresponding version of fmap.

```
fmap :: (a -> b) -> (r -> a) -> (r -> b)
```

The easiest solution in this case is to apply the first function after the second to get a result of the desired type.

```
instance Functor ((->) r) where
  fmap f g = f . g
```

In this case, the concept behind the type class implementation is that of *computational context*. This adds to any expression an extra value of type r that can be used to control the behavior of such an expression. You will see in Chapter 6 how this mimics the existence of a constant of type r in your code.

Note   Set cannot be made an instance of Functor. The reason is that the mapping function for sets has the type Ord b => (a -> b) -> Set a -> Set b, which is not compatible with that of Functor, which doesn't have any restriction. The Haskell language provides enough tools nowadays for creating another type class for functors that would allow Set inside it. However, this would make using the Functor type class much more complicated and would break a lot of already existing code. For that reason, the simpler version of Functor is the one included in the libraries.

Foldables

The other basic operation you can do with containers is computing some aggregate information from all the held elements, that is, a fold. This concept has its corresponding type class, called `Foldable`, which can be found in module `Data.Foldable`. To differentiate between folds and functors, you can think of folds in two different ways:

- Like the list `foldr`, a fold takes an initial value and a combining function and, starting with the initial value, applies the combining function to the current value and the next element in the structure.

- You can see that a type with a binary function and some special value matches exactly the definition of a monoid. Furthermore, you have seen how combining functions in `foldr` should be associative, just like (`<>`) from `Monoid` is.

These two definitions allow for two different ways of instantiating the `Foldable` class. You need to give a definition of either `foldr` (the version with the combining function) or `foldMap` (the version with monoids).

```
class Foldable t where
  foldMap :: Monoid m => (a -> m) -> t a -> m
  foldr   :: (a -> b -> b) -> b -> t a -> b
  fold    :: Monoid m => t m -> m
  foldr'  :: (a -> b -> b) -> b -> t a -> b
  foldl   :: (a -> b -> a) -> a -> t b -> a
  foldl'  :: (a -> b -> a) -> a -> t b -> a
  foldr1  :: (a -> a -> a) -> t a -> a
  foldl1  :: (a -> a -> a) -> t a -> a
```

The rest of the operations correspond to default definitions that could be overridden for performance reasons. `fold` is a version of `foldMap` that just combines a container full of monoid values without previously applying any function. `foldl` corresponds to folding over the elements starting from the "other side" of the structure. You've already seen how the result of `foldr` and `foldl` are different if the combining function is not commutative. The versions ending with prime (`'`) are strict versions of the functions; they will play a central role in the next chapter.

Foldables are also ubiquitous in Haskell code, like functors. Exercise 4-9 asks you to provide instances of this class for the same types you did in Exercise 4-8.

EXERCISE 4-9. FOLDABLE FUN!

Maybe and binary trees can also be folded over. Write their corresponding Foldable instances. The warnings and hints from Exercise 4-8 also apply here.

As you saw in the previous chapter, a lot of different algorithms can be expressed using folds. The module Data.Foldable includes most of them, such as maximum or elem. One easy way to make your functions more general is by hiding the functions with names from the Prelude module and importing the similarly named ones using Foldable.

Note   You may wonder why Prelude includes specialized definitions for lists instead of the most general versions using Functor and Foldable. The reason is that, for a beginner, having the functions working only on [a] helps you understand the first error messages that Haskell may encounter because they don't involve type classes. But now that you know about them, you should aim for the largest degree of abstraction that you can achieve.

In this section, you wrote instances of Functor and Foldable for various data types. Because Functor and Foldable are so heavily used, the GHC developers also decided to include automatic derivation of these type classes. However, since this is not indicated in the Haskell Report, you need to enable some extensions, namely, DeriveFunctor and DeriveFoldable, for them to work. Note that if you have a type with several parameters, the one chosen for mapping or folding over is always the last one in the declaration.

TYPECLASSOPEDIA

Several of the type classes discussed here, such as Monoid, Functor, and Foldable, are deeply documented in Typeclassopedia, the encyclopedia of Haskell type classes. You can find it online at wiki.haskell.org/Typeclassopedia. It's an important source of information and examples.

Summary

In this chapter, you looked at several features of the Haskell ecosystem.

- You learned about how packages are specified as dependencies, and then used by either Cabal or Stack, allowing the reuse of many libraries already available in the repositories Hackage and Stackage.

- Several new containers were introduced, including maps, sets, trees, and graphs. The quest for understanding their commonalities led to the discovery of the concepts of `Functor` and `Foldable`.

- I covered the reason why (+) could work on several numeric types, namely, through ad hoc polymorphism and type classes. You learned both how to declare a new type class describing a shared concept between types and how to instantiate that class for a specific type. Furthermore, you saw how both classes and instances can depend on class constraints on other types or parameters.

- You learned about the built-in classes `Eq`, describing equivalence; `Ord`, describing ordering; `Num` and its derivatives, describing numbers; and `Default`, describing default values for a data type.

- I covered the design of a special binary tree with a cache, including how to incrementally improve the design of such a data type. In particular, you saw how type classes allow you to generalize the values it can take, looking specifically at the monoidal structure that is common in Haskell data types.

CHAPTER 5

Laziness and Infinite Structures

In previous chapters, I introduced several of the pillars of Haskell programming: the pure functional paradigm and the strongly typed nature of the language, which nevertheless allows powerful type constructs such as parametric polymorphism and type classes. This chapter will be devoted to understanding the unique evaluation model of Haskell, based on *laziness*, and the consequences of that choice.

In short, *lazy evaluation* means that only the necessary parts of an expression are computed, and this is done at the last possible moment. For example, if you have an expression such as head [2+3, 5*7], the multiplication is never performed at runtime because that value is irrelevant for the result of the expression. head uses only the first element in the list. As you may know, this way of performing evaluation is quite different from other programming languages. That opens the door to some interesting new idioms, such as working with infinite and cycling structures without caring about their special nature.

However, as a developer, you also need to be conscious of the trade-offs this model has, especially in the area of memory usage and performance. You will see the most typical problems that arise because of the laziness in Haskell code and learn about Haskell's *strictness* to overcome them. Strictness annotations are available in pattern matching and in data declarations. The time and memory profiler that comes bundled with GHC will be an incredible tool to spot these problems; in this chapter, you will look at its basic usage.

© Alejandro Serrano Mena 2022
A. Serrano Mena, *Practical Haskell*, https://doi.org/10.1007/978-1-4842-8581-7_5

An Infinite Number of Time Machines

First, you are going to see how Haskell can cope with infinite and cyclic structures without imposing any burden on the developer. In this section, you will look at the declaration and usage of these kinds of values in an intuitive way. The next section will discuss how Haskell is able to represent this information so that the code works.

As I have mentioned, some kinds of time machines allow travel to only certain years in history. But the store is known for always having the time machines to travel to any particular point in time. The problem here is that the world may never end, so the set of all time machines is infinite! Let's declare a small data type for holding time machines, with the manufacturer and the year to which travel is permitted.

```
data TimeMachine = TM { manufacturer :: String, year :: Integer }
                 deriving (Eq, Show)
```

You can write a function to return all the time machines from a year n on. Check that there's no guard or base case that stops the production of more time machines.

```
timeMachinesFrom :: String -> Integer -> [TimeMachine]
timeMachinesFrom mf y = TM mf y : timeMachinesFrom mf (y+1)
```

And from there, here are all the time machines made by Timely Inc. from year 100 on:

```
timelyIncMachines :: [TimeMachine]
timelyIncMachines = timeMachinesFrom "Timely Inc." 100
```

If you now load the file in the GHC interpreter, you can get the first elements of the list, using the built-in take function. The system doesn't enter into any kind of infinite loop while evaluating the Timely Inc. machines.

```
*Chapter5.Infinite> take 3 timelyIncMachines
[TM {manufacturer = "Timely Inc.", year = 100}
,TM {manufacturer = "Timely Inc.", year = 101}
,TM {manufacturer = "Timely Inc.", year = 102}]
```

You can also try to find the first of those machines that travels after 2021.

```
*Chapter5.Infinite> import Data.List
*Chapter5.Infinite Data.List> find (\(TM { year = y }) -> y > 2021)
timelyIncMachines
Just (TM {manufacturer = "Timely Inc.", year = 2022})
```

But if you try to compute the length of the list or to find an element that does not exist (in this case, a time machine that travels to year 10), the interpreter will enter into an infinite computation and will never return. To halt the execution in the console, you should press Ctrl+C.

```
*Chapter5.Infinite> length timelyIncMachines
-- Never stops
*Chapter5.Infinite> find (\(TM { year = y }) -> y == 10) timelyIncMachines
-- Never stops
```

Somehow, Haskell knows how to treat an infinite list, given that you observe only a finite part of it during runtime. On the other hand, the evaluation of an expression such as length timelyIncMachines involves traversing the entire list, so it doesn't end.

Infinite lists are useful in some other situations. For example, in a previous chapter you wrote a function that, given an input list, returned a new list of tuples where each element was decorated by its position in the list. For that matter, you used the zip function.

```
*Chapter5.Infinite> (\list -> zip [1 .. length list] list) "abcd"
[(1,'a'),(2,'b'),(3,'c'),(4,'d')]
```

But to do so, you had to traverse the list twice, once to get its length and once again to zip both. A better way to do it is to remember that zip stops when one of the lists ends. Then, you can use an infinite list of numbers as the first argument to zip. Let's write a function that holds the list of all numbers from 1 on.

```
allNumbers :: [Integer]
allNumbers = allNumbersFrom 1
allNumbersFrom :: Integer -> [Integer]
allNumbersFrom n = n : allNumbersFrom (n+1)
```

Now you can write the same function easily.

```
*Chapter5.Infinite> zip allNumbers "abcd"
[(1,'a'),(2,'b'),(3,'c'),(4,'d')]
```

Or even better, you can use Haskell infinite list ranges. The notation [1 ..] describes a list starting from 1 until the end of the integer elements (which in this case does not exist, because integer numbers are infinite).

```
*Chapter5.Infinite> zip [1 .. ] "abcd"
[(1,'a'),(2,'b'),(3,'c'),(4,'d')]
```

Note   The notation [e ..] does not necessarily imply that an infinite list is created but rather that the list will hold all the elements larger than e. For example, [False ..] is equivalent to writing [False, True] because the ordering in Bool is False < True and there are no more elements in that type.

There are even more tricks with infinite lists. Let's look now at an interesting way to define Fibonacci numbers. If you remember from previous chapters, the nth Fibonacci number is defined as the sum of the Fibonacci numbers of steps $n-1$ and $n-2$. Let's look it from a different perspective. Say you already have the list of all the Fibonacci numbers. The position n in this list holds that Fibonacci number. If you take the tail of that list, the list is moved one step forward; position n holds the Fibonacci number $n+1$. And finally comes the magic: if you sum the elements one by one, you get the Fibonacci numbers but moved two positions. This is depicted in Figure 5-1.

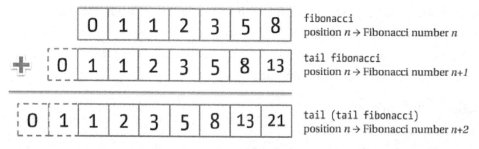

Figure 5-1. *Properties of the list of Fibonacci numbers, graphically*

You can use this remark to define the list of all Fibonacci numbers. The first two elements will be 0 and 1 (this is fixed by the definition). Then, you obtain the rest of the list by adding elements one at a time, with the list moved one element forward. This element-by-element addition is what you get using zipWith (+).

```
fibonacci :: [Integer]
fibonacci = 0 : 1 : zipWith (+) fibonacci (tail fibonacci)
```

Obtaining the nth Fibonacci number is now equivalent to obtaining the element in position n-1 (like in C or Java, lists are indexed starting with 0). The (!!) function in Data.List is exactly the function you need.

```
*Chapter5.Infinite> import Data.List
*Chapter5.Infinite Data.List> fibonacci !! 20
6765
```

In addition to using list ranges and constructing functions by hand, an approach that returns infinite lists, the Prelude module includes some built-in functions to generate the needed results. As a special offer, Timely Inc. supplies an infinite number of time machines to travel to the year 2021. One way to define this could be as follows:

```
infinite2020Machines :: [TimeMachine]
infinite2020Machines = TM "Timely Inc." 2020 : infinite2020Machines
```

But another way to do so would be using the repeat combinator, which just creates infinite copies of the same value in a list.

```
*Chapter5.Infinite> take 3 $ repeat $ TM "Timely Inc." 2020
[TM {manufacturer = "Timely Inc.", year = 2020}
,TM {manufacturer = "Timely Inc.", year = 2020}
,TM {manufacturer = "Timely Inc.", year = 2020}]
```

In addition to one value, you can also repeat a set of values in order. In a special offer, you may have a set of time machines with a 20 percent discount but with the particular property so that you have to sell one for 2005, then one for 1994, then one for 908, and then again from 2005. You declare this infinite list with cycle.

```
specialOffer :: [TimeMachine]
specialOffer = cycle [TM m 2005, TM m 1994, TM m 908]
               where m = "Timely Inc."
```

You can see how values are repeated by looking at the first four values.

```
*Chapter5.Infinite> take 4 specialOffer
[TM {manufacturer = "Timely Inc.", year = 2005}
,TM {manufacturer = "Timely Inc.", year = 1994}
,TM {manufacturer = "Timely Inc.", year = 908}
,TM {manufacturer = "Timely Inc.", year = 2005}]
```

Values don't need to always be equal. The `iterate` function generates values by applying a function to a value to get a second, then applying the same function to this second value to get the third, and so on. You can see the infinite list that will be generated as follows:

```
iterate f x = [ x, f x, f (f x), f (f (f x)), ... ]
```

This gives you another way to implement Fibonacci. In particular, the `fibonacci2` list will hold pairs of values; for example, in position *n*, you can find (*n* Fibonacci number, *n+1* Fibonacci number). From one of these tuples, you can build the next element by shifting one position to the left and adding the two numbers to get the *n+2* Fibonacci number. In code, this translates to the following:

```
fibonacci2 :: [Integer]
fibonacci2 = map fst $ iterate (\(n,n1) -> (n1,n+n1)) (0,1)
```

You can use this new function like you used the previous one.

```
*Chapter5.Infinite> fibonacci2 !! 20
6765
```

In Exercise 5-1, you will see how infinite lists can even give you a glimpse into history.

EXERCISE 5-1. THE SIEVE OF ERATOSTHENES

Eratosthenes was a Greek mathematician from the third century BC. One of his most known inventions is the *prime sieve*. This sieve gives an algorithm for getting the list of all the primes. It works in the following way:

- Start with a list of all the numbers from 2 on.

- Take the first number, in this case 2, and drop from the list of numbers all its multiples, that is, all numbers *n* such that the remainder of *n* and 2 is 0.

- Now take the next number (in this case, it will be 3) in the filtered list and repeat the operation: filter out all the multiples of that number.

- Repeat the previous step with the first number left in the previous one.

Implement the sieve of Eratosthenes using the techniques outlined in this section. The solution should take the form of a declaration `primes :: [Integer]`, which contains all the prime numbers.

Lazy Evaluation Model

At this point, you should be convinced that Haskell can indeed work with infinite values (or, at least, with infinite lists). However, it may seem a bit like black magic. Of course, this is not the case: the ability to work in this way is the result of the strategy that Haskell follows for evaluating expressions, which departs greatly from other programming languages. In this section, I will introduce this lazy strategy and point out some of the most common problems with it.

Understanding Evaluation in Haskell

Most of the programming languages follow a *strict evaluation model*. In other words, whenever a compound expression is found, it's immediately transformed into a simpler version (maybe including calls to functions of methods) before the larger expression is evaluated. Most importantly, arguments to a function are evaluated before the control flow enters the body of the function. Here's an example of the steps that would be followed in this model to evaluate a simple expression:

```
head [3+2, 7*5] => head [5, 35]  -- we evaluate the arguments to head
                => 5             -- and then we execute the function itself
```

Under this kind of evaluation, an expression like head timelyIncMachines would cause an infinite loop because there's no point at which to stop going further and further in the list. In the following code, I reproduce the first steps of this infinite loop, which will continue as shown with three dots. Take the time to understand this example until you are completely sure about why this example loops.

```
head timelyIncMachines
    => head (timeMachinesFrom "Timely Inc." 100)
    => head (TM "Timely Inc." 100 : timeMachinesFrom "Timely Inc." 101)
    => head (TM "Timely Inc." 100 : TM "Timely Inc." 101 :
            timeMachinesFrom "Timely Inc." 102)
    => head (TM "Timely Inc." 100 : TM "Timely Inc." 101 :
            TM "Timely Inc." 102 : ...)
```

In contrast, Haskell tries to evaluate expressions as late as possible. In this example, it won't initially evaluate the expressions that make the elements in the list. When it finds a call to head, it obtains the first element, which will still be an unevaluated expression, 3+2. Since you want to print the result of this expression on the screen, it will continue only by computing the addition, until it arrives at the same final value, that is, 5. This kind of evaluation is known as *nonstrict* or *lazy*.

I have been intuitively using the idea of "evaluating as late as possible." But that approach is not directly applicable to the example of the infinite list because for getting the head you have to enter the body of timeMachinesFrom, which would then give rise to a loop. The extra bit of information you need to know is that, by default, Haskell evaluates an expression only until a constructor is found. The rest of the value will be left unevaluated. Its spot will be occupied by a placeholder indicating how that specific field can be computed. This placeholder is called a *thunk*.

Applying what I've just described to the evaluation of the head of the infinite list, timeMachinesFrom will just produce a (:) constructor with a thunk for the element and another thunk for the rest of the list. When you apply head to it, you get back the first of the thunks. If you want to show the value on the screen, the thunk has to be unwrapped, and the recipe to create the value that is held in the thunk must be followed. Figure 5-2 shows these steps graphically. The first three transitions are the actual evaluation of thunks. In the fourth state, you arrive at a point where you can evaluate the case expression because you can choose a pattern based on the already evaluated value. The final steps are already plain evaluation of thunks. The next thunk to be evaluated in each step is shown with a bolder frame.

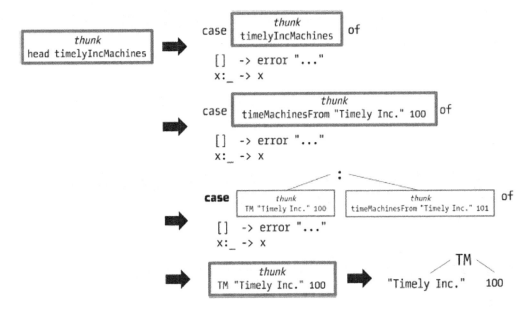

Figure 5-2. *Evaluation of head* `timelyIncMachines`

One important feature of lazy evaluation is that once a thunk has been evaluated, the result is saved, and the thunk is not evaluated again if the result of that expression is needed elsewhere. This is a great feature because it means you pay only once for the cost of evaluating each expression in your application. Furthermore, the pure nature of Haskell also helps in sharing thunks that refer to the same expressions, which means it can reuse the evaluation in some part of the program in other places. For example, Figure 5-3 shows how the memory layout changes when executing (`head allNumbers,` `head (tail allNumbers), tail allNumbers`). Since `allNumbers` is a list, the Haskell runtime environment keeps a reference to the same expression from all the appearances of that value. This is shown in Figure 5-3 as different arrows pointing to the same expression. Exercise 5-2 allows you to try this sharing.

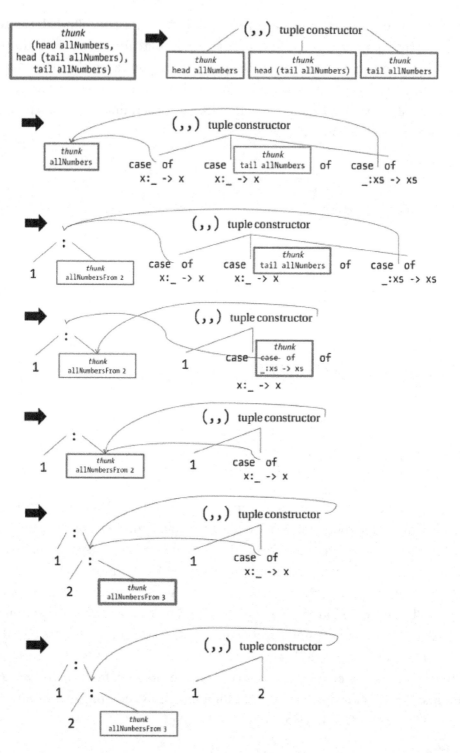

Figure 5-3. *(head allNumbers, head (tail allNumbers), tail allNumbers)*

EXERCISE 5-2. EVALUATING FIBONACCI

Write down the evaluation steps of the expression `fibonacci !! 3`, where `fibonacci` is the infinite list of the Fibonacci numbers, as defined previously in this chapter.

This would be impossible in a language that allows printing while computing a value. Let's assume that during its evaluation, `allNumbers` outputs `"Natural numbers rule!"`. If you share the same value for `allNumbers`, the string would be printed only once. But in many languages, including C and Java, what you would expect is to show it three times, one per reference to `allNumbers`. You have seen that side effects make it impossible to apply these sharing optimizations, which are key to good performance in Haskell programs.

It should be noted that only expressions will be shared. This should not be confused with memorizing a function, that is, caching the results for arguments that have already been provided. Here's an example:

```
(allNumbersFrom 1, allNumbersFrom 2)
```

Even though `allNumbersFrom 1` will call `allNumbersFrom 2`, the evaluation of `allNumbersFrom 2` in `allNumbersFrom 1` and in the previous expression will not be shared.

One final issue that remains to be explained is how cyclic structures are represented. Haskell maintains a cycle in memory when declarations are the same. For example, for the case of `repeat e`, Figure 5-4 shows the evaluation.

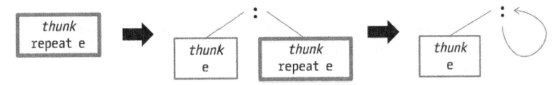

Figure 5-4. *Evaluation of* `repeat e`

EVALUATION STRATEGIES

In this section, you saw two examples of *evaluation strategies*: ways in which the computation proceeds and the order in which parts of the expressions are evaluated. In addition to those two, more strategies have been developed.

What I have called *strict evaluation* is also known as *call by value*. Sometimes, especially in object-oriented languages, this is changed to *call by reference*, where you don't receive values as arguments but boxes holding those values.

Lazy evaluation is sometimes referred to as *call by need*, which is a special case of the more general strategy of *call by name*, in which function arguments are not evaluated before the body of the function but are substituted directly. The difference is that, in general, *call by name* may evaluate the same expression more than once, whereas *call by need* uses thunks to do it only once.

Problems with Laziness

Laziness is often a blessing, but sometimes it can also be a curse. As usual in computer science, there's a trade-off in lazy evaluation. In this case, delaying the evaluation until needed may result in less computation and also allow some programming idioms unavailable in other languages. On the other hand, it may create many thunks, causing the memory to become quite full so that the operating system starts to paginate, which makes the program slower. Let's look at this problem with the help of your old friends, the folds.

Let's build a picture showing how foldr (+) 0 [1,2,3] is evaluated, showing explicitly the thunks. Each thunk will hold the recipe to convert it into a proper value inside it. This is depicted in Figure 5-5.

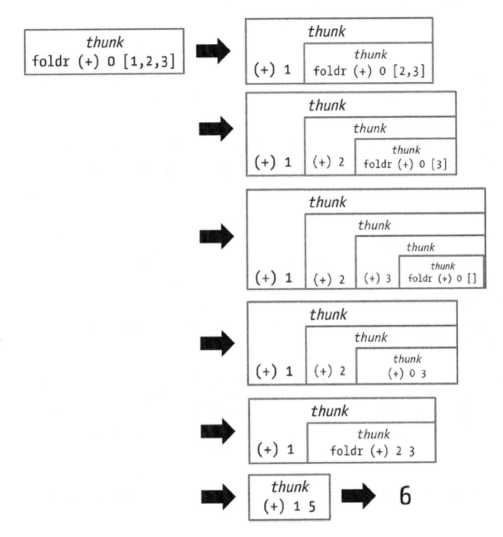

Figure 5-5. *Evaluation of foldr (+) 0 [1,2,3]*

Until the interpreter reaches the final step of foldr, it cannot proceed with the additions. This means that for each element in the list, a new thunk is created. Now you understand why, when requested to interpret the following line of code, the computer starts to sweat and later halts with an error.

*Chapter5.Problems> **foldr (+) 0 [1 .. 1000000000]**

Depending on your system, you may get one of these errors:

<interactive>: out of memory (requested 1048576 bytes)

```
** Exception: stack overflow
Killed
Note
```

Note   At first sight, the culprit could also be the big length of the list. However, if you perform some other computation over it that doesn't create thunks in between, such as length [1 .. 1000000000], you can see that the system responds correctly (the actual speed will depend on the capacity of your computer to hold big integers).

The shape of the evaluation using foldr is something like (1 + (2 + (3 + (... + <thunk>)))), so it cannot continue because at each point during evaluation it knows about only one argument to (+). So, if you use parentheses in another way, making the evaluation look like ((((1 + 2) + 3) + ...) + <thunk>), the problem may be gone. You already know how to do it: using foldl.

```
*Chapter5.Problems> foldl (+) 0 [1 .. 1000000000]
<interactive>: out of memory (requested 1048576 bytes)
```

But here you face a similar situation: (+) has at each step all of its arguments, but since you do not request the result until the end of the list, many thunks have to be created.

The solution is to *force* evaluation. Basically, you need to tell Haskell to evaluate the (n+m) thunks before proceeding with the rest of the computation, overriding the default lazy behavior. The function seq in the Prelude module allows you to do so. In the most general form, a force expression is written as a `seq` b. Haskell ensures that the expression a is evaluated before b. Usually, a is part of the expression b. Let's write an addition operation using the force operator that doesn't suffer from memory problems.

```
sumForce :: [Integer] -> Integer
sumForce xs = sumForce' xs 0
   where sumForce' []     z = z
         sumForce' (y:ys) z = let s = z + y in s `seq` sumForce' ys s
```

When executing sumForce [1 .. 1000000000], the interpreter may take a lot of time, but no memory problem will arise, and eventually an answer will be given. The idiom x `seq` f x is so common that there is a special operator, $! (*strict application*), to perform this task. So, you can rewrite the bold expression in the previous piece of code as sumForce' ys $! (z+y).

Note Once again, you see a familiar foldlike pattern in the previous code. Prelude includes a foldl' function that forces the accumulated value before passing it into the next step. To avoid a memory leak, you could have written the previous example as foldl' (+) 0 [1 .. 1000000000].

Once again, I stress that Haskell evaluates something only until a constructor is found. The fields are left as thunks until some further computation needs the information enclosed by them. This is true also for seq. If you want to be sure that some part of a larger value is evaluated before continuing, you should explicitly get that value and force it (you will see by the end of the chapter that if you don't want *any* thunk inside a value, you can use deep strict evaluation with deepseq). This is enough for this case because the first constructor that will be encountered will be the integer value coming from the addition.

Now that you know about forcing evaluation, you should resist the temptation to use it everywhere you think a memory problem could be found. Forcing expressions destroys the lazy nature of the language and may also lead to cases where a previously terminating expression no longer is. Think of the case of taking the head of an infinite list. If you make Haskell force the entire list, it will never reach the end, thus entering into an infinite computation chain. If you suspect a memory leak, you should first use profiling to find the correct spot and then think carefully whether using seq will not hurt the applicability of your functions to the kind of arguments that are expected.

Pattern Matching and Laziness

As you can see, this interplay of delays using thunks and forcing their evaluation is important. For that reason, you should have a clear idea of when computation takes place. In addition to explicit seq or ($!), another place where the compiler or interpreter needs to evaluate thunks is on pattern matching; it needs to evaluate up to the point that it knows which of the corresponding branches has to be taken.

There's a GHC extension to patterns, called `BangPatterns`, which allows you to force the evaluation of some parts of the pattern. Concretely, you can write ! before any part of the pattern, and then when matching is tried against that pattern, the expression in that point will be evaluated up to a constructor, and then the match will be tried. For example, you can write a function that adds all the years from a list of time machines, using the following syntax both to force the addition of each step and to ensure that the year in each time machine is also evaluated (so the addition does not have a thunk like the second argument):

```
{-# LANGUAGE BangPatterns #-}

sumYears :: [TimeMachine] -> Integer
sumYears xs = sumYears' xs 0
  where sumYears' []              z = z
        sumYears' (TM _ !y :ys) z = let !s = z + y in sumYears' ys s
```

Interesting enough, and because of this evaluation forcing in pattern matching, Haskell also includes a way to *delay* evaluation in matching phases. The way to do it is to use an *irrefutable pattern*. Matching upon it never fails, but it's destructured only when some of its constituent parts are needed. One use case for irrefutable patterns involves a function that always returns a value given the same input. For example, you are finding an element in a list, and you have made sure that the element you are searching for already exists, so `find` will always return the same result. In that case, you can delay the computation of `find` a bit and just evaluate it when you need the constituent value.

For a more explicit example, suppose you have this function:

```
lengthyOperation = if lengthyPredicate then Just something else Nothing
```

Say you know that the `lengthyPredicate` will be true in some situation. If you write a regular matching as follows, then you will force the `lengthyOperation` to be evaluated just to choose the branch:

```
case lengthyOperation of
  Just something -> ...
  Nothing        ->
```

But since you know that the first one will be the selected one, you can delay the computation a bit more using an irrefutable pattern, like so:

```
case lengthyOperation of
  ~(Just something) -> ...
```

Remember that a pattern such as that never fails. So, if you come to a situation where lengthyOperation returns Nothing and you use something inside the body of the match, you will get an error.

Prelude> **case Nothing of ~(Just e) -> "hello, " ++ e ++ "!"**
"hello, *** Exception: Irrefutable pattern failed for pattern (Just e)

Note   Irrefutable patterns are rarely used, but in some cases they are the key to code that performs well. You shouldn't worry too much about understanding all the cases where they may be applicable, but knowing of their existence may become handy, especially if reading the source of some built-in function.

STRICT FUNCTIONS

It won't be long until you read in the documentation of some package that a function is *strict* on one or several of its arguments. At a high level, this means the argument will have to be evaluated if it is still in thunk form, so you should take care of providing in that place an expression that won't lead to nontermination.

Formally, in Haskell there is a canonical value called undefined that represents all those computations that don't end. Because undefined never returns, it can be typed as you want, so you can have undefined :: a. By the way, this typing makes undefined a perfect placeholder in the place of code you haven't yet written, such as when you want to check that your current code passes type checking.

A function f is then called strict on its argument if f undefined = undefined; that is, if given a nonterminating argument, the function itself does not terminate. One example of a strict function is head. But a function defined as g x = 1 isn't, because, given any argument, it returns 1.

Intuitively, the notion of being strict on something means that it doesn't inspect that something. The way a function is strict may be subtler than in the previous examples. For example, head undefined is undefined, but head (1 : undefined) isn't.

Profiling with GHC

The GHC compiler can be used to generate statistics about runs of your program to get more insight on where computation effort is spent. In this section, you will focus on two kinds of profiling: *time profiling*, which gets information about the amount of time spent in each of the functions in the system, and *memory profiling*, which allows you to look at the values holding the larger amount of memory. The profiling output in GHC assigns time or memory to the so-called *cost centers*, and the information and summaries are always related to them. By default, cost centers are assigned to functions, but more can be added using annotations.

To use profiling, you can no longer build the code as a library. You need to build a full executable that could be run from the command line. So, let's first look briefly at the modifications you need to do in the Cabal file to include an executable.

Each Haskell project may include several executables, identified by a name, and with a reference to the file that includes the entry point of the application as a function `main` of type `IO ()`. For now, it's only important to know that `IO` allows you to perform side effects such as printing onto the screen; you will take a closer look at this type in Chapter 9. Each of these executables is defined as a new block in the Cabal file. The name is specified after the `executable` keyword that heads the block, and the file containing the entry function is declared inside the `main-is` property. It's important to note that the `main-is` property needs a reference to the file itself (including the extension), not a module name like other properties. The auxiliary modules are defined inside the `other-modules` property, and dependencies are specified in the `build-depends` property, as in library blocks.

For example, the following declaration includes an executable `profiling-example` whose `main` function is defined in the `Main.hs` file and that uses the `Chapter5.Annotations` module. The only dependency is the `base` package.

```
executable profiling-example
  build-depends:   base >= 4
  hs-source-dirs:  src
  main-is:         Main.hs
  other-modules:   Chapter5.Annotations
```

To check that it works, create the Main.hs file. It's mandatory for the module name that defines an entry point to be called Main and to contain the main :: IO () function, so the file should be named accordingly. In this example, the executable just prints "Hello!" using the putStrLn function.

```
module Main where

main :: IO ()
main = putStrLn "Hello!"
```

Then, call cabal build or stack build in the project folder. Now you can run it in the console. Both tools provide a shortcut for running the executable in the package being built.

```
$ cabal run profiling-example    # for Cabal
$ stack exec profiling-example   # for Stack
Hello!
```

To enable profiling, you must tell the compiler that's what you want to do. In Cabal, you do so by running cabal configure --enable-profiling. This creates a new cabal.project.local file with a single line.

```
Profiling: True
```

Setting up Stack is quite similar. You need to include the following two lines in the stack.yaml file which specifies the resolver of the project:

```
Build:
  library-profiling: true
  executable-profiling: true
```

Then you need to run cabal build or stack build to apply the new configuration options. Once your executable is compiled with runtime options support, you specify the runtime options for your program in the command line between +RTS and -RTS. Time and allocation profiling is specified with -p. Thus, for calling the previous executable while gathering time information, you need to run the following:

```
$ cabal run profiling-example -- +RTS -p -RTS    # for Cabal
$ stack exec profiling-example -- +RTS -p -RTS   # for Stack
Hello!
```

At first sight, nothing has changed in the execution. But if you look carefully at the project folder, a new file called profiling-example.prof has been created. Since the running time of the program is near zero, no interesting profiling output will be generated. Thus, let's better profile a program that computes the factorial of 100,000 and outputs it to the screen. You should change Main.hs to read as follows:

```
module Main where
main :: IO ()
main = putStrLn $ show result
result :: Integer
result = foldr (*) 1 [1 .. 100000]
```

Now run cabal build and the executable in profiling mode. The contents of profiling-example.prof should be similar to the following:

```
        total time  =          5.68 secs   (5680 ticks @ 1000 us, 1
processor)
        total alloc = 9,981,322,816 bytes   (excludes profiling overheads)
COST CENTRE MODULE   %time %alloc
result     Main      94.1   99.7
main       Main       5.9    0.3
```

COST CENTRE	MODULE	no.	entries	individual		inherited	
				%time	%alloc	%time	%alloc
MAIN	MAIN	42	0	0.0	0.0	100.0	100.0
main	Main	85	0	1.2	0.0	1.2	0.0
CAF	Main	83	0	0.0	0.0	98.8	100.0
result	Main	86	1	94.1	99.7	94.1	99.7
main	Main	84	1	4.7	0.3	4.7	0.3
CAF	GHC.IO.Encoding	79	0	0.0	0.0	0.0	0.0
CAF	GHC.Conc.Signal	77	0	0.0	0.0	0.0	0.0
CAF	GHC.IO.Handle.FD	71	0	0.0	0.0	0.0	0.0
CAF	GHC.IO.Encoding.Iconv	66	0	0.0	0.0	0.0	0.0
CAF	GHC.Show	63	0	0.0	0.0	0.0	0.0

The information is divided into three parts. The first part is a summary of the total time and memory used by the program. The second part shows the cost centers (in this case, functions) that contribute the most to that cost. In this case, it's obvious that result takes most of the time and memory, and `main` uses a smaller part of it. The last part is a more detailed view that shows the information about time and allocation in a tree. In this case, a lot of internal functions dealing with file handles and encoding are shown, but in a larger application, fewer of these will be shown because they will be buried in a larger call stack.

However, the most interesting part is *heap profiling*, which allows for the production of a graph stating the consumption of memory throughout the program. The most important ways to run heap profiling are breaking it down by cost centers, which is specified using the -h runtime option, and breaking it down by type, whose option is -hy. Other ways to group consumption, such as by module, by closure, and so on, are available but not used often. If you run the previous program with any of those options, a new file is produced, called `profiling-example.hp`. This file is raw information; to convert it to a graph, you have to use the `hp2ps` tool that comes bundled with the Haskell Platform. Running `hp2ps -c profiling-example.hp` will produce a (color) PostScript file that can then be viewed.

Figure 5-6 shows the output of running `profiling-example -- +RTS -h -RTS` at the command line and then processing the resulting heap profile.

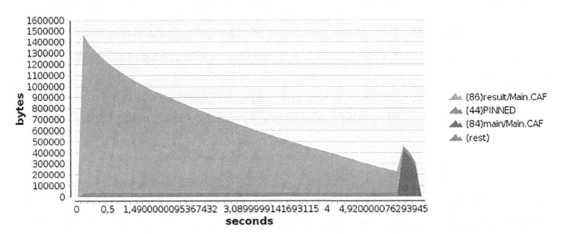

Figure 5-6. *Graphical output of heap profiling by cost centers (run with -h)*

You can see here that there is a big increase in memory usage in the first tenths of a second, shown in orange. This reflects the large creation of thunks I spoke about in the "Problems with Laziness" section. Then, the memory decreases as the thunks are evaluated. A second spike, shown at the extreme right edge of the graph, highlights the increase in memory when the resulting number has to be converted to a string.

The breakdown by types can illustrate the way memory is used in the system. Now run the application with the -hy runtime option and produce the graph. The result looks like Figure 5-7.

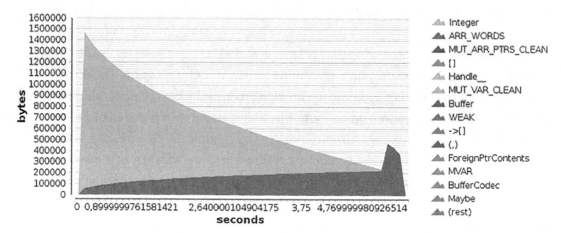

Figure 5-7. *Graphical output of heap profiling by types (run with -hy)*

As you can see, at the beginning most of the memory belongs to elements of type Integer, which corresponds to those thunks I talked about. As you go further in the execution, the ARR_WORDS type uses more memory. This encompasses the memory used by basic types such as evaluated integers (you see that it grows as the number gets larger) and strings.

Let's profile the other versions to see how the profiling output confirms my initial thoughts on the problem of memory exhaustion. Replace the code using foldl' instead of foldr.

```
Import Data.List (foldl')

result :: Integer
result = foldl' (*) 1 [1 .. 100000]
```

The graph in Figure 5-8, obtained by running this new version through heap profiling by types, shows that now intermediate thunks are not created because evaluation is forced at each step, so you don't see the initial spike of Integer values. Memory is used only in ARR_WORDS.

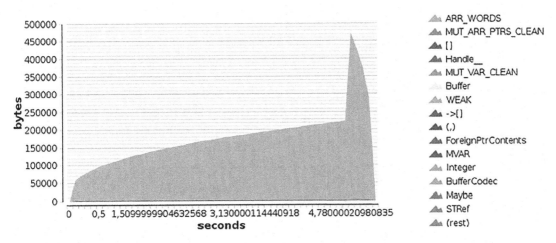

Figure 5-8. *Graphical output of heap profiling by types,* `foldl'` *version*

As you have seen, profiling is a great tool for spotting problems both in time and in memory because it allows focusing on those points that are really wasting those resources, instead of having to guess where the leak comes from. I suggest profiling some larger programs to get confident with the profiler and its output in order to be productive with the tool in the near future.

Strictness Annotations

This section gives more insight into GHC internals. You may safely skip this section in a first reading, but you should return to it later because you will greatly benefit from this information. This section will help you understand the memory and time used by your problem, and it gives you the tools to enhance your application in those aspects.

In general, you can think of a value in Haskell as being represented in memory as some header stating its type and the constructor used to build it, followed by references to each of the fields composing that value. Basic types, such as integers or characters, deviate from this layout and are represented just by the header and the value itself. One `Individual` client, as defined in the previous chapters, would then conform to the representation shown in Figure 5-9.

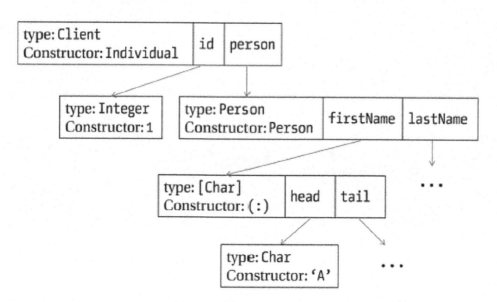

Figure 5-9. *Representation of* `Individual 1 (Person "Andrea" "Blacksmith")`

Remember that before being completely evaluated, expressions in Haskell are represented by thunks. Figure 5-9 shows the memory representation when an expression is completely evaluated. If some parts of it were still to be computed, the references will point to thunks containing the code to be executed.

This representation is flexible but suffers from some performance penalties. First, you may be creating thunks for values that you know will be used in the future or that may be needed to ensure good performance for that data type. For example, if you implement a new kind of list that stores its length, it doesn't make much sense to not store the length directly and instead evaluate it lazily because at the moment you need to query it, a long chain of computations will happen and performance will suffer.

In that case, you want the length to be a *strict field*. Following the same syntax of bang patterns in matching, strict fields are declared by writing ! before the type of the field itself. As a result, every time a new value of that type is created, the expressions in the strict positions will be forced to evaluate in the same fashion as if you had included an explicit `seq`. A possible implementation of your lists with length could be as follows:

```
data ListL a = ListL !Integer [a]
```

The memory representation of values also makes generous use of references to associate values with field positions. This means every time you want to access a field in a value, you need to traverse one reference. Once again, this is flexible and allows you to have potentially extensive structures in memory. However, it can be overkill for accessing small fields, such as integer ones, whose value could be directly encoded in the space that is taken by the reference (the size of a pointer in the target architecture). A field in that situation is said to be *unpacked*.

Unpacking fields is a special feature of the GHC compiler, and it's declared via an {-# UNPACK #-} annotation right before the field declaration. For example, you could decide to unpack the identifiers of all the constructors of the Client data type to make it more efficient.

```
data Client = GovOrg     {-# UNPACK #-} !Int String
            | Company    {-# UNPACK #-} !Int String Person String
            | Individual {-# UNPACK #-} !Int Person
            deriving Show
```

Note that not all fields can be unpacked; it depends on the type of field. Basic types, such as integers or characters, are eligible. Other data types can be used only if they consist of just one constructor and all their fields are also unpacked. This makes it possible to unpack a tuple of types that are unpackable themselves but forbids unpacking a list. Trying to unpack a String field will also produce a warning since it's just a list of Char.

In many cases, you should consider whether for your particular application you prefer a lazier or a stricter implementation of your data structures. Laziness delays the moment of evaluation and allows you to compute only what is strictly needed for the program but has the trade-offs of larger memory consumption and more uncertainty over when the evaluation will take place.

Some packages, such as containers, provide both lazy and strict implementations of the data structures. For example, you have both implementations of maps living in different modules: Data.Map.Lazy and Data.Map.Strict. By default, the module Data. Map uses the lazy versions. The difference in this case, stated in the documentation, is that in the strict version both keys and values are forced before being saved in the map, whereas in the lazy version this is done only for keys.

EVEN DEEPER

In some cases, you need to evaluate an expression until no thunks are left. For that matter, the Haskell Platform provides the deepseq package, which in its module Control.DeepSeq provides the deepseq and ($!!) functions, similar to seq and ($!), respectively, but that also takes care of forcing the subexpressions, not stopping at the layer of constructors.

If you want your data types to support deep evaluation with deepseq, you have to make them instances of the NFData type class. Implementing them is quite easy; you just need to force all the fields and then return (). Here's an example, in Client:

```
import Control.DeepSeq

instance NFData Client where
  rnf (GovOrg i n) =
    i `deepseq` n `deepseq` ()
  rnf (Company i n (Person f l) r) =
    i `deepseq` n `deepseq` f `deepseq` l `deepseq` r `deepseq` ()
  rnf (Individual i (Person f l)) =
    i `deepseq` f `deepseq` l `deepseq` ()
```

The same warnings for forcing with seq apply to deepseq, but they are even stronger because the latter forces even more evaluation to take place.

Summary

In this chapter, you looked at several ways to use the evaluation model of Haskell, based on *laziness*.

- You saw how lazy evaluation allows you to work with seemingly infinite or cyclic structures, making for elegant patterns in the code.

- I explained the lazy evaluation model, explaining the special role of thunks for delaying evaluation until a value is needed and at the same time increasing sharing of evaluated computations.

- You looked at the shortcomings of lazy evaluation, the most important being increased memory consumption and uncertainty about the moment in which a thunk will become evaluated.

- You learned how to annotate the code using `seq`, or strictness annotations in both pattern matching and data types, to work around these problems.

- The GHC profiler is a powerful tool for detecting time and space leaks. I covered its basic usage and the interpretation of its results in this chapter.

PART II

Data Mining

CHAPTER 6

Knowing Your Clients Using Monads

Remember that you have been commissioned to build a Time Machine Store. Apart from a beautiful design and an intuitive user experience, a good web store should adapt itself to the customers' likes and needs by keeping track of clients and analyzing their behavior. With that information, better campaigns, such as discounts or targeted ads, can be developed, increasing sales. For these tasks, many *data mining* algorithms have been developed. In this chapter, you will focus on *clustering* algorithms, which try to find groups of related clients. You will use a specific implementation of clustering, called *K-means*, using Haskell.

The K-means algorithm is better understood in terms of a set of vectors. Each vector is an aggregation of numeric variables describing a client, product, or purchase, and each vector changes in every iteration. In an imperative language, these vectors would be modeled as a set of variables that are updated in a loop. The solution presented in this chapter will start with a basic implementation where you will keep track of all the information. I'll then introduce *lenses*, which are used to manipulate and query data structures in a concise way; you'll refine the code and split it into a set of basic combinators that glue together the different parts.

Looking at those combinators and their relation to other data types will lead to the notion of *monad*, one of the central idioms (and type classes) in Haskell code. You will explore its definition and laws and compare it to the other pervasive type class, the *functor*. Many instances of the Monad class are available in the Haskell Platform; in this chapter, I will focus on those related in some way to keeping track of *state*.

The idea of monad is not complex, but it has enormous ramifications in Haskell. For that reason, both this chapter and the next one are devoted to understanding monads in depth.

© Alejandro Serrano Mena 2022
A. Serrano Mena, *Practical Haskell*, https://doi.org/10.1007/978-1-4842-8581-7_6

Data Mining

Data mining is a wide field and comprises many kinds of algorithms that use statistics, machine learning, and artificial intelligence; data mining is about discovering different patterns in the data. The following are two concrete tasks that you will consider in this chapter and the next:

- Discovering the different types of clients that use the time machine store, based on their user information and their purchase history. *Clustering* tries to discern groups (or *clusters* in data mining jargon) of elements that share common properties. The hope is that, using this information, the marketing team can better target their campaigns.

- Detecting the purchase habits of each type of client. This will allow you to tailor the discounts (there will be more discussions about discounts in the last part of the book). For that matter, the idea is to learn *association rules* and later use them to derive conclusions.

Note   Since the store is selling time machines, you could use the machines to travel in time and look at trends in the future. However, this is sort of dishonest, so you should try to use current data and technology to perform better in the market.

Implementing K-means

K-means is one of the simplest algorithms for performing clustering on a set of data. The information in this case is represented as a set of points in n-dimensional space, with each of them representing a different observed fact. The similarity between two facts corresponds to the proximity of the points. The concrete task of the algorithm will be dividing the whole set of points into k partitions, such that the aggregated distance of the points in each partition is minimized.

Note   The number of partitions to create is usually represented as *k* and must be explicitly given as input to the algorithm. This need to specify the number of partitions up front is one of the shortcomings of K-means. Different methods are proposed in the literature to determine the best value to provide. The Wikipedia article at `http://en.wikipedia.org/wiki/Determining_the_number_of_clusters_in_a_data_set` summarizes the different approaches.

For example, Figure 6-1 shows a set of 2D points. The K-means algorithm has been executed over that set of points with *k=3*. The output of the algorithm (i.e., the three clusters of points) is distinguished in the figure by a common shape used to draw them. Cluster 1 is drawn with circles, cluster 2 uses triangles, and cluster 3 uses crosses.

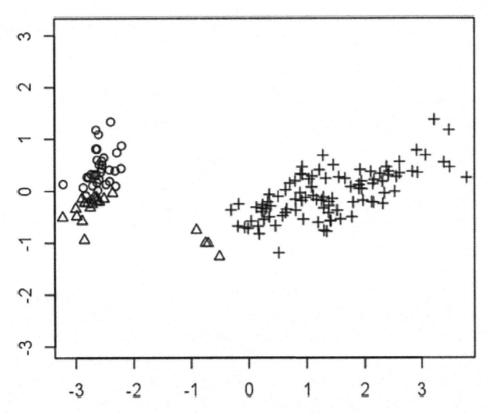

Figure 6-1. *Clusters obtained for an example data set*

This example shows a main characteristic of K-means: it works only on vectors for which you can define a notion of distance and proximity. Another approach would be using a tuple for representing that information, but using a tuple poses the problem that the number of components of the vectors should be constant among all the uses of the algorithm. This is not a reasonable assumption because taking into account some new information (e.g., deciding to cluster also depending on the age) would require changing all the type definitions. Another possibility would be to use lists, but then you lose the safety enforced by tuples (because lists can have different numbers of elements). The best option then is to define a new type class, `Vector`, which will have as instances all data types supporting the `distance` operation you need.

```
class Vector v where
  distance :: v -> v -> Double
```

The following is one possible implementation for numeric pairs using the Euclidean distance measure:

```
{-# LANGUAGE FlexibleInstances #-}
instance Vector (Double, Double) where
  distance (a,b) (c,d) = sqrt $ (c-a)*(c-a) + (d-b)*(d-b)
```

Note   The Haskell Report allows instance declarations only for types whose shape is a name followed by a list of distinct type variables. The previous definition doesn't follow that lead, so the compiler complains. However, GHC supports those declarations if you enable the `FlexibleInstances` extension.

Furthermore, you also need to specify how to translate one item in your data into its corresponding vector. Again, doing so using a type class is the best way to go. But this time you need to specify two types taking part in the type class: the type of the items to convert and the type of the vectors in which they are translated. You can do so by using *multiparameter type classes*, which follow the same syntax as one-parameter ones, and by enabling the `MultiParamTypeClasses` extension. However, the concept of type classes with two or more parameters departs from being just like an interface in an object-oriented language and looks more like a contract between two different types.

Working with these type classes can be tricky; you will explore the implications of them throughout the book. The name given to elements translatable to vectors will be, no surprise here, Vectorizables. Here's the definition and a simple instance for performing the identity conversion between Double pairs:

```
{-# LANGUAGE MultiParamTypeClasses #-}
class Vector v => Vectorizable e v where
  toVector :: e -> v
instance Vectorizable (Double,Double) (Double,Double) where
  toVector = id
```

The way in which the K-means algorithm describes a cluster is via one vector for each, called the *centroid* of the cluster. Each element in the data set is assigned to the cluster whose centroid is nearer to the data point. After knowing this fact, you already have an initial idea of how the type of K-means should look.

```
kMeans :: (Vector v, Vectorizable e v)
       => Int  -- number of centroids
       -> [e]  -- the information
       -> [v]  -- centroids after convergence
```

The K-means algorithm is simple. In a first phase, it generates k vectors, which will be used as the initial centroids. Then, each point is assigned to the cluster of the nearest centroid. In that way, a first partition of the data points is created. After all points have been assigned, the algorithm computes new centroids. The updated centroid of each cluster will be the average of all the points in that cluster. These new centroids will be the input of the new cluster-point assignment and centroid updating phases, and so on. At some point, the clusters will be stable: the partition and the clusters won't change anymore. Thus, the procedure stops and returns the centroids as the final ones. Figure 6-2 pictures this process as a diagram.

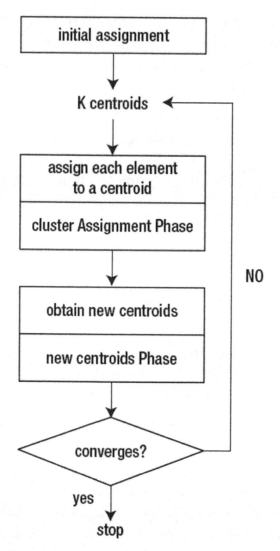

Figure 6-2. *K-means algorithm*

Let's work on each of the steps and finally join everything together into a big algorithm. There are several options for generating the initial vectors. One possibility is generating random vectors; another one is choosing *k* of the vectors in the data set (this is called the Forgy method). The best option is to abstract this choice and include an extra argument to the kMeans function for the function generating the initial values. The type of the function in this case would turn into this:

```
kMeans :: (Vector v, Vectorizable e v)
      => (Int -> [e] -> [v]) -> [e] -> [v]
```

190

The cluster assignment phase should receive the current centroids and the elements of the set and decide which centroid each element corresponds with. This is done based on the proximity. Since you have a key (cluster) to values (points) mapping, it makes sense to use a Map to hold the assignments. This implies that you need to include an extra Ord v constraint in the Vector type class because Map keys must fulfill that requirement.

This cluster assignment phase can be divided into two different tasks. The first one is creating the Map with all the keys assigned to empty lists. At this point, there's an implicit assumption that no two keys will be the same at any point of the algorithm, but in a more complete implementation, this should be taken care of. The second task should go element by element and find the centroid closer to it and then add the element to the list of the chosen centroid. Remember that you must first translate the element to a vector using the toVector function. The following code uses folds both for creating the initial maps and for updating each element in the data set:

```
import Data.List
import qualified Data.Map as M
clusterAssignmentPhase :: (Ord v, Vector v, Vectorizable e v)
                       => [v] -> [e] -> M.Map v [e]
clusterAssignmentPhase centroids points =
  let initialMap = M.fromList $ zip centroids (repeat [])
   in foldr (\p m -> let chosenC = minimumBy (compareDistance p) centroids
                      in M.adjust (p:) chosenC m)
            initialMap points
  where compareDistance p x y = compare (distance x $ toVector p)
                                        (distance y $ toVector p)
```

Finally, you have to compute the new centroid of each cluster. To do so, you need to map from the elements in a cluster to a vector. You can see now that an extra function was left out in the type class for Vectors: computing the centroid of a set of them. Thus, let's augment that type class and implement it for Double pairs. We also add Ord v as a superclass of Vector, since it is required by the Map operations.

```
class Ord v => Vector v where
  distance :: v -> v -> Double
  centroid :: [v] -> v
instance Vector (Double, Double) where
  distance (a,b) (c,d) = sqrt $ (c-a)*(c-a) + (d-b)*(d-b)
```

```
centroid lst = let (u,v) = foldr (\(a,b) (c,d) -> (a+c,b+d)) (0,0) lst
                   n = fromIntegral $ length lst
               in (u / n, v / n)
```

With this new function, it's straightforward to implement the computation of new centroids. The idea of the code is the following: for each cluster (so you need to use fmap), convert the list of associated elements to vectors (so inside the function to apply to each element, you need to have a map toVector) and then get the centroid of this set. Finally, you convert the map into a list of *(old,new)* elements.

```
newCentroidPhase :: (Vector v, Vectorizable e v) => M.Map v [e] -> [(v,v)]
newCentroidPhase = M.toList . fmap (centroid . map toVector)
```

Even though the algorithm is known to converge, you may want to stop iterating when the amount of change between successive centroids is less than a threshold. For that reason, the code includes a function that computes the total amount of change and compares it with a predefined value.

```
shouldStop :: (Vector v) => [(v,v)] -> Double -> Bool
shouldStop centroids threshold =
  foldr (\(x,y) s -> s + distance x y) 0.0 centroids < threshold
```

With all these parts, you can finally wrap up the initial code for K-means.

```
kMeans :: (Vector v, Vectorizable e v)
       => (Int -> [e] -> [v])  -- initialization function
       -> Int                  -- number of centroids
       -> [e]                  -- the information
       -> Double               -- threshold
       -> [v]                  -- final centroids
kMeans i k points = kMeans' (i k points) points
kMeans' :: (Vector v, Vectorizable e v)
        => [v] -> [e] -> Double -> [v]
kMeans' centroids points threshold =
  let assignments      = clusterAssignmentPhase centroids points
      oldNewCentroids = newCentroidPhase assignments
      newCentroids     = map snd oldNewCentroids
```

```
in if shouldStop oldNewCentroids threshold
   then newCentroids
   else kMeans' newCentroids points threshold
```

To test kMeans, here's a small function that generates *k* vectors *(i, i)*, where *i* goes from 1 to *k*:

```
initializeSimple :: Int -> [e] -> [(Double,Double)]
initializeSimple 0 _ = []
initializeSimple n v = (fromIntegral n, fromIntegral n)
                     : initializeSimple (n-1) v
```

With that piece of code, you can run a first example of K-means in the interpreter.

```
*Chapter6.KMeans> let info = [(1,1),(1,2),(4,4),(4,5)]::[(Double,Double)]
*Chapter6.KMeans> kMeans initializeSimple 2 info 0.001
[(1.0,1.5),(4.0,4.5)]
```

To check whether you've understood how all the pieces of this initial implementation of K-means fit together, complete Exercise 6-1, where the code is instrumented to produce some statistics of a run of the algorithm.

EXERCISE 6-1. COUNTING THE NUMBER OF STEPS

While profiling the performance of iterative algorithms, it's common to look at the number of recursive steps that have been done until reaching the threshold. Enhance the previous implementation of K-means to provide this value as an extra output of the kMeans function.

Lenses

The K-means algorithm is usually expressed in a more imperative way, in which the centroids and the error are variables that are updated in each iteration until the threshold is greater than the error. One of the big differences between more usual languages and Haskell is the query and access to data structures, which should be made using either pattern matching or records, with the record update syntax or via the helper functions that are created automatically by the compiler.

Lenses allow you to query and update data structures using syntax much closer to the typical dot notation found in other languages. However, that notation is defined completely in a library, not as part of the language. This should give you a taste of the great power of the Haskell language, which allows you to express the scaffolding of data access and update the language.

A lens wraps together a getter and a setter for a specific field in a data structure. In that way, it's similar to a JavaBean or a C# property. Apart from that, a particular lens library includes a number of combinators to mix together several lenses (e.g., for chaining accesses to deeper parts of a structure) and to provide more recognizable syntax (e.g., using += to update a numeric field by adding some amount).

You may have noticed that in the previous paragraph, I used the phrasing *a* lens library instead of *the* lens library. The Haskell community doesn't have a preferred or definite library for this task. Some of the lens packages are `lens`, `fclabels`, `data-accessor`, and `data-lens`. The most commonly used one is the `lens` library by Edward A. Kmett. There's one problem, though: that library is huge. For that reason, we shall start with the `microlens` library, which provides the most common features from `lens` in a more digestible fashion. In any case, the main ideas remain the same among all the packages. They differ in the theoretical basis (how lenses are represented internally and composed) and in the implementation itself, but not much in the external interface.

Although I speak of "the `microlens` library," there is in fact a constellation of libraries. The `microlens` library proper provides just the core abstractions. Instead, I assume that you have added `microlens-platform` as a dependency to your project or installed the library before starting a GHCi session. That library exposes the most important functionality from the `microlens` library under a single `Lens.Micro.Platform` module, the one you need to import.

After this introduction, let's focus on the use of lenses in your own code. The following are the definitions of `Client` and `Person` from Chapter 3:

```haskell
data Client i = GovOrg      i String
              | Company     i String Person String
              | Individual i Person
data Person   = Person String String
```

Previously, the definitions used record syntax, but I have included here the raw ones because once you create lenses for them, the usefulness of using record assessors disappears.

There are two approaches for generating the lenses for each field. The first approach involves writing the lenses by hand. Even though it sounds difficult, it's really simple; you just need to write the getter and the setter, which you can define via pattern matching. Let's do it for the Person data type.

```
firstName :: Lens' Person String
firstName = lens (\(Person f _) -> f)
                 (\(Person _ l) newF -> Person newF l)
lastName :: Lens' Person String
lastName = lens (\(Person _ l) -> l)
                (\(Person f _) newL -> Person f newL)
```

These are examples of simple lenses, in which the type of the structure does not change when the value changes. Therefore, we use the type Lens' instead of Lens. However, there are cases when you want the type to change. For example, say you have a Client Int, and you want to update the identifier to a Double value. Now the client would have a Client Double type. So, you need full lenses, which take as extra type variables the different types of the inner values. Here's an example:

```
{-# LANGUAGE LambdaCase #-}
identifier :: Lens (Client i) (Client j) i j
identifier = lens (\case (GovOrg i _)      -> i
                         (Company i _ _ _) -> i
                         (Individual i _)  -> i)
                  (\client newId -> case client of
                       GovOrg _ n       -> GovOrg newId n
                       Company _ n p r -> Company newId n p r
                       Individual _ p  -> Individual newId p)
```

The lenses don't need to reflect only fields in the data definition. Every time you have a well-defined way to get and return values, you can generate a lens. For example, assume that names for a Person don't contain spaces. Then, you can create a lens for the full name: getting it will concatenate the first and last names with a space in between, and setting a value would split the name in two parts and assign a part to each field.

```
fullName :: Lens' Person String
fullName = lens (\(Person f l) -> f ++ " " ++ l)
                (\_ newFullName -> case words newFullName of
                                      f:l:_ -> Person f l
                                      _     -> error "Incorrect name")
```

But most of the time, you want to generate the basic lenses that just get and set a field in a structure, and this task involves a lot of boilerplate code. The Haskell philosophy wouldn't allow writing so much repetitive code, so the writer of the library has included a facility for automatically creating lenses. To use it, you need to write your data declarations using the record syntax, but use an underscore in the field names. For example:

```
data Client i = GovOrg     { _identifier :: i, _name :: String }
              | Company    { _identifier :: i, _name :: String
                           , _person :: Person, _duty :: String }
              | Individual { _identifier :: i, _person :: Person }
              deriving Show
data Person   = Person { _firstName :: String, _lastName :: String }
              deriving Show
```

Now you need to ask the library to create the lenses for you. First, you need to enable the TemplateHaskell extension, which allows the automatic generation of code. Then, you need to call makeLenses over each data type. Notice the use of two single quotes before the type name.

```
{-# LANGUAGE TemplateHaskell #-}
makeLenses ''Client
makeLenses ''Person
```

Et voilà! The code you wanted has been written for you in the background.

TEMPLATE HASKELL

Template Haskell is the name of a metaprogramming facility included in GHC. Metaprogramming is the name given to those techniques that allow you to modify the code that will be generated by a compiler, usually generating new code automatically. In the language Lisp, metaprogramming is a form of compile-time macros.

You saw an example of metaprogramming: the `deriving` mechanism for built-in type classes. Template Haskell provides an extensible interface to the GHC compiler and allows library authors to provide their own code modification facilities, like the `microlens` library does. There are many other libraries in Hackage making use of Template Haskell; for example, `derive` includes the automatic derivation of many other type classes, such as `NFData`.

Template Haskell is not part of the Haskell 2010 Report so, as usual, your code won't be easily portable to other Haskell compilers as it stands. However, GHC provides a command-line argument, `-ddump-splices`, which outputs the code that Template Haskell generated, and you can copy it back if you need full compatibility.

Now that you know how to create lenses, it's time to use them. One of the basic operations you can do with a lens is query a value. For that, you can use either the `view` function or the (`^.`) operator.

```
*Chapter6.Lenses> let p = Person "John" "Smith"
*Chapter6.Lenses> (view firstName p, p^.lastName)
("John","Smith")
```

The best thing about lenses is that they can be composed with the (`.`) operator (the same used for function composition) to create new lenses. This in particular gives a very C-like feeling to field access.

```
*Chapter6.Lenses> let client = Individual 3 (Person "John" "Smith")
*Chapter6.Lenses> view (person . lastName) client
"Smith"
*Chapter6.Lenses> client^.person.fullName
"John Smith"
```

Updating is done using the `set` function or the (`.~`) operator. As you will notice, the semantics here are compatible with a pure language like Haskell. A new copy of the data structure with the field updated is returned; the element is not updated in place.

```
*Chapter6.Lenses> set identifier 4 client
Individual {_identifier = 4,
            _person = Person {_firstName = "John", _lastName = "Smith"}}
*Chapter6.Lenses> person.lastName .~ "Kox" $ client
Individual {_identifier = 3,
            _person = Person {_firstName = "John", _lastName = "Kox"}}
```

While it's useful in terms of composing lens operations, having the structure that will be updated being the last argument of the function may be a bit difficult to read sometimes. For that reason, lens includes the (&) operator, which flips the order of the parameters and allows you to use the value at the beginning.

```
*Chapter6.Lenses> client & person.fullName .~ "Marianne Kox"
Individual {_identifier = 3,
            _person = Person {_firstName = "Marianne", _lastName = "Kox"}}
```

The good thing about lens is the inclusion of a lot of combinators that resemble the typical combined update operators in C or Java (i.e., += or *=). They always follow the same name schema: the name of the operator that will combine the current value and the new one, followed by a tilde.

```
*Chapter6.Lenses> client & identifier +~ 2
Individual {_identifier = 5, _person = Person {_firstName = "John", _
lastName = "Smith"}}
```

All of these operators are specific instances of the more general function over or its infix form (%~), which takes a function to apply to the field pointed by the lens.

```
*Chapter6.Lenses> client & over identifier (+2)
Individual {_identifier = 5,
            _person = Person {_firstName = "John", _lastName = "Smith"}}
*Chapter6.Lenses> import Data.Char  -- for bringing toUpper into scope
*Chapter6.Lenses> client & person.fullName %~ (map toUpper)
Individual {_identifier = 3,
            _person = Person {_firstName = "JOHN", _lastName = "SMITH"}}
```

Lenses for many different types are included in the library. For example, there's a family of lenses _1 to _9 that go in each component of a tuple, provided it is long enough.

```
*Chapter6.Lenses> ("a","b") & set _1 "c"
("c","b")
*Chapter6.Lenses> ("a","b") & set _3 "c"
<interactive>:
    No instance for (Field3 ([Char], [Char]) b0 a0 [Char])
      arising from a use of `_3'
```

```
Possible fix:
  add an instance declaration for
  (Field3 ([Char], [Char]) b0 a0 [Char])
In the first argument of `set', namely `_3'
In the second argument of `(&)', namely `set _3 "c"'
In the expression: ("a", "b") & set _3 "c"
```

Sometimes, the value in the mentioned field may not be available. This happens, for example, in the lenses[1] for obtaining the head and tail of a list. In this case, you have two options: either use the (^?) operator, which returns its value wrapped on Maybe, or use (^?!), which doesn't wrap the value but signals an error if the element is not available. The update is performed using the same operators as before:

```
*Chapter6.Lenses> "abc"^?_head
Just 'a'
*Chapter6.Lenses> "abc"^?!_tail
"bc"
*Chapter6.Lenses> "abc" & (_head .~ 'd')
"dbc"
*Chapter6.Lenses> "abc" & (_tail %~ map toUpper)
"aBC"
```

In Haskell, the most usual way to split a list is between its head and the rest of the list (the tail), but you can also split from the end. The lens library provides lenses for accessing the last element in the list and the list without that last element, namely, _last and _init.

```
*Chapter6.Lenses> "abc"^?_init
Just "ab"
*Chapter6.Lenses> "abc" & (_last %~ toUpper)
"abC"
```

As mentioned, many other lenses are included in the library distribution for lists, maps, and sets. If you decide to use microlens, don't forget to check these instances.

---

[1] Technically, they are not a Lens, but a Traversal.

Finally, I will discuss the `traversed` lens. This lens allows you to go inside a list (or in general any instance of the `Traversable` type class, which also includes trees and maps) and update each of the elements using a further lens. For example, if you have an array of people, you can change all the first names to uppercase by using that lens.

```
*Chapter6.Lenses> let people = [Person "Jack" "Smith", Person "Mary" "B."]
*Chapter6.Lenses> people & traversed.firstName %~ map toUpper
[ Person {_firstName = "JACK", _lastName = "Smith"}
, Person {_firstName = "MARY", _lastName = "B."} ]
```

Exercise 6-2 applies the information about the `microlens` library to time machines. I encourage you to go through that exercise to get a good idea of lenses.

EXERCISE 6-2. TIME MACHINE LENSES

Generate lenses for the `TimeMachine` data type you created in previous chapters, including all the information mentioned before and also a price. Using the operators introduced here, create a function that, given a list of time machines, increases the price by a given percentage.

Let's use lenses to rewrite the implementation of K-means. Instead of having different arguments for each piece of information that it needs to hold, let's create a data type holding all of them. The lenses will be derived automatically using Template Haskell.

```
data KMeansState e v = KMeansState { _centroids :: [v], _points :: [e]
                                   , _err :: Double, _threshold :: Double
                                   , _steps :: Int }
makeLenses "KMeansState
```

Note   The derivation of lenses via Template Haskell must appear *before* any use of them in other code. Thus, you must be careful about writing the previous code before the definition of the new kMeans code.

As you can see, the error will be saved in a field, and also you are saving the number of steps, something that you were asked to include in a previous exercise. The new algorithm kMeans' will be seen as a series of changes in that state. It first creates the assignments and then updates the centroids, the error, and the number of steps. These three last steps are implemented using lenses. Finally, the algorithm must check the stopping condition by comparing the error to the threshold, which is also a field in the state data type. The kMeans function also changes to return only the centroids from the full state.

```
initializeState :: (Int -> [e] -> [v])
                 -> Int -> [e] -> Double -> KMeansState e v
initializeState i n pts t = KMeansState (i n pts) pts (1.0/0.0) t 0
clusterAssignmentPhase :: (Vector v, Vectorizable e v)
                    => KMeansState e v -> M.Map v [e]
clusterAssignmentPhase = undefined   -- See exercise 6.3
kMeans :: (Vector v, Vectorizable e v)
       => (Int -> [e] -> [v]) -> Int -> [e] -> Double -> [v]
kMeans i n pts t = view centroids $ kMeans' (initializeState i n pts t)
kMeans' :: (Vector v, Vectorizable e v)
        => KMeansState e v -> KMeansState e v
kMeans' state =
  let assignments = clusterAssignmentPhase state
      state1 = state  & centroids.traversed
                    %~ (\c -> centroid
                                $ fmap toVector
                                $ M.findWithDefault [] c assignments)
      state2 = state1 & err .~ sum (zipWith distance (state^.centroids)
                                                      (state1^.centroids))
      state3 = state2 & steps +~ 1
  in if state3^.err < state3^.threshold then state3 else kMeans' state3
```

Notice that the way in which you compute the error has also been changed. Instead of return pairs of *(old centroid, new centroid)* when updating the centroids, it takes the centroids in the current and previous stats and performs the aggregation of their distance using sum and zipWith. Exercise 6-3 asks you to finish this implementation with lenses by writing the code of the cluster assignment phase.

EXERCISE 6-3. K-MEANS LENSES

The implementation of the algorithm using lenses is not yet complete. The function `clusterAssignments` is missing. Starting from the version shown in the previous section, write these functions (which now operate on full states) using lenses.

Discovering Monads

One of the pillars of Haskell philosophy is reusability. For that reason, while learning the language and its libraries, it's useful from time to time to step back and look at the code you've already written, looking for common patterns that could be abstracted. In this section, you will think about abstractions related to Maybe values and to state handling. The same kind of structure will appear in both cases, leading you to the notion of a *monad* that will be the core of this section.

Watching Out for Incomplete Data

In the previous section, there's an explicit assumption that you already have all the information that will be input to the K-means algorithm in a nice way so that the only transformation you need to do is convert that information to vectors. However, this is rarely the case with a data set from the real world. Usually, you need an initial preprocessing stage to gather all the information, do some aggregation, and maybe fix some inconsistences.

Usually, the raw information will come from some sort of database system. You will see later how to communicate with these systems using the Persistent library; here, only some aspects of its use will be needed. In many cases, a table may contain NULL as a value for a column, meaning that there's no information (or it hasn't been recorded). The way that the Persistent library represents a nullable column of type T is via a value of type Maybe T. For example, say you want to compute the average value of all the items purchased by a given client. The following is a possible way to code that:

```
meanPurchase :: Integer -- the client identifier
             -> Double  -- the mean purchase
meanPurchase clientId = let p = purchasesByClientId clientId
                        in foldr (+) 0.0 $ catMaybes $ map purchaseValue p
purchaseValue :: Integer -> Maybe Double
purchaseValue purchaseId =
  case numberItemsByPurchaseId purchaseId of
    Nothing -> Nothing
    Just n  -> case productIdByPurchaseId purchaseId of
                 Nothing    -> Nothing
                 Just prId -> case priceByProductId prId of
                                Nothing    -> Nothing
                                Just price -> Just $ (fromInteger
                                n) * price
```

The previous example used catMaybes from the Data.Maybe module. This function filters out every Nothing element in the list, and it's convenient when working with a list of Maybe values.

Note   In the previous example and in the next examples in this section, I've factored out the code for accessing the database, which is not relevant to the current discussion. If you want to try the code, just include a simple return value. For example, purchasesByClientId could return [1,2,3], and numberItemsByPurchaseId, productIdByPurchaseId, and priceByProductId could return a constant value.

Clearly, this code is neither elegant nor maintainable. You have to write explicitly a waterfall of checks for Nothing or Just. Furthermore, in the event you want to add some new query in between the other ones, you would need to re-indent all the code you had already written. What you are going to do is to develop a combinator[2] that will allow you to write better, more maintainable code.

---

[2] At this moment, you can think of *combinator* as just a fancy name for function.

The main idea is that the combinator should take a value wrapped by Maybe. This value will be taken into consideration only if it's constructed using Just. In other cases, you just return Nothing. If you decide to continue, you should apply a function to the element enclosed in Just, which itself returns another Maybe value. At the end, you should end in any case with a Maybe value resulting from the application. Once you know what is wanted, the combinator is straightforward to write.

```
thenDo :: Maybe a -> (a -> Maybe b) -> Maybe b
thenDo Nothing  _ = Nothing
thenDo (Just x) f = f x
```

Now let's rewrite the initial purchaseValue using that combinator, which has been applied infix to increase clarity. Here's the new solution:

```
purchaseValue :: Integer -> Maybe Double
purchaseValue purchaseId =
  numberItemsByPurchaseId purchaseId `thenDo` (\n ->
  productIdByPurchaseId purchaseId   `thenDo` (\productId ->
  priceByProductId productId         `thenDo` (\price ->
  Just $ fromInteger n * price       )))
```

The new code is definitely cleaner and much more maintainable. Furthermore, you have hidden the low-level operation of unwrapping Maybes into a combinator, leading to more reusability.

Note   Take some time to parse the previous function. The style of writing the argument to a function in a different line from the body is called *hanging lambdas*. It's common when using function combinators such as your thenDo.

One fair question is why you need to write a new combinator thenDo. At first, it seems that the task of that function is similar to the fmap in a functor. Let's write its type, specialized for Maybe.

```
fmap :: (a -> b) -> Maybe a -> Maybe b
```

The problem here is that the result being Nothing or Just cannot depend on the function to be applied; it's completely determined by the input value. If you tried to use a function with an output type of Maybe b, you would have a specialized type.

```
fmap :: (a -> Maybe b) -> Maybe a -> Maybe (Maybe b)
```

And a value wrapped twice in Maybe is not what you want. The opposite case is possible, though: you can express fmap in terms of your thenDo combinator.

```
fmap f x = x `thenDo` (\y-> Just $ f y)
```

Thus, the newly defined combinator is strictly more powerful than fmap. It can be used to write a version of fmap for Maybe values because fmap cannot express the behavior of thenDo. The optional Exercise 6-4 asks you to verify that your new definition of fmap is indeed correct.

EXERCISE 6-4. PROVING THAT YOUR FMAP IS CORRECT

Using the equational reasoning introduced in Chapter 3, prove that this implementation of fmap is correct. To do so, you should check that fmap as defined in this section works the same as the instance of Functor for Maybe values, which maps Just x to Just (f x) and Nothing to Nothing. Hint: Split the solution into cases, depending on the constructor for the Maybe value. In other words, start by using a case expression in which you pattern match on the two possible values of an expression of Maybe type, namely, Nothing and Just v.

Combinators for State

Based on your success of building a combinator for chaining functions that may fail and return Nothing, you can think of doing the same to refactor a bit of your code for the K-means algorithm. It would be interesting to hide the management of the states found in the last version of the code.

Let's think about how to represent a function that manipulates a state. Each function will be the real building block that will later be chained using the combinator that you will develop. The state prior to the execution of the function could be seen as an extra argument to the function. So, if in general you have a function of type a -> b, a function that also consumes a state of type s should be typed as a -> s -> b. This function must also be decorated with the state at the end of the execution, which could be later passed to the next function expecting a state. Given that the function returns a value of type b, you can pair it up with a value of type s. In conclusion, functions that manipulate a state have type a -> s -> (b,s). Using your previous knowledge of working with Maybe values, you would expect your combinator to have a type similar to this:

```
thenDo :: (s -> (a,s)) -> (a -> s -> (b,s)) -> (s -> (b,s))
```

This seems a bit awkward at first because it seems more natural to choose (a,s) -> (a -> s -> (b,s)) -> (b,s), that is, to thread the state directly from the initial computation through the second function. However, the version that generates a function that still needs an initial state is more useful because it allows you to combine stateful computation for which the initial state is not yet present, and it will also make clearer the pattern that will emerge from these examples. Since the code will be using s -> (a,s) a lot, it makes sense to introduce a type synonym for it.

```
type State s a = s -> (a, s)
```

Now the parallelism with the Maybe case is more obvious in the type of the combinator.

```
thenDo :: State s a -> (a -> State s b) -> State s b
```

The implementation of the combinator is simple. You just need to apply the state to the first function to get a result and a new state, which is passed to the second function. I have also included the type signature without synonyms in the Haskell code.

```
   thenDo :: State s a     -> (a -> State s b)  -> State s b
-- thenDo :: (s -> (a,s)) -> (a -> s -> (b,s)) -> s -> (b,s)
thenDo f g s = let (resultOfF, stateAfterF) = f s
                 in g resultOfF stateAfterF
```

In the version that will be developed from now on, only the information about the centroids, the error threshold, and the number of steps will be recorded. That way, there will be two separate sets of information: the state itself, which is threaded by the State combinators, and the vectors you run the algorithm over, which are explicitly passed as arguments. Furthermore, I will present the code here without lens combinators to focus the discussion on the combinators related to state. The new KMeansState definition is as follows:

```
data KMeansState v = KMeansState { centroids :: [v]
                                 , threshold :: Double
                                 , steps :: Int }
```

As for Maybe values, let's rewrite the code using the thenDo combinator. The main kMeans function will just call kMeans', which is the one using the combinator with an initial state. The result of the computation is a pair of the final centroids and the last state; you need to return only the first one using fst.

```
newCentroids :: (Vector v, Vectorizable e v) => M.Map v [e] -> [v]
newCentroids = M.elems . fmap (centroid . map toVector)
clusterAssignments :: (Vector v, Vectorizable e v)
                   => [v] -> [e] -> M.Map v [e]
clusterAssignments centrs points =
  let initialMap = M.fromList $ zip centrs (repeat [])
   in foldr (\p m -> let chosenC = minimumBy (compareDistance p) centrs
                      in M.adjust (p:) chosenC m)
            initialMap points
  where compareDistance p x y = compare (distance x $ toVector p)
                                        (distance y $ toVector p)
kMeans' :: (Vector v, Vectorizable e v) => [e] -> State (KMeansState v) [v]
kMeans' points =
  (\s -> (centroids s,s))                              `thenDo` (\prevCentrs ->
  (\s -> (clusterAssignments prevCentrs points, s)) `thenDo` (\
assignments ->
  (\s -> (newCentroids assignments, s))                `thenDo` (\newCentrs  ->
  (\s -> ((), s { centroids = newCentrs }))            `thenDo` (\_          ->
  (\s -> ((), s { steps = steps s + 1 }))              `thenDo` (\_          ->
  (\s -> (threshold s, s))                             `thenDo` (\t          ->
  (\s -> (sum $ zipWith distance prevCentrs newCentrs, s))  `thenDo`
(\err  ->
  if err < t then (\s -> (newCentrs, s)) else (kMeans' points) )))))))
initialState :: (Vector v, Vectorizable e v)
             => (Int -> [e] -> [v]) -> Int -> [e] -> Double
             -> KMeansState v
initialState i k pts t = KMeansState (i k pts) t 0
kMeans :: (Vector v, Vectorizable e v)
       => (Int -> [e] -> [v]) -> Int -> [e] -> Double -> [v]
kMeans i k pts t = fst $ kMeans' pts (initialState i k pts t)
```

Fair enough, it seems that making this change for handling states didn't give as much clarity as before; you need to write explicitly the s argument all the time. Let's try then to refine your combinators to be more specific to this situation. Notice that you have three kinds of functions working on the state: those in which the state remains the same, those that access a particular member of the state and return the result, and those that update the state. Let's write a definition for each of them.

```
remain :: a -> (s -> (a,s))
remain x = \s -> (x,s)
access :: (s -> a) -> (s -> (a,s))
access f = \s -> (f s, s)
modify :: (s -> s) -> (s -> ((), s))
modify f = \s -> ((), f s)
```

Note   In the previous pieces of code, I used the unit type, ( ). It's a type that has only one element, the empty tuple, ( ). It's customarily used when you need to return something in a function but don't really have a good value for it.

The rewritten version of kMeans' is as follows:

```
kMeans' :: (Vector v, Vectorizable e v)
        => [e] -> State (KMeansState v) [v]
kMeans' points =
  access centroids                                `thenDo` (\prevCentrs ->
  remain (clusterAssignments prevCentrs points) `thenDo` (\assignments ->
  remain (newCentroids assignments)               `thenDo` (\newCentrs   ->
  modify (\s -> s { centroids = newCentrs })    `thenDo` (\_           ->
  modify (\s -> s { steps = steps s + 1 })      `thenDo` (\_           ->
  access threshold                                `thenDo` (\t          ->
  remain (sum $ zipWith distance prevCentrs newCentrs) `thenDo` (\
err      ->
  if err < t then remain newCentrs else kMeans' points )))))))
```

Dissecting the Combinators

At the beginning of the section, I presented the way to deal with function chains involving Maybe values, and you learned that developers can benefit from a combinator called thenDo. You also successfully applied that idea to State values. Following the same approach used with functors, you should wonder whether this pattern can be abstracted into a type class.

The answer is affirmative: the thenDo combinator is exactly the (>>=) (pronounced "bind") function of the Monad type class. This type class encompasses all those types that allow you to combine computations of a certain kind between them. You have already seen two examples:

- The Maybe monad combines functions that may fail.

- The State s monad combines functions that keep track of an internal state of type s.

However, the Monad type class includes more functionality than just binding.

```
class Monad m where
  return :: a -> m a
  (>>=)  :: m a -> (a -> m b) -> m b
  (>>)   :: m a -> m b -> m b
  f >> g = f >>= (\_ -> g)
```

Caution   The return function in Monad has nothing to do with the return keyword in C or Java. However, it was an unfortunate choice from the designers of this type class because it resembles imperative programming. Before continuing, try to free your mind from this idea. Monads have essentially no relation to imperative programming, state, or mutability (although specific Monad instances cover these use cases).

The role of (>>=) has already been explained, so let's move to return. This function describes how to wrap a pure value using a monad. Usually, it also describes the simpler element you can get (just returning a value) for each kind of computation. At first, this might seem extremely vague, so let's look at the implementation for your Maybe and State monads.

The specific type for the `return` implementation of State s is a -> State s a or, equivalently, a -> s -> (a,s). This is the only implementation I can think of that returns the value that was passed, with the internal state unchanged. This is the same purpose of the `remain` combinator in the previous section. It also complies with the idea of being the "simplest" computation with state – one that does not change the state at all.

For `Maybe`, the type of return looks like a -> Maybe a. So, you have two alternatives: either return the value wrapped in Just or return Nothing. In the definition of `return`, you already have a value to wrap, so it makes more sense to have `return` = `Just`. Furthermore, if you look at the final example in the section where incomplete data was discussed, you can see that in the last step you used Just, and now you could change it to a `return`.

The next function in the type class is (>>). As you can see from its definition, it combines two computations such that the second one doesn't use the return value of the first one. This may sound strange, but you have already encountered such a situation. When you modify the state in your State s monad, you don't use the return value of this operation (which is always the empty tuple, ()). Like in many other default implementations, this function is defined here because it's expected that some instances could give a much faster definition for (>>) than the default one.

Note   Historically, the Monad type class also contained a `fail` method. As its name suggests, it allows you to define special behavior of the monad when some part of its computation fails. For example, failing into the Maybe monad should intuitively return Nothing. However, not all monads have sensible definitions for `fail`, State being a prime example. For that reason, it has been decided to move this function to its own type class, called MonadFail.

Right now, you have enough information for using a monad instead of a custom combinator in the previous examples. Exercise 6-5 shows you how to do so.

EXERCISE 6-5. MONADS FOR INCOMPLETE DATA AND K-MEANS

All the parts that make up the Monad instance for Maybe have already been discussed. Write the `instance` declaration for it. Then, rewrite the `purchaseValue` function using (>>=) and return.

Another interesting fact that you discovered in your combinator for Maybe is that by using it you can write a correct implementation of fmap. Let's look first at how the type of fmap specialized for State s looks.

```
fmap :: (a -> b) -> State s a -> State s b      -- with type synonyms
fmap :: (a -> b) -> (s -> (a,s)) -> (s -> (b,s))  -- without type synonyms
```

The implementation should be clear; just apply the function to the returned value and leave the state as is.

```
instance Functor (State s) where
  fmap f gWithState = \s -> let (gResult, gState)
                            in g s in (f gResult, gState)
```

In a previous section, you saw that you could also define it for Maybe using the combinators in that section, which you have seen are functions of the Monad type class.

```
fmap f g = g >>= (\x -> return $ f x)
```

Indeed, this definition is equivalent to the previous handwritten definition. The good news is that this implementation works for any monad; that is, every Monad instance gives rise to a Functor instance by defining fmap as shown earlier. It's included in the Control.Monad module of the base package, under the name liftM.

Note   If any Monad instance is also an instance of Functor, why is this relation not shown in the declaration of those classes? The truth is that in the library this relation exists but includes the Applicative type class in between. That is, Applicative is a superclass of Monad, and Functor is a superclass of Applicative. Chapter 10 contains a thorough description of the Applicative type class and its uses.

---

do Notation

The monad concept, brought from a branch of mathematics called *category theory* into Haskell by Phil Wadler (among others), is ubiquitous in Haskell libraries. Many computational structures have been found to be instances of Monad. Given its success, the Haskell designers decided to include special syntax for monads in the language: the so-called do notation.[3]

A do block starts with the do keyword and then is followed by a series of expressions. At compile time, those expressions are translated into regular code using (>>=), (>>), and fail. So, the best way to understand what this notation means is by looking at the possible ways you could use monadic functions and see how do notation approaches it.

The first case has two computations f and g such that the second doesn't consume any input from the first. You have already seen that this corresponds to the expression sequencing those computations f >> g. In do notation, this is written as follows:

```
do f
   g
```

However, there's also the possibility that the second function uses the result value of the first one. For that matter, you have the bind function: f >>= g. Usually, the way you use bind is not like that, but rather using an anonymous function and giving a name to the result of f: f >>= (\x -> g x). do notation also introduces a name for the resulting value but using <-. In particular, the expression f >>= (\x -> g x) is written as follows:

```
do x <- f
   g x
```

There's also support for introducing computations that are not done inside a monadic context. For example, you may need to call (+) over a number that has been obtained before. But if you do the following, the compiler will complain because the addition doesn't have the required return type, which should be m a, where m is a monad:

```
do number1 <- obtainNumber1   -- or any Maybe value, such as Just 3
   number2 <- obtainNumber2   -- or any Maybe value, such as Just 5
   sum      <- number1 + number2
   return $ sqrt sum
```

One solution is changing the previous-to-last line to sum <- return $ number1 + number2, but this introduced an unnecessary burden. The best thing is to use a let expression.

---

[3] The inclusion of this special notation is a great incentive for library authors to discover whether their types form a monad so that their users approach their library with an already-known syntax.

```
do number1 <- obtainNumber1
   number2 <- obtainNumber2
   let sum = number1 + number2
   return $ sqrt sum
```

Notice that you don't have to write in after this kind of let expression.

Previously, I explained that you could use pattern matching directly on let and where blocks and function declarations. This possibility is also available when using <- or let in a do block. If you remember, this had the risk of the returning value not matching the pattern. In those cases, the compiler added automatically a call to error with the appropriate message. When using do notation, the behavior deviates a bit from this. Instead of calling error, the compiler will call the fail function of the monad. For example, the following code:

```
do True <- willThatHold  -- placeholder for a function returning Maybe Bool
   f 5
```

would be transformed by the compiler to a version with an explicit branch for those values that are not True, even if that part didn't appear in the code.

```
willThatHold >>= \x ->
  case x of
    True -> f 5
    _ -> fail "error"
```

In turn, this call to fail implies that the type of that piece of code does not only require a Monad but the more restrictive MonadFail. Any time that you check the shape of the return value of a monadic computation, you should expect a MonadFail constraint to appear.

The great power of do blocks comes from the fact that they are not limited to just two expressions; the syntax is desugared also for more expressions. For example, if you have this:

```
do x <- f
   g
   y <- h x
   return y
```

The preceding version is more readable than its corresponding translation, as shown here:

```
f >>= (\x -> g >> (h x -> (\y -> return y)))
```

The example of Maybe looks much nicer when using do notation.

```
purchaseValueWithDo :: Integer -> Maybe Double
purchaseValueWithDo purchaseId
  = do n          <- numberItemsByPurchaseId purchaseId
       productId <- productIdByPurchaseId purchaseId
       price     <- priceByProductId productId
       return $ fromInteger n * price
```

For the K-means implementation, you can stop using your home-baked data type and start using the State implementation that you can find in the Control.Monad.State module of the mtl package. mtl (from Monad Transformers Library) is one of the basic libraries, along with base or containers, that make up the Haskell Platform. It contains instances of many different monads and utility functions for all of them.

In particular, it includes equivalents to the access and modify combinators that were written. Instead of using a function for getting part of the state, this implementation gives access to the full state via the get function. Using the fact that State is also a functor, you can write access by lifting the accessor function to the result of get.

```
access :: (s -> a) -> State s a
access f = fmap f get
```

Since obtaining only part of the state in that way is used often, mtl includes a gets function for that task.

This particular implementation also allows you to change completely the internal state via the put function. There's also the possibility of using a function to update it via a function that's also named modify. With all this information, the implementation of kMeans' reads as follows:

```
kMeans' :: (Vector v, Vectorizable e v)
        => [e] -> State (KMeansState v) [v]
kMeans' points = do prevCentrs <- gets centroids
                    let assignments = clusterAssignments prevCentrs points
                        newCentrs   = newCentroids assignments
```

```
modify (\s -> s { centroids = newCentrs })
modify (\s -> s { steps = steps s + 1 })
t <- fmap threshold get
let err = sum $ zipWith distance prevCentrs newCentrs
if err < t then return newCentrs else kMeans' points
```

Finally, when using the State data type from mtl, you have several options for giving an initial state and thus performing the full computation. These can be summarized via their types; each of them returns a different set of information.

```
runState :: State s a -> s -> (a,s)   -- return value and final state
evalState :: State s a -> s -> a      -- return only value
execState :: State s a -> s -> s      -- return only final state
```

For K-means, the interest lies only in the return value, so you need to use the second alternative.

```
kMeans :: (Vector v, Vectorizable e v) => Int -> [e] -> Double -> [v]
kMeans n pts t = evalState (kMeans' pts) (initializeState n t)
```

Monad Laws

Beware that not all definitions of (>>=) and return will make a true monad. As with functors, the Monad type class imposes some laws over the behavior of their instances. These laws are not checked by the compiler but must be satisfied if you don't want the user or the compiler to introduce subtle errors in the code. Don't worry if in a first read you don't understand all the details. This information is useful only if designing new monads, but it's not needed at all for their usage.

The first two laws relate the bind operation with return:

- return a >>= f must be equivalent to f a, or in do notation, do { x <- return a; f x} must be equivalent to bare do { f a }. That is, nothing changes if you apply a computation to a value wrapped into the monad via return, or without it.

- x >>= return must be equivalent to x, or in do notation, do { y <- m; return y } must be equivalent to do { m }. This means that return just unwraps and wraps again a value when bound from another computation.

> **Note**   The second law is important for good Haskell coding style. Remember that computing a value inside a monad to immediately call `return` is not needed; just include the value computation as an expression.

The next law tells you about the associativity of the (`>>=`) operation, although it's better stated using the do notation. It specifies that the following code, where one do block is sequenced after another one:

```
do x <- m
   do y <- f x
      g y
```

is equivalent to performing some computation first, nesting the do block, and then doing the second part, as shown here:

```
do y <- do x <- m
              f x
   g y
```

This means you can nest do blocks in any way you like, and the result should be the same. This resembles the fact that (`1 + 2`) `+ 3` is equal to `1 + ` (`2 + 3`). This allows you to write that code as follows:

```
do x <- m
   y <- f x
   g y
```

The final law makes explicit that the definition of `fmap` that was given based on a monad must indeed be the `fmap` of its `Functor` instance. That is, `fmap f g` must be equivalent to `g >>= (\x -> return $ f x)`.

MONADS EVERYWHERE

If you look at the available information about Haskell on the Internet, you will notice that there are a large number of tutorials devoted to monads. This might imply that monads are difficult to grasp, but they shouldn't be.

Using monads is much more common than *designing* monads. You have already looked at the Maybe and State monads, and you will continue looking at more instances of this type class throughout the book. If you understand how to use each of them, you'll be ready for real Haskell programming and on the path to fully understanding the concept of a monad.

Different Sorts of State

It's important to know the most common instances of monads. In this section, you will look at those monads that have some relation to keeping or using an internal state. Two of them, Reader and Writer, could be seen as restricted versions of State. However, they have their own uses, and it's interesting to know in which scenario you should apply each of them. Then the discussion will move to the ST monad, which is a special one that allows you to use mutable references (as variables in an impure language) but in a controlled way so you don't surpass the purity of the language.

State and Lenses

Before going in depth into the other monads, I will highlight a special feature of the microlens library, among other lens libraries: its special combinators for using lenses inside the State monad. Using these combinators, code resembles a more sequential style of programming but keeps all the purity.

Instead of using get and then applying a lens with view, you can directly access part of a data structure with the function use. This function already gives the result in the State monad, so you don't need to call any extra fmap or return to get the value.

Remember that when you used the update functions for lenses, you always had to write the structure to be applied by explicitly using either $ or &. But inside a State monad, there's always a special value to count on: the internal state. For each update function ending in tilde (such as `.~`, `%~`, or `+~`), we have a corresponding function ending in an equal sign (`.=`, `%=`, or `+=` in the previous cases), which changes the internal state.

If you use a data type with several fields as your state and have lenses for it, you can use syntax close to the C one to change the state. For example, in K-means you need the following state to keep track of the centroids, the threshold, and the number of steps:

```
data KMeansState v = KMeansState { _centroids :: [v]
                                 , _threshold :: Double
                                 , _steps :: Int }
makeLenses ''KMeansState
```

The following code shows how to rewrite the implementation of `kMeans'` via the `use` function to get information or temporarily save it and shows how to rewrite the (`.=`) and (`+=`) functions to update centroids and steps in each iteration:

```
kMeans' :: (Vector v, Vectorizable e v)
        => [e] -> State (KMeansState v) [v]
kMeans' points = do prevCentrs  <- use centroids
                    let assignments = clusterAssignments prevCentrs points
                        newCentrs = newCentroids assignments
                    centroids .= newCentrs
                    steps    += 1
                    let err = sum $ zipWith distance prevCentrs newCentrs
                    t <- use threshold
                    if err < t then return newCentrs else kMeans' points
```

Now that you know about `State`, you can also stop a bit on the *zooming* functionality of `lens`. Zooming takes a lens as an input and a computation that now uses as internal state the information contained in that lens. In some sense, it's like focusing your attention on a small part of the structure for some time. Suppose you have a simple function that will increment all the identifiers of a list of `Clients` by some number and update its names to uppercase. Given the following state declaration:

```
data ExampleSt = ExampleSt { _increment :: Int
                           , _clients :: [Client Int] }
                 deriving Show
makeLenses ''ExampleSt
```

The following function implements the mentioned functionality, zooming in on each of the clients:

```
zoomCl :: State ExampleSt ()
zoomCl = do n <- use increment
            zoom (clients.traversed) $ do
              identifier    += n
              person.fullName %= map toUpper
```

Here's an example of using the function over a list of clients in the interpreter:

```
*Chapter6.StateLenses> :{
*Chapter6.StateLenses| let client1 = Individual 4 (Person "John" "Smith")
*Chapter6.StateLenses|     client2 = Individual 3 (Person "Albert"
"Einstein")
*Chapter6.StateLenses|   in execState zoomCl (ExampleSt 2 [client1,
client2])
*Chapter6.StateLenses| :}
ExampleSt { _increment = 2, _clients = [
  Individual { _identifier = 6
             , _person = Person { _firstName = "JOHN"
                                , _lastName = "SMITH"}}
             , Individual { _identifier = 5
                          , _person = Person { _firstName = "ALBERT"
                                             , _lastName = "EINSTEIN"}}]}
```

Reader, Writer, and RWS

In many cases, the global state does not change through the execution of the code but contains a bunch of values that are taken as constants. For example, in the K-means algorithm, the number of clusters to make, the information in which the algorithm is executed, or the error threshold can be seen as constant for a concrete run. Thus, it makes sense to treat them differently than the rest of the state. You aren't going to change it, so let's ask the Haskell compiler to ensure that absence of modification for you.

If you recall, Chapter 4 introduced (->) r as a functor. If you look at context as an extra, hidden argument to functions, you can also see it as a monad, representing exactly those computations that take an extra context that cannot change. Let's try to write its

Monad instance to get some practice and focus on the monadic structure. The simplest function is return, which should have type a -> (r -> a). Thus, you have only one option for it.

```
return x = \r -> x
```

The types can also help you write the implementation of (>>=) for this monad.

```
(>>=) :: (r -> a) -> (a -> r -> b) -> (r -> b)
```

You know that the result of (>>=) is a function that takes the context. Using this context, you can use the first function to retrieve a value of type a. Then, you can just pass it to the second function, along with the context, to get the final result of type b.

```
f >>= g = \r -> g (f r) r
```

Now you have all the code needed to get the Monad instance you were looking for, and you can put it together in an instance declaration.

```
instance Monad ((->) r) where
  f >>= g = \r -> g (f r) r
  return x = \r -> x
```

As in the case of State, this monad is already packaged in the mtl library. It's known under the name Reader because the context can be read only, not written. But apart from the monad structure, you also need a way to retrieve the context. The library provides two different functions:

- ask retrieves the complete context, similarly to the get function for mtl's State.

- asks applies a function to the context and returns the result. This function is similar to the access function you developed for your handwritten State monad and to the gets function in mtl, and it's useful for querying a specific field in a structure.

A typical example of Reader usage is handling the settings of an application. Usually, these settings are read at the beginning of the application from some configuration file, but through the lifetime of the application, it doesn't change. It would be really annoying to include an explicit Settings parameter in every single function of the application, so wrapping it on the Reader monad is an elegant solution.

```
data Settings e v = Settings { i :: Int -> [e] -> [v], k :: Int
                             , th :: Double, user :: Person }
kMeansMain :: (Vector v, Vectorizable e v)
           => [e] -> Reader (Settings e v) [v]
kMeansMain points = do i' <- asks i
                       k' <- asks k
                       t' <- asks th
                       return $ kMeans i' k' points t'
```

As happened with State, you also need a function to execute the monad, to which you give the context. In this case, it is called runReader and just takes as an argument the initial unchangeable state.

Even though the main idea of Reader is to describe some immutable context, the mtl implementation also provides the option of executing a piece of code with a context only for that subcomputation. To do so, use the local function, providing it with the function to modify the current state and the computation to perform. Inside the inner block, calls to ask or asks refer to the modified context, which will return to the original once the call to local has ended. For example, you may want to compare the run of K-means when you increase the number of clusters by 1. If you want to use the previous Settings context, you need change it for the enlarged cluster set.

```
compareClusters :: (Vector v, Vectorizable e v)
                => [e] -> Reader (Settings e v) ([v], [v])
compareClusters points = do c1 <- kMeansMain points
                            c2 <- local (\s -> s { k = k s + 1 })
                                        (kMeansMain points)
                            return (c1, c2)
```

You have just seen functions that *consume* a state but don't modify it. The other side of the coin comprises those functions that *generate* some state but never look back at it. This is the case of a logging library. You are always adding messages to the log, but you never look at the previous messages; you are interested only in increasing the log. For that, you should use the Writer monad, as usually available in mtl.

The key design decision that was made for this particular implementation of the Writer monad is that every time you want to add some new value to the output state, the way it is combined with the previous state is specified by an instance of Monoid. Here are two examples that can help you understand better this fact:

1. If you are building a log composed of strings, the monoid structure is that of the list type. The neutral element is the empty list, and the operation to combine two strings is their concatenation. So, if you want to build a log, you should use String as type parameter to Writer.

2. Another place where some information can be seen as an output parameter is in the case of counting the number of iterations for the K-means algorithm. In that case, every time you perform some number of iterations, you want it to be added to the current value. So, the monoid structure is that of the integer with sum. Remember that since numbers have usually two monoidal structures (one for addition and another one for product), you need to wrap the values inside the Sum newtype to use addition as an operation.

The way in which you modify the output state with a new value (which will get combined with the previous value) is by using the tell function with that new value as an argument.

```
accessDatabase :: Writer String ()
accessDatabase = do tell "Start database access"
                    info <- readInformation
                    computeValue info
                    tell "Finish database access"
```

Since the initial value for the output information must be taken as the neutral element of the corresponding monoid, you don't need any extra argument to run a Writer monad value using runWriter, which returns a tuple with both the return value of the computation and the output information.

Writer is an example of a monad whose instance declaration is still accessible while learning. Exercise 6-6 asks you to do so, taking care of some tricks needed to write the correct types.

EXERCISE 6-6. INTERNALS OF THE WRITER MONAD

The `Writer` monad is simply the one corresponding to the type `(a,m)` for any `Monoid` instance `m`. However, you cannot write directly `instance Monoid m => Monad (a,m)` because the type parameter `a` must not be written in the declaration, or the kind won't fit. Thus, you need to use a newtype for the declaration.

`newtype MyWriter m a = MyWriter (a,m)`

Now you can write the declaration starting with `instance Monoid m => MyWriter m`. Also, provide a definition for the `tell` function. Remember to first write down the specific types of the `return` and `(>>=)` functions; it will make things a lot easier.

Haskell tries to carefully delimit how much power should be given to each function, making the compiler able to detect more kinds of errors than in other languages. This philosophy can be transported to the context or state of a particular function. You should give only read access to the information that should be seen as constant, write-only for output that won't be queried, and read and write to the internal state that will be manipulated. It seems that in many cases what you need is a combination of the `Reader`, `Writer`, and `State` monads.

How monads can be combined is a topic for the next chapter, but for this specific case, the `mtl` developers have designed the RWS monad (the acronym comes from the initial letter of each functionality it includes), which you can find in the `Control.Monad.RWS` module. A specific value of this monad takes three type parameters: one for the read-only context, one for the write-only output, and one for the mutable state. The operators needed to access each component remain the same: `ask` and `asks` get the `Reader` value, `tell` includes a new value in the `Writer` monad, and `get`, `put`, and `modify` are used to query and update the `State` value.

Using RWS, you can create your final version of K-means, which keeps the threshold as the context, retains the number of iterations using the `Writer` monad, and uses the centroids as the internal state to update. Notice how you need to wrap the integer values into the `Sum` newtype to tell the compiler which monoid structure for integers you want to use.

```
import Control.Monad (unless)
import Data.Monoid (Sum(..))
kMeans' :: (Vector v, Vectorizable e v)
        => [e] -> RWS Double (Sum Int) [v] ()
kMeans' points = do prevCentrs  <- get
                    let assignments = clusterAssignments prevCentrs points
                        newCentrs = newCentroids assignments
                    put newCentrs
                    tell (Sum 1)
                    t <- ask
                    let err = sum $ zipWith distance prevCentrs newCentrs
                    unless (err < t) $ kMeans' points
kMeans :: (Vector v, Vectorizable e v)
       => (Int -> [e] -> [v]) -> Int -> [e] -> Double -> ([v], Sum Int)
kMeans i n pts t = execRWS (kMeans' pts) t (i n pts)
```

As you can see, RWS provides an elegant way to design your functions, separating explicitly the purpose of each piece of information. This monad is especially useful when porting algorithms that have been developed before in an imperative language without losing any purity in the process.

Mutable References with ST

You have seen how a clever combination of extra arguments to functions and combinators allows for easier descriptions of computations with state. Furthermore, these abstractions can be turned into monads, which enable you to use the do notation, making the code more amenable to reading. But apart from this, Haskell also provides true mutable variables, in the same sense of C or Java, using the ST monad.

Caution   There's a chance that after reading this section you will start using the ST monad everywhere in your code. It's interesting to know how this monad works, because it can lead to more efficient implementations of some algorithms and because it gives a glimpse of the full range of possibilities of the Haskell Platform.

One question that may come to mind is, does the use of ST destroy the purity of the language? The answer is that it does not. The reason is that the way ST is implemented restricts the mutable variables from escaping to the outside world. That is, when you use ST at a particular point, you can create new mutable variables and change them as much as you want. But at the end of that computation, all the mutable variables are destroyed, and the only thing that matters is the return value. Thus, for the outside world, there's no mutability involved. Furthermore, the Haskell runtime separates the mutable variables from different ST instances, so there's a guarantee that mutable variables from different realms won't influence each other.

Let's present the actors in the ST play. The first one is, of course, the ST monad from the `Control.Monad.ST` module, which takes two type parameters, but only the second is important for practical use. It's the type of the return value of the computation (following the same pattern as other state monads). The first argument is used internally by the compiler to assign a unique identifier that will prevent different ST computations from interfering. Once the computation is declared, it's run simply by using it as an argument to the `runST` function.

Inside ST computations, you can create mutable variables, which have the type `STRef a`, from the `Data.STRef` module, where a is the type of the values that will be held in the cell. All the definitions and functions related to STRefs live in the `Data.STRef` module of the base package. Each new variable must be created with a call to `newSTRef`, which consumes the initial value for the variable (uninitialized variables are not supported). The result value is the identifier for that specific mutable variable, which will be used later to access and modify its contents.

The value of a variable can be queried using `readSTRef`, which just needs the variable identifier to perform its task. For updating a variable, as in the case of `State`, you have two different means. You can either specify the new value using the `writeSTRef` function; or you can specify a function that will mutate the current value of the STRef cell into a new value. For that matter, you can use `modifySTRef`. However, since `modifySTRef` is lazy on its application, there's a strong recommendation against its use, because it may lead to memory leaks similar to the ones shown in the previous chapter. Use instead `modifySTRef'`, which is strict.

For example, the following code computes the length of a list using ST. It starts by creating a new mutable variable initialized to the value 0. Then, it traverses the list, updating the value by 1 in each iteration. Notice that the code passes the specific identifier for the mutable variable to be accessible in the `traverseList` function that you defined.

```
listLength :: [a] -> Integer
listLength list = runST $ do l <- newSTRef 0
                             traverseList list l
                             readSTRef l
              where traverseList []      _ = return ()
                    traverseList (_:xs) l = do modifySTRef' l (+1)
                                               traverseList xs l
```

Note   You cannot use map of fold directly on the list because you are in a monadic context, and the types of those functions do not allow this. In the next chapter, you will see how monadic counterparts to these exist, such as mapM, foldM, and forM.

K-means is one of the algorithms which benefit from using mutability. Exercise 6-7 asks you to reimplement the algorithm.

EXERCISE 6-7. K-MEANS USING ST

Implement the K-means algorithm using the ST monad. In particular, you must create one STRef for holding the centroids that will be updated and another one for the number of iterations.

Summary

In this chapter, you finally got in touch with the notion of a *monad*.

- Several implementations of the K-means clustering algorithm were presented, starting with a handwritten one, then refining it using your own combinators, and finally creating versions using the State and RWS monads.

- The chapter defined combinators for working with Maybe values in an easier way.

- The chapter explained the monad, which is a way to combine computations with some special characteristic, such as being able to fail or having an internal state.

- Monads are one of the most important constructions in Haskell and come with a custom syntax, called do notation, which you studied in depth in this chapter. This is the most used style of writing monadic code.

- You saw several other monads: Reader, which holds a read-only context; Writer, which outputs a write-only value that is combined using a monoid structure; RWS, which combines the three Reader, Writer, and State monads; and ST, which implements controlled mutable variables.

- Apart from monads, in this chapter *lenses* were introduced as a way to query and update data structures in a common and powerful way.

CHAPTER 7

More Monads: Now for Recommendations

The previous chapter introduced monads. In particular, the tasks of handling errors using Maybe, constants using Reader, logging using Writer, and state were presented through the same point of view, making clear how monad functions form the scaffolding that combines code for all of them.

The list monad can also represent multiple outcomes of a function. This is useful for modeling paths between years in time machines. However, you must be careful to ensure that the code does not enter an infinite loop. You can avoid that problem by using the Logic monad. As you can see, lists are important in Haskell programming; many ideas and algorithms depend on their special structure. This chapter will also clarify the interactions between lists and other monads.

Data mining is going to be an integral part of this chapter too. You will implement the Apriori algorithm, which learns association rules from a data set. In short, *association rules* express relations between variables, such as "most of the people who buy a time machine also buy a travel guide." Expressing the Apriori algorithm using the *list monad* will unveil a new type class, called MonadPlus, which introduces choice to the mix.

You have so far been looking at examples that use one monad at a time. And that is generally what you'll encounter as you program in Haskell. However, more complex applications sometimes require the power of several monads, such as Maybe for handling errors and Writer for logging information about the process. The most common way to combine multiple monads is by using *monad transformers*, and that will be one of the topics in this chapter.

© Alejandro Serrano Mena 2022
A. Serrano Mena, *Practical Haskell*, https://doi.org/10.1007/978-1-4842-8581-7_7

Returning More Than One Value

In the previous chapter, you saw how the Maybe monad models functions that may fail. Their monad functions allow you to thread successful values and stop as soon as the first failure has been detected. If you look at lists with the same ideas, it can be said that a function returning a list is really returning several possible values for the same input arguments; an empty list will model failure, a singleton list will model a deterministic computation that returns just a value, and a longer list will model many possible outputs or paths of execution, usually expressed by saying that it models *nondeterministic* behavior.

Caution   The term *nondeterministic* is used differently when speaking about lists in Haskell than when speaking about other kinds of systems in computer science. The term was chosen because when simulating a nondeterministic computation, several outputs are possible, and this can be represented using a list. However, the computation in a list monad is completely deterministic and pure, and it doesn't add any uncertainty in the way results are computed or ordered.

The List Monad

Maybe forms a monad, so a fair question is whether lists also form one. One way to check is by opening GHCi and calling return, a function that you know must be implemented by any monadic type, and asking it to return a list. If the expression runs successfully, it means that the type [] (remember, this is the name of the type of lists) is a monad. Let's do it with an easy example.

```
Prelude> return 1 :: [Integer]
[1]
```

You can see from the output not only that lists form a monad but also that the Monad instance for lists is compatible with the previous discussion; a deterministic computation with just one value is modeled as a singleton list. The second function found in all monad instances is (>>=), the bind operator. Let's first look at the bind operator's type when instantiated for this case.

```
(>>=) :: [a] -> (a -> [b]) -> [b]
```

To check the bind operator's behavior, let's apply to a simple number list a function that, given a number, will produce the double and the triple of that number in a list.

```
Prelude> [1,2,3] >>= \x -> [2*x,3*x]
[2,3,4,6,6,9]
```

As you can see, the function is applied to each element of the list, and all the results are gathered again into a new list. You have already seen a function with this "application plus gathering" behavior. It is the composition of mapping over a list, which would return a list of lists, and then flattening the result using concat.

```
Prelude> map (\x -> [2*x,3*x]) [1,2,3]
[[2,3],[4,6],[6,9]]
Prelude> concat $ map (\x -> [2*x,3*x]) [1,2,3]
[2,3,4,6,6,9]
```

However, the best way to understand why it's said that the list monad models nondeterminism is using some code with do notation. For example, the following piece of code takes values from two lists and then computes the product of each pair. Check the result carefully.

```
Prelude> :{
Prelude| do x <- [1,2,3]
Prelude|    y <- [7,8,9]
Prelude|    return $ x * y
Prelude| :}
[7,8,9,14,16,18,21,24,27]
```

The code has taken all possible values from the first list and all possible values from the second list and has returned the application of the product function to each pair. This example shows how the monadic notation may hide some surprises. You may not expect from the <- syntax to take each of the values in the list in order. Exercise 7-1 will help you fully grasp the behavior by explaining broken time machines.

EXERCISE 7-1. BROKEN TIME MACHINES

More often than should happen, time machines break. Imagine, for example, that you have a time machine that jumps randomly between the previous year, three years into the future, and five years into the future. Consider that to move four years into the future, you would need to make a five-year leap followed by a one-year jump into the past.

Imagine that you have such a machine like this. Write a function named brokenThreeJumps that, starting for a year, returns all possible years in which you can arrive after three jumps in time with your broken time machine. Use the list monad and do notation.

Afterward, design a function called brokenJumps that generalizes the former and returns the possible years after a specified number of jumps.

A New View over Monads

From the previous discussion, you can easily get the declaration of the monad instance for lists. If you remember, a monad is composed of a return function, which wraps a single value, and a bind function (>>=), which threads several computations in the monad. The corresponding instance for a list reads as follows:

```
instance Monad [] where
  return a = [a]
  x >>= f  = concat $ map f x
```

However, there's another possible way to define a monad, and lists are the perfect example of this different view. Instead of (>>=), you define fmap and additionally a join function, which should have the type m (m a) -> m a for each monad m. In the case of lists, join boils down to having the type [[a]] -> [a]. And there you can find again our old friend concat, which flattens lists.

Defining a monad in terms of these functions is equivalent to declaring it using return and bind. In particular, every monad has a sensible definition for fmap and join. You already know the definition of fmap for Maybe. Here's the corresponding code implementing join:

```
join :: Maybe (Maybe a) -> Maybe a
```

```
join Nothing          = Nothing
join (Just Nothing)   = Nothing
join (Just (Just x))  = Just x
```

Since I'm talking about the equivalent of definitions, I should tell you how to define (>>=) in terms of fmap and join, and vice versa. Let's start with the bind operator. This is the definition that I'm giving:

```
x >>= f = join $ fmap f x
```

As an exercise to build confidence in the validity of this rule, you can apply the left side to the list monad and check whether the result is the same as the definition of (>>=). The equational reasoning looks like the following example for the list case:

```
join $ fmap f x = concat $ map f x = x >>= f
```

So, at least for the list case, the equivalence holds. Now, let's go for the converse equivalences.

```
fmap f x = x >>= (\y -> return $ f y)
join x   = x >>= id  -- id is the identity function, id x = x
```

A good exercise to refresh your knowledge about equational reasoning is checking that the converse definitions hold for the list monad, as I just did in the preceding code.

Note   You have just seen another way in which you can get a definition of fmap using the monad functions, apart from using liftM as explained in the previous chapter. Every type that belongs to the Monad type class can also be made an inhabitant of the Functor type class in a uniform way. As I have already explained, this is reflected in the actual definition of the Monad type class, but for the time being, we look at those two classes in isolation.

Failures and Alternatives

Some monads implement a concept of failure, which is supported by the fail function in the MonadFail type class. But in some cases, apart from failure, you have the concept of multiple successes, as happens with [ ]. For them, the standard library includes the

MonadPlus type class, which extends Monad with two operations. This type class is found in the Control.Monad module, which also includes a lot of utility functions that will be discussed later. The full declaration of the type class is shown here for reference:

```
class Monad m => MonadPlus m where
  mzero :: m a
  mplus :: m a -> m a -> m a
```

The mzero function is the one supporting failure. Note that this function returns a value that is parametric on every possible element wrapped by the monad, without any input from outside. In the case of lists, this means that only one kind of value can be returned, the empty list, because it is the one that you can build in such a way. You can verify the empty list by using the interpreter as follows:

```
*Chapter7.MonadPlus> import Control.Monad
*Chapter7.MonadPlus Control.Monad> mzero :: [Integer]
[]
```

Successes from multiple branches of execution can be joined together using the other operation, mplus. Since lists model the multiple success values as their elements, joining several paths should be like concatenating both lists. For example, let's define two different ways in which a time machine could be broken: one traveling randomly between the previous year and the next year and another traveling randomly between the year 1024 and two years into the future.

```
broken1 :: Integer -> [Integer]
broken1 n = [n-1, n+1]
broken2 :: Integer -> [Integer]
broken2 n = [1024, n+2]
```

You might have a time machine and not know how it is broken. Thus, it makes sense to put together all possible years to which such a machine may travel, either as broken1 or as broken2. This disjunctive behavior is exactly what is captured by the mplus function in MonadPlus.

```
*Chapter7.MonadPlus Control.Monad> broken1 73 `mplus` broken2 73
[72,74,1024,75]
```

The most important function using the failure behavior of a monad is guard. You will see examples of its use in the implementation of the Apriori algorithm. But first, let's introduce its type and definition, which is quite small but has big implications on the way you use it.

```
guard :: MonadPlus m => Bool -> m ()   -- for list, Bool -> [()]
guard True  = return ()   -- for list, [()]
guard False = mzero       -- for list, []
```

Notice that the function returns some value, but there's no interesting value saved within as it is an empty tuple. Thus, in practice guard is never used in conjunction with <- to get its value. To understand the function's behavior, let's focus on the following piece of code:

```
do guard condition
   return 1
```

This code will be translated by the compiler into a form without do notation, as shown in the previous chapter.

```
guard condition >>= (\_ -> return 1)
```

Going a step further and replacing the monad functions by the specific definitions for lists, the code reads as follows:

```
concat $ map (\_ -> [1]) (guard condition)
```

The first possible case is that the condition is satisfied. Then, guard condition is equivalent to [()]. The evaluation steps in that case are as follows:

```
concat $ map (\_ -> [1]) [()] = concat [[1]] = [1]
```

However, when the condition is False, then the guard condition is equivalent to an empty list. This means that when performing the map operation, the resulting list will also be empty. In this way, the guard ensures that when the condition is not fulfilled, no values are returned.

Creating a new type class, MonadPlus, and including it in the basic distribution wouldn't make sense if lists are the only type for which an instance exists. But this is not the case because an instance for Maybe is also included, and it's convenient to use. Until now, you have learned how a do block with a bunch of Maybes returns a Just only if all its intermediate computations have also returned a Just value. This was useful for writing code that accesses a database and tries to get a final result by joining different pieces of information; if any of it fails, the whole process should be considered as failed. In the previous chapter, you saw the following code:

```
do n        <- numberItemsByPurchaseId purchaseId
   productId <- productIdByPurchaseId purchaseId
   price     <- priceByProductId productId
   return $ fromInteger n * price
```

Sometimes, the behavior you want to obtain is not a series of accesses, all of which should be done correctly. Instead, you might want one main way to get the information along with a fallback case. Only if both fail would the entire process fail. Once again, this possibility of falling back when one Maybe operation fails is an example of a disjunctive behavior captured by the MonadPlus type class. For example, let's see what the interpreter gives back when you model the first computation as failed using Nothing.

```
*Chapter7.MonadPlus Control.Monad> Nothing `mplus` Just 5
Just 5
```

The code falls back to the second option, which is the one returned. In the case that both computations are correct, the Monad instance for Maybe gives priority to the leftmost one, as shown in this example:

```
*Chapter7.MonadPlus Control.Monad> Just "first" `mplus` Just "second"
Just "first"
```

While reading the previous presentation of MonadPlus, another type class may come to your mind: Monoid. In some sense, mzero is a bit like mempty on monoids, and mplus is a bit like mappend. However, these two type classes should not be confused. The mplus one works over a specific data type, whereas mzero is to be applied over data types that admit a type variable. That means [Integer], a specific data type with no type variables, can be made a Monoid but not a MonadPlus. On the other hand, a polymorphic type such as [a] can be made a MonadPlus but never a Monoid. In the language of kinds, you would say that the Monoid type class applies to types of kind *, whereas MonadPlus applies to types of kind * -> *.

In the same line of this relation, Control.Monad features a couple of functions similar to monoidal ones. msum is one of those, which corresponds to the mconcat in the Monoid case and which folds over a list of values using the combination operation (mappend for monoids or mplus for MonadPlus). Once again, the difference in kinds can be observed in the types of these functions. mconcat has type Monoid m => [m] -> m, and msum is typed as MonadPlus m => [m a] -> m a. You can find two examples of its use here. Think carefully about the results.

```
*Chapter7.MonadPlus Control.Monad> msum [[1],[2,3],[],[1,2]]
[1,2,3,1,2]
*Chapter7.MonadPlus Control.Monad> msum [Nothing, Just 1, Just 2, Nothing]
Just 1
```

The other specific function for MonadPlus is mfilter. In this case, the function being generalized is filter. The function mfilter returns all the values satisfying a condition but joined using the mplus operation of MonadPlus. Exercise 7-2 shows how you can use the msum function to implement a related functionality: searching for an element in a list.

EXERCISE 7-2. SEARCHING WITH MONADPLUS

Write a find_ function with type (a -> Bool) -> [a] -> Maybe a that returns the first element in the list that fulfills the given condition. Do so using the function msum introduced in this section and the behavior of the MonadPlus instance of Maybe.

Association Rule Learning

In the previous chapter, the focus was on discovering similar kinds of clients in order to create better advertising campaigns targeting one or more of these groups. Now, the aim is to perform data mining over the data set in order to be able to suggest new products to buyers while they are surfing the web store. To do so, one simple option is to use association rules.

In association rule learning, you assume that your data is composed of a series of *transactions*, each of them being a set of *items*. You can think of each transaction as coming from a row or set of associated rows in a regular database. For example, you can begin from the following piece of information:

The company Wormhole Inc. bought the travel guide with product iden-
tifier 3.

From this bit of information, you can derive the following transaction:

```
{ company, name "Wormhole Inc.",
  purchased travel guide,
  purchased product 3 }
```

These items are generated from a set of possible ones. Since information is usually represented in Haskell as a tree of values, you will first need to implement a way to translate those values into a flat representation made of transactions.

From those transactions, your aim is to create *association rules*. These rules are formed by two sets of items, the antecedent A and the consequent C, and are represented by A => C. The meaning of such a rule is that, often, when a transaction contains the items in A, it also contains the items in C. An example may be { `individual, purchased time machine` } => { `purchased travel guide` }, telling that usually when an individual has bought a time machine, it will also buy a travel guide, so you can do better by suggesting the available guides.

To finish this overview, I need to introduce two measures associated with sets of items and rules. The *support* of a set of items is defined as the ratio of transactions that contain the mentioned set of items. For example, if your transactions are [{`a, b`}, {`a, c`}, {`b, c`}], the support of {`b`} is computed by dividing the number of transactions that contain b (in this case, 2) by the total amount of transactions (here, 3). So, *support*({`b`}) = 2/3 = 0.66.

The *confidence* of a rule A => C is defined as *support*(A and C) / *support*(A). This measure quantifies how many transactions support the rule by looking at the ratio of those transactions that fulfill the entire rule and those transactions that fulfill the antecedent.

Flattening Values into Transactions

As explained earlier, the process of learning the association rules works over flat sets of items instead of composite values. In this section, I will introduce those functions that will turn composite values into flat sets of items. As a reminder, here is the description of clients and the data types for products:

```
-- Clients
```

```
data Client = GovOrg     { clientName :: String }
           | Company     { clientName :: String
                         , person :: Person, duty :: String }
           | Individual { person :: Person }
           deriving (Show, Eq, Ord)
data ClientKind = KindGovOrg | KindCompany | KindIndividual
               deriving (Show, Eq, Ord)
data Person = Person { firstName :: String, lastName :: String
                     , gender :: Gender }
           deriving (Show, Eq, Ord)
data Gender = Male | Female | UnknownGender deriving (Show, Eq, Ord)
-- Products
data Product = Product { productId :: Integer, productType :: ProductType }
           deriving (Show, Eq, Ord)
data ProductType = TimeMachine | TravelGuide | Tool | Trip
               deriving (Show, Eq, Ord)
```

A purchase in the database is then just the aggregation of a client and a set of products.

```
data Purchase = Purchase { client :: Client, products :: [Product] }
             deriving (Show, Eq, Ord)
```

The items in a transaction will reflect useful information about a purchase, such as the kind and identifier of purchased product and the kind of client (government organization, company, or individual). In the case of companies, there's also interest in knowing the role of the person responsible for the purchase and, in the case of individuals, of knowing the gender if that information is available.

```
data PurchaseInfo = InfoClientKind          ClientKind
                 | InfoClientDuty          String
                 | InfoClientGender        Gender
                 | InfoPurchasedProduct    Integer
                 | InfoPurchasedProductType ProductType
                 deriving (Show, Eq, Ord)
```

To make the code clearer and type safer, let's create a newtype to tag those sets used as transactions.

```
import Data.Set (Set)
import qualified Data.Set as S
newtype Transaction = Transaction (Set PurchaseInfo)
                      deriving (Eq, Ord)
```

As an example, here is the code that converts the information in a product/purchase into a real transaction. Check that most of the work is just transposing some fields into values of the PurchaseInfo type. In Exercise 7-3, you will be asked to write the clientToPurchaseInfo function that is missing in the declaration of purchaseToTransaction.

```
productsToPurchaseInfo :: [Product] -> Set PurchaseInfo
productsToPurchaseInfo = foldr
  (\(Product i t) pinfos -> S.insert (InfoPurchasedProduct i) $
                            S.insert (InfoPurchasedProductType t) pinfos)
  S.empty
purchaseToTransaction :: Purchase -> Transaction
purchaseToTransaction (Purchase c p) =
  Transaction $ clientToPurchaseInfo c `S.union` productsToPurchaseInfo p
```

EXERCISE 7-3. CLIENTS INTO ITEMS

Write the missing clientToPurchaseInfo function. It should have type Client -> Set PurchaseInfo and should satisfy the requirements for obtaining items from clients that I explained while defining the PurchaseInfo data type. Here's an example showing the return value for a test:

*> **clientToPurchaseInfo (Company "1984 Inc." (Person "George" "Orwell" Male) "Director")**

fromList [InfoClientKind KindCompany,InfoClientDuty "Director"]

As you can see, from a simple Client you get a whole set of items.

The Apriori Algorithm

One of the simplest algorithms for mining association rules is Apriori, introduced in 1994 by Agrawal and Srikant. The Apriori algorithm works in two phases:

- First, it generates sets of items that fulfill the condition of minimum support, called *frequent sets*.

- Then, from those sets, it derives association rules with a minimum confidence.

The result is a set of association rules known to satisfy some minimum value for both measures. By changing those values, you can experiment by creating more or fewer rules. Creating many rules has the problem of overfitting; the rules are true in the specific data set you are using, but they cannot be generalized and applicable to new scenarios. Thus, creating fewer rules increases the confidence in the further applicability of them. The main flow of the Apriori algorithm is pictured in Figure 7-1, along with the types involved in each step.

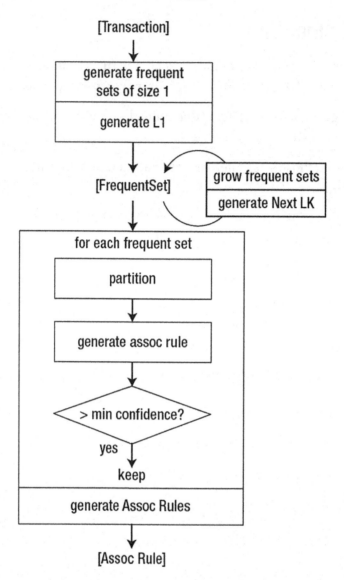

Figure 7-1.   *Apriori algorithm*

The way in which the first phase works is derived from an observation: if you have a set of items *I* with a support *s*, any subset of *I* will have a support equal or greater than *s* (because all the transactions that made *I* have such support, thus it will also be counted for any of its subsets). This means you can reuse the sets with *n* items to create larger sets of *n+1* items by taking those that have an intersection of *n-1* items, joining them, and then looking to see whether they fulfill the required support. From what I have just explained, it does not make sense to join sets of items that have a support below the minimum because the join will never satisfy the condition.

Note   The actual algorithm performs some nice tricks at this point in order to generate a smaller number of item sets from the previous ones and thus have to do fewer checks.

Let's introduce the data type for association rules and sets of items in this phase. Remember, they are called *frequent sets*. Here is the code to review:

```
newtype FrequentSet = FrequentSet (Set PurchaseInfo)
                      deriving (Eq, Ord)
data AssocRule = AssocRule (Set PurchaseInfo) (Set PurchaseInfo)
             deriving (Eq, Ord)
instance Show AssocRule where
  show (AssocRule a b) = show a ++ " => " ++ show b
```

Along with the data type definitions, you will need helper functions for computing the confidence and support measures for frequent sets and association rules, respectively. As you can see, this code is not tuned for performance because it calls length repeatedly on lists. Thinking about how to increase the speed of the following code is a good exercise:

```
setSupport :: [Transaction] -> FrequentSet -> Double
setSupport trans (FrequentSet sElts) =
  let total = length trans
      f (Transaction tElts) = sElts `S.isSubsetOf` tElts
      supp  = length (filter f trans)
   in fromIntegral supp / fromIntegral total
ruleConfidence :: [Transaction] -> AssocRule -> Double
ruleConfidence trans (AssocRule a b) =
  setSupport trans (FrequentSet $ a `S.union` b)
  / setSupport trans (FrequentSet a)
```

The first thing to do is to generate the initial sets of one element that are frequent. In the following code, instead of using list functions or comprehensions, I'm using list as a monad. Don't get confused by the conversions from set to list via S.toList. Also, do not be confused by the wrapping of the singleton set into a FrequentSet. That is just boilerplate and not the real point of this code.

```
import Control.Monad
generateL1 :: Double -> [Transaction] -> [FrequentSet]
generateL1 minSupport transactions =
  noDups $ do Transaction t <- transactions
              e <- S.toList t
              let fs = FrequentSet $ S.singleton e
              guard $ setSupport transactions fs > minSupport
              return fs
-- noDups removes duplicates in a list
noDups :: Ord a => [a] -> [a]
noDups = S.toList . S.fromList
```

The relevant parts are how the code uses <- from the do notation to resemble the list comprehension syntax (as you will see later, this is not by chance) and the guard function that was introduced in the previous section.

The previous code also uses a special definition of a function that removes duplicates, namely, noDups. In Chapter 4, I discussed how the basic function in the Prelude for this task, named nub, is quite slow. Converting to a set and from it back to a list is a more performant way to accomplish this same task.

The next step in the algorithm is how to generate the frequent sets of level $k+1$ from the frequent sets of level k. As I discussed earlier, this can be done in two steps. First, check whether each pair of sets of level k shares $k-1$ elements and then check whether the combined set fulfills the minimum support condition. Before looking at the code, let's see briefly what it's going to be doing with this function. You need to create more and more levels from the previous ones until you find an empty frequent set. You already know this pattern of generating elements until some condition is reached; it's an "unfold."

Since you already know that you want to use the unfoldr function to generate the list, it's time to plug in the information specific to this case. As you know, unfoldr uses a seed value that is changed and threaded while creating new elements. Which pieces of information will be held in this value? You need at least the frequent sets of the previous level. But, to be able to know whether two frequent sets share $k-1$ elements, it's also useful to thread the level you are working with at that moment (in other cases, you would have to recompute it from the number of elements in the sets). So, the seed value will have type (Int, [FrequentSet]).

In each level, the algorithm will produce a list of frequent sets, so the element type in unfoldr needs to be [FrequentSet]. This poses a problem: the result of unfolding will have type [[FrequentSet]] instead of a plain list called [FrequentSet]. The easiest way to solve this problem is by including a call to concat, which flattens the list. In conclusion, a new function generateNextLk is defined next. Check how guard is used to cut from the list of frequent sets all those that don't fulfill the conditions.

```haskell
generateNextLk :: Double -> [Transaction] -> (Int, [FrequentSet])
                          -> Maybe ([FrequentSet], (Int, [FrequentSet]))
generateNextLk _ _ (_, []) = Nothing
generateNextLk minSupport transactions (k, lk) =
  let lk1 = noDups $ do FrequentSet a <- lk
                        FrequentSet b <- lk
                        guard $ S.size (a `S.intersection` b) == k - 1
                        let fs = FrequentSet $ a `S.union` b
                        guard $ setSupport transactions fs > minSupport
                        return fs
  in Just (lk1, (k+1, lk1))
```

At this point, you have all the ingredients for generating the frequent sets of all levels. You only need to have repeated calls to generateNextLk, threading the previous frequent sets and the level number. This is a perfect job for unfoldr. Thus, a possible way to generate the frequent sets, given l1 as the initial frequent set returned by generateL1, is the expression shown next. This expression will be part of the whole implementation of the Apriori algorithm.

```haskell
concat $ unfoldr (generateNextLk minSupport transactions) (1, l1)
```

The final step is to generate association rules with a minimum confidence. The way in which the Apriori algorithm works at this point is as follows: take a frequent set *I* from the previous steps. Then, partition the set into two disjointed sets *A* and *B* such that *A* is not empty. Each partition will give rise to a rule A => B, which should be checked for minimum confidence. This should be done for each possible partition of each frequent set, which would be obtained by the powerset function. This is a perfect job for the list monad. The Haskell code is a straightforward translation of this description:

```
generateAssocRules :: Double -> [Transaction] -> [FrequentSet]
                   -> [AssocRule]
generateAssocRules minConfidence transactions sets =
  do FrequentSet fs <- sets
     subset@(_:_) <- powerset $ S.toList fs
     let ssubset = S.fromList subset
         rule = AssocRule ssubset (fs `S.difference` ssubset)
     guard $ ruleConfidence transactions rule > minConfidence
     return rule
powerset :: [a] -> [[a]]
powerset [] = [[]]
powerset (x:xs) = powerset xs ++ map (x:) (powerset xs)
```

The only thing left is gluing all these functions into an actual apriori function, which should take the data set along with the minimum support and confidence values and should return the association rules that fulfill those requirements. I have chosen to use a direct style, passing the result of each function to the next one, but it could also be written using lets for each step or in a point-free form.

```
import Data.List (unfoldr)
apriori :: Double -> Double -> [Transaction] -> [AssocRule]
apriori minSupport minConfidence transactions =
  generateAssocRules minConfidence transactions
    $ concat $ unfoldr (generateNextLk minSupport transactions)
                       (1, generateL1 minSupport transactions)
```

Search Problems

Many problems in computer science can be better solved when looking at them as *search problems*. In a search problem, you don't know how to come to an answer directly, but you have a way to explore the space of possible solutions, and you can do so until you find the correct answer. Usually, the way to explore the space resembled the shape of a tree. From a possible solution, you can create a set of other possible solutions to check. In this way, looking for the wanted value is pretty similar to traversing the tree.

Paths in a Graph

Graphs are a good source of problems that can be solved using this approach. In this section, you will look at one instance of it. Previous chapters introduced the idea of time machines that can travel only to specific points in time. The problem you need to solve now is finding all possible journeys between two years. As in the previous examples, the model will be a graph given by a list of edges, (start, end). Assume also that there are no self-loops in it (i.e., there are no edges (y,y) with the same year y in both components). Let's think about the function signature. You are looking for a list of paths, each of them represented as a list of years, between the node start and the node end. Thus, you need the graph and two nodes, and the results will be a list of a list of nodes.

```
paths :: [(Int,Int)] -> Int -> Int -> [[Int]]
paths edges start end = undefined -- code here
```

Remember that in real life, you would use instead the much more performant Data. Graph module that was introduced in Chapter 4. However, for ease of exposition, in this section I'm using a bare list of pairs to model the graph.

Note   The Prelude function undefined is customarily used as a placeholder for code that hasn't been written yet. Trying to execute this function will result in an error, but it's handy for designing the overall structure of the code, marking with undefined those holes that will be filled later.

As in any search algorithm, there are several cases to tackle. In the general case, you must take all the nodes (o,t) whose origin is start (i.e., o coincides with the parameter start) and find those paths between the target of that edge and the year you want to end in. This logic can be coded easily with a combination of the list monad and the guard function. As you can see, the following code is almost a transliteration of the logic that has just been described:

```
import Control.Monad
paths :: [(Int,Int)] -> Int -> Int -> [[Int]]
paths edges start end =
  do (e_start, e_end) <- edges
     guard $ e_start == start
```

```
    subpath <- paths edges e_end end
    return $ start:subpath
```

However, this code is not yet right because you need to manage the case in which you have reached the target year of your journey. In that case, you need to add to those paths an extra one consisting of just one year, the one that is at the same time start and end. To do so, you can use the (:) constructor to append the element at the beginning of e_paths. However, in the following code, I've rather chosen return and mplus in order to show how MonadPlus functions can be used in this scenario:

```
paths :: [(Int,Int)] -> Int -> Int -> [[Int]]
paths edges start end =
  let e_paths = do (e_start, e_end) <- edges
                   guard $ e_start == start
                   subpath <- paths edges e_end end
                   return $ start:subpath
  in if start == end
        then return [end] `mplus` e_paths
        else e_paths
```

If you take a graph like the following:

```
graph1 :: [(Int, Int)]
graph1 = [(2013,501),(2013,1004),(501,2558),(1004,2558)]
```

you can easily get all paths from year 2013 to 2558 in GHCi.

```
*Chapter7.Graph> paths graph1 2013 2558
[[2013,501,2558],[2013,1004,2558]]
```

The Logic Monad

However, loops can create problems when the search space is explored in a naïve way. For example, take this other graph, where there's a cycle between years 501 and 1004:

```
graph2 :: [(Int, Int)]
graph2 = [(2013,501),(501,2558),(501,1004),(1004,501),(2013,2558)]
```

The list of paths between years 2013 and 2558 is infinite (you can always loop once more between years 501 and 1004). But you can still get a finite set of those paths, as this example shows:

```
*Chapter7.Graph> take 3 $ paths graph2 2013 2558
[[2013,501,2558],[2013,501,1004,501,2558],
 [2013,501,1004,501,1004,501,2558]]
```

The problem you have here is that the path [2013,2558] will never be found because the search strategy embodied in the list monad will first need to find all subpaths that go through year 501 (because it was found earlier while exploring the list of edges). This is due to the fact that every time the list is traversed, it is done in the order in which they appear. However, the list of those subpaths is infinite, so the computation never reaches the point at which the (2013,2558) edges are considered. In this case, writing (2013,2558) before (2013,501) would solve the problem, but we do not want to depend on those details in general.

To get much better control over how the search proceeds, I will introduce the Logic monad, which can be found in the Control.Monad.Logic module of the logict package from Hackage (remember that you can install it using cabal install or adding it as a dependency of a project). By default, this monad behaves as the list one, so almost all the code from the previous example is valid now just by changing the type signature of the function.

```
import Control.Monad.Logic
pathsL :: [(Int,Int)] -> Int -> Int -> Logic [Int]
pathsL edges start end =
  let e_paths = do (e_start, e_end) <- choices edges
                   guard $ e_start == start
                   subpath <- pathsL edges e_end end
                   return $ start:subpath
  in if start == end then return [end] `mplus` e_paths else e_paths
choices :: [a] -> Logic a
choices = msum . map return
```

The only important addition is the call to a newly defined choices[1] function. This function allows you to turn a list into a set of successes in your Logic computation. This is done by returning each of the elements in the list (via map return) and then joining these successes together with msum.

At this stage, the definition using the Logic monad suffers from the same problem of the one implemented using lists. If you take the first three solutions, using the observeMany function from the Control.Monad.List module, you can observe the same behavior of traversing first all paths that go through year 501.

```
*Chapter7.Graph> import Control.Monad.Logic
*Chapter7.Graph Control.Monad.Logic> observeMany 3 (pathsL graph2
2013 2558)
[[2013,501,2558],[2013,501,1004,501,2558],
 [2013,501,1004,501,1004,501,2558]]
```

To solve this problem, Logic introduces a set of operators that are fair, that is, a set of operators that do not give priority to any of the possible branches in the computation. You can see the difference between mplus, the usual function for joining results that first takes all those from the first argument and then those of the second, and interleave, which takes one from each time it needs a further element.

```
*Chapter7.Graph Control.Monad.Logic> [1,2] `mplus` [3,4]
[1,2,3,4]
*Chapter7.Graph Control.Monad.Logic> [1,2] `interleave` [3,4]
[1,3,2,4]
```

There's also a fair replacement of (>>=), called (>>-). However, since the bind operator is different, you can no longer use do notation. Thus, you need to desugar the pathsL function and write it using the monad primitives, as Exercise 7-4 asks.

---

[1] The definition of choices is taken from the article "Adventures in Three Monads" by Edward Z. Yang.

EXERCISE 7-4. DESUGARING MONAD NOTATION

Using the rules explained in Chapter 6, rewrite the pathsL function using (>>=) and return instead of the do notation. Remember that guard is a normal function, not special syntax, so you don't need to do anything differently than when using any other function.

The replacement of (>>=) by (>>-) gives the next iteration of the path algorithm.

```
pathsLFair :: [(Int,Int)] -> Int -> Int -> Logic [Int]
pathsLFair edges start end =
  let e_paths = choices edges >>- \(e_start, e_end) ->
                guard (e_start == start) >>
                pathsLFair edges e_end end >>- \subpath ->
                return $ start:subpath
  in if start == end then return [end] `interleave` e_paths else e_paths
```

And now the problem is gone. Edges are visited in a different order, which gives fair priority to all the elements, and you get the [2013,2558] path.

```
*Chapter7.Graph Control.Monad.Logic>
    observeMany 3 $ pathsLFair graph2 2013 2558
[[2013,501,2558],[2013,2558],[2013,501,1004,501,2558]]
```

This example has given just a shallow exposition of the features in logict. This package provides many more combinators that allow the programmer to program in a logical programming style, with backtracking, cuts, conditionals, and so on, so I encourage you to look at its documentation if you need to implement solutions to other search problems. Logic is also a sample of how monads can be used to embed other paradigms of computation inside Haskell, without losing the native taste.

Monads and Lists, Redux

Up to this point, you have seen examples of lists considered as monads being used in a model that returns multiple values. In this section, you will learn about two other ways in which monads can relate to lists: first, functions performing operations like the usual list ones (e.g., maps and folds) but that work in a monadic environment; then, how the list comprehension syntax can be extended to work under any monad.

Combining Values Under a Monad

In some cases, you want to execute a computation over all elements of a list, but this computation happens inside a monad, instead of being a pure function. For those cases, the Control.Monad module contains a bunch of functions ending in M, which provide similar functionality to usual list functions. In this section, you will get a high-level overview of them and see examples of where to apply them.

The first of these functions is mapM, and the type is Monad m => (a -> m b) -> [a] -> m [b]. The mapM function applies a monadic function to each element of the list, chaining the execution of each element inside the monad you are working on. For example, say you have a simple function that prepends one string to another. But instead of using an extra parameter, you want to use some global context modeled with the Reader monad.

```
import Control.Monad.Reader
addPrefix :: String -> Reader String String
addPrefix s = ask >>= \p -> return $  p ++ s
```

If you now have a list of strings to which you want to prefix with that first string, your intuition may be to use map. However, map wouldn't be a solution. Let's try to spot the reason by looking at the type of the expression you want to execute.

```
*Chapter7.UnderAMonad> :t map addPrefix
map addPrefix :: [String] -> [Reader String String]
```

What you get using map is not a function that prefixes all the strings in the list. Rather, the return value is a list of computations, with each of them needing a context in which to perform its actions. If you use mapM, all those computations would go under the same Reader monad and thus share a context. That, it turns out, is exactly what you need.

```
addPrefixL :: [String] -> Reader String [String]
addPrefixL = mapM addPrefix
```

You can check that the function works as expected by testing it in the interpreter.

```
*Chapter7.UnderAMonad> runReader (addPrefixL ["one","two"]) "**-"
["**-one","**-two"]
```

In some cases, you are not interested in the results of the computations but just in the other effects the functions have on the elements of a list. For example, say you want to log a series of data using the Writer monad. You don't really care in this case about what to return, just about the fact that the strings are appended in the log of the computation. For these cases, there is a version of mapM called mapM_ that doesn't return such values. Here's how the log function would look using it:

```
import Control.Monad.Writer
logInformation :: [String] -> Writer String ()
logInformation = mapM_ (\s -> tell (s ++ "\n"))
```

And again you can use the interpreter to check that the function is working as expected.

```
*Chapter7.UnderAMonad> runWriter $ logInformation ["one","two"]
((),"one\ntwo\n")
```

The Control.Monad module also provides functions forM and forM_, which are simply mapM and mapM_ with their arguments reversed. That is, the list goes first and then the function. Using forM, you can write code that looks a lot like a for-each loop in Java or C#. The previous function can be rewritten as follows:

```
logInformation infos = forM_ infos $ \s -> tell (s ++ "\n")
```

mapM and forM are really specializations of the more general sequence function, which executes all actions of a set of monad values under the same monad context. The type of sequence is Monad m => [m a] -> m [a]. Exercise 7-5 provides hints for you to write a definition of sequence and mapM.

EXERCISE 7-5. A DEFINITION FOR SEQUENCE AND MAPM

Try to write the definition of sequence. Do it using do notation and pattern matching. Like with any other list function, you should consider the cases of the empty list and the list with some head and tail. Remember that x <- v "extracts" the value wrapped in a monad from v :: m a into a binding x :: a.

For the mapM function, the hint is to write it as a composition of two other functions. The ones you should use have already been showcased in the example of prefixing a list of strings with a common prefix from a shared context.

Be aware that the behavior of sequence (and hence mapM and forM) is determined mostly by the monad in which computation will happen. For example, if what you are sequencing is a list of Maybe values, the behavior is to return Just only if all the elements in the list are Just values and to return Nothing if any of the elements in the list is a Nothing. This is derived from the way (>>=) works for Maybe.

The same way the module provides "upgraded" maps, it also provides folds that work under a monad umbrella. The function that performs the task is foldM :: Monad m => (a -> b -> m a) -> a -> [b] -> m a. Notice that there are no right and left fold versions: foldM always performs a left fold (if you need to perform it rightward, just reverse the list before applying the function). Once again, a logging facility provides you with an example in which you would use this function. In this case, I'm going to present you with a version of factorial that, in addition to calculating the result, takes care of the number of folding steps needed for evaluation. The code uses (>>) instead of the do notation because in this case it leads to much more concise code.

```
factorialSteps :: Integer -> Writer (Sum Integer) Integer
factorialSteps n = foldM (\f x -> tell (Sum 1) >> return (f*x)) 1 [1 .. n]
```

The last function in the walk-through is filterM, which filters some values on the list based on a monadic predicate. It's folklore in the Haskell community to use filterM and the list monad to provide a concise definition of a function returning the *powerset* of a list.

```
powerset :: [a] -> [[a]]
powerset = filterM (\_ -> [False,True])
```

This function works by using at its core the nondeterministic nature of computations under the list monad. Instead of returning merely True or False as whether to include an element in the filtered list, the powerset function uses an expression that returns both choices (these can be seen more clearly if you rewrite [False,True] to return False `mplus` return True). All the possible choices for each of the elements will create a set of possible states: one for each subset of the original list.

In addition to mapM, forM, sequence, foldM, and filterM, there are other functions such as zipWithM and replicateM that behave as counterparts of list functions and that can be useful in a wide variety of situations. I encourage you to read their documentation in Hackage.

LIFTM AND AP

In the previous chapter, you saw how every monad admits a function called `liftM` of type `Monad m => (a -> b) -> m a -> m b`. This function allows you to convert any pure function into a function working on a monad (usually called *lifting*). As you already saw, this makes every `Monad` a `Functor`. This goes on until you find a function with more than one parameter that you want to be lifted. For that case, the `Control.Monad` module provides the functions `liftM2`, `liftM3`, and so on, which convert into monadic form functions with two, three, or more arguments.

However, it seems that the need of a family of functions, one for each number of arguments, is not very coherent with the elegance that Haskell code usually has. One would expect a solution that works for every number of arguments.

This solution exists, and it's called ap. This function has type `Monad m => m (a -> b) -> m a -> m b`. This small change in signature allows you to chain several of these functions together. For example, say you want to lift the `compare` function. First, you wrap the entire function into a monad to satisfy the type of the first argument. You do so via the following:

```
Prelude> :t return compare
return compare :: (Monad m, Ord a) => m (a -> a -> Ordering)
```

Next, you use ap to feed the first argument. Then, you get back another function that expects one parameter less. You can think of ap as a replacement of (`$`) when using monads. So, assuming x has type m a, then you get this:

```
return compare `ap` x :: (Monad m, Ord a) => m (a -> Ordering)
```

Finally, you can use ap again to feed the last argument and get the final result.

As a rule of thumb, you can replace any call of the form `liftMn f x1 x2 ... xn` by returning `f `ap` x1 `ap` x2 `ap` ... `ap` xn`. The ability to do so will play an important role in another important Haskell type class, `Applicative`, which will be introduced in Chapter 10.

Monad Comprehensions

The similarity between list comprehension syntax and do notation is not a coincidence. Indeed, in the olden days of Haskell, back in 1992, Philip Wadler proposed a general syntax that worked for any monad. However, it was decided to keep the do notation for arbitrary monads separate and to use comprehension syntax only for lists. In 2011, redesigned monad comprehensions were introduced in the GHC compiler, which can be enabled using the MonadComprehensions extension.

The best way to understand the monad comprehension syntax is by comparing it to the do notation, which should be familiar to you at this point. The first translation rule says that generators in a syntax comprehension correspond to bindings in do notation. Or more easily, e <- m is kept as is between both syntaxes. The expression at the beginning of the comprehension is translated into a call to return in do notation. With these two rules, you can translate the example with Maybe in the previous chapter, which read as follows:

```
purchaseValueWithDo :: Integer -> Maybe Double
purchaseValueWithDo purchaseId
  = do n         <- numberItemsByPurchaseId purchaseId
       productId <- productIdByPurchaseId purchaseId
       price     <- priceByProductId productId
       return $ fromInteger n * price
```

into comprehension syntax as follows:

```
{-# LANGUAGE MonadComprehensions #-}
purchaseValueWithDo :: Integer -> Maybe Double
purchaseValueWithDo purchaseId =
  [ fromInteger n * price
  | n         <- numberItemsByPurchaseId purchaseId
  , productId <- productIdByPurchaseId purchaseId
  , price     <- priceByProductId productId ]
```

On the other hand, you have seen that comprehensions allow for a much richer syntax than merely generators. Monad comprehensions can also be used with that other syntax, but in many cases doing so requires the monad to implement a type class stronger than a mere Monad. Guards are an example and are translated into calls to the guard function, so the expression must be wrapped in a MonadPlus instance. Here's an example:

```
[ price | price <- priceByProductId productId, price > 5.0 ]
```

The previous code would be translated into the following:

```
do price <- priceByProductId productId
   guard price > 5.0
   return price
```

Grouping and parallel comprehensions also require a monad that instantiates the MonadGroup (providing mgroupWith) and MonadZip (providing mzip) type classes, respectively. However, these instances are provided in the Haskell Platform only for the list monad, and third-party packages implement only those type classes for data types that resemble that structure (such as database tables), so I won't delve into more detail at this point.

Transformations are a bit tricky to understand with list comprehensions. In general, an expression such as [g x1 ... xn | x1 <- m1, ..., xn <- mn, then f by e] is translated into the following:

```
do (x1, ..., xn) <- f (\(x1, ..., xn) -> e)
                      (do x1 <- m1
                           ...
                          xn <- mn
                          return (x1, ..., xn))
   return g x1 ... xn
```

This code is quite complex, but it can help you to understand why a complex expression works. For example, in Chapter 3 you can find the following expression: [x*y | x <- [-1,1,-2], y <- [1,2,3], then sortWith by x]. Using the translation rules, this expression is equivalent to the following:

```
do (x, y) <- sortWith (\(x, y) -> x)
                      (do x <- [-1,1,2], y <- [1,2,3], return (x,y))
   return $ x*y
```

These translations (even when in appearance they are just different ways to tell the same thing and thus repetitive) can help by shedding light on what monads really are and on their relation to other computational structures. For example, if you know Scala, you may be aware that an expression such as the following:

```
for (x <- List(-1,1,2) ; y <- List(1,2,3)  if x < y) yield x*y
```

is translated by the compiler as follows. Consider that Scala uses object-oriented notation, so map and flatMap are written as methods of the lists, and anonymous functions are introduced with => instead of ->.

```
List(-1,1,2).flatMap(x => List(1,2,3).withFilter(y => x < y).map(y => x*y))
```

What you can see here is that the idea is the same as monad comprehensions in Haskell. The main difference between both languages is that Scala decided to model monad-like structures using flatMap, which is equivalent to the join combinator introduced at the beginning of the chapter. But, as you saw earlier, both definitions are equivalent.

You can find monad ideas in other, unexpected places. For example, recent versions of C# introduce a SQL-like syntax. In the language reference, you'll find a translation from this syntax to standard function calls. One of the important methods involved in such translation is SelectMany, whose signature is as follows:

```
public static IEnumerable<TResult> SelectMany<TSource, TResult>
  ( this IEnumerable<TSource> source
  , Func<TSource, IEnumerable<TResult>> selector )
```

The syntax is a bit verbose, but it can be easily understood. The type parameters to parametric types are given between < and >. Furthermore, all type parameters in a method signature must be given explicitly (that's why you have <TSource, TResult> after the method name). There's no special syntax for the function type; it's just called Func. So, if I had to translate this signature into Haskell, it would read as follows:

```
selectMany :: IEnumerable TSource
              -> (TSource -> IEnumerable TResult)
              -> IEnumerable TResult
```

But this is just the type signature of the (>>=) monad function! This shows you can also come to monads starting with basic SQL syntax. Indeed, this SQL-like syntax is now used in ways that were not expected at the beginning, such as for managing tasks, but that makes sense when you consider their relation to monads.

My hope with these last examples in other languages is that you relate one of the core concepts in Haskell, the monad, to what you may already know from your programming experience in other languages.

Combining Monads

In this chapter and the previous one, I've been careful about selecting examples that use only one monad (even RWS, which works as a union of Reader, Writer, and State, is just one single monad). It's clear, though, that in some cases you will need the combination of several monads to architect your code. There are many algorithms that are better explained as a combination of State for keeping some internal data and the possibility of failure that Maybe gives you. In this section, you will see how monads can be combined, with a special focus on *monad transformers.*

In some cases, you could roll your own monad combination. Let's take as an example a function that will get all possible paths between two points in a graph (like the paths function introduced earlier) but will manage the path as the output of a Writer monad.

```
import Control.Monad
import Control.Monad.Writer
pathsWriter :: [(Int,Int)] -> Int -> Int -> [[Int]]
pathsWriter edges start end = map execWriter (pathsWriter' edges start end)
pathsWriter' :: [(Int,Int)] -> Int -> Int -> [Writer [Int] ()]
pathsWriter' edges start end =
  let e_paths = do (e_start, e_end) <- edges
                   guard $ e_start == start
                   subpath <- pathsWriter' edges e_end end
                   return $ do tell [start]
                               subpath
  in if start == end then tell [start] : e_paths else e_paths
```

Notice two things in this code. First, it uses the Monoid instance of lists and uses it in the Writer. Second, you must explicitly manage the change in monad. You can see that clearly in this code because there is a nested do block. In this case, this block is just creating a new Writer computation by telling the start year before executing the Writer computation for a subpath. Finally, you also need to manually consider how to execute the computations that were created; in this case, the solution has been to map execWriter over every element returned by pathsWriter'.

In this case, the code is still quite readable, and the places where you use each monad are clearly delimited (the first part of the do block uses the list monad to span several possible paths, and the Writer part is confined to the nested block). However, if the code turns more complex, you may need to manually call execWriter in the middle of the code and feed the resulting state from that computation into the next Writer block. Clearly, a better solution is needed for monad composition.

Monad Transformers

Monad transformers are the preferred way in Haskell to combine the effect of several monads into a new one. Other approaches to combining computational effects (failure, state, etc.) have been (and continue to be) proposed, but transformers continue to be the most used option. The transformers and mtl packages (short for Monad Transformer Library) have hundreds of packages depending on them. In short, a monad transformer takes some *base monad* and transforms it into a *new monad* with some extra computational effects. For example, in the previous code, I used the type [Writer [Int] ()], which can be seen as the list monad [()] (which adds nondeterminism) being transformed to add extra output (in the form of the Writer [Int] monad). Formally, a monad transformer is a data type with the following structure:

MonadT e_1 ... e_n m a

Let's go element by element through the general transformer type to understand the common structure:

- MonadT is the name of the monad transformer. It usually coincides with the name of the monad whose effects the transformer adds. For example, StateT adds state functionality to other monads, ListT adds nondeterminism, ReaderT adds a read-only context, and so on.

- e1 ... en represent any extra type variables that the monad transformer may need. In most cases, it is none, like MaybeT or ListT, or just one, like the transformers for state that need the type of the internal state; but in some cases, like the RWST transformer, it needs more (RWST needs one for read-only context, one for write-only output, and one for state).

- Then the monad to be transformed or wrapped (both terms are used interchangeably) comes in the position of the m type variable.

- The result of MonadT e1 ... en m must be a monad itself, so it takes an extra parameter a to make it of kind * -> *, as expected.

As a result of this structure, a monad obtained by transformation looks a lot like an onion, with an inner monad in its heart and several layers adding extra functionality to this base monad. The downside of this is that computations in an inner layer must be "brought up" until you reach the outermost layer. This functionality is provided by the only function of the MonadTrans type class, which is the class of all monad transformers, named lift.

```haskell
class MonadTrans t where
  lift :: Monad m => m a -> t m a
```

For example, if you want to translate the previous code into using monad transformers, you must include a lift in the access to the edges argument in order to use the do notation. With that extra call, the type changes into the monad used in the example.

```haskell
lift edges :: WriterT [Int] [] ()
```

This way, you can rewrite the example using monad transformers. Check how the nested do block has disappeared. As explained earlier, a lift on edges was needed; but notice how it is not needed when using tell because this is functionality in the outermost layer of the monad. Also, the code was changed to use the MonadPlus function mplus instead of the more concrete (:) list constructor.

```haskell
import Control.Monad.Writer
pathsWriterT' :: [(Int,Int)] -> Int -> Int -> WriterT [Int] [] ()
pathsWriterT' edges start end =
  let e_paths = do (e_start, e_end) <- lift edges
                   guard $ e_start == start
                   tell [start]
                   pathsWriterT' edges e_end end
  in if start == end then tell [start] `mplus` e_paths else e_paths
```

Like with other monads, each monad transformer has a corresponding function for running the computation given the extra information that such a monad would need. In this example, instead of execWriter, the code uses execWriterT, which returns the write-only output wrapped in the inner monad, in this case, a list.

```haskell
pathsWriterT :: [(Int,Int)] -> Int -> Int -> [[Int]]
pathsWriterT edges start end = execWriterT (pathsWriterT' edges start end)
```

One important thing to remember is that monad transformers are not *commutative*. That is, the computational effect of the resulting monad depends on the other transformations. For example, the monad StateT s [] can represent those nondeterministic computations where each of the paths has a different result and a different internal state. But ListT (State s) represents those computations where several results can be returned, but the state is shared among all the branches.

One rule of thumb is that effects are stacked intuitively in reverse order in which they appear in the transformer onion. This coincides to the previous description: StateT s [] first adds state to the mix and then the results with state are wrapped into nondeterminism, whereas ListT (State s) first adds nondeterminism to the result and then a state to the whole.

Consider the following example that combines Reader and Writer, the former being the outer layer (and thus requiring a lift for using tell, which works on the Writer layer):

```
import Control.Monad.Reader
readerWriterExample :: ReaderT Int (Writer String) Int
readerWriterExample = do x <- ask
                         lift . tell $ show x
                         return $ x + 1
```

The aforementioned fact that effects are stacked in reverse order can be seen when you execute the function. The outer call corresponds to runWriter (which is the inner monad), and the inner call is for runReaderT (which "peels" one layer).

```
*Chapter7.CombiningMonads> runWriter (runReaderT readerWriterExample 3)
(4,"3")
```

Exercise 7-6 helps you understand how lifting works in an example case that uses a complex monad stack and learn more about the order in which effects are stacked.

EXERCISE 7-6. TWO STATES AT A TIME

Write a function that computes the factorial of a number. But instead of the usual implementation, use one based on two states: one for keeping a decreasing counter and another one for keeping the factorial. One approach is to keep the state as a tuple, but for this exercise I want you to implement the state using a StateT Integer (State Integer) monad. Thus, you must use `lift` to access one of the internal states. The final code to run the monad computation should be similar to `execState (execStateT factorial x) 1`.

Table 7-1 shows the way each of the most common monads is represented internally and how the monad transformer changes a base monad `m`. This information will be the key to understanding the previous example with list and state.

Table 7-1. *Commonly Used Monads and Their Associated Transformers*

Monad	Transformer	Internal Repr.	Transformation	Description
Identity	IdentityT	A	m a	Represents no transformation.
[]	ListT	[a]	m [a]	Represents nondeterminism. As mentioned, for more control over the search strategy, use `Logic` and `LogicT` from package `logict`.
Maybe	MaybeT	Maybe a	m (Maybe a)	Represents computations that may fail. This transformer is not found in `mtl` but in a separate package `MaybeT`.
Reader r	ReaderT r	r -> a	r -> m a	A read-only context of type `r` is available.
Writer w	WriterT w	(a, w)	m (a, w)	Computation outputs a write-only value of type `w`, where `w` must be a `Monoid`.
State s	StateT s	s -> (a, s)	s -> m (a, s)	An internal state of type `s` is kept internally.

To use this table, take the monad onion you want to describe. Apply the rules recursively, replacing the type variable `m` in each case with the inner monad. For example, let's do it to describe the differences between `StateT s Maybe` and `MaybeT` `(State s)`:

- `StateT s Maybe a = s -> Maybe (a, s)`, so the failure affects both the result and the state. The entire computation fails or not.

- MaybeT (State s) a = (State s) (Maybe a) = s -> (Maybe a, s), where the failure affects only the result, not the internal state being kept.

You have surely noticed the inclusion of a monad called Identity (which is available in module Control.Monad.Identity) that I hadn't introduced previously. This monad adds no effect to the computation. return is the identity, and binding is the mere function application. The purpose of this monad is to serve as the innermost monad of the onion, which allows you to build the entire stack of monads using only monad transformers. For example, in the mtl package, Reader r is actually defined as ReaderT r Identity.

Monad Classes

Up to this point, the transformers functionality is available in both the transformers and mtl packages. But the mtl package is built in a clever way and includes a type class hierarchy to eliminate the need of most calls to lift. In that way, working with transformers is no more difficult than using monads built from scratch.

As an example, take the Reader monad. The basic operations with this monad are ask, local, and reader, which are the functions to be generalized (others, such as asks, can be written using them). In the Control.Monad.Reader, you can find the MonadReader type class, which consists of those functions.

```
class Monad m => MonadReader r m | m -> r where
  ask    :: m r
  local  :: (r -> r) -> m a -> m a
  reader :: (r -> a) -> m a
```

Note   In the type class declaration, you can see an extra bit of information: m -> r. This is called a functional dependency and will be discussed in detail in Chapter 13.

Then, mtl defines instances of MonadReader for every combination of monad transformers, which include ReaderT as a layer. Using them, you don't need to write explicit lift for using ask, local, and the rest of context handling functions. The same combination of a type class and several instances is defined for the rest of monad transformers: MonadWriter, MonadState, and MonadLogic (MonadLogic lives in the logict package). The type class corresponding to the functionality in lists and Maybe is obtained through MonadPlus.

For example, if you work with transformers using the mtl package, you can rewrite the previous example without the explicit call to lift for accessing the Writer layer, as follows:

```
readerWriterExample :: ReaderT Int (Writer String) Int
readerWriterExample = do x <- ask
                         tell $ show x
                         return $ x + 1
```

But those type classes help not only by lowering the need of calls to lift but also by enabling you to give type signatures that cover a certain structure of monad layers as well as any of them that supports some amount of functionality. Here's an example. Say you want to include the previous readerWriterExample function in your utilities library, and you do so using the type signature given previously. What you would get is a function with an over-concrete example. You will be able to run the function using only the exact combination of monads stated in the signature. But the code you've written supports being run in any "onion" given that it includes the functionality of ReaderT and WriterT. Thus, you should strive for generality, something you can gain by using monad classes instead of an explicit stack.

```
readerWriterExample :: (MonadReader Int m, MonadWriter String m) => m Int
readerWriterExample = do x <- ask
                         tell $ show x
                         return $ x + 1
```

Note   The preceding code needs the FlexibleContexts extension to be enabled. Otherwise, you get an error Non type-variable argument in the constraint: MonadReader Int m. The reason is that the Haskell standard does not admit a ground type like Int to appear in a constraint; the aforementioned extension drops this restriction.

The important part is the one shown in bold. The information about monadic functionality used inside the function is encoded in the type class constraints. In the example, m represents a monad, which supports both Reader and Writer functionality.

To show that this code is indeed general, the following interpreter session runs the same monadic function using both the ReaderT Int (Writer String) and the RWS Int String Int monad (here, the state part is not used, but it's still a monad that supports the operations from MonadReader and MonadWriter):

```
*Chapter7.CombiningMonads> runWriter (runReaderT readerWriterExample 3)
(4,"3")
*Chapter7.CombiningMonads> runRWS readerWriterExample 3 0
(4,0,"3")
```

Thus, if you need to expose a function that produces a monadic value, instead of using an explicit monad (such as Reader, Writer, etc.), it is better to program against the corresponding type class. In that way, you get much better reusability because the users of your library can use any transformed monad they want whenever it has the corresponding functionality embedded.

TRANSFORMERS VS. MTL

As stated at the beginning of the section, there are two different packages in the Haskell Platform that support monad transformers. The transformers package is the core one; it provides all the monad transformers and the MonadTrans type class. The mtl package includes that functionality, plus the monad classes. If you are exporting functions whose type includes monads, you should try using the monad classes and thus mtl.

The examples in this section are to be used with mtl. If you want to use transformers instead, you need to change the imports from Control.Monad.Something to Control. Monad.Trans.Something.

In Exercise 7-7, you'll create a function paths that uses several monad transformers. Remember to program it using the corresponding type classes like I have just explained.

EXERCISE 7-7. PATHS ON MONAD TRANSFORMERS

Write a new version of `pathsWriter` that holds the graph in a read-only context. This means you need to use functionality from both `MonadReader` (for handling the graph) and `MonadWriter` (for handling the paths) wrapping the base list monad. To check that the function is general, use two different monads to provide the requested functionality: `ReaderT r (WriterT w [])` a and `RWST r w s a`.

I want to stress the importance of monad transformers for the Haskell programmer. It's common to design a monad stack for your application and add or remove layers during the development process. However, this doesn't mean your code should become tangled spaghetti where every function calls any monad functionality. The `mtl` solution for abstraction using type classes allows you to explicitly tell which monad layers are used in each function, leading to better composability and higher reusability.

Summary

This chapter went deeper into the notion of monad, which was introduced in the previous chapter.

- The chapter explained the *list monad*, which models nondeterministic computations that may return more than one value. You saw how this monad can be used to implement search problems.

- In cases where the list monad doesn't give enough control over the search, the `Logic` monad can implement fair conjunction and disjunction.

- You learned about an important extension of `Monad`, called `MonadPlus`, which allows you to model failure and choice. Using its functions `mzero` and `mplus`, you now know how to implement the Apriori rule-learning algorithm.

- The chapter covered a high-level view of monad utility functions, such as `sequence`, `mapM`, and so on.

- You learned how the *comprehension* syntax can be generalized to work on any monad with the `MonadComprehensions` GHC extension. This enabled you to relate Haskell monads with other notions in Scala and C#.

- Finally, you learned how to combine monads using *monad transformers*.

CHAPTER 8

Working in Several Cores

One of the main advantages of the purity that Haskell embodies is the ability to run code in parallel easily. The absence of side effects means that all data dependencies are explicit in the code. Thus, the compiler (and you) can schedule different tasks with no dependencies between them to be performed in parallel.

The Par monad enables you to make explicit which parts of your code would benefit from being run in parallel. The model supported by Par allows you to write code using both the *futures* model and the *dataflow parallelism* approach. Then, a scheduler takes care of running your code using parallel threads. Par is a powerful abstraction because you don't need to take care of managing the creation and destruction of threads; just let the library do what it does.

In some cases, though, several parallel tasks need to share resources in a way not expressible using Par. In the Time Machine Store, for example, several clients may be buying some items, which implies that several database updates will be happening at the same time. In those scenarios, ensuring that the resources are accessed concurrently in the right way is essential. Haskell features *Software Transactional Memory* as the way to control this behavior, using the idea of transactions brought from database systems.

Finally, you may want to split the computation between several nodes that are distributed across a network. One of the many ways to communicate those nodes is to use a *message queue*. In this chapter, we look at how to use AMQP, a message queuing protocol, to exchange simple messages.

Parallelism, Concurrency, and Distribution

There's always some confusion between the terms *parallel programming*, *concurrent programming*, and *distributed programming*. *Concurrency* is a programming model where the computation is designed as several, mostly independent, threads of control. The system may either interweave the computations or run them in parallel, but in

269

© Alejandro Serrano Mena 2022
A. Serrano Mena, *Practical Haskell*, https://doi.org/10.1007/978-1-4842-8581-7_8

any case the illusion is that all of them work asynchronously. One archetypal example of a concurrent application is a web server. Many clients request services at the same time, and from programmers' point of view, each of these requests is independent and happens asynchronously.

In most cases, those threads need access to some shared resource. At this point, you must ensure that concurrent access does not leave the system in an inconsistent way. For that purpose, many programming techniques have been developed, including locks, semaphores, and channels. In the case of Haskell, a model called *Software Transactional Memory* (STM) brings the concept of atomic transactions from databases into your code to enable optimistic concurrency with rollback.

Parallelism refers to a way of executing code in more than one computer core at once. Concurrent tasks are often run in parallel to achieve much better performance. This increment in speed can also be applied to tasks that were not thought of as concurrent but whose data dependencies enable running parts of the algorithm independently of each other. Think of the QuickSort algorithm for sorting: at each step, the list is divided into two parts, and each of them is sorted separately. In this case, the subsequent sorting of the two lists can be made in parallel.

For this second case, Haskell is the perfect field. Pure computations can't interfere with each other, and their data dependencies are completely explicit. The Par monad, which will be introduced later, follows this line of thought and enables parallelism for tasks.

In many cases, the confusion between parallelism and concurrency comes from languages with side effects. In languages such as Java or C, any piece of code can access and change global state. For that reason, any amount of parallelism must also take care of the access to those shared resources and thus is required for concurrent programming. You cannot really separate both in that context.

Parallel programming is usually associated with running tasks in different cores (microprocessors or GPUs) on the same computer system. But the work can also be split between different computers that communicate across a network. That's where *distributed programming* comes into play. Since each of the actors in the system is independent from any other, the coordination of tasks must happen in a different way from one-system parallel programming. Furthermore, communication through a network imposes constraints in case of failure or big latency. For all these reasons, distributed programming needs other techniques.

One of the biggest challenges is to ensure reliable communication: in a network, messages may be lost, duplicated, or come out of order. In some cases, routing messages to different actors or choosing an actor among an available pool is required to perform efficiently. A standard approach to this problem is to introduce an intermediate *message broker*. AMQP is a common protocol for dealing with message queues. There are several implementations; RabbitMQ is a widely used one. The `amqp-worker` package provides a simple interface for exchanging messages via this protocol and leverages several Haskell-specific techniques.

Tip   "Concurrency is about *dealing* with lots of things at once. Parallelism is about *doing* a lot of things at once." – Rob Pike

---

The fields of parallel, concurrent, and distributed programming in Haskell are much wider than what will be shown in this chapter. The libraries explained here can be used in many other ways, and many other packages are available in Hackage. For parallel programming, you have the `parallel` package, which features the strategy approach. Parallelism is not only available for processors. Accelerate builds code to be run in a GPU. Haskell's `base` package features low-level functionality for concurrency in the `Control.Concurrent` module, including mutable memory locations (`MVars`) and semaphores. The `distributed-process` set of packages introduces Erlang-style actors which can share both code and data. The book *Parallel and Concurrent Programming in Haskell* by Simon Marlow describes several of these techniques in much more depth than this chapter.

The Par Monad

This section will focus on the parallel programming package called `monad-par`. The functions in that library revolve around the `Par` monad and the use of `IVars` for communication results. As you will see, computation can be modeled in two ways with this package: as futures or as dataflow programs.

Futures

Let's start with a simple task that aims to produce the factorization into primes of several numbers. The algorithm for factorizing one number is simple. You try to divide by increasing natural numbers. If at some point the division has zero remainder, that number is a prime factor. Thus, the original number can be divided by that prime factor, and the process can start over again. If at some point you reach the same number you started with, that means you've reached the last prime factor. In Haskell, the code for that approach reads as follows:

```
findFactors :: Integer -> [Integer]
findFactors 1 = [1]
findFactors n = let oneFactor = findFactor n 2
                in oneFactor : (findFactors $ n `div` oneFactor)

findFactor :: Integer -> Integer -> Integer
findFactor n m | n == m        = n
               | n `mod` m == 0 = m
               | otherwise      = findFactor n (m + 1)
```

At some point in the program, you'll be asked to factorize two different numbers. The code for such a function is straightforward to write.

```
findTwoFactors :: Integer -> Integer -> ([Integer],[Integer])
findTwoFactors x y = (findFactors x, findFactors y)
```

However, the efficiency of this function won't be very high. Even in the case where more than one processor is available, the computation of the prime factors of x and of y will be done sequentially (assuming that they will be fully evaluated at the same time). You would aim for computing findFactors x at the same time as findFactors y, as Figure 8-1 shows.

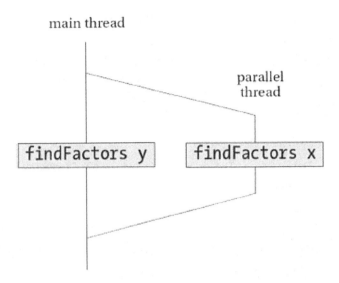

Figure 8-1. *Parallel computation of two prime factorizations*

You can easily tell the system to run both findFactors calls in parallel by using the monad-par package. In Control.Monad.Par, there's a function called spawnP. Let's look closely at its type.

```
spawnP :: NFData a => a -> Par (IVar a)
```

The purpose of spawnP is just running a computation in parallel with the rest of the program. However, there are three things to notice from that signature. First, it requires the computation to be run to have a type supporting the NFData type class. If you remember, this is a type found in the deepseq package, which ensures that the computation is fully evaluated. spawnP imposes this constraint because it's the only way to ensure that the code will actually run in parallel. If that constraint wasn't there, the lazy evaluation model may make it run at any other time, losing the benefit of parallelism. Since the use of spawnP fully determines when some computation will be executed, the parallel model of monad-par is called *deterministic*.

The second thing you may notice is that the result is wrapped inside Par. This type is the monad in which parallelism is run. Finally, instead of just a value, the result of spawnP is an IVar. An IVar is a *future*, a promise that the result of the computation will be available when requested. To get the result of the computation inside an IVar, you must call the get function. This function returns immediately if the computation has finished or blocks execution until the result is available. This is the same model used in Scala or in the Task Parallel Library in C#.

You can call spawnP and get only inside the Par monad. To run all the tasks, you call runPar with the whole trace of parallelism. A version of findTwoFactors that spawns a parallel task for computing the factors of x while keeping the factorization of y in the current thread would read as such:

```
import Control.DeepSeq
import Control.Monad.Par

findTwoFactors :: Integer -> Integer -> ([Integer],[Integer])
findTwoFactors x y = runPar $ do
  factorsXVar <- spawnP $ findFactors x
  let factorsY = findFactors y
      _        = rnf factorsY
  factorsX <- get factorsXVar
  return (factorsX, factorsY)
```

Notice the call to rnf from the deepseq library to fully evaluate the factorization of y.

Following these steps does not immediately result in parallel tasks being created; you need to follow two extra steps. First, you must compile your program with the *threaded runtime*, which enables GHC to create code that uses several threads. To do so, add the –threaded options in the Cabal file.

```
executable chapter8
  hs-source-dirs:  src
  main-is:         Main.hs
  build-depends:   base >= 4, monad-par, deepseq
  ghc-options:     -Wall -threaded
```

In addition, you have to pass options to your program for using several cores. Remember that when using cabal or stack, you need to add two dashes before the options that are passed to the executable.

```
$ cabal run chapter8 -- +RTS -N2
```

The +RTS option indicates the start of the options given to the Haskell runtime. In particular, -N2 indicates that two processors should be used. You can indicate at most the number of processors in your system. If you like, you can specify –N by itself, without a number, and allow the Haskell runtime to make the decision on the number of processors to use.

Dataflow Parallelism with IVars

The monad-par package not only provides futures but also a wider model of declaring parallel computations. Instead of just spawning parallel computations, you specify several steps of computation, which share intermediate results via IVars. These variables are created via new. Tasks can write to an IVar via the put function and obtain a result via get. Notice that an IVar is a write-once variable.

Let's consider the example of building a letter for a client with their bill of a product. There will be four different tasks. One will search the client information in the database, and another one will do the same for a product. Each of these tasks will communicate with the other tasks using corresponding IVars. The other two tasks will take that information and generate the text of the letter and the text of the envelope. Figure 8-2 shows the graph.

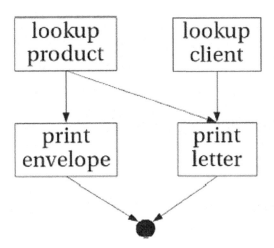

Figure 8-2. *Dataflow graph of letter building*

Computations built in this way always follow the shape of a graph of tasks joined by IVars to communicate. For that reason, the model is called *dataflow programming*. The main benefit of this approach is that all data dependencies are explicit; they are exactly those specified by the IVars. The monad-par library takes advantage of that information for scheduling the tasks in a parallel way.

The following code implements the dataflow graph of Figure 8-2. Notice that when using this model and IVars, instead of spawnP, one uses fork, which expects a computation of type Par ().

```
printTicket :: Int -> Int -> [(Int,String)] -> [(Int,String)] -> String
printTicket idC idP clients products = runPar $ do
  clientV  <- new
  productV <- new
  fork $ lookupPar clientV  idC clients
  fork $ lookupPar productV idP products
  envV     <- new
  letterV <- new
  fork $ printEnvelope clientV envV
  fork $ printLetter   clientV productV letterV
  envS    <- get envV
  letterS <- get letterV
  return $ envS ++ "\n\n" ++ letterS

lookupPar :: (Eq a, NFData b) => IVar (Maybe b) -> a -> [(a,b)] -> Par ()
lookupPar i _ []                   = put i Nothing
lookupPar i x ((k,v):r) | x == k    = put i $ Just v
                        | otherwise = lookupPar i x r

printEnvelope :: IVar (Maybe String) -> IVar String -> Par ()
printEnvelope clientV envV = do
  clientName <- get clientV
  case clientName of
    Nothing -> put envV "Unknown"
    Just n  -> put envV $ "To: " ++ n

printLetter :: IVar (Maybe String) -> IVar (Maybe String)
            -> IVar String -> Par ()
printLetter clientV productV letterV = do
  clientName  <- get clientV
  productName <- get productV
  case (clientName, productName) of
    (Nothing, Nothing) -> put letterV "Unknown"
    (Just n,  Nothing) -> put letterV $ n ++ " bought something"
    (Nothing, Just p)  -> put letterV $ "Someone bought " ++ p
    (Just n,  Just p)  -> put letterV $ n ++ " bought " ++ p
```

One interesting benefit of separating the dataflow dependencies from the actual parallel execution is that several strategies for scheduling the tasks can be used. By default, monad-par uses the so-called Direct scheduler. Two others are available; just import Control.Monad.Par.Scheds.Spark or Control.Monad.Par.Scheds.Trace instead of Control.Monad.Par, and the corresponding scheduler will be used.

Parallelizing the Apriori Algorithm

Let's finish this section by looking at how the Apriori algorithm could be enhanced to perform in parallel. The code will be based on the implementation in Chapter 7.

If you're working with lists, the monad-par package includes a parMap function. The purpose of this function is executing a function over each element of the list, parallelizing each of the applications. Spawning a task for each element may seem overkill, but the scheduler will take into account the number of cores available in the system. To apply this parMap function, let's first rewrite generateL1 from the monadic style to explicit calls to map and concatMap. The following code is completely equivalent to that in Chapter 7:

```
generateL1 minSupp transactions =
  let c1 = noDups $
          concatMap (\(Transaction t) ->
                      map (FrequentSet . S.singleton) $ S.toList t)
                  transactions
      l1NotFiltered
        = map (\fs -> (fs, setSupport transactions fs > minSupp)) c1
  in concatMap (\(fs,b) -> if b then [fs] else []) l1NotFiltered
```

Since most of the time in the algorithm is spent in calculating supports, this is the part that has been chosen for parallel execution. Beforehand, calculating supports was done inside filter, which both computed the support and decided whether to keep a transaction in the list. Now those two tasks are split: set supports are computed at l1NotFiltered, and then deciding whether to include an element is done in the final concatMap. Afterward, you need only to change map to parMap and wrap the entire computation with runPar to take advantage of dataflow parallelism in the Apriori algorithm. The result in this case is as follows:

```
generateL1 minSupp transactions = runPar $ do
```

```
let c1 = noDups $
         concatMap (\(Transaction t) ->
                       map (FrequentSet . S.singleton) $ S.toList t)
                 transactions
    l1NotFiltered
      <- parMap (\fs -> (fs, setSupport transactions fs > minSupp)) c1
    return $ concatMap (\(fs,b) -> if b then [fs] else []) l1NotFiltered
```

Note   Remember that to use monad-par, your data types must
instantiate NFData.

In some cases, this may not be the best strategy for creating parallel tasks. Instead
of parMap, you can divide the list in halves until you reach some minimal length.
Once the list is small enough, it's better to execute the mapping in a sequential way
because creating parallel tasks has some overhead. This is done in a new version of the
generateNextLk function.

```
generateNextLk :: Double -> [Transaction] -> (Int, [FrequentSet])
               -> Maybe ([FrequentSet], (Int, [FrequentSet]))
generateNextLk _ _ (_, []) = Nothing
generateNextLk minSupp transactions (k, lk) =
  let ck1 = noDups $ [ FrequentSet $ a `S.union` b
                     | FrequentSet a <- lk, FrequentSet b <- lk
                     , S.size (a `S.intersection` b) == k - 1 ]
      lk1 = runPar $ filterLk minSupp transactions ck1
  in Just (lk1, (k+1, lk1))

filterLk :: Double -> [Transaction] -> [FrequentSet] -> Par [FrequentSet]
filterLk minSupp transactions ck =
  let lengthCk = length ck
  in if lengthCk <= 5
     then return $ filter (\fs -> setSupport transactions fs > minSup) ck
     else let (l,r) = splitAt (lengthCk `div` 2) ck
          in do lVar <- spawn $ filterLk minSupp transactions l
                lFiltered <- get lVar
```

```
rVar <- spawn $ filterLk minSupp transactions r
rFiltered <- get rVar
return $ lFiltered ++ rFiltered
```

As you can see, the monad-par library makes it easy to add parallelism to your current code. The focus of this library is futures and dataflow programming. There are other approaches, though. The parallel library, for example, uses another monad called Eval that helps to define how a specific data structure can be traversed in parallel. You can find more information about this and other packages on the Haskell wiki.[1]

PARALLELIZING TASKS WITH SIDE EFFECTS

Computation with arbitrary side effects hasn't been introduced yet. However, as a reference, it's interesting to know that the monad-par package provides another monad for parallelism, called ParIO and available in the Control.Monad.Par.IO module, in which side effects are allowed. The interface is the same as pure Par, except for running the computation, which is achieved via the runParIO function.

Note that the implementation does not guarantee any ordering on the execution of the tasks, and thus the outcome will show nondeterministic ordering of the side effects.

Many algorithms that work on lists or have a divide-and-conquer skeleton can be easily turned into parallel algorithms via the monad-par library. In Exercise 8-1, you're asked to do this with the other data mining algorithm introduced in this book: K-means.

EXERCISE 8-1. PARALLEL K-MEANS

Write a parallel version of the K-means algorithm developed in Chapter 6. To make the task a bit easier, you may look at the first implementation, which didn't use monads. Remember, when using functions such as parMap, think about when the overhead of creating parallel tasks will exceed the benefits.

---

[1] See, for example, wiki.haskell.org/Applications_and_libraries/
Concurrency_and_parallelism.

Software Transactional Memory

In this section, you will look at problems where several threads of execution interact with each other and share resources; that is, *concurrency* comes into play. Haskell allows you to design concurrent tools in the classical way, using locks, semaphores, and so on, but in this section you will see how the functional style of programming enables you to use a much more powerful abstraction called *Software Transactional Memory*.

Before starting, you should be aware that code using concurrency is considered side-effect code. When several threads are executing asynchronously and sharing resources, the order in which they do this affects the observable outcome. In contrast, in pure code the order in which functions are evaluated is irrelevant because the result will be the same.

You will learn more about how to deal with arbitrary side effects in the next chapter. For the time being, you just need to know that Haskell uses a special monad called IO, in which you can use side effects. In the code, the only difference you will see between programming with and without side effects is that do notation is used.

Concurrent Use of Resources

Let's begin the journey through concurrent programming in Haskell with a simple example: a simulation of several clients buying products from the store. In the first approximation, only the change in the money that the Time Machine Store has earned will be considered. The code to create these three threads is as follows:

```haskell
import Control.Concurrent

main :: IO ()
main = do v <- newMVar 10000
          forkIO $ updateMoney v
          forkIO $ updateMoney v
          forkIO $ updateMoney v
          _ <- getLine
          return ()

updateMoney :: MVar Integer -> IO ()
updateMoney v = do m <- takeMVar v
                   putStrLn $ "Updating value, which is " ++ show m
                   putMVar v (m + 500)   -- suppose a constant price
```

The first thing you need to know is how to create a new thread of execution. You achieve this via the forkIO function in the Control.Concurrent module. This function takes as an argument an action of type IO () and starts executing that code in parallel.

Note   forkIO returns a thread identifier that allows you to pause and stop the thread that was just created. However, the functionality of the Control. Concurrent module won't be covered in this book.

As you can see, the main function creates three threads running the same code. The next question is how to make those threads cooperate and share resources because by default they cannot communicate between them. The answer is via an MVar, a box that can hold a mutable variable, which can be read or updated. One of those boxes is created before forking the threads using the newMVar function and is given as an argument to each of them. Thus, the threads have access to a shared resource in the form of a mutable variable.

Each thread can read the value of the MVar using takeMVar and to write a new one using putMVar. What makes this type useful for concurrency is the special behavior that it shows in the presence of multiple threads. You should think of an MVar as a box that either is holding some element or is empty. When you use takeMVar, you either read the value being held and make the box empty or block until some element is put in there. Conversely, putMVar either writes a new value if the box is empty or waits. Furthermore, those functions guarantee that only one thread will be woken up if it is blocked and that threads will be served in a first-in, first-out order, which means that no thread can swallow the events of all the rest.

Notice that the code includes a call to getLine at the end. The purpose of this function is to wait for some user input. The reason you need it is because when the main thread ends its computation, any other thread created by forkIO dies with it. Thus, if you want to see the effect of the other threads, you need to add a way to make the main thread continue execution. Waiting for user input is one way to do this.

To add some different actions, let's add a new kind of thread that will just read the current money value and print it on the screen. Since you don't need to perform any computation, you can use the readMVar function, which is equivalent to readMVar followed by putMVar with that same value. Then, it would read as follows:

```
readMoney :: MVar Integer -> IO ()
```

```
readMoney v = do m <- readMVar v
                 putStrLn $ "The current value is " ++ show m
```

To make things even more interesting, let's add some random delay between 3 and 15 seconds. The following function just computes that random number (more on random numbers will be presented in the next chapter) using randomRIO and then calls threadDelay, which pauses a thread for a number of microseconds. Be aware that when using the randomRIO function, you need to add a dependency on the random package.

```
import System.Random

randomDelay :: IO ()
randomDelay = do r <- randomRIO (3, 15)
                 threadDelay (r * 1000000)
```

Finally, you can write a forkDelay function that spawns *n* threads with a random waiting time before.

```
import Control.Monad

forkDelay :: Int -> IO () -> IO ()
forkDelay n f = replicateM_ n $ forkIO (randomDelay >> f)
```

Creating five new updaters and five readers will then be implemented in the following way:

```
main :: IO ()
main = do v <- newMVar 10000
          forkDelay 5 $ updateMoney v
          forkDelay 5 $ readMoney v
          _ <- getLine
          return ()
```

Note   None of the MVar-related functions forces the evaluation of the data inserted in them. This may cause problems because the price of executing some code may be paid much later, in the context of another computation. You may want to look at the `strict-concurrency` package to obtain a strict version of MVar.

Atomic Transactions

Let's move on to a more complex example. The main idea continues to be a client who is buying a particular product, but in this case more than one resource will be involved. The first one will be the money the Store has earned, as before, and the second one will be current stock of the Store, which should be updated to reflect that one item has been sold. As in the previous case, some extra threads reading the money and the stock will be added:

```
main :: IO ()
main = do v <- newMVar 10000
          s <- newMVar [("a",7)]
          forkDelay 5 $ updateMoneyAndStock "a" 1000 v s
          forkDelay 5 $ printMoneyAndStock v s
          _ <- getLine  -- to wait for completion
          return ()

updateMoneyAndStock :: Eq a => a -> Integer
                    -> MVar Integer -> MVar [(a,Integer)] -> IO ()
updateMoneyAndStock product price money stock =
  do s <- takeMVar stock
     let Just productNo = lookup product s
     if productNo > 0
       then do m <- takeMVar money
               let newS = map (\(k,v) -> if k == product
                                         then (k,v-1)
                                         else (k,v)) s
               putMVar money (m + price) >> putMVar stock newS
       else putMVar stock s

printMoneyAndStock :: Show a => MVar Integer -> MVar [(a,Integer)] -> IO ()
printMoneyAndStock money stock = do m <- readMVar money
                                    s <- readMVar stock
                                    putStrLn $ show m ++ "\n" ++ show s
```

Your first impression may be that the code is quite complex. However, you want to update the stock and the price only when there are enough items to sell. And if you cannot perform the purchase, you wouldn't want to block the access to the money shared variable. Thus, you need to plan for both possibilities and restore the initial stock if the transaction is not successful.

Apart from its apparent complexity, there are other problems in the code related to several concurrent scenarios. It may be the case that one of the updateMoneyAndStock threads takes the stock variable, and then printMoneyAndStock threads get access to the money variable. At this point, the whole execution is blocked; the updater thread must be blocked because it cannot get the ownership of the money variable, and the printer thread cannot continue because of denial of access to stock. This is an archetypical instance of *deadlocking*. Figure 8-3 depicts this situation: each vertical line represents the execution of one thread.

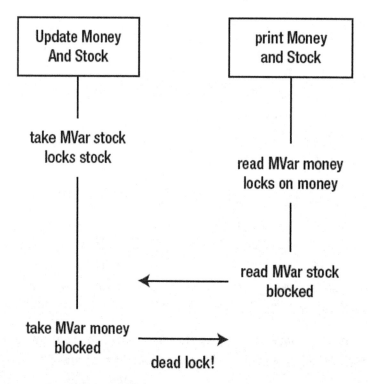

Figure 8-3. *Example of deadlock*

Another problem may occur in the following case of two updater threads, U1 and U2, and one reader thread that I'll call R. It is possible that U1 updates the money variable and immediately afterward R reads that variable, obtaining the money after selling the item in U1. However, afterward U1 can proceed, and the whole U2 is executed as well. By that time, the stock variable will contain the changes of both U1 and U2, and R will get stock information that is not consistent with the value it got from money. In this case, the problem is that a thread can get an *inconsistent view of the world.*

Both problems are common in systems where many agents update and query some data in a concurrent way. The best example of this pertains to database systems. The solution comes in the form of *transactions.* A transaction is a computation guaranteed to be run reliably independent from other transactions, and it always has a coherent view of the data. Transactions provide the illusion that a whole computation runs as an atomic block inside the database and ensure that data maintains its integrity.[2]

The stm package brings this idea into the realm of Haskell programming. Using this library, you can define blocks of code that will be run as an atomic unit by the system. In the code, each transaction is translated into a computation inside the STM monad. This name is an acronym for Software Transactional Memory, which is the implementation of transactions that the library uses. As an example, here's a version of the updater thread but using STM instead of MVars:

```
import Control.Concurrent.STM

updateMoneyAndStockStm :: Eq a => a -> Integer
                       -> TVar Integer -> TVar [(a,Integer)] -> STM ()
updateMoneyAndStockStm product price money stock =
  do s <- readTVar stock
     let Just productNo = lookup product s
     if productNo > 0
       then do m <- readTVar money
               let newS = map (\(k,v) -> if k == product
                                         then (k,v-1)
                                         else (k,v)) s
               writeTVar money (m + price) >> writeTVar stock newS
```

---

[2] Here, I am talking about ACID transactions, which ensure atomicity and consistency after each transaction. Most SQL databases follow the ACID model. Other database systems follow the BASE paradigm, which guarantees eventual consistency instead.

```
        else return ()
```

When using stm, instead of MVars you should use TVars. In contrast to the former, TVars can be read and written as many times as you want. Thus, you don't need to write back the stock if the purchase could not be done.

Computations in the STM monad are not directly executable. Instead, you must call the atomically function, which moves the transaction to the IO monad instead. For example, to execute the updater transaction five times, with delay, you would change the main function to read as follows:

```
main :: IO ()
main = do v <- newTVarIO 10000
          s <- newTVarIO [("a",7)]
          forkDelay 5 $ atomically $ updateMoneyAndStockStm "a" 1000 v s
          _ <- getLine  -- to wait for completion
          return ()
```

The great advantage of having a function such as atomically is that you can delimit which parts of your code need to be run as a transaction and which don't. This is important for performance. Keeping the guarantees of transactionality is expensive, and you should make minimal use of it.

Rolling Back Transactions

When working with databases, you often find scenarios in which your current transaction cannot be performed. Usually, this comes into play when considering the constraints that your data should maintain. For example, selling an item from the Store stock can be done only when the corresponding number of items of that product is larger than zero. When you abort a transaction, you want the state of the world to return to the previous moment in time, as if no computation has happened at all. This operation is called a *rollback*.

The stm package not only brings the atomicity guarantees of transactions to the Haskell world but also offers the ability to roll back some piece of code. To signal that a transaction cannot continue, you need to use the retry function. For example, let's consider the scenario where a client wants to pay by card. First, you need to check that the card system is working. In the negative case, you cannot continue.

```
payByCard :: Eq a => a -> Integer
            -> TVar Integer -> TVar [(a,Integer)] -> STM ()
payByCard product price money stock =
  do working <- isCardSystemWorking
     if not working
     then retry
     else updateMoneyAndStockStm product price money stock

isCardSystemWorking :: STM Bool
isCardSystemWorking = ...   -- code to check card system status omitted
```

Code using retry has special behavior. As a first description, the transaction is executed repeatedly until it finally finds a scenario in which it succeeds. Of course, such an approach would be overkill. Internally, stm keeps track of which TVars influence the transaction and executes the code again only if any of them change. Not having to implement that functionality by hand makes your code much more modular and maintainable.

Another feature that the previous example demonstrates is the *compositionality* of transactions. Since a transaction is just a value of the STM monad, you can put several of them together to create a larger transaction. In the example, the check for the card system and the money and stock update are defined separately and then joined to make the larger payByCard transaction.

While retry is a powerful tool, in some cases you may want to follow a path different from waiting until the variables change and the invariants are satisfied. For those occasions, stm provides the orElse combinatory. In general, t1 `orElse` t2 behaves as t1. However, in the case in which t1 calls retry, the effects of t1 are rolled back, and t2 is run. If t2 ends successfully, no more work is done. If t2 also calls retry, the *whole* t1 `orElse` t2 transaction is restarted.

The following example uses orElse to implement the behavior of trying first to pay by card and, when that doesn't work, then starting a cash-based transaction:

```
pay :: Eq a => a -> Integer
     -> TVar Integer -> TVar [(a,Integer)] -> STM ()
pay product price money stock
   = payByCard product price money stock `orElse`
     payByCash product price money stock
```

```
payByCash :: Eq a => a -> Integer
          -> TVar Integer -> TVar [(a,Integer)] -> STM ()
payByCash = ...  -- code that asks for cash omitted
```

In Exercise 8-2, you can use your knowledge of transactions to build a Time Machine system.

EXERCISE 8-2. TRAVELING THROUGH TIME

The Time Machine Store also provides the service of time traveling. However, there are some restrictions that customers must abide by: at most *n* people can be traveling at the same moment (because the company owns only *n* time machines), and by no means should two people be on the same year at the same time.

Develop a small application where customers are simulated by different threads and the restrictions are always satisfied via a careful use of the `stm` library. Hint: Use a shared `TVar` for saving the years that people are traveling to, and use `retry` to block customers from traveling without satisfying the rules.

Producer-Consumer Queues

Up to this point, the focus has been on threads that communicate using shared variables. But in the world of concurrency, there are many other ways in which two threads can share some data. Even more, data can be shared not only among threads but also across different processes or different parts of the network. In this section, you'll see how to use a queue to implement a producer-consumer model.

One way to architect the Store, for example, is to have multiple front-end threads or processes and just one back end. The front ends are responsible for asking all the information that may be needed to perform a transaction. However, they are not responsible for processing the orders. That responsibility belongs to the back end.

Single-Process Queues

If you want to keep all your computation within a single process, you may think of using STM to handle concurrent access to the data. If you could use only TVars to implement this solution, you would have a tough time. You would need a concrete amount of possible front ends that may communicate, and the back end should always be on the lookout to see whether some of those variables have new information. The better solution is to stop using a TVar and instead use a *queue*.

The stm package provides several kinds of queues. The easiest one is called TQueue. You can put a new element on the queue using writeTQueue. This queue does not impose any limit on the number of elements that may be waiting in the queue (apart from the obvious constraints on memory available in the system), so the writeTQueue function will never block a thread. The converse operation, getting the first element from the queue, is done via readTQueue. If the queue is empty, the thread will be blocked.

In this model, the front end behaves as a *producer*; it creates new elements for the queue, whereas the back end is the *consumer* that takes information from the queue. The implementation of the full orchestration using queues can be done as follows:

```haskell
import Control.Monad
main = do q <- newTQueueIO
          forkIO $ backend q                    -- create one backend
          replicateM_ 10 $ forkIO (frontend q)  -- create 10 frontends
          _ <- getLine
          return ()

backend :: TQueue (String,Integer) -> IO ()
backend q = do
  m <- newTVarIO 10000
  s <- newTVarIO [("a",7)]
  forever $ atomically $ do (product,price) <- readTQueue q
                            pay product price m s

frontend :: TQueue (String,Integer) -> IO ()
frontend q = do (product,price) <- ...  -- get purchase info from client
                atomically $ writeTQueue q (product,price)
```

Other kinds of queues can be classified into two axes. Table 8-1 shows the name of each of the four possibilities. The table also gives the package where each queue can be found. The two dimensions are as follows:

- Whether a queue has a *bounded* size or is *unbounded*. In the case of bounded queues, the creation of such a queue needs the maximum number of elements as a parameter. When calling the corresponding write function, if the queue is full, the thread is blocked until more space becomes available.

- Whether a queue is *closable*. A queue that is closed cannot receive any more items. When this happens, every call to the write function is effectively discarded, and every read returns Nothing. Note that the behavior when the queue is closed and when it's empty is completely different.

Table 8-1. *Types of STM Queues*

	Unbounded	Bounded
Not closable	TQueue (package stm)	TBQueue (package stm)
Closable	TMQueue (package stm-chans)	TBMQueue (package stm-chans)

These two dimensions can be combined in the four ways in Table 8-1.

Using queues can help in the design of the system from Exercise 8-2. Indeed, Exercise 8-3 asks you to use queues to make the management of clients in the store fairer.

EXERCISE 8-3. QUEUING TRAVELERS

In the previous exercise, all customers were trying to access the finite number of time machines at the same time. This may pose a problem of fairness because stm does not guarantee which thread will be woken up from retry if several are waiting.

An alternative solution involves using a queue where customers put their requests and where a master thread assigns time machines when they are free. Implement this solution using TBQueue.

Message Queues Using AMQP

The main caveat of the previous solution is that the queue can only be used by threads coming from the same process. But in many cases, you would like the front end and the back end to be different, isolated programs, maybe even running on different machines in the network. The main problem in that case is communication and sharing of resources: how to ensure that messages are transported correctly between processes and how to ensure that all of them have a consistent view of the message queue.

There are many libraries available in Haskell to communicate through the network, starting with the network package. Alas, rolling your own messaging protocol does not seem like a good idea. Communication is known to be a tricky area of computer science, since many things can go wrong: messages can be lost, duplicated, or arrive out of order or simply very late. Fortunately, we do not need to write any of that code if we introduce a message broker to the mix.

A *message broker* is simply a program whose only role is to manage communication between nodes and processes. Their most basic functionality is to connect endpoints, sometimes by forwarding a message to more than one recipient. Many brokers also introduce a notion of message queue, where messages are saved until they are handled somehow. Most deployed message brokers with support for queues use the *Advanced Message Queuing Protocol*, or AMQP, which is the focus of this section.

INSTALLING RABBITMQ

In order to run the code in this section, you need to have an AMQP-compatible broker in your machine. My suggestion is to use RabbitMQ, available at `www.rabbitmq.com`. The server runs in Linux, Windows, and Mac OS X, and you can also get it as a Docker image. In the following code, I assume that you have RabbitMQ running in the default port, 5672, with the default security configuration, so we can access it as guests.

The simplest messaging model of AMQP involves four elements, all of them shown in Figure 8-4. The first one is *queues*, which store a sequence of messages. Each queue is identified by a name. Then we have *producers* and *consumers*, which write and read messages to a particular queue. Note that the distinction is not clear-cut, since the same program may send and receive messages from the same queue. These three elements are obviously involved whenever we talk about queuing.

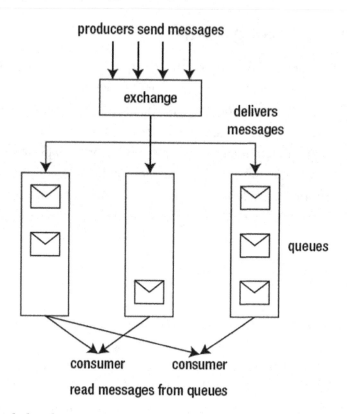

Figure 8-4. *High-level view of the AMQP messaging model*

On top of those, AMQP defines the concept of exchange. An *exchange* is an intermediary between producers and queues. In this messaging model, producers never write directly to queues. Instead, each message is sent to an exchange which decides in which queue or queues the message should be delivered. Take, for example, a logging message: different processes may want to listen to only specific severity levels. We can model each of them as a queue. The exchange in this case distributes the messages according to our specific logging policy.

AMQP handles many more communication needs. For example, you can use a message queue as a work queue: in that case, many processes may consume messages, but each message should only be consumed once. As a result, consumers must acknowledge that they have handled a message to get it removed from the work queue. The notion of exchange is also greatly generalized: you can have queues with different topics, to which consumers may subscribe. If you are interested on the possibilities, I strongly suggest looking at RabbitMQ tutorials.

AMQP in Haskell

There are several libraries in Hackage for communication using AMQP. The amqp package gives access to the full set of features of the protocol, at the expense of a more complicated interface. On top of this, we have amqp-conduit, which exposes the message queues as streams (the conduit streaming library is discussed in the next chapter). In this section, we look at amqp-worker, which exposes a simple functional interface.

Note   At the time of writing, amqp-worker is only compatible with the 0.2.x series of resource-pool, so you need to constrain the latter to version < 0.3 in your Cabal file.

One of the main characteristics of amqp-worker is its use of type-level mechanisms to ensure that access to queues is done in the right way. In particular, messages are not seen as a mere sequence of bytes, but as a representation of a concrete Haskell type. To achieve its goal, amqp-worker requires you to declare queues before using them. You do so by creating a value of the Queue type.

```haskell
{-# LANGUAGE OverloadedStrings #-}

import Network.AMQP.Worker
import Control.Exception  -- needed later

type Order = (String, Integer)

ordersQueue :: Queue Direct Order
ordersQueue = let testExchange = exchange "test"
                  in queue testExchange "orders"
```

The queue function receives two arguments. The second one is the name of the message queue to connect to, which will be created if it does not exist yet. As we have discussed earlier, each queue is associated with an exchange, so we also need to declare it beforehand by giving it a name. Any client connecting to the same exchange and the same queue will be able to send and receive messages. Something which is only explicit in the type signature is that ordersQueue deals with messages of type Order. In this case, our data is expressed using a simple tuple, but amqp-worker can deal also with programmer-defined types.

OVERLOADEDSTRINGS

You may have noticed that we need to enable the OverloadedString extension to compile this code. This is required because the literals "test" and "orders" are not of type String (the default in Haskell) but of type Text (a different representation often used when interoperating with other languages). We discuss the differences between the two and how to convert between them in Chapter 10.

The next step is to initialize the connection. The simplest way is to use a big string containing all the connection data (although you should not use this in real production environments, since the password is visible in the code). Once the connection is created, we need to initialize the exchange and the queue we want to use, just writing the code defining them is not enough. The result of this process is a connection identifier which we use afterward to communicate with the RabbitMQ server.

```haskell
initialize :: IO Connection
initialize = do
  conn <- connect (fromURI "amqp://guest:guest@localhost:5672")
  initQueue conn ordersQueue
  return conn
```

The simplest operation to perform over a queue is to send a message. In our case, this is what the front end does. Once you have the data, you just need to call publish. The compiler ensures that the type of the message you want to send matches the one declared for the queue.

```haskell
frontend :: Connection -> IO ()
frontend conn = do (product, price) <- ... -- get info
                   publish conn ordersQueue (product, price)
                   putStrLn "Message sent"
```

The other side of the coin is the back end. In this case, the code is slightly longer. Let me show it and then discuss it step by step:

```haskell
import Control.Concurrent.STM

backend :: Connection -> IO ()
```

```
backend conn = do
  m <- newTVarIO 1000
  s <- newTVarIO [("a", 7)]
  putStrLn "Starting backend..."
  worker def conn ordersQueue onBackendError (onBackendMessage m s)

onBackendMessage :: TVar Integer -> TVar [(String, Integer)]
                -> Message Order -> IO ()
onBackendMessage m s Message { value = (product, price) }
  = do putStrLn $ "Received order " ++ show (product, price)
       atomically $ pay product price m s
onBackendError :: WorkerException SomeException -> IO ()
onBackendError e = putStrLn $ "ERROR: " ++ show e
```

Building on the code we had before, we are still using two TVars to handle the state of the program. The money is represented by the m variable, and the current stock by the s variable. This is a very common pattern in Haskell programs: whenever you need to keep some mutable state, throw a transactional variable to ensure that your program is free from deadlocks and any kind of data race.

The novelty from amqp-worker comes from the call to worker. This function receives the connection and the queue to listen to. Additional options may be provided, but in this example are set to the default by using def. Every time a message arrives to the queue, two events may be raised:

- There might be some error when dealing with the message. Then the error handler is called, in this case onBackendError. The function is called with the description of the problem so that it can be further inspected, although in the preceding code we just print it.

- If the message arrives successfully, the other handler is called. In the preceding code, it is called onBackendMessage. The information, of type Order in this case, is wrapped in a Message type which includes additional information about the delivery. If we are not interested in that extra information, we can just get the inner message as the value field. Note that the actual work of calling pay remains equal to our older version using TQueues.

To finish our program, we need put all these parts together. To ease our testing, we are going to have one single executable which works as the back end or front end depending on how it is called from the command line. In Haskell, command-line arguments are available by calling the getArgs function from System.Environment. Do not worry if you do not fully understand our use of monadic notation here; the next chapter is devoted to input and output with the IO monad.

```haskell
import System.Environment

main :: IO ()
main = do conn <- initialize
          args <- getArgs
          case args of
            "backend"  : _ -> backend  conn
            "frontend" : _ -> do frontend conn
                                 _ <- getLine
                                 return ()
```

Note   The extra getLine after calling frontend is required to give some time for amqp-worker to send the message before exiting. If the process ends right after the call to publish, the message may not be correctly delivered.

Scaling this simple example to a real network requires a bit more work in order to configure RabbitMQ correctly. If your communication patterns are simple, the amqp-worker library may cover your needs quite well. The only caveat of this library is that it fixes a simple messaging pattern; if you need something more complex, you can switch to the broader amqp.

Summary

In this chapter, you learned about some parallelism, concurrency, and distribution packages from the Haskell ecosystem.

- The Par monad provides simple parallelism via *futures*, which are computations started in parallel that you can ask for the result of at some later point.

- You saw how monad allows spawning parallel computations around the concept of a *dataflow* graph, where dependencies are defined via IVars.

- Basic *concurrency* can be achieved in GHC via forkIO for creating new threads and via MVars for sharing information.

- In some cases, you need to perform longer access to shared resources as an atomic operation. In that case, you can use *transactions* via the stm library.

- In addition to simple TVar variables, the stm library provides abstractions over several types of *queues*. The examples have focused on TQueue, the nonbounded nonclosable one.

- Finally, you learned the basics of communication using message queues using the amqp-worker package.

PART III

Resource Handling

Dealing with Files: IO and Conduit

In Parts 1 and 2, you learned the basics of pure evaluation and how it helps in parallelizing and distributing code. However, sometimes you need to step out to the wild world of side effects. You'll start by looking at simple input and output in Haskell. At the beginning, the information will be input in the console, and the output will be printed on the screen. Afterward, you'll learn how to use a permanent means of storing data and reading and writing from files in disk.

Computations with side effects may turn out wrong in many ways; maybe the data is corrupted, or perhaps the network connection goes down. Haskell includes an exception mechanism that signals these conditions and allows you to react. In pure computations, you've been handling erroneous scenarios using `Maybe` and `MonadPlus`. The relation between the different ways of handling errors in Haskell will be clear by the end of this chapter.

One problem with Haskell's lazy evaluation model is that it brings some unpredictability to input and output. The Haskell community has come up with several streaming data libraries to solve this problem. This chapter discusses `conduit`, as well as some applications of this library to deal with file handling and networking. After learning all this information, you'll be ready to save the client and product data on disk using a binary serialization format. For that matter, the `binary` library will also be presented.

Basic Input and Output

To begin the journey through side effects in Haskell programs, let's create some simple interactions with the console. These small examples will help you to discover the concepts involved. The first bit of code to look at is an executable program that just prints "Hello Beginning Haskell!" at the console.

301

© Alejandro Serrano Mena 2022
A. Serrano Mena, *Practical Haskell*, https://doi.org/10.1007/978-1-4842-8581-7_9

```
module Main where
main :: IO()
main = putStrLn "Hello Beginning Haskell!"
```

A second example is a bit more involved. In this case, the program asks for a place and decides which point in time you should travel to, based on the given name. The algorithm is fairly easy; the important part of this code is how the information is taken from the user and threaded through the program.

```
main = do putStrLn "Where do you want to travel?"
          place <- getLine
          let year = (length place) * 10
          putStrLn $ "You should travel to year " ++ show year
```

If you run the program, the output will be like the following. (As usual, bold denotes those parts that are to be input, while the program font is used for output from the program.)

```
Where do you want to travel?
India
You should travel to year 50
```

BUFFERING

In some systems, especially in Windows, you may find that there's no output at all upon executing a program. This issue is related to *buffering*. To gain efficiency, the information you send to a file (or to the console) is not directly written (or shown) but instead is buffered until a certain amount of data is gathered. You can change the way in which each handle uses buffering via hSetBuffering. The most common use of this function, making the system flush the contents after each newline character, is coded as follows:

```
import System.IO
main = do hSetBuffering stdout LineBuffering  -- enable line buffering
          -- continue with the rest
```

There's another possible value for hSetBuffering, namely, NoBuffering, that makes the system use no buffering at all. However, you should be wary. Problems can result from using NoBuffering in combination with console functions in Windows.

It's interesting to look at the signature of the functions that have been used in the examples. The easiest way to get the signature is to ask the interpreter with its :t command.

```
*Chapter9.BasicInputOutput> :t putStrLn
putStrLn :: String -> IO ()
*Chapter9.BasicInputOutput> :t getLine
getLine :: IO String
```

The do notation that has been used and the data types wrapped inside another type (in this case, IO) should give you a clue that you're indeed working inside a monad. In the previous chapters, you saw that State represents computations that carry a state, Maybe computations that may fail, and so on. IO brings to a certain bit of code the ability to perform side effects. In the previous examples, it was used to print to and get information from the console.

There's one important difference between IO and the rest of the monads that have been considered up to this point. For the other monads, there was some way to inspect the resulting value (e.g., using pattern matching with Maybe) or run the monad (with functions similar to runState). In that way, you could get back to a context without the corresponding monad.

By contrast, IO has *no escape hatch*. There's no operation that converts an IO t value into a plain t value.[1] This is how Haskell imposes a barrier between the computations that involve side effects and must work inside the IO monad, as well as the rest. You want to be sure that a function without IO in its signature is pure, free of side effects, and referentially transparent. Furthermore, every call to IO in a certain application must span from the initial main function, which has IO () type.

Note   For the Haskell compiler, an expression that is pure must be treated differently than an expression involving side effects and that lives in IO. However, from a programmer's point of view, IO is no different from any another monad. It just happens to introduce side effects into computations.

---

[1] This assertion is not completely true. There are ways you can perform such a conversion. However, it's considered extremely unsafe because it may break several of the invariants that Haskell code counts on. The main use of this unsafe conversion is interoperation with languages that don't make a distinction between pure and side-effectful functions.

Haskell's Prelude module offers several functions for interacting with the console. In addition to the aforementioned putStrLn, which prints a line of text and then starts a new line, you have at your disposal putStr, a variant of printing a string but without any final newline character, and putChar, which prints just one character on the screen. For the common case where the data to print is not yet a string but can be converted into one by the show function, you can use print. Here's a brief example where the user is requested to input a first name and a last name, and the system shows a value of the type Person:

```haskell
main = do putStrLn "First name?"
          fName <- getLine
          putStrLn "Last name?"
          lName <- getLine
          putChar '>' >> putChar ' '
          print $ Person fName lName
```

For the record, the Person and Client data types were declared as follows in Chapter 4:

```haskell
data Person   = Person { firstName :: String, lastName :: String }
                deriving (Show, Eq, Ord)
data Client i = GovOrg  { clientId :: i, clientName :: String }
              | Company { clientId :: i, clientName :: String
                        , person :: Person, duty :: String }
              | Individual { clientId :: i, person :: Person }
                deriving (Show, Eq, Ord)
```

All these output functions have IO () as the return type. Remember, () is the *unit type* and there's only one value of that type, which is confusingly also named (). It's customarily used in Haskell programming to identify those monadic computations that don't have a value to return but that has effects on the context that you're interested in. In addition to putStr and friends, other functions that use () in their return types are tell (from the Writer monad) and put (from the State monad).

The counterparts to the previous functions are the ones that receive information from the user. The most common one is getLine; its task is to gather all the input up to the moment in which the user presses Enter. You may be interested, however, in getting the input character by character, which you can do using getChar. Finally, in some cases you want to get all input up to an end-of-file marker. This is common when piping data between processes in a Unix-like shell. The getContents function provides this functionality.

HASKELINE

If you're planning to create a command-line application, the simple functions that Prelude includes won't offer the best experience to the end user. In particular, you may want to provide command history or autocompletion.

The haskeline library is specifically designed for this task. The core of the library is the InputT monad transformer, which provides those features. The previous example asking for a person could be rewritten as follows:

```
import System.Console.Haskeline
main = runInputT defaultSettings $ do
  fName <- getInputLine "First name? "
  lName <- getInputLine "Last name? "
  case (fName, lName) of
    (Just f, Just l) -> outputStrLn $ show (Person f l)
    (_     , _     ) -> outputStrLn "I cannot identify you"
```

One difference with standard Prelude is that input functions return their value wrapped on a Maybe, anticipating the case in which the input may stop earlier than expected.

Since IO is a monad, you can use the enormous set of functions that were presented in Chapters 6 and 7. As you may remember, any monad is a functor, so you can use fmap directly on IO. For example, you may refactor the following use of variable s since it's used only to thread the information to upperS:

```
import Data.Char
main = do s <- getLine
          let upperS = map toUpper s
          putStrLn upperS >> putStrLn upperS
```

into a more concise form which directly generates upperS:

```
main = do upperS <- fmap (map toUpper) getLine
          putStrLn upperS >> putStrLn upperS
```

Another possibility is accumulating some information using foldM. The following code goes through a whole list of clients, and for each of them, it asks the user whether they should be included in a special VIP list:

```
import Control.Monad (foldM)
createVIPList :: Show a => [Client a] -> IO [Client a]
createVIPList = foldM (\lst c -> do
                          putStrLn $ "\nShould " ++ show c
                                                 ++ "be included as VIP? "
                          answer <- getLine
                          case answer of
                            'Y':_ -> return $ c:lst
                            _     -> return lst)[]
```

It's interesting to consider what happens when IO values are *inside* a certain container. For example, you may want to create a list of actions and, based on some user input, execute one of them. This is exactly what is done in the following piece of code:

```
main = do actionName <- getLine
          case lookup actionName listOfActions of
            Just action -> action   -- execute action
            Nothing     -> putStrLn "Unknown action"
listOfActions :: [(String, IO ())]
listOfActions = [
  ("greet", do name <- getLine
               putStrLn $ "Hello " ++ name),
  ("sum"  , do putStrLn "First number:"
               n1 <- fmap read getLine
               putStrLn "Second number:"
               n2 <- fmap read getLine
               putStrLn $ show n1 ++ "+" ++ show n2
                                  ++ "=" ++ show (n1+n2))]
```

It's important to think for a moment how the execution of such code differs from what you may expect. In most programming languages, the call to lookup would have triggered the evaluation of listOfActions. Then, all the calls to getLine or putStrLn would have been executed since they appear in the body of listOfActions. However, in the Haskell code the side effects aren't executed until you've unwrapped the action to be of type IO t for some t and asked for its execution, which happens in the line in bold with the "execute action" comment. One important implication is that IO values are *first-class citizens* of Haskell, like functions are, and can be combined, can be passed as arguments, and can be returned as any other value.

Randomness

Let's take a break from input and output and consider the issue of randomness in Haskell. For that purpose, I present a simulation of a time machine breaking in the middle of a journey. When this breakdown happens, the time traveler is involved in a disturbing experience: ending in a random place, at a random point in time, with no clue of what is outside the machine.

The following code uses the randomRIO function from the System.Random module in the random package to simulate a random walk from an initial point, that is, a series of random jumps in time made by a broken time machine. The randomRIO function needs upper and lower bounds for the value to obtain, which in this case have been set to 0 and 3000. Since the walk may be infinite, the code just prints the ten initial hops.

```
{-# LANGUAGE ScopedTypeVariables #-}
import Control.Monad.Loops
import System.Random
main = do (initial :: Int) <- fmap read getLine
          jumps <- unfoldrM (\_ -> do next <- randomRIO (0, 3000)
                                      if next == initial
                                        then return Nothing
                                        else return $ Just (next, next))
                           initial
          print $ take 10 jumps
```

Note   In the preceding code, I'm using the monadic counterpart of unfolding, namely, unfoldrM. However, you won't find it in the usual Control.Monad module. Instead, you need to import Control.Monad.Loop from the monad-loops package. This is an interesting module, which you should add to your list of tools for monadic programming.

Since you know how to read and write from the console and how to generate random values, you can now develop small console games. Exercise 9-1 asks you to do this.

EXERCISE 9-1. WIN A TIME TRAVEL TRIP

Develop a small game in which you can win a time travel trip in one of the machines in the store. The game should generate a random number between 3 and 17. Then, the user has five possibilities of guessing the number. If the user guesses correctly, the program will show a message congratulating them. In case of failure, the program will show a message encouraging the user to try again.

While developing the game, try to think about how to modularize and abstract the code; the range of numbers or the number of guesses can be turned into parameters.

The previous code did its job in the main function, which has the IO () type. The call to randomRIO is not made on a let block, which points out that this function works also in IO contexts. You can see that this is the case by asking the interpreter its type.

```
*Chapter9.Randomness> import System.Random
*Chapter9.Randomness System.Random> :t randomRIO
randomRIO :: Random a => (a, a) -> IO a
```

Let's think for a moment why randomness needs an IO context to work. The main reason is that randomRIO *breaks the referential transparency* property found in pure Haskell code; not every call to randomRIO will return the same result. That fact implies that the compiler may not be able to perform certain optimizations. For example, in pure code if you have a piece of code like g (f x) (f x), it may be rewritten to let h = f x in g h h, which involves one call less to f and thus less work to be done. But if instead you write this:

```
do x <- randomRIO (0, 10)
   y <- randomRIO (0, 10)
   return g x y
```

this cannot be rewritten to the following:

```
do z <- randomRIO (0, 10)
   return g z z
```

The code cannot be rewritten because the two calls to randomRIO may return a different random value. Many other good properties of Haskell code break in the presence of side effects, and thus you cannot use tools such as equational reasoning. This is another reason, in addition to maintainability, for keeping pure and IO code apart.

Furthermore, any call to that function must update the *global random generator*, which is kept in memory by the system. This is an important side effect. If you don't want to use that global variable and being forced to use IO, you can create pure functions that involve random values given that you provide the initial random generator, which is a value of type StdGen. The corresponding pure functions return both a random value and the generator for the next value. For example, the previous code can be "purified" to work on StdGen values as follows:

```
import Data.List
getJumps :: StdGen -> Int -> [Int]
getJumps gen initial = unfoldr (\g -> let (next, nextG) = randomR (0, 3000) g
                                      in if next == initial
                                         then Nothing
                                         else Just (next, nextG))
                    gen
```

You can either create a StdGen value with a fixed seed via mkStdGen or obtain the global one via getStdGen. Thus, the initial random code, which also outputs the result, can be written as follows:

```
main = do (initial :: Int) <- fmap read getLine
          gen <- getStdGen
          print $ take 10 $ getJumps gen initial
```

This example holds a valuable lesson; in many cases, you can split your functions with side effects in several pure functions. There is also a driver function that operates in IO and takes care of threading the information between the others. In that way, your code will be easier to maintain.

Working with Files

The next step after knowing how to deal with side effects and how to communicate with the console is to read and write on a durable location. In other words, you will learn how to read and write files on the system. At some point, the files turn into objects that can perform certain operations, such as moving files from one location to another or deleting one file from disk. This section will delve into the functions that provide this functionality in the Haskell Platform.

Reading and Writing

The Prelude provides functions for bulk operations on files, either writing from or reading an entire string into a file. The involved functions are writeFile or appendFile for output and readFile for input. One possibility is reading a list of clients and, for each of them, deciding whether they've won a time travel to a point in time (for this second part, the code uses randomRIO). The main assumption is that each line of the file will contain a client, so you can use the lines function in Data.String, which separates a string between newline boundaries.

```
{-# LANGUAGE ScopedTypeVariables #-}
import Data.String
import System.Random
main = do clients <- fmap lines $ readFile "clients.db"
          clientsAndWinners
                  <- mapM (\c -> do (winner :: Bool) <- randomIO
                                    (year    :: Int ) <- randomRIO (0, 3000)
                                    return (c, winner, year))
                          clients
          writeFile "clientsWinners.db" $ concatMap show clientsAndWinners
```

However, working only with these operations has a severe performance impact: the information read from the file is kept entirely in memory, and the data to write to the file must be assembled into a string before writing it. In many cases, you will want further control. For example, you will want to read just a line or a file or write information to the disk as you go, instead of waiting for the entire process to finish. The module you should look at is System.IO.

Like in most programming languages, the flow of work with a file involves first opening a *handle* to it, then performing any operation that you need on the file, and finally closing the access to the file. The handle keeps track of all internal information that the system may need to work on the file.

The first step is handled by the openFile operation. The arguments for this function are the path to the file (the documentation shows that the type of this argument is FilePath, but it's just a synonym for String) and the opening mode, which can be for reading, writing (or both), or appending. The result will be a file handle. In addition to opening your own files, you can use any of the predefined handles, such as stdin, stdout, or stderr, which map to standard input, output, and error, usually from the console.

The inverse operation, *closing* a file, is done via the hClose functions. As in any other programming language, it's important that you close the file after you've finished working with it because an open handle consumes resources from the machine.

To *read or write*, you can use the generalizations of the previous console functions, which work on any file handle. These are all prefixed by h, and thus you get hGetChar, hGetLine, hGetContents, hPutChar, hPutStr, and hPutStrLn. Additionally, you can query the system as to whether you've finished reading the file with hIsEOF. Armed with these weapons, you can write a more efficient version of the previous example, which reads one line from the file at a time.

```
import System.Environment
import System.IO
main = do (inFile:outFile:_) <- getArgs
          inHandle  <- openFile inFile  ReadMode
          outHandle <- openFile outFile WriteMode
          loop inHandle outHandle
          hClose inHandle
          hClose outHandle
       where loop inHandle outHandle = do
```

```
            isEof <- hIsEOF inHandle
            if not isEof
                then do client <- hGetLine inHandle
                        (winner :: Bool) <- randomIO
                        (year   :: Int ) <- randomRIO (0, 3000)
                        hPutStrLn outHandle $ show (client, winner, year)
                        loop inHandle outHandle
                else return ()
```

You may have noticed that instead of hard-coding the input and output file names, the code obtains them via the getArgs function. This function, found in System. Environment, returns a list of all the command-line parameters that have been given to the executable command.

Since opening a file, working with it, and closing the handle afterward are common tasks, the Haskell Platform includes a special withFile function that takes care of the file and expects only the action to perform. For example, the previous code could have been written as follows:

```
main = do (inFile:outFile:_) <- getArgs
          withFile inFile  ReadMode  $ \inHandle ->
            withFile outFile WriteMode $ \outHandle ->
              loop inHandle outHandle
        where loop inHandle outHandle = do ...
```

Additionally, withFile will protect against possible errors while processing the file, ensuring that the file handle is always closed. In the next section, you will learn how to treat possible errors that may occur while working with files (e.g., data corruption, files that do not comply a certain schema, etc.).

Knowing how to read and write information from files, in addition to marshaling to and from strings with show and read, provides a way to save information about clients and products on disk. In Exercise 9-2, you are asked to classify clients in several files based on their category.

EXERCISE 9-2. CLIENT CLASSIFICATION

Remember that clients in the time machine store can be individuals, companies, or government organizations. Right now, the store keeps the records for all clients in a single file. Each line contains a client, and it's encoded by using the show function on them.

In this exercise, write a small executable that reads the information of those clients and generates another three files. Each of these files should contain all the clients of one of the three possible categories.

Up to this point, the code has just read the data in every file as a string. But in reality, two different scenarios may occur. The first one is that the file contains text; the other is that the information in the file is raw binary data. Furthermore, in the first case different encodings may have been used to translate from text data into a sequence of bytes. The hSetEncoding function is used to change the current encoding of a handle. The System. IO module includes many encoders, including latin1, utf8, utf16, and utf32, as well as its big-endian and little-endian versions. If you want to be sure that the contents of the output file for winners are written in UTF-8, you ought to change the code before going into the loop.

```
withFile outFile WriteMode $ \outHandle -> do
  hSetEncoding outHandle utf8
  loop inHandle outHandle
```

Anyway, in the next chapter you'll see that using Strings is rarely the best option when dealing with files. Instead, you should use ByteString and Text values. In that case, the encoding problem comes first, and you always need to specify how to convert from sequences of bytes to text values.

Handling Files

Let's move now to another range of operations you can do with files. Moving, copying, and deleting don't involve the data stored in files but rather the files themselves. For these operations, the Haskell Platform includes the directory package, which is quite straightforward to use.

The functions `renameFile`, `copyFile`, and `removeFile`, from the `System.Directory` module, take care of moving, copying, and deleting files from the system, respectively. It's important to note here that none of these operations supports working on directories, only on files.

Because of the inability of the previous functions to work on folders, `directory` provides a different set of functions for them. The following list enumerates the most important ones:

- `getDirectoryContents` returns a list of all the elements inside the folder.

- `createDirectory` makes a new folder on the system. However, it may fail if the directory already exists or if some of the parent directories are not present. `createDirectoryIfMissing` takes care of those two conditions.

- `renameDirectory` allows you to move a folder in the system. Notice that errors may happen if the path where you want to move already exists.

- `removeDirectory` deletes a folder from the system. Usually, the directory cannot be removed if it's not empty. `removeDirectoryRecursive`, on the other hand, deletes every element inside the folder and then the folder itself.

In addition to encoding, the other big issue when handling files is the format of the file paths, which changes depending on the underlying operating system. For example, Windows uses drive letters to prefix the paths and allows both \ and / to separate parts, whereas Unix and Mac OS X systems allow only / as a separator. Since the Haskell community considers interoperability between systems an important issue, a library has been included in the Haskell Platform that abstracts from these issues; its name is `filepath`.

The most important function in this library is (), which combines two path segments into a larger one. For example, if you want to read some database configuration found in the `database.settings` file in the `config` folder, the most correct way to do so is as follows:

```
withFile ("config" </> "database.settings") ReadMode $ \handle -> ...
```

Conversely, you may want to split a certain file path in the directory between where the file resides and the file name. You can do this with `splitFileName`. As an example, here's some code that gets an input file name from command-line arguments and writes into a file named `example` within the same folder:

```
import System.FilePath
main = do (file:_) <- getArgs
          let (folder, _) = splitFileName file
          withFile (folder </> "example") WriteMode $ \handle -> ...
```

In some cases, it may be interesting not to split only between the folder and the file name but rather get a list of all the path segments. In that case, you can use `splitDirectories` instead.

Finally, `filepath` includes functions for dealing with extensions. You can use (`<.>`) to add an extension to an existing file path. The other way around, you can use `splitExtensions` to generate a tuple of the file name and all the extensions attached to it. The package includes many other little utilities, such as replacing an extension, dropping just the last extension, and so on. It's useful to look at the `filepath` documentation when you need to handle file paths in your application.

Note   Again, never roll your own ways to combine extensions, add extensions, or do any other task involving file paths. Instead, use the `filepath` package to ensure that your code is correct and interoperable.

Error Handling

When dealing with input and output or many other kinds of side effects such as printing or communicating through a network, many kinds of errors can occur. In all the previous examples, the program would just crash when trying to open a file that doesn't exist on the system. It's important to know how to detect and recover from those error conditions.

But before proceeding with handling errors in IO contexts, I'm going to discuss how errors are handled in pure code, a topic you've already heard about previously in this book. In that way, you'll notice the differences between pure errors and exceptions. The latter is the mechanism for signaling anomalous conditions in IO.

Pure Errors

Until now, when an operation could not be performed, the most common way to cope with it was to return a Maybe value. This happened, for example, when a function was not applicable to some of the constructors of the value, such as head to empty lists, [ ], or getting the company name of an Individual client. In that way, the calling function would get Nothing as a result if any problem happened.

Unfortunately, Maybe is not a precise way to specify what error has occurred. You can declare that the operation was not successful but cannot specify the reason. And in many cases, that information is relevant; it's not the same failure that happens on a database transaction because the connection is not available as the failure that happens because some constraint has been violated. A useful type for these scenarios is Either, which is declared simply as follows:

```
data Either a b = Left a | Right b
```

For example, if x :: Either Int String, x can contain either an integer value, in which case the Left constructor would have been used, or a string value, which is wrapped on the Right constructor.

Conventionally, using Either for errors uses Right when the computation is successful and Left for failing scenarios. Thus, if r is the type of correct results and e is the type you would use for specifying the possible errors, Either e r is the customary type to use in functions. As an example, let's define a version of companyName that tells you the specific error why it couldn't retrieve the name of a company client.

```
data CompanyNameError = GovOrgArgument | IndividualArgument
companyName :: Client i -> Either CompanyNameError String
companyName Company { clientName = n } = Right n
companyName GovOrg     { }                = Left GovOrgArgument
companyName Individual { }                = Left IndividualArgument
```

A user of this function can now pattern match on the result and find the type of error in case it's needed.

```
printCompanyName :: Client i-> IO ()
printCompanyName c = case companyName c of
  Right n -> putStrLn n
```

```
Left GovOrgArgument-> putStrLn "A government organization was given"
Left IndividualArgument -> putStrLn "An individual was given"
```

The dichotomy between using Maybe and Either for specifying when an operation was not successful is usually a source of headaches. This becomes especially painful when you're using a library that uses a different style of error specification than the one you've decided to use in your application. Thankfully, the errors package, in its Control.Error.Util module, contains helpful functions to convert between styles. The signatures of those functions involved in the conversion are as follows:

```
hush :: Either a b -> Maybe b
note :: a -> Maybe b -> Either a b
```

Essentially, you use hush to forget about any concrete error in an Either value and just return Nothing if the computation fails. In the other direction, you need to tell which error value to return in case the Maybe value turns out to be Nothing. The name of the function is a reminder of its usage; you need to "add a note" to the possible error value.

Since deciding whether to use Maybe or Either is difficult but also may have ramifications throughout your application, so you may think about abstracting over the way errors are handled. Haskell type classes are the tool you need here.

In Chapter 7, you learned how to use MonadPlus to return values that declared an erroneous condition and its mplus operation to combine several of those values and returned the ones that were not errors. If you use MonadPlus, you can use Maybe or lists, signaling errors with Nothing and empty lists, respectively. Unfortunately, Either cannot be made an instance of MonadPlus. The problem is that the mempty operation in that type class must not have any parameter. Thus, you cannot specify which value to wrap in the Left constructor if an error should be returned.

The mtl package includes a generalization of MonadPlus to which both Maybe and Either can be given instances; its name is MonadError. Any type that supports this type class must provide two different operations, as its declaration needs.

```
class Monad m => MonadError e m | m -> e where
  throwError :: e -> m a
  catchError :: m a -> (e -> m a) -> m a
```

The first operation is the one responsible for signaling failure. As you can see, it satisfies the requirement that mempty didn't; it takes an extra parameter that is the error value to return. For example, the companyName function could be generalized to work on both Maybe and Either as follows:

```
{-# LANGUAGE FlexibleContexts #-}
import Control.Monad.Except
companyName :: MonadError CompanyNameError m => Client i -> m String
companyName Company { clientName = n } = return n
companyName GovOrg      { }             = throwError GovOrgArgument
companyName Individual { }              = throwError IndividualArgument
```

In the case of MonadPlus, the mplus function serves well for recovering from an error. Essentially, x `mplus` y was described in this context as returning the value of x if it represents success, or otherwise returning y if x represents failure.[2] This operation has also been generalized: catchError has the same task but has access to the error value of the corresponding throwError if the operation fails. For example, let's create a function that calls companyName and in case of failure returns a predefined empty value using MonadError.

```
companyNameDef :: MonadError CompanyNameError m => Client i -> m String
companyNameDef c = companyName c `catchError` (\_ -> return "")
```

Along with the MonadError type class, mtl and transformers include an ExceptT monad transformer you can add to your stack. The best way to understand its task is by thinking of the MaybeT transformer, in other words, of computations that may fail, with the addition of a tag specifying the error in the appropriate case. The errors package also encourages the use of ExceptT and provides conversion functions between stacks using MaybeT and ExceptT.

```
hushT :: Monad m => ExceptT a m b -> MaybeT m b
noteT :: Monad m => a -> MaybeT m b -> ExceptT a m b
```

---

[2] This analogy doesn't apply as much in the case of lists, where a `mplus` b is the concatenation of both lists and thus returns all the successful values from both branches.

Note   There is a historical reason for the breakage of the naming convention in the case of `Either`, `MonadError`, and `ExceptT`. Older versions of transformers contained an `ErrorT` monad transformer, along with the `MonadError` class. This type has been deprecated, because it imposed unnecessary constraints in the type of errors, and has been replaced by `ExceptT`.

SAFE FUNCTIONS

Because of the historical development of the Haskell libraries, some of the functions in the `Prelude` module don't have a pure-friendly way to cope with errors. An archetypical example is head. In the case of applying it to [ ], this function raises an exception (which can be caught only inside the `IO` monad, as you will see in the next section) instead of returning some representation of the error.

To alleviate this problem, the `safe` package provides a lot of versions of common functions that fail in a more pleasant way. For example, head has a version called headMay, which returns the value wrapped in a `Maybe`, and thus allows you to return `Nothing` for empty lists; and headDef, which takes an extra argument with a default value to return in the case of an empty list.

Catching Exceptions

I've already discussed how dealing with the outer world opens the door to a whole new category of errors, such as nonexistent files or lost connections. For that kind of events, Haskell provides an *exception mechanism*. There are two main differences between exceptions and the pure errors discussed:

- Pure errors can be thrown and caught in any place, usually by simply pattern matching on the final value of the computation. In contrast, exceptions can be handled only inside an IO context (but still be thrown from any place).

- When using `Either`, you need to specify in advance every possible error that may happen in the execution of some code. On the other hand, Haskell's exception mechanism is extensible. This decision allows new side effects to fail in new ways but hurts the analysis of the code because you cannot tell in advance which exception may be thrown.

The entry point of any work with exceptions is the `Control.Exception` module. The code examples in the rest of the section will assume that this module is included in the import list. In many cases, you need to specify exception types inside function bodies and `let` declarations; the `ScopedTypeVariables` GHC extension will be assumed to be enabled in all the samples.

Let's start with an example that adds exception handling to the initial function that wrote a list of winners from the database of clients by using `readFile` and `writeFile`.

```
import Control.Exception
import System.IO.Error
import System.Random
main = do clients <- fmap lines $ readFile "clients.db"
          clientsAndWinners
                <- mapM (\c -> do (winner :: Bool) <- randomIO
                                  (year   :: Int ) <- randomRIO (0, 3000)
                                  return (c, winner, year))
                   clients
          writeFile "clientsWinners.db" $ concatMap show clientsAndWinners
       `catch` (\(e :: IOException) -> if isDoesNotExistError e
                                       then putStrLn "File does not exist"
                                       else putStrLn $ "Other error: "
++ show e)
```

The first thing to notice is the use of the `catch` function. The idea is simple; you declare the main code to run and then a handler for a specific class of exceptions. The second thing to notice is that the code explicitly mentions the *type of exceptions* to be handled using that code.

In this particular case, the type you're interested in is `IOException`, which describes those exceptions that have something to do with input and output. A value of type `IOException` encodes extra information about the kind of problem that occurred. You can query it via a set of functions in the System.IO.Error module. In the example, our interest is nonexistent files and checks via the isDoesNotExistError function.

The fact that the Haskell exception mechanism is dynamic and extensible makes the type specification an important part of handling erroneous scenarios. The predefined set of exceptions that is raised by functions in the Haskell Platform is also included in the Control.Exception module. This set includes, among others, ArithException, which signals that a numerical error such as underflow or division by zero has occurred; ErrorCall, which allows handling calls to error; and PatternMatchFail, which is thrown when no pattern matches a specific value.

The following code asks the user for two integer numbers and shows the quotient of the two. Two kinds of exceptions may be raised. First, the user may input something that is not a number, which will cause a call to error inside read. Second, the other possible problem is division by zero. As you can see, each exception has its own handler.

```haskell
main = do (n1 :: Int) <- fmap read getLine
          (n2 :: Int) <- fmap read getLine
          putStrLn $ show n1 ++ " / " ++ show n2
                      ++ " = " ++ show (n1 `div` n2)
    `catch` (\(_ :: ErrorCall) -> putStrLn "Error reading number")
    `catch` (\(e :: ArithException) -> case e of
                DivideByZero -> putStrLn "Division by zero"
                _            -> putStrLn $ "Other error: " ++ show e)
```

These exception types are different from IOException in one sense. Whereas an IOException value needs to be queried through special-purpose functions about the kind of problem that happened, these types are defined as simple ADTs, and thus you can use pattern matching to discover the source of problems.

The Control.Exception module includes many other variations of catch for handling exceptions. One of them is catches, which receives a list of handlers for different exceptions. For example, the previous code could have been written without several calls to catch using that function.

```haskell
main = do ...
        `catches`
          [ Handler (\(_ :: ErrorCall) -> putStrLn "Error reading number")
          , Handler (\(e :: ArithException) -> case e of ...)]
```

Another possibility is using handle, which is just catch with reversed arguments. It's common to use it when the code to execute is long but the code to handle the errors is short because it makes the exception handling apparent up front. The following is a third way to write the same quotient code:

```
main = handle (\(_ :: ErrorCall)      -> ...) $
       handle (\(e :: ArithException) -> ...) $
       do (n1 :: Int) <- fmap read getLine
          ...
```

In some cases, you want to treat an exception in a similar way to an error in a pure computation. This may lead to code that is easier to read if other sources of errors are pure. Think of a scenario when you're validating some values from a database. In that case, exceptions can be raised in the database connection code, but validation will use Maybe or Either. The way to bridge both worlds is via the try function, which returns an Either value that may contain a result in its Right or a thrown exception in its Left.

For every exception handling function, there's a corresponding one ending in Just: catchJust, handleJust, and tryJust. Those functions take as an extra parameter an *exception filter*, which decides whether a particular exception should be caught by that handler or rethrown. These filters take the exception value as a parameter and must return a Maybe value. If it's Nothing, the exception should be rethrown; if the result is Just e, the exception is handled by the code corresponding to that catch. You've already found a case where this is interesting to do. From all the possible ArithException values, the real interest lies only in DivisionByZero. Thus, you can use catchJust to ensure that any other exception is correctly rethrown.

```
main = catchJust (\e -> if e == DivideByZero then Just e else Nothing)
          (do (n1 :: Int) <- fmap read getLine
              (n2 :: Int) <- fmap read getLine
              putStrLn $ show n1 ++ " / " ++ show n2
                      ++ " = " ++ show (n1 `div` n2)
           `catch` (\(_ :: ErrorCall) -> putStrLn "Error reading number") )
          (\_ -> putStrLn "Division by zero")
```

Note As you can see, the exception mechanism in Haskell is much more powerful than those in other languages. In addition to defining handlers by type, functions such as catchJust allow you to perform a dynamic check on whether to catch a particular exception. Using catchJust and similar functions ensures that you handle only the exceptions you know how to deal with, and the rest are properly rethrown to subsequent handlers.

Combinators such as catchJust enable you to be specific about which exception each handler should catch. In some cases, a handler has the opposite intention, though: catching every exception that might have been thrown in the code. The solution comes after looking closely at how different types of exceptions relate to each other. In particular, Haskell exceptions form a *hierarchy*. Each exception type E has a parent exception type P, describing the fact that E exceptions are a subset of P exceptions. At the root of this hierarchy, you find the SomeException type. In conclusion, if you want to add a handler that catches all possible exceptions that may arise in your application, your code should look like this:

```
main = do ...
      `catch` (\(e :: SomeException) -> ...) -- uncaught exceptions
```

Most programming languages that use exceptions as their error mechanism include, in addition to ways of throwing and catching them, a way to ensure that a certain piece of code runs even in the case of an exception. The usual purpose is to include some cleanup code or release some resource. For example, if you open a file handle, you want to ensure that it's closed even if some exception arose in its processing. In Haskell, this functionality is provided via the finally function. It can be used to create a more resilient version of the code that writes the winner clients in a file.

```
main = do (inFile:outFile:_) <- getArgs
          inHandle  <- openFile inFile  ReadMode
          outHandle <- openFile outFile WriteMode
          ( loop inHandle outHandle
            `finally` (do hClose inHandle
                          hClose outHandle) )
      where loop inHandle outHandle = ...
```

However, this code is not completely correct. In particular, it may be the case that an exception is thrown *while* opening any of the files. In that case, you cannot use `finally` because the call to hClose without opening the handle is incorrect. A three-stage flow is usual when dealing with resources: you acquire the resource, you perform some operation, and you release it. Even in the case of an exception during processing, you want to release the resource, but you don't want to run that code if the acquisition failed. This pattern is made explicit in Haskell by the `bracket` function. The most correct way to write the previous code is as follows:

```
main = do (inFile:outFile:_) <- getArgs
          bracket (openFile inFile  ReadMode)  -- acquisition of inHandle
                  hClose                       -- release of inHandle
                  (\inHandle -> bracket (openFile outFile WriteMode)
                                hClose
                                (\outHandle -> loop inHandle outHandle))
       where loop inHandle outHandle = ...
```

In Exercise 9-3, you can apply your new knowledge about exceptions by taking Exercise 9-2 and improving on it.

EXERCISE 9-3. BETTER CLIENT CLASSIFICATION

Add exception handling to the code you wrote for Exercise 9-2.

Throwing Exceptions

Now that you've seen how to catch exceptions, it's time to learn how to *throw* them. If you want to reuse any of the predefined exception types in `Control.Exception`, you just need to call `throwIO` if you are within the IO monad, or you can call `throw` if you want to throw an exception from pure code (but remember that the handler still needs to be inside the IO monad). This simple example does so by reusing the `NoMethodError` exception type.

```
main = do throw $ NoMethodError "I don't know what to do"
          `catch` (\(e :: SomeException) ->
                      do putStr "An exception was thrown: "
                         putStrLn $ show e)
```

Usually, you will want to raise an exception of a new custom type, which describes those exceptions that may happen in your code. To use a type as an exception, you need to create instances for it of the Show, Typeable, and Exception type classes. Thankfully, Haskell's deriving mechanism saves you from writing all the boilerplate code. The following code declares a type of exceptions in an authentication system:

```
{-# LANGUAGE ScopedTypeVariables, DeriveDataTypeable #-}
import Data.Typeable
data AuthenticationException = UnknownUserName  String
                            | PasswordMismatch String
                            | NotEnoughRights  String
                            deriving (Show, Typeable)
instance Exception AuthenticationException
```

Now you can use your new exception type as any built-in one.

```
main = do throw $ UnknownUserName "Alejandro"
          `catch` (\(e :: AuthenticationException) -> ...)
```

THE TYPEABLE TYPE CLASS

Haskell's exception mechanism makes heavy use of the Typeable type class. This class allows you to get information about the type of a value at runtime (because usually Haskell erases all type information after compiling in order to increase performance). Typeable can also be used, in the Data.Dynamic module, to create an interface for dynamic values, which you can cast at runtime to other types.

Like on other occasions, having the exception functionality wrapped in a type class makes it easier to write code so that it's reusable among several monad stacks and users of your library. In most cases, the MonadError type class introduced before should be enough to cover stacks with exceptions. If you want a real generalization of the Control. Exception functions and interface, I recommend the MonadCatch type class from the exceptions package.

> **Caution**   Throwing exceptions in pure code is not recommended at all. Instead, you should strive to use other kinds of error propagation mechanisms, such as Maybe or Either. Inside IO code, exceptions may result in code that is more concise and clearer (such as having a last-chance exception handler that logs all critical errors) but still shouldn't be overused.

Streaming Data with Conduit

The input/output framework that has been shown in the previous sections is usually known as *classic I/O* or *lazy I/O*. It has been included in Haskell since the first versions. However, the way it works does not interact well with the laziness inherent to the Haskell language, giving rise to the so-called *streaming data problem*. For that reason, several *stream libraries* have been developed, which solve the problems related to this interaction in an elegant and efficient way.

Problems with Lazy Input/Output

Let's consider the following simple piece of code. You open a file, get its contents, close the file, and then work with the information you've just obtained. At first sight, this should be OK: hGetContents reads all the information, and you ensure that the handle is closed with hClose.

```
main = do h <- openFile "/some/text/file" ReadMode
          s <- hGetContents h
          hClose h
          print s
```

However, if you run this code, you'll either get an empty string on the screen or an error message.

```
$ cabal run chapter9-stream
file: hGetContents: illegal operation (delayed read on closed handle)
```

But if you exchange the order of the printing and closing operations, everything works fine. That a simple change in order makes the difference pinpoints a problem in the interaction between input/output operations and the time at which each element in the program is evaluated. Because of the lazy nature of Haskell, the s value won't be evaluated until it's needed, something that happens in the call to print. But at that point, the handle has already been closed, so hGetContents is not able to bring any kind of information from the file. In this case, the behavior of your program doesn't match your expectations.

One possible solution is to force the evaluation of s using seq or deepseq. While this is a working solution, it has two problems. The first one is efficiency: forcing the entire string brings it into memory, consuming scarce system resources. If you want to be clever and force only the string you need, you run into problems of maintenance and composability. For example, which function should be responsible for bringing into memory a determinate value? How can you know up front which of the values will be needed in the entire application?

An even worse solution is keeping the file handle open through the life of the application. But this would have the obvious problem of acquiring resources without releasing them. Files may be cheap resources, but when speaking about network or database connections, this becomes an impossible way to go.

Laziness and IO may bring even more surprises. Suppose that during the execution of hGetContents in the previous code, an exception is thrown. This exception won't be seen by the block of code that generated the string but rather where the value is being used. That means in the middle of some pure computation that uses s, an exception may get in the way, and there's no way to handle it without resorting to IO. Furthermore, your code loses its predictability because you can't always be sure whether using some value would entail running some IO computation.

As you can see, using the simple model of handles that System.IO exposes brings unpredictability to when resources may be released and when exceptions could be thrown. The possible solutions such as forcing evaluation or keeping handles open are definitely inefficient. This is called the *streaming data problem.*

The Haskell community has come up with some solutions to this problem in the form of stream libraries. These libraries usually provide an abstraction of data that comes from a resource in the form of a *stream*. Furthermore, the way in which the resource that generates the data is acquired and released is made much more predictable. In many cases, stream libraries also introduce a boost in performance because they can ensure that only the necessary data for performing an operation is brought into memory.

Several libraries in Hackage are built around this idea. An initial approach, developed by Oleg Kiselyov, is shown in the iteratee and enumerator packages.

Afterward, other libraries provided a more convenient and easy-to-use interface, including pipes, io-streams, and conduit. All those three libraries are used in the wild.

I will now focus on the conduit library because it's been used in other libraries that will be presented later, such as Persistent for database connections. In addition to the core library, there are many other libraries connecting conduit to different sources of data. In any case, the notions that appear in the conduit library are similar to those in any other libraries.

Introducing Conduits

conduit is based on streams of data that are produced, modified, and consumed by different actors. For example, if the "winner clients" example was modeled using conduit, there would be an actor providing a stream of strings from a file, another actor modifying that stream to add the information about whether each client has won or not, and finally another actor converting that stream into a new file in the system.

There are three kinds of actors which take part in processing data. Sources provide streams of values to be consumed. Examples of sources are obtaining text data from a file in disk, reading from a network connection, and obtaining each of the elements in a list. The converse behavior, consuming a stream of values and not producing any further stream (but maybe some final value), is modeled by sinks, for example, writing data into disk or sending it via a network connection. Summing a list could also be seen as a sink, since it turns a list of values into a single one. Finally, we have stream transformers (originally known as conduits) that consume an input stream and produce an output stream.

One important feature is that each actor can take care of acquiring and releasing its resources in a safe and predictable way. For example, a "write to file" sink may open a handle when the stream of data starts and can safely close the handle when the input stream is finished. Furthermore, data is only requested when the next parts of the stream need them, which enables better performance.

The separation between sources, sinks, and conduits used to be part of the public interface of the conduit package, but it is no more. In its current incarnation, the library uses a single type ConduitT i o m r. The first argument i represents the type of values in the input stream; the second argument o represents that of the output stream. The third argument m should be a monad which defines which side effects may occur while processing the stream (in fact, ConduitT is a monad transformer). For example, a source that reads data from a file would have the m parameter equal to IO. Finally, the r argument defines the type of the final result. The trick to only need one type is to set an argument to Void when no output is generated or to ( ) if no input is required or no interesting result is produced.

A complete flow of data is established via the (. |) *connect* or *fuse operator*. Of course, you can only combine two ConduitTs if the output type of one matches the input type of the next one. Finally, to run the operations in a stream, you call runConduit, or runConduitPure if no side effects are involved.

Let's look at some examples involving the simplest kind of stream: a list. All the functions related to using lists in this way are found in the Data.Conduit.List module. The sourceList function produces a stream that gives each of the elements in the list in order. The fold function consumes the list and produces the result of folding a specific function over all the elements. Let's look at an example in the interpreter.

```
*Chapter9.Stream> import Data.Conduit
*Chapter9.Stream Data.Conduit> import qualified Data.Conduit.List as L
*Chapter9.Stream Data.Conduit L> let c = L.sourceList [1 .. 5] .|
L.fold (+) 0
*Chapter9.Stream Data.Conduit L> runConduitPure c
15
```

The Data.Conduit.List includes many other actors over streams that have a similar interface to list functions. A useful one is map, which applies a function to each element in the stream, producing a new stream with the result of each application. You also can use filter on a stream to eliminate those values that are not interesting. As an example, let's compute the sum of the squares of all odd numbers from 1 to 20.

```
> :{
| runConduitPure $ L.sourceList [1 .. 20] .| L.filter odd
|                   .| L.map (\x -> x*x) .| L.fold (+) 0
| :}
1330
```

As in the case of lists, unfolding is another way to generate streams, provided in this case by the unfold function. In the next example, you'll see how it is used to generate an infinite stream of natural numbers, from which it takes only the first ten via isolate. The example also showcases the use of consume, which converts a stream to a simple list.

```
> :{
| runConduitPure $ L.unfold (\x -> Just (x,x+1)) 1
|                     .| L.isolate 10 .| L.consume
| :}
[1,2,3,4,5,6,7,8,9,10]
```

The operations that are similar to lists give you lots of possibilities, but it's interesting to know how to create your own conduits. Inside a ConduitT context, you gain access to four functionalities that are used to build streams:

- await tries to take the next element in the input stream. If it is successful, it's returned wrapped in Just. If the stream doesn't have any more elements, it returns Nothing.

- Input streams can be manipulated also inside a ConduitM. leftover allows you to put back some value on the input stream. At this point, the documentation discourages you from putting back elements that haven't been obtained from a call to await.

- yield is the function used to send values to the output stream.

- The return value of the ConduitT you're coding is stated simply as using the return method of monads.

As an example, let's create a simple conduit that takes a stream of Clients and returns every person, whether an individual or part of a company, which appears in that stream.

```
people :: Monad m => ConduitT (Client i) Person m ()
people = do client <- await
            case client of
              Nothing -> return ()
              Just c -> do case c of
                             Company { person = p }    -> yield p
                             Individual { person = p } -> yield p
                             _                          -> return ()
                           people
```

Notice that the code doesn't have to return one element in the output stream per element in the input stream; government organizations are not yielded. In that way, you can implement filters. You can check that this can be used as a normal Conduit in the interpreter.

```
> :{
| runConduitPure $
|    L.sourceList [ GovOrg 1 "NASA", Individual 2 (Person "A" "S")]
|    .| people .| L.consume
| :}
[Person {firstName = "A", lastName = "S"}]
```

It's important to notice that if you wrap some monad m in ConduitT, the result of streaming data will live inside such monad m. Say that you want to count the number of government organizations that are clients. You can build this with a simple counter, but for illustration purposes let's do so using State. Since ConduitT is a monad transformer, you need to insert calls to lift before the State actions. Also, this conduit does not produce any output stream, so we set the second type argument to Void to indicate this fact.

```
import Control.Monad.State
countGovOrgs :: MonadState Int m => ConduitT (Client i) Void m Int
countGovOrgs = do client <- await
                  case client of
                    Nothing -> do n <- lift $ get
                                  return n
                    Just c  -> do case c of
                                    GovOrg { } -> lift $ modify (+1)
                                    _          -> return ()
                                  countGovOrgs
```

Once you connect countGovOrgs to a source and execute it using runConduit (not runConduitPure since we use the effects of a monad), what you get still needs to be executed on a monad supporting MonadState. In this case, you're interested only in the state, so execState is the function you need to get the result.

```
main = let clients = [ GovOrg 1 "Zas"
                     , Individual 2 (Person "Alejandro" "Serrano")]
           conduitGovOrgs = L.sourceList clients .| countGovOrgs
       in print $ execState (runConduit conduitGovOrgs) 0
```

As an extra example of conduit in which you take advantage of the ability to use other monads underneath, let's implement the "winner clients" intermediate step in this framework. In the same way that the code uses randomRIO, you can use print or any other IO action.

```
import Control.Monad.Trans
import System.Random
winners :: ConduitT (Client i) (Client i, Bool, Int) IO ()
winners = do client <- await
             case client of
               Nothing -> return ()
               Just c  -> do (w :: Bool) <- lift $ randomIO
                             (y :: Int)  <- lift $ randomRIO (0, 3000)
                             yield (c, w, y)
                             winners
```

Exercise 9-4 should help you get fluent with conduit idioms.

EXERCISE 9-4. CONDUIT UTILITIES

Port the list functions that were presented in Chapter 3 to work with streams. In particular, write the definitions of unfold, which should generate a stream of values based on a generator, map that applies a function to all elements of a stream, filter for dropping some of them, and fold that computes a fold of a binary operation over a whole stream.

Accessing Files via Conduit

The problem that pushed you to consider conduit was not about lists but about accessing files better, getting improved performance, and gaining much more predictability. It's time to consider the functions that the conduit ecosystem provides for these tasks, which are available in the Data.Conduit.Binary module of the conduit-extra package.

The interface is simple: the functions sourceFile and sourceHandle generate a stream from a file, whereas sinkFile and sinkHandle consume a stream, writing it into a file. The difference between the two kinds of functions is that those ending in File take care of opening and closing the handle to the corresponding file, whereas the ones ending in Handle must be provided with an already open handle and *do not* close the file at the end. The first ones provide all the features of conduit, whereas the second set enables easy interoperation.

One small tidbit is that those streams do not provide String values but rather ByteString values. This latter type is a more efficient way to treat bytes of data. The next chapter includes a complete treatment of ByteString, which is defined in the bytestring package, along with ways to convert it from and to String. But for the simple example of "winner clients" where each line must be enlarged with some extra information, the only thing you need to know is that pack converts a String into a ByteString. Here's the corresponding code:

```
import qualified Data.ByteString.Char8 as BS
import qualified Data.Conduit.Binary as B
import Data.Monoid
winnersFile :: (Monad m, MonadIO m)
            => ConduitT BS.ByteString BS.ByteString m ()
winnersFile = do
  client <- await
  case client of
    Nothing -> return ()
    Just c  -> do (w :: Bool) <- liftIO $ randomIO
                  (y :: Int ) <- liftIO $ randomRIO (0, 3000)
                  yield $ c <> BS.pack (" " ++ show w ++ " " ++ show y)
                  winnersFile
```

As you may notice, the winnersFile code does not refer directly to the IO monad but rather to a type class called MonadIO. This is the class of all monad stacks that support calling IO actions inside its body. The particular feature that the MonadIO type class adds is lifting computations via liftIO.

With the information you have, putting all the actors to work reading and writing the file should be as simple as the following code. Notice the lines function, which separates a file into parts delimited by newlines.

```
main = runConduit $
         B.sourceFile "clients.db" .| B.lines .| winnersFile
                                   .| B.sinkFile "clientsWinners.db"
```

But the compiler will refuse such code. At this point, you need the extra generality introduced earlier via the MonadIO constraint. The operations that create sources or sinks in the Data.Conduit.Binary module use an extra facility from the conduit package (or to be more precise, from the resource package), to handle the opening and closing of resources in a safe fashion. The only difference is that you need to use runConduitRes instead of runConduit:

```
main = runConduitRes $
          B.sourceFile "clients.db" .| B.lines .| winnersFile
                              .| B.sinkFile "clientsWinners.db"
```

Now you are sure that your files will be opened and closed when required.

THE RESOURCET PACKAGE

In the previous example, you saw how conduit uses ResourceT to manage the allocation and release of resources. This monad transformer, which lives in the resourcet package, is a generalization of the bracket function in Control.Exception. In particular, you can use its allocate function to acquire a resource along with a release action that is ensured to be called when the control exists from the ResourceT block.

If only that functionality is provided, you will gain nothing from using ResourceT instead of bracket. But the former also allows you to release resources explicitly by calling the release function along with an identifier that allocate returns.

This package is useful for implementing managers of scarce resources. If your intention is to use a pool of resources for sharing them, you should also look at the resource-pool package, which can be easily combined with resourcet.

Looking Further Than Text Files

At the beginning of the chapter, I mentioned that IO allows you to access a large variety of resources and perform many kinds of side effects. However, the only focus until now has been interacting with the console and accessing text files in the disk. This section presents two examples of work inside conduit but that relate to networking and binary serialization of Haskell data.

Basic Networking

The conduit-extra package does not only provide a conduit-based interface to the file system. Its Data.Conduit.Network module provides ready-to-use sources and sinks for network programming. There is one simplification though; when using this interface, an actor in the network is either a server, which listens for incoming connections, or a client, which connects to a server, but not both. Furthermore, the connection always runs through TCP. The network interface provided by lower-level packages allows a much wider range of behavior, but in practice these two modes are enough for most applications.

In both the server and the client, the module expects a value of type AppData -> IO r, where the result r differs in the server and client, in addition to the connection parameters. That value of type AppData is used to retrieve the source and sink in which you can read and write the connection, respectively. There are also generalized versions which use AppData -> m r, where m supports IO operations, but I do not consider them here.

The network application to develop will be yet another way to look at the "winner clients." In this case, the client will send its name, obtained from the console, and the server will return information about whether the client has won. The main Conduit in the server is like the previous exercises. The only addition is a call to putStrLn to print the name of the user on the screen.

```
{-# LANGUAGE ScopedTypeVariables #-}
import Control.Monad.Trans
import qualified Data.ByteString.Char8 as BS
import Data.Conduit
import Data.Monoid
import System.Random
isWinner :: ConduitT BS.ByteString BS.ByteString IO ()
isWinner = do client <- await
              case client of
                Nothing -> return ()
                Just c  -> do
                  lift $ BS.putStrLn c
                  (w :: Bool) <- liftIO $ randomIO
```

```
(y :: Int ) <- liftIO $ randomRIO (0, 3000)
yield $ c <> BS.pack (" " ++ show w ++ " " ++ show y)
isWinner
```

The next step is to create the conduit which will tie together the input flow of data to the server and the output to each client. For that matter, you can access the source and sink representing the connection via the appSource and appSink functions.

```
import Data.Conduit.Network
serverApp :: AppData -> IO ()
serverApp d = runConduit $ appSource d .| isWinner .| appSink d
```

The last step is to start the server in the entry point. runTCPServer is the one with that task and needs as parameters both the port in which it will keep listening and the kind of connections to accept. You can restrict connections through IPv4 or IPv6 or from a specific address. In this case, any client is welcome.

```
{-# LANGUAGE OverloadedStrings #-}
import Network.Socket
main :: IO ()
main = withSocketsDo $ runTCPServer (serverSettings 8900 "*") serverApp
```

Note   On Windows systems, you need to initialize the networking subsystem before doing any communication over that channel. You can achieve this by wrapping your main code with a call to withSocketsDo from the Network. Socket module in the network package, as done earlier. The function itself has no effect on other operating systems, so you should always include it to retain maximum compatibility between platforms.

The other side of the coin, the client, is much simpler. After the connection is created by the runTCPClient function, it must write the name given by the command line to the appSink, which will send that information to the server. Once some information is returned, it just prints it to the screen. In total, the code looks like this:

```
{-# LANGUAGE OverloadedStrings #-}
import Network.Socket
import System.Environment
```

```
main :: IO ()
main = withSocketsDo $ do
        (name:_) <- getArgs
        runTCPClient (clientSettings 8900 "127.0.0.1") (clientApp name)
clientApp :: String -> AppData -> IO ()
clientApp name d = do runConduit $ (yield $ BS.pack name) .| appSink d
                      runConduit $ appSource d .| (do Just w <- await
                                                      lift $ BS.putStrLn w)
```

As you can see, conduit allows you to treat both files in disk and network connections with the same abstractions. This makes it easy to reuse data transformation functions between different resources, as this example has done with isWinner.

Note   The network package provides an interface to networking using the more conventional approach of sockets. You can create the sockets using that package and still access the data using the sourceSocket and sinkSocket functions.

Binary Serialization

In the Haskell ecosystem, there are two main libraries to automatically serialize Haskell values into binary data. That is, it converts some value to a stream of bytes that can later be read to reconstruct such value. This data can be sent through a network, written to disk, or in general used as any other byte-encoded information.

These libraries are binary and cereal. Both provide almost the same interface. The only difference is that when using binary, you reference the Binary type class from the Data.Binary module; and when using cereal, you should use the Serialize type class in the Data.Serialize module. There are also corresponding packages to perform the serialization via streams: binary-conduit and cereal-conduit. The difference, which is important in terms of laziness and performance, is that cereal is strict, whereas binary is lazy. This implies, for example, that binary can cope with infinite streams of data (e.g., provided through a network connection), whereas cereal cannot. On the other hand, the lazy behavior of binary may give surprising results in some cases.

Since both are so similar, in this section the focus will be just on binary and binary-conduit. The first thing you must do to be able to serialize your own data types is instantiate the Binary type class. Prior to GHC 7.2.1, you had to write the code for the instance by hand, but since that version, the compiler can write the instance for you. Thus, I won't delve into the details of Binary instances.

Let's say you want to serialize values of the Person data type introduced in Chapters 2 and 3 using the automatic derivation of Binary. First, you need to enable the DeriveGeneric extension to GHC. Then, you can include Generic in the deriving clause of the data type. An instance of Generic contains information about the constructors and arguments that a specific data type declares. Using that information, binary can build a whole Binary instance, so you need only to declare it, but you need to do this without providing any implementation of the functions. For Person, the whole code reads as follows:

```
{-# LANGUAGE DeriveGeneric #-}
import Data.Binary (Binary)
import GHC.Generics (Generic)
data Person = Person { firstName :: String, lastName  :: String }
            deriving (Show, Read, Generic)
instance Binary Person
```

Another alternative is to enable a small GHC extension which allows us to indicate that we want to derive Binary directly in the data definition.

```
{-# LANGUAGE DeriveAnyClass #-}
data Person = Person { firstName :: String, lastName  :: String }
            deriving (Show, Read, Generic, Binary)
```

Once you have a Binary instance, you get access to the functions decode and encode, which convert from and to ByteStrings to the corresponding values, respectively. The binary-conduit package wraps those functions, allowing you to provide a stream of values from encode or to consume a stream of values, serializing each of them in turn, from decode. The following example serializes a list of people to disk. The specific code that brings binary into the game is shown in bold.

```
import Data.Conduit
import qualified Data.Conduit.List as L
import qualified Data.Conduit.Binary as B
import qualified Data.Conduit.Serialization.Binary as S
main = runConduitRes $
```

```
      L.sourceList clients.| S.conduitEncode .| B.sinkFile "people.db"
where clients = [Person "Alejandro" "Serrano", Person " Doctor" "Who?"]
```

Doing the converse is also simple. The only difference is using conduitDecode instead of conduitEncode. The following example gets a stream of Person elements and outputs them to the screen:

```
import Control.Monad.Trans
main = runConduitRes $
  B.sourceFile "people.db"
  .| S.conduitDecode
  .| L.mapM_ (\(p :: Person) -> lift $ putStrLn $ show p)
```

It's important that binary knows which kind of value it's deserializing, either from using other functions on them or by explicitly writing a signature (like in the example). In the version of binary used when writing this book, if you change Person to String, the code still works OK but generates a stream of four strings instead of two Persons.

Comma-Separated Values

Another simple format to save or transmit data is comma-separated values, usually shortened to CSV. Turning Haskell values into this format is as simple as doing binary serialization as described earlier, thanks to the cassava package and the cassava-conduit bridge to encoding and decoding.

In fact, the only difference is that instead of Binary, you have to write instances for ToRecord and FromRecord. As in the previous case, all these instances can be automatically generated. Remember that you need to choose only one of the following options: either independent instance declarations or using the DeriveAnyClass extension and adding FromRecord and ToRecord to the deriving clause. If you add the code as it is, GHC complains about duplicate instances.

```
import Data.Csv (FromRecord, ToRecord)
-- option 1: using a separate instance
instance FromRecord Person
instance ToRecord Person
-- option 2: using DeriveAnyClass
data Person = Person { firstName :: String, lastName  :: String }
            deriving (Show, Read, Generic, FromRecord, ToRecord)
```

Encoding to CSV instead of a binary format translates to replacing the conduitEncode function from the latter with toCsv of the former. Decoding takes slightly more work, as shown in the following code:

```
import qualified Data.Csv as Csv
import qualified Data.Csv.Conduit as Csv
import System.IO.Error
main = runConduitRes $
  B.sourceFile "people.db"
  .| Csv.fromCsvLiftError (userError . show)
                          Csv.defaultDecodeOptions Csv.NoHeader
  .| L.mapM_ (\(p :: Person) -> lift $ putStrLn $ show p)
```

When decoding from CSV, problems may arise. The number or format of the data in the file may not be as required to create a value of the corresponding type. As with other parts of the Haskell ecosystem, cassava-conduit forces you to decide what to do with those errors. The simplest strategy is to map the errors from CSV decoding into those understood by the monad in which the conduit runs. In the preceding code, that monad is IO, and its error type is IOException. We use the simplest mechanism: turn the error into a string using show and then throw the exception with that string, without further inspection.

In addition to this error mapping, the decoder also needs to know several options, including how values are separated, and whether the file contains a first row with headers or not. In the preceding example, we use the default, which means that values are separated by commas.

BETTER SERIALIZATION

None of the serialization mechanisms presented in this chapter is very efficient when you need to query and transform a lot of data because the full set of data must be brought into memory and decoded. A better solution is to use a database management system for storing the information. Chapter 12 is devoted to connecting to databases in Haskell and storing and querying the data saved in them. In Chapter 11, I consider another common interchange format: JSON.

Summary

This chapter covered how to interface with the "outer world" and explained how to deal with side effects.

- The IO monad was presented as the one that gives context for *side effects* in computations. Furthermore, we looked at the way in which Haskell separates pure computations from those with side effects.

- You learned how to read and write from the *console* and from *files* in the disk using the "classic I/O" approach.

- Another source of side effects is *randomness*, which is provided by the random package.

- The chapter covered the way in which *errors* are handled in pure code. In particular, I talked about the Either type.

- Side-effect computations open the door to *exceptions*, an extensible but impure way to treat erroneous scenarios inside IO.

- The "classic I/O" exhibit has several deficiencies in its interaction with laziness. The conduit library is a solution for those problems based on the stream abstraction.

- Finally, you learned how to use conduit in several scenarios, such as reading and writing to files, communicating through the network, and serializing Haskell values to various formats.

Building and Parsing Text

The previous chapter opened the door to side effects, including, among others, saving data from your Haskell application on disk or sending it through the network. However, the only true serialization mechanism that was introduced was the binary one, through the binary package.

In many cases, a *textual representation* of data is preferable to a binary one. Even though it is usually much larger, data encoded in text is more readable for a human consumer, making your programs much easier to inspect and debug. Furthermore, many interchange formats such as XML or JSON encode the data in text, adding to the plain information tags to structure it.

Haskell has great features for working with text, which are the focus of this chapter. As you will see, the built-in String data type is not the best option in many cases and should be replaced by much more efficient alternatives such as ByteString and Text. You shouldn't use plain concatenation to build output text either; your programs should use *builders*.

The converse operation, decoding some information from a textual representation, is called parsing. Haskell offers an approach to parsing that uses combinators, which is exemplified by the attoparsec library. Interestingly, parsing introduces new type classes, the most important one being Applicative.

The Five Textual Data Types

Treating text correctly is a difficult task in almost any programming language. Behind the simple concept of textual data, there are always subtle issues related to encoding and representation in memory. This section discusses how to deal with text in the most correct and efficient way in your Haskell code.

Until now, you've worked with text values represented within the String data type, which is just a synonym for [Char], a list of characters. The main benefit of String is

© Alejandro Serrano Mena 2022
A. Serrano Mena, *Practical Haskell*, https://doi.org/10.1007/978-1-4842-8581-7_10

the simple model that allows any function working on lists to work also on text. Since lists are an integral part of Haskell, this is an important feature. Another good quality of String is its support for Unicode. You may not have tried it, but any of the code you've written with String would work perfectly with Chinese, Greek, or Cyrillic characters.

The downside is that this ease of use comes at the expense of performance. Even though GHC performs extensive optimizations on Strings, there's some overhead both in time and in memory compared to the raw representation as used in other languages. When you are dealing with large quantities of text (e.g., generating output for a web application), you need the best performance possible.

At this point, two functionalities collide, and you need to balance them:

- You want to see the string as a bare *stream of bytes*. If you don't confer any extra meaning to the raw bytes, you can substantially increase the performance because operating systems usually provide specialized operations for moving bulk blocks of bytes quickly both on memory and to disk.

- Those bytes have an *intended meaning*. To recover the meaning, you need to consider the encoding the data uses. The same bytes may mean different things when interpreted as a set of Latin-only characters or when using UTF-8 to decode them. Thus, if you care about the actual characters encoded in the string, you have to be careful when performing operations on them. The aim should be to have a data type that is as performant as possible while still maintaining correctness.

In the case of Haskell, the Haskell Platform splits the String data type in two other different types. When you need a fast implementation but are looking only at the text as raw bytes, you should choose the ByteString type from the bytestring package. The Text type, bundled in the text package, focuses on describing Unicode strings while keeping up good performance.

Note   String is good for experimentation and for the prototyping phases of development because Haskell makes the String easy to use. However, when writing actual code, you should use ByteString or Text. Furthermore, making this choice will make you consider other important issues such as encoding.

In addition to this distinction in focus, the two libraries provide both strict and lazy versions of their corresponding data types. Remember the subtle balance that strictness and laziness expose. Using a strict ByteString or Text means that you might end up evaluating chunks of text that are larger than expected. On the other hand, laziness may bring back some of the problems that were discussed in the previous chapter.

Table 10-1 shows the two dimensions and the module you should import to get each set of features. Notice that for lazy Unicode data, you can use both lazy Text and built-in [Char].

Table 10-1. *Haskell Platform Modules for Textual Data*

	Strict	**Lazy**
Raw stream of bytes	Data.ByteString	Data.ByteString.Lazy
Unicode data	Data.Text	Data.Text.Lazy or [Char]

As important as deciding which type to use is knowing how to convert between those different representations. For example, you may need to insert some String obtained by calling getLine inside a Text value. Another common scenario is getting some input from a file or from a network as a stream of bytes, which is described as a ByteString value, and decoding it to a Text value. Figure 10-1 summarizes all possible paths between the types.

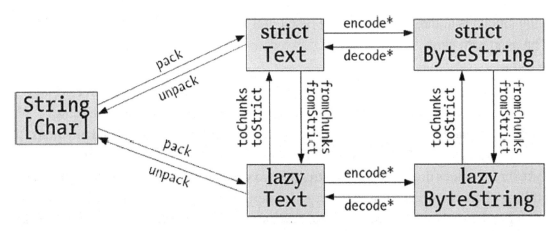

Figure 10-1. *Conversions between textual data types*

There are two points to be made about Figure 10-1. The first one is that conversion between strict and lazy types can be done via toStrict and fromStrict, but also via toChunks and fromChunks. All these functions are available in the modules corresponding to lazy versions, that is, Data.Text.Lazy or Data.ByteString.Lazy. The difference is that the functions ending in Strict consume or produce strict versions, whereas the Chunks functions consume or produce *lists* of strict values. Here are two of these signatures:

```
toStrict :: Data.ByteString.Lazy.ByteString -> Data.ByteString.ByteString
toChunks :: Data.ByteString.Lazy.ByteString -> [Data.ByteString.ByteString]
```

This small distinction allows you to retain some degree of laziness even with strict versions because the elements in the list will be evaluated only when needed.

There's no single conversion between Text and ByteString but rather a family of them, found in the Data.Text.Encoding and Data.Text.Lazy.Encoding modules. Each of the functions includes in its name the encoding that should be used to give meaning to the raw stream of bytes. For example, encodeUtf8 converts some text to the byte representation using UTF-8; decodeLatin1 does the converse operation but with Latin-1 encoded text.

Note   There are direct conversions from String to ByteString defined in the modules Data.ByteString.Char8 and Data.ByteString.Lazy. Char8. However, they treat each character as an 8-bit value, dropping any extra information (most characters need more than one byte to be encoded). Thus, using the functions in those modules may result in a loss of information, so they should be used with care.

In addition to conversions between them, the external interface to ByteString and Text is almost the same. For that reason, it's common to import the corresponding modules in qualified form. Functions are also rather similar to the list-based functions that you would use for String. The main difference with them is that Text and ByteString values do not define constructors, so you need to substitute the use of (:) to add one character with cons and the use of pattern matching with head and tail. On the other hand, usual functions such as map, reverse, foldr, or foldl maintain their names, as this example shows:

```
*Chapter10.Text> import qualified Data.Text as T
*Chapter10.Text T> :t T.pack "Hello Text type"
```

```
T.pack "Hello Text type" :: T.Text
*Chapter10.Text T> import Data.Char
*Chapter10.Text T Data.Char> T.map toUpper (T.pack "Hello Text type")
"HELLO TEXT TYPE"
*...> T.intercalate (T.pack ",") (map T.pack ["apples","oranges"])
"apples,oranges"
*Chapter10.Text T Data.Char> T.length (T.pack "A Text example")
14
```

Both Text and ByteString are instances of the Monoid type class. This is quite useful because the (<>) operator is equivalent to concatenation, a quite common operation to do on these types.

```
*...> (T.pack "Hello ") <> (T.pack "Beginning Haskell")
"Hello Beginning Haskell"
```

There's still one drawback to using Text or ByteString instead of String: the code becomes full of calls to T.pack to convert from literals. Because of the popularity of these packages, the GHC developers have introduced an extension that allows you to write constant values directly as string literals, making the compiler responsible for inserting the corresponding calls to pack (in many cases, the call to pack is further optimized, and the literal is compiled directly to its Text or ByteString representation). This extension is called OverloadedStrings. The following example enables such an extension in GHCi and uses it to construct directly a Text value:

```
*Chapter10.Text T Data.Char Data.Monoid> :set -XOverloadedStrings
*Chapter10.Text T Data.Char Data.Monoid> T.map toUpper "Hello Text type"
"HELLO TEXT TYPE"
```

Be aware that in some cases you may need to introduce an explicit type signature in order to fix the type of text value you're creating. But in most cases, Haskell type inference will be able to make the decision.

In the previous chapter, I introduced the functions in Data.Conduit.Binary that work with files on the disk, as well as Data.Conduit.Network that does the same but with a network connection. In that case, the type of input and output streams was ByteString, which is compatible with the treatment of raw bytes, which was discussed here. If you want to treat Text data, you need to convert it via an encoding, using the

Conduits in Data.Conduit.Text. The functions in that module take a codec, like utf8, as a parameter. This is the final version of the "winner clients" application using conduit:

```
{-# LANGUAGE OverloadedStrings #-}

import Control.Monad.Trans
import Data.Conduit
import qualified Data.Conduit.Binary as B
import qualified Data.Conduit.List as L
import qualified Data.Conduit.Text as T
import Data.Text

main :: IO()
main = runConduitRes $
  B.sourceFile "clients.db" .| T.decode T.utf8 .|
  T.lines .| winnersFile .| L.concatMap (\x -> [x, "\n"]) .|
  T.encode T.utf8 .| B.sinkFile "clientsWinners.db"

winnersFile :: (Monad m, MonadIO m) => ConduitT Text Text m ()
winnersFile = ...   -- same as previous chapter, but using Text
```

Note   In addition to using conduit, you can also access files directly as Text or ByteString using the "classical I/O" approach. Those functions live in the Data.Text.IO and Data.ByteString.IO packages and have the same name as their String counterparts.

Building As Fast As the Wind

Until now, the examples have shown how to deal with chunks of text data in several ways, but no complete example has been shown that stores the list of clients on disk. But this shouldn't be complicated; one way to do it is just to generate a big Text value and then save it using conduit.

Since the purpose of the data is to be read back by other applications, you should impose some structure to the representation. In particular, the encoding that I've chosen for Client is the following:

- Each client is written as its own line. So, the file has a list of clients delimited by newline characters. This allows faster reading via lines afterward.

- Each client's data starts with client, and the fields composing the information will be written between parentheses and as a list separated by commas.

- The first field in each line specifies the kind of client. gov, com, or ind will be used in each case.

- Since newline, comma, and parenthesis characters are used for special purposes, these will be replaced by \n, \,, \(, and \) inside each representation.

- The rules for the embedded Person data type are the same, but with the information prepended by person instead of client.

The implementation using Text is straightforward.

```
{-# LANGUAGE OverloadedStrings #-}

import Data.Conduit
import qualified Data.Conduit.Binary as B
import qualified Data.Conduit.List as L
import qualified Data.Conduit.Text as T
import Data.Monoid
import Data.Text

saveClients :: FilePath -> [Client Int] -> IO ()
saveClients fpath clients = runConduitRes $
  L.sourceList clients .| L.map clientToText
    .| L.concatMap (\x -> [x, "\n"])   -- write '\n' between clients
.| T.encode T.utf8 .| B.sinkFile fpath

clientToText :: Client Int -> Text
clientToText (GovOrg  i n)     =
```

```
      "client(gov," <> escapeString (show i) <> "," <> escapeString n <> ")"
clientToText (Company i n p d) =
      "client(com," <> escapeString (show i) <> "," <> escapeString n <> ","
        <> personToText p <> "," <> escapeString d <> ")"
clientToText (Individual i p)  =
      "client(ind," <> escapeString (show i) <> "," <> personToText p <> ")"

personToText :: Person -> Text
personToText (Person f l) = "person(" <> escapeString f <> "," <>
escapeString l <> ")"

escapeString :: String -> Text
escapeString = replace "\n" "\\n" . replace "," "\\," .
               replace "(" "\\(" . replace ")" "\\(" . pack
```

However, while its simplicity cannot be denied, this code is highly inefficient. Every time two elements are concatenated, a new Text value has to be created, and this comes with some overhead to allocate memory, to copy data, and also to keep track of the value and release it when it's no longer needed. Furthermore, the conversion of integer values to Text entails an intermediate conversion to String via the show function.

Both the text and bytestring packages provide a Builder data type that can be used to efficiently generate large text values. The trick is that a Builder is not itself a value but instead encodes how to build the large text value from its constituent parts. Then, you execute the Builder, which finally generates the string you were looking for. In this last step of executions, many optimizations can be done. For example, the Builder knows how long the final result will be, so it can allocate the whole memory it needs just once.

Builders are built from three basic blocks. You can build one out of a single character using the singleton function or build it from a larger string value using one of fromString, fromText, or fromLazyText. The following code, however, takes advantage of the OverloadedStrings extension, which allows you to create a Builder from a literal string. Finally, Builders are concatenated via the Monoid (<>), like Text values are. The following code is a complete replacement of the previous one, where Builders are used instead of Text:

```
import qualified Data.Text.Lazy.Builder as B
import qualified Data.Text.Lazy.Builder.Int as B
```

```
clientToText :: Client Int -> B.Builder
clientToText (GovOrg i n) =
  "client(gov," <> B.decimal i <> B.singleton ','
                <> B.fromText (escapeString n) <> B.singleton ')'
clientToText (Company i n p d) =
  "client(com," <> B.decimal i <> B.singleton ','
                <> B.fromText (escapeString n) <> B.singleton ','
                <> personToText p <> B.singleton ','
                <> B.fromText (escapeString d) <> B.singleton ')'
clientToText (Individual i p) =
  "client(ind," <> B.decimal i <> B.singleton ','
                <> personToText p <> B.singleton ')'

personToText :: Person -> B.Builder
personToText (Person f l) =
  "person(" <> B.fromText (escapeString f) <> B.singleton ','
            <> B.fromText (escapeString l) <> B.singleton ')'
```

You may have noticed that the Data.Text.Lazy.Builder.Int has also been imported into the code. This module gives you access to the decimal combinator, which is a fast Builder for converting integer values into text. If you prefer to use base 16, you may use hexadecimal instead.

To get the final Text value, you just need to call toLazyText on the Builder. As the name suggests, you won't get a strict Text value but rather a *lazy* one. Remember that in any case you have the toStrict function to convert that value to a strict one when needed. Let's see an example of building a client description in GHCi.

```
> let co = (Company 1 "Black Hole" (Person "John" "Smith") "Traveller")
> B.toLazyText $ clientToText co
"client(com,1,Black Hole,person(John,Smith),Traveller)"
```

Since conduit uses strict ByteStrings instead of lazy ones, the new version of saveClients using Builders must call toStrict at some point. The implementation shows that fact.

```
import qualified Data.Text.Lazy as LT
saveClients fpath clients = runConduitRes $
  L.sourceList clients .| L.map clientToText
```

```
.| L.map (LT.toStrict . B.toLazyText)
.| L.concatMap (\x -> [x, "\n"])  -- write '\n' between clients
.| T.encode T.utf8 .| B.sinkFile fpath
```

The bytestring library provides Builders for both strict and lazy ByteStrings in the Data.ByteString.Builder and Data.ByteString.Lazy.Builder modules, respectively. Note that the purpose of ByteString Builder is not to produce some text content but rather a stream of raw bytes. Thus, you can use it to create your own *binary* format via new combinators. For example, the library provides functions such as in16LE and word64BE, which directly include some value of a specific number of bits (8, 16, 32, or 64) with big-endian or little-endian formats directly as raw data.

Note   Remember, use Builders when you want to generate a large Text value or a big stream of bytes. They provide much more efficiency than bare concatenation of strings, without any loss in expressiveness.

You can use the same techniques shown here to allow clients to write information about products and purchases in disk. Exercise 10-1 guides you in the process of doing so.

EXERCISE 10-1. BUILDING PRODUCTS AND PURCHASES

Write Builders for the following data types that encode products and purchases in the Time Machine Store:

```
data Product  = Product  { id :: Int, name :: String, price :: Double
                         , description :: String }
data Purchase = Purchase { client :: Client Int, products :: [Product] }
```

You can use any representation you want. However, make sure to escape characters correctly so that later other applications can read the file.

Parsing with attoparsec

While generating output efficiently is useful, it's often necessary to read back those values in your application. You can use a textual format to interchange information between applications, such as a web front end, an accounting program, an inventory application, and so on.

The most efficient way to deal with the problem of recognizing patterns is using a *parser*. Often, you create a description of the grammar (in other words, of the structure that strings will follow) in a file separate from your source code. Then, a parser generator converts the description into executable code written in a specific programming language. The best-known examples of these parser generators are bison or yacc for C, ANTLR and JavaCC for Java, and Happy for Haskell.

The focus in this section won't be on these parser generators but rather on the attoparsec package that you can find in Hackage. When using attoparsec, you describe your grammar using a set of combinators *within* your Haskell code. The benefit of this approach is that you can take advantage of the modularization and reuse features of the Haskell programming language when writing your parser. For example, you may declare a function that takes as a parameter a parser and generates another one that is the same one given as an argument but run twice.

Note In the following examples, the code will use the Data.Attoparsec.Text module, which creates parsers that work on Text values. If you're interested in parsing ByteStrings instead, you should use the Data.Attoparsec module.

The simplest example of a parser is one that needs to match an exact string to succeed. The corresponding combinator is called, quite naturally, string and takes as a parameter the string to match. In the interpreter, let's try to run a parser that succeeds only with hello on some different strings.[1]

```
*Chapter10.Parsing> :set -XOverloadedStrings
*Chapter10.Parsing> import Data.Attoparsec.Text
*Chapter10.Parsing Data.Attoparsec.Text> parse (string "hello") "hello"
Done "" "hello"
```

---

[1] The messages in the case of failure may differ depending on your version of attoparsec.

```
*Chapter10.Parsing ...> parse (string "hello") "hello world"
Done " world" "hello"
*Chapter10.Parsing ...> parse (string "hello") "bye bye"
Fail "bye bye" [] "string"
*Chapter10.Parsing ...> parse (string "hello") "he"
Partial _
*Chapter10.Parsing ...> feed (parse (string "hello") "he") "llo"
Done "" "hello"
```

As you can see, the function that ultimately executes a parser is called parse. It takes as a first argument the description of the format to decode and as a second argument the string that should be matched. However, the results from parsing may be a bit surprising.

- Execution of the parser *consumes* only *part* of the string; the remainder is left for further work. The Done constructor for results wraps both that part that hasn't been used in the parsing process, along with the string that successfully matched. In the example, parsing "hello" returns no leftover strings, whereas doing so on "hello world" makes " world" still available.

- In some cases, the execution of the parser just fails; this is described by the Fail constructor of the result.

- A third possibility to be returned is Partial. This highlights one important feature of attoparsec: it parses strings *incrementally*. In this example, when you provide "he", attoparsec does not have enough data to finish running the parser, so it gives you a callback you can use to provide more input. This is done via feed. In this example, if you provide "llo", you get a successful parse.

attoparsec includes some built-in parsers for different kinds of numbers, such as decimal, hexadecimal, or signed for integer values; rational for exact fractions; and double for floating-point values. Let's try to use one of them.

```
*Chapter10.Parsing Data.Attoparsec.Text> parse decimal "78 cents"
Done " cents" 78
```

As you can see, the returned value is not a string but rather the *actual integer value* that could be parsed from the start of the string. This is another important characteristic of attoparsec: the parsers you create build Haskell values as they go. The type of the result is encoded in the type variable of the Parser type, which represents the basic attoparsec blocks. For example, the type of decimal is Integral a => Parser a.

The string and numeric parsers are basic blocks you can use to build larger ones. For that, you need combinators that combine parsers in certain ways. The first one is (<|>), which represents the *disjunction* of two parsers. If the first one doesn't succeed on some input, the second one is tried. Let's say you want to match either hello or bye. The following GHCi output shows how to do that. Notice that the (<|>) combinator lives in the Control.Applicative module (you'll soon learn why) and that the code is using a variant of parse named parseOnly, which returns the success or failure of the parser using Either.

```
*> import Control.Applicative
*> parseOnly (string "hello" <|> string "bye") "hello"
Right "hello"
*> parseOnly (string "hello" <|> string "bye") "bye!"
Right "bye"
*> parseOnly (string "hello" <|> string "bye") "aloha"  -- should fail
Left "string"
```

Note   The result types of the parsers being conjoined must coincide.

The next step is to combine several parsers in *sequence*. There's one small tidbit: since each parser returns a result, you need to tell attoparsec how to combine those results. This is done via the (<$>) and (<*>) combinators. The first one is used just after the function, which should combine the results, and the second one is used to thread each of the arguments, in case the function has more than one. To make things clear, let's define a parser that accepts hello or bye followed by a number and builds a value of type GreetingYear.

```
{-# LANGUAGE OverloadedStrings #-}

import Control.Applicative
import Data.Text
import Data.Attoparsec.Text
```

```
data GreetingYear = GreetingYear Text Int

greetingYearParser :: Parser GreetingYear
greetingYearParser = GreetingYear <$> (string "hello" <|> string "bye")
                                  <*> decimal
```

The code without any parsing involved could be written using the ($) application function instead of (<$>) and simply a space instead of (<*>). As you can see, the interface of parser combinators resembles regular Haskell code, which makes it easy to use. With (<$>) and (<*>), you *lift* your normal functions to work on values wrapped in Parser. Let's look at the types of those two operations.

```
(<$>) :: (a -> b)         -> Parser a -> Parser b
(<*>) :: Parser (a -> b) -> Parser a -> Parser b
```

The first one is essentially your old friend fmap, which makes a pure function work on elements of a functor. Parser is an instance of Functor. In the previous example, you have the following:

```
GreetingYear                          :: Text -> (Int -> GreetingYear)
(string "hello" <|> string "bye")  :: Parser Text
GreetingYear <$> (string "hello" <|> string "bye")
                                      :: Parser (Int -> GreetingYear)
```

The (<*>) function is the one helping you supply more arguments to the function. Or, from another point of view, (<*>) unwraps the function inside a Parser and applies one argument.

```
GreetingYear <$> (string "hello" <|> string "bye")
                                      :: Parser (Int -> GreetingYear)
decimal                               :: Parser Int
GreetingYear <$> (string "hello" <|> string "bye") <*> decimal
                                      :: Parser GreetingYear
```

Thanks to curried functions, you can iterate (<*>) to apply each of the arguments of a multiparameter function.

Sometimes, working with (<$>) and (<*>) alone is not enough for creating a maintainable Parser. For example, say you want to recognize the same pattern as shown earlier but with a space between the greeting and the number. You have almost all the building blocks to do so, but how do you recognize a single character? This is achieved via the char function. Now, you could write code similar to the following:

```
greetingYearParserS :: Parser GreetingYear
greetingYearParserS = (\g _ y -> GreetingYear g y)
                        <$> (string "hello" <|> string "bye")
                        <*> char ' ' <*> decimal
```

Notice how the better-looking application of GreetingYear has been replaced with an abstraction whose only matter is dropping some of its arguments. If you were to change this parser (e.g., requiring an extra ! character after the greeting), you would need to assemble a new abstraction and take care that you drop the new unnecessary data. Clearly, this is not maintainable. The Control.Applicative module offers a version of (<*>), namely (<*), which describes the case where some input should be parsed but won't be used to build any larger structure. Using it, the previous becomes the following:

```
greetingYearParserS :: Parser GreetingYear
greetingYearParserS = GreetingYear
                        <$> (string "hello" <|> string "bye")
                        <*  char ' ' <*> decimal
```

It's time to start building the parser for the Client output generated in the previous section. The first thing you need is some way to parse names, taking into account the rules of escaping that were outlined (remember, the characters , \n ( ) were replaced by a backslash and the character itself). Let's create a parser that returns a single character, the satisfy combinator, that matches any character that satisfies a particular predicate; the notInClass function, which returns True only when an element is not in some set, will become handy. Also, when \, and similar combinations are found, you want to return the corresponding single character, for which the const function is used.

```
aChar :: Parser Char
aChar =    (const ',') <$> (string "\\,")
       <|> (const '\n') <$> (string "\\n")
       <|> (const '(')  <$> (string "\\(")
       <|> (const ')')  <$> (string "\\)")
       <|> satisfy (notInClass ",\n()")
```

The idea is to call this parser repeatedly until some nonmatching input is found. One way to do this would be to create a new `Parser` that calls itself recursively. In each step, it prepends a character to the `String` value to be returned later. But you also need a base case, which will be applied when a nonmatching character is found. The way to create a `Parser` that returns some value, without consuming any input, is via `pure :: a -> Parser a`. With all these ingredients, the code reads as follows:

```
aString :: Parser String
aString = ((:) <$> aChar <*> aString) <|> (pure "")
```

This pattern is common in parsers (if you know some grammar theory, the operation is called *Kleene star*, and it's one of the basics in that theory), so `Control.Applicative` offers a `many` function that just iterates a parser until no matching input is found. The result is a list of the type of inner parsers, in this case `[Char]`.

```
aString = many aChar
```

Once you know how to parse the escaped strings and integer numbers, you can create a parser for `Person` and `Client`. The following code is straightforward; the only new function introduced is (`<$`), which is the application function that drops its first argument. The purpose is similar to (`<*`).

```
aPerson :: Parser Person
aPerson = Person <$ string "person(" <*> aString
                 <* char ',' <*> aString <* char ')'

aClient :: Parser (Client Int)
aClient =     GovOrg     <$ string "client(gov," <*> decimal
                         <* char ',' <*> aString <* char ')'
          <|> Company    <$ string "client(com," <*> decimal
                         <* char ',' <*> aString <* char ','
                         <*> aPerson <* char ',' <*> aString <* char ')'
          <|> Individual <$ string "client(ind," <*> decimal
                         <* char ',' <*> aPerson <* char ')'
```

You can check that the parser works on the builder output using the interpreter.

```
*> let co = Company 1 "Black Hole Inc." (Person "John" "Smith") "Traveller"
*> let b = clientToText co
*> let c = Data.Text.Lazy.toStrict $ Data.Text.Lazy.Builder.toLazyText b
*> parseOnly aClient c
Right (Company {clientId = 1, clientName = "Black Hole Inc.",
               person = Person {firstName = "John", lastName = "Smith"},
               duty = "Traveller"})
```

To finish this brief introduction to attoparsec, I'll introduce the Data.Attoparsec.Combinator module. In that module, you can find parser combinators that match many other typical patterns. For example, you have option, which helps you build parsers with optional input. A call to option has two parameters. The second one is the parser that is tried for matching on the input; if the matching is unsuccessful, the call to option returns the value given as the first parameter.

Many other combinators help in matching lists of elements in many different ways. For example, sepBy parses a list with some separator between them. This is the case of the list of clients; a Parser for it would call aClient repeatedly, but it would expect newline characters between them.

```
parseClients :: Parser [Client Int]
parseClients = sepBy aClient (char '\n')
```

That module also features functions for parsing lists that end in 1, such as many1, sepBy1, and so on. In that case, the lists must contain at least one element to be successful.

Exercise 10-2 asks you to parse the products and purchases in Exercise 10-1. You can use this task to master the attoparsec interface and the many combinators it provides.

EXERCISE 10-2. PARSING PRODUCTS AND PURCHASES

Create parsers for the output that could be generated by the functions you wrote for Exercise 10-1. You might want to read the attoparsec documentation in Hackage beforehand to have a better idea of the built-in parsers that it provides.

In the same way that a `Builder` could work with `conduit`, a `Parser` can be used to produce a stream of values from the textual input. In this case, it may become either a sink, returning the values themselves, or provide the information for further processing. This functionality is provided in the `Data.Conduit.Attoparsec` module of the `conduit-extra` package.

Using this package, building a function that loads all the clients in a file generated by the `Builder` in the previous section becomes just a simple concatenation of three actors: first, we read a file as a `ByteString`, then decode it into `Text` values, and finally parse that information.

```
loadClients :: FilePath -> IO [Client Int]
loadClients fPath = runConduitRes $
  B.sourceFile fPath .| T.decode T.utf8 .| sinkParser parseClients
```

Introducing New Type Classes

The fact that (`<$>`) and (`<*>`) do not live in some `attoparsec`-specific module but rather in their own `Control.Applicative` offers a hint about those combinators being useful in other scenarios. It would be interesting to study how the lifting works with other types. For example, suppose they would also work on `Maybe` values. Then the types would be as follows:

```
(<$>) :: (a -> b)        -> Maybe a -> Maybe b
(<*>) :: Maybe (a -> b) -> Maybe a -> Maybe b
```

In combination, these functions provide a way to lift a function on possibly empty values, returning `Nothing` when some of the arguments are left and returning `Just` if every argument is available. Let's confirm this by running some examples in the interpreter.

```
*Chapter10.TypeClasses> import Control.Applicative
*Chapter10.TypeClasses Control.Applicative> (+) <$> Just 2 <*> Just 3
Just 5
*Chapter10.TypeClasses Control.Applicative> (+) <$> Just 2 <*> Nothing
Nothing
```

If both Parser and Maybe can be used with the same functions, it indicates you're in the presence of a new type class, namely, Applicative. In this section, you'll get a look at Applicative and several other related type classes. I already spoke about how (<$>) is quite like fmap, which opens the door to discussing the relation to the Functor type class, and you saw how Maybe an instance of Applicative is too, so maybe there's also some relation with Monad.

Applicative

I will now introduce the basic Applicative type class. The (<*) and (*>) functions are also part of the type class, but they have default definitions and will be treated later. The basic functions in the type class are defined as follows:

```
class Functor f => Applicative f where
  pure  :: a -> f a
  (<*>) :: f (a -> b) -> f a -> f b
```

You already have some intuition about (<*>); it allows you to extract some function that is inside a context of type f and applying one argument to it. This is the main strength of the Applicative type class: being able to compute when everything you have is inside the same context. In the following examples, both functions and arguments are wrapped inside Maybe, and (<*>) allows you to perform the application:

```
*Chapter10.TypeClasses ...> Just (+) <*> Just 2 <*> Just 3
Just 5
*Chapter10.TypeClasses ...> Just (+) <*> Just 2 <*> Nothing
Nothing
*Chapter10.TypeClasses ...> Nothing <*> Just 2 <*> Just 3
Nothing
```

As you can see in the third example, both the function to be applied and the arguments can be Just or Nothing. Intuitively, when you have no function to apply, you cannot return any result, as shown earlier.

The second function in the type class is pure. Looking at its type, a -> f a, you can guess what the function does; it wraps some pure value inside the context f. For example, when using Maybe, pure is equivalent to Just. Thus, you may write the first two examples in the previous code as follows:

```
*Chapter10.TypeClasses ...> (pure (+) <*> pure 2 <*> pure 3) :: Maybe Int
Just 5
*Chapter10.TypeClasses ...> pure (+) <*> Just 2 <*> Nothing
Nothing
```

The combination of wrapping some pure function and then applying it to several arguments is common when using Applicative. For that reason, the (<$>) was created with that simple definition.

```
(<$>) :: (a -> b) -> f a -> f b
f <$> x = pure f <*> x
```

APPLICATIVE LAWS

As is the case with Monoid, Functor, Monad, and many other type classes, Applicative not only mandates some functions but also has some laws that must be fulfilled. In this case, the laws are as follows:

```
pure id <*> x = x, or id <$> x = x
(.) <$> x <*> y <*> z = x <*> (y <*> z)
f <*> pure x = pure ($ x) <*> f
f <$> pure x = pure f <*> pure x = pure (f x)
```

The first three rules make Applicatives work nicely with regular functions. The identity function is still identity inside f, and function composition and application are also reflected inside Applicative. The last law is telling that pure computations do not change whether they are performed outside and then lifted or lifted in parts.

Up to now, you've seen that Parser and Maybe are instances of Applicative. Your old friend [ ] is also part of that group. As in Chapter 7, lists can be used to model nondeterminism, and this is exactly what its Applicative instance does. For example, if you have a set of functions that may be applied and a set of data that could be used as arguments, (<*>) returns a list with all pairwise applications.

```
*> import Data.Char
*> [("Hello, " ++), \x -> "HEY, " ++ map toUpper x] <*> ["Alex",
"John", "Paul"]
["Hello, Alex","Hello, John","Hello, Paul","HEY, ALEX","HEY,
JOHN","HEY, PAUL"]
```

The (<$>) function is useful to describe computations where a fixed function may be given several different arguments. For example, let's create several greetings for several people.

```
*> (++) <$> ["Hello, ", "Good bye, "] <*> ["Alex", "John", "Paul"]
["Hello, Alex","Hello, John","Hello, Paul","Good bye, Alex","Good bye,
John","Good bye, Paul"]
```

Functors, Applicatives, and Monads

There are some interesting things going on with the use of (<$>) in the preceding section. The signature of (<$>) is equal to that of fmap of a Functor.

```
(<$>) :: Applicative f => (a -> b) -> f a -> f b
fmap  :: Functor     f => (a -> b) -> f a -> f b
```

Also, (<*>) looks close to the (=<<) function (which is just (>>=) but with arguments reversed) in a Monad.

```
(<*>) :: Applicative f => f (a -> b) -> f a -> f b
(=<<) :: Monad        f => (a -> f b) -> f a -> f b
```

And indeed, you've seen that Maybe and [], which are both monads, are instances of Applicative. In this section, I'll shed some light on the relation of these important type classes.

First, the Applicative type class mandates that every Applicative also be a Functor. Furthermore, the laws of the first type class imply that the definition of fmap must be exactly equal to (<$>). However, as discussed in the context of parsers, Applicative is stronger than Functor. This is because with Functor you can move functions with only one parameter inside the appropriate context. If you want to apply a function f with two parameters instead, applying fmap once to get rid of one parameter gives you the following type:

```
fmap      :: (a -> b -> c) -> f a -> f (b -> c)
fmap f    :: f a -> f (b -> c)
fmap f x :: f (b -> c)
```

You cannot do anything more with only Functor because it's not able to get the function within the f context. But if f were Applicative, you could use (<*>) to continue supplying parameters. The extension from Functor to Applicative gives you the power of using functions with any number of arguments.

The Monad and Applicative type classes are also related in a direct way. In short, every Monad is also an Applicative, which means that every monad that has been presented until now can be used also with the Applicative interface. You can verify this by remembering the function ap that was introduced in Chapter 7 as a way to generalize liftM to any number of parameters.

```
ap :: Monad m => m (a -> b) -> m a -> m b
```

This is exactly the signature of (<*>) in Applicative, and it works the same. In Chapter 7, I also discussed how liftMn f x1 ... xn could be changed into the more extensible version shown here:

```
return f `ap` x1 `ap` ... `ap` xn
```

This follows the same pattern that you use in the definition of (<$>) in terms of pure and (<*>). In particular, it shows that if a type is an instance of Monad, you can define the pure function in its Applicative instance by making it equal to return.

Of course, since Applicative and Monad are not equal and Applicative is higher in the hierarchy of classes, there must be something you can do with Monads that cannot be done using only Applicatives. The answer to that question comes by looking at the different signatures of (<*>) and (=<<) that were introduced earlier in the section. There you can spot the difference; the function provided as the first argument to (<*>) must be of type f (a -> b), whereas in (=<<) this type is a -> f b.

The implication here is that using monads as an argument to a function can change the function to be executed in the next step (because you return f b), whereas in Applicatives an argument to a function may affect the current step to be executed but not the remaining ones. To make it clear, consider the following case, where you want to use the following function that, depending on whether the first parameter is 1 or not, would result in adding one or doubling one number:

```
\x -> if x == 1 then Just (+ 1) else Just (* 2)
```

If you apply one parameter using (`<*>`), you get the following type:

```
(\x -> if x == 1 then pure (+ 1) else  pure (* 2)) <$> Just 1
  :: (Num a) => Maybe (Maybe (a -> a))
```

And at this point, the `Applicative` type class is of no help; there's no way you can unwrap those two layers of `Maybe` using either (`<$>`) or (`<*>`). However, in Chapter 7, a join function on monads was introduced, with exactly the signature that you need: `Monad m => m (m a) -> m a`. So, if you're using a monad, you can "fuse" the two layers into one and continue execution.

This doesn't necessarily mean that a monadic interface is always better than an `Applicative` one. The fact that when using monads you can influence the flow of execution via the values that are computed at runtime makes it much harder to analyze what's going on inside. But in a parsing library, you are willing to inspect the structure of the computation, and in doing so, you may apply many optimizations that make the parsing process much more efficient. For that reason, the `Applicative` interface was chosen for `attoparsec`.

WRITING MORE READABLE MONADIC CODE

In this chapter and Chapter 7, you've seen many different ways to express the same concepts in `Functor`, `Applicative`, and `Monad`.

```
fmap f x = f <$> x = do y <- x; return (f x) = liftM f x
f <$> x <*> y = return f `ap` x `ap` y
pure x = return x
```

These equalities can help you write more readable code, especially when using monads. For example, consider the following code:

```
do name <- getLine
   let upperName = map toUpper name
   putStrLn upperName
```

In previous chapters, I advocated for removing the intermediate let step with fmap, but it can be written even more closely to a regular function application with (<$>).

```
do upperName <- map toUpper <$> getLine
   putStrLn upperName
```

Or it can even be much shorter using the Monad functions.

```
putStrLn =<< (map toUpper <$> getLine)
```

Finding the best way to write the code, balancing both readability and conciseness, is always important.

Alternative

I have already discussed the (<$>) and (<*>) functions, but while using Parsers you saw another important function: (<|>). It is part of the Alternative type class, which is reproduced here:

```
class Applicative f => Alternative f where
  empty :: f a
  (<|>) :: f a -> f a -> f a

  some  :: f a -> f [a]
  some v = (:) <$> v <*> many v
  many  :: f a -> f [a]
  many v = some v <|> pure []
```

As you can see, the Alternative type class resembles MonadPlus a lot. It gives you the possibility of failure via empty and a choice via (<|>), much like mempty and mplus worked. For example, you can use it to return one of several Maybe possibilities, namely, the first, which is Just.

```
*Chapter10.TypeClasses> import Control.Applicative
*Chapter10.TypeClasses Control.Applicative> Nothing <|> Just 2 <|> Just 3
Just 2
```

Note   Indeed, anything that is MonadPlus is both Monad and Alternative.

The some and many functions are intended to be used in parser-like environments. If you have a computation v that holds or returns elements of type t, you can use many and some to run it repeatedly and get a list of elements of type t instead. The difference is that with many you may get an empty list, whereas some enforces that at least one element is returned. These functions are not used outside of parsers because in many cases the recursive definition does not allow them to terminate.

Traversable

Now that many new type classes have been introduced, it is a good time to look at the last of the "structural" type classes of which containers and context are examples. The name is Traversable, and here's the definition:

```
class (Functor t, Foldable t) => Traversable t where
    traverse :: Applicative f => (a -> f b) -> t a -> f (t b)
    traverse f = sequenceA . fmap f
    sequenceA :: Applicative f => t (f a) -> f (t a)
      sequenceA = traverse id

    mapM :: Monad m => (a -> m b) -> t a -> m (t b)
    mapM f = unwrapMonad . traverse (WrapMonad . f)
    sequence :: Monad m => t (m a) -> m (t a)
    sequence = mapM id
```

It looks scary, so let's first make some simplifications. If you look closely, the Traversable type class defines two sets of functions, one for Applicative (containing traverse and sequenceA) and another one for Monad (with mapM and sequence), with the same signature in addition to the type class constraints. Thus, you need to learn about only one of the two sets.

One example of Traversable is [ ]. The types of sequence and sequenceA for that case are as follows:

```
sequenceA :: Applicative f => [f a] -> f [a]
sequence  :: Monad       m => [m a] -> m [a]
```

The functions are telling you how to go from a list of computations of type f a to a single computation with a list in its core. Say you want to make f or m equal to Maybe, which is both Applicative and Monad. Then the specific type in that case is as follows:

```
sequenceA, sequence :: [Maybe a] -> Maybe [a]
```

If you look at Maybe as having some effect, what both sequence and sequenceA are doing is bringing all those effects "out of the list." Since the effect Maybe entails is the possibility of failure, you would expect that running any of those functions will succeed only when every element in the list is a Just; otherwise, it needs to bring the failure "out of the list," which can be done only by returning Nothing altogether. You can check that this is indeed the case in the interpreter.

```
*Chapter10.TypeClasses> import Data.Traversable
*Chapter10.TypeClasses Data.Traversable> sequenceA [Just 2, Just 3, Just 4]
Just [2,3,4]
*Chapter10.TypeClasses Data.Traversable> sequenceA [Just 2,
Nothing, Just 4]
Nothing
```

A more specific version of sequence in Control.Monad (only for lists) was already used in Chapter 7 for this same purpose: executing all the actions in a list of monadic values and returning the results of those actions.

The sequence and sequenceA functions are often described also as "commuting two functors." If you look at their type, you can see that you start with t (f a) and end up with f (t a). The order of t and f has been reversed; this is what *commuting* means. Furthermore, since t is Traversable, it ought to be a Functor, and since f is Applicative, it needs to be a Functor as well. This means there are some kinds of structures (such as lists and Maybes) that are able to go "inside" every possible effect in a normal way.

Let's look at the other set of functions: traverse and mapM. In this case, it might be important for you to recall the usage of the mapM function in Control.Monad. Usually, the way to look at these functions is thinking of "fmap with extra effects." The first argument is a function that returns some value and along the way has some extra computational effects. This function is applied in every element contained in the Traversable value, and the effects are all joined and taken outside the returned structure.

Once again, let's look at the special case of the `Traversable` t being [] and the `Applicative` f being Maybe. The specific signature for `traverse` and `mapM` becomes the following:

```
traverse, mapM :: (a -> Maybe b) -> [a] -> Maybe [b]
```

In this case, the first argument is applied to every element of the list. Alas, since you need to return a Maybe value at the end, the only thing you can do is return `Just` only if every application of that first argument returned `Just`.

One important characteristic of all these functions is that they respect the structure of the `Traversable` being worked on. For example, if `traverse` is applied to a list with five elements, the resulting list will also have five elements, plus any extra effect. This is important because it means that the functions may change only the values contained but not the pattern they follow. This brings it closer to `fmap` and spans a variety of applications. For example, in Chapter 6 I spoke about the `traversed` lens that allowed you to go inside a container and retrieve or update the value of each of its elements. Now you can see the reason behind the name and why `Traversable` is exactly the type class you need.

The documentation of `Traversable` also specifies that the structures are traversed from left to right. This small detail was not important for `Functor` (because no extra effect was produced) or for `Foldable` (because the monoid you use underneath is associative). But in the case of `Traversable`, it may not be the same to execute the actions in one or another order. Think of the case of `Applicative` f or `Monad` m being the IO monad or the `Writer` monad.

Implementing `Traversable` for a specific container seems like a complex task, but it's easy in practice. Take as an example the `BinaryTree2` type, which was introduced in Chapter 4.

```
data BinaryTree2 a = Node2 a (BinaryTree2 a) (BinaryTree2 a)
                   | Leaf2
                   deriving Show
```

In Exercises 4-8 and 4-9, you were asked to implement its `Functor` and `Foldable` instances. `Functor` instances usually follow the pattern of applying the corresponding function to each value in the structure and then calling `fmap` recursively on each substructure. Foldable instances do a similar job, but they apply the monoid operations in between. Thus, the instances looked like this:

```
instance Functor BinaryTree2 where
  fmap f (Node2 x l r) = Node2 (f x) (fmap f l) (fmap f r)
  fmap _ Leaf2         = Leaf2

instance Foldable BinaryTree2 where
  foldMap f (Node2 x l r) = (f x) <> (foldMap f l) <> (foldMap f r)
  foldMap _ Leaf2         = mempty
```

The best way to write the Traversable instance is via traverse, which makes itself a minimal complete definition. The function traverse was introduced before as "fmap with effects." The only thing you need to do is follow the same structure as fmap but ensure that Applicative is used along the way.

```
instance Traversable BinaryTree2 where
  traverse f (Node2 x l r) = Node2 <$> f x
                                   <*> traverse f l
                                   <*> traverse f r
  traverse _ Leaf2         = pure Leaf2
```

Since these instances always follow the same structure, GHC is able to automatically derive it. You do this by enabling a bunch of extensions in your source file.

```
{-# LANGUAGE DeriveFunctor, DeriveFoldable, DeriveTraversable #-}
```

Then you change the deriving part of the BinaryTree2 definition.

```
deriving (Show, Functor, Foldable, Traversable)
```

Don't Overengineer: Just Use JSON

The focus of this chapter has been building and parsing text, which are usually tedious and error-prone activities. Every time you want to add some new data, you have to change both parts and keep them synced so that the output generated by the Builder can be consumed by the Parser.

Instead, it would be nice to use a library that helps to interchange information in a textual way. If possible, it would be nice to use a format that is common to many languages and platforms because future interoperation between tools may be a requirement. The JSON format provides all those features. It has almost universal support between languages and platforms, and it uses a simple textual representation that makes it easy for both humans and computers to process it. Furthermore, JSON is the *de facto* standard for data interchange in the Web, so using it opens the door to creating web applications in Haskell.

A Client can be represented in JSON in the following way:

```
{ "type": "company", "id": 1, "name": "Black Hole Inc."
, "person": { "first": "John", "last": "Smith" }, "duty": "Traveller" }
```

In this brief example, you can see almost every possible way to build a JSON value. First, you have basic types, such as numbers, Booleans, and strings, which are represented by their literals. From these basic values, you can build either arrays (not shown here, but written using the same syntax as Haskell lists) or objects, which are key-value maps. In addition, you also have the null special value. In this case, the full value is an object with four keys and values, of which the person key contains a nested object.

The good news is that the Haskell community has come up with a simple yet efficient library for reading and writing JSON values. Its name is aeson, and its use revolves around a small data type.

```
data Value = Object Object
           | Array  Array
           | String Text
           | Number Number
           | Bool   Bool
           | Null
```

Each of the constructors corresponds to a type of value you can find in JSON, as explained earlier.

Let's start by writing functions for converting JSON representations and
Client values. Most of the conversion to a JSON value entails wrapping data in the
corresponding constructor. In the case of creating Objects, the easiest way to do this is
via the object function, which takes a list of pairs as an argument. Each of these pairs is
defined as key .= value. The conversion to JSON then reads as follows:

```
{-# LANGUAGE OverloadedStrings #-}

import Data.Aeson
import Data.Text

clientToJSON :: Client Integer -> Value
clientToJSON (GovOrg i n) =
  object [ "type"   .= String "govorg"
         , "id"     .= Number (fromInteger i)
         , "name"   .= String (pack n) ]
clientToJSON (Company i n p d) =
  object [ "type"   .= String "company"
         , "id"     .= Number (fromInteger i)
         , "name"   .= String (pack n)
         , "person" .= personToJSON p
         , "duty"   .= String (pack d) ]
clientToJSON (Individual i p) =
  object [ "type"   .= String "individual"
         , "id"     .= Number (fromInteger i)
         , "person" .= personToJSON p ]

personToJSON :: Person -> Value
personToJSON (Person f l) = object [ "first" .= String (pack f)
                                   , "last"  .= String (pack l) ]
```

If you now want to re-create a Person from a JSON value, you need to check that
every key is present. You can do this via the KeyMap[2] functions (similar to those in Map)
that aeson Value uses.

---

[2] This module was introduced in aeson 2.0; before that, the regular HashMap from unordered-
containers was used. At the momento of writing, the Haskell ecosystem is still transitioning from
the previous aeson 1.5 version.

```
import qualified Data.Aeson.KeyMap as M

jsonToPerson :: Value -> Maybe Person
jsonToPerson (Object o) = do String f <- M.lookup "first" o
                             String l <- M.lookup "last"  o
                             return $ Person (unpack f) (unpack l)
jsonToPerson _            = Nothing
```

There's more than one approach to accessing the fields in the JSON value. As you saw in Chapter 6, lenses are useful for this kind of navigation inside an object. The `microlens-aeson` package provides a set of functions that aim to make the work with `aeson` `Value`s easier. In this particular case, you can use key, which provides access to a named field in the object. Since the key may be unavailable, you do not use (^.) but its counterpart (^?), which may return `Nothing`. The previous code can be rewritten as follows:

```
import Lens.Micro ((^?))
import Lens.Micro.Aeson

jsonToPerson :: Value -> Maybe Person
jsonToPerson j = do String f <- j ^? key "first"
                    String l <- j ^? key "last"
                    return $ Person (unpack f) (unpack l)
```

Another interesting member of the `Lens.Micro.Aeson` module is nth, which given an index obtains the element in that position if the JSON value being considered is an array. For the rest of the primitive JSON types, `microlens-aeson` provides the combinators _Number (with its two variants _Double and _Integer for automatically converting into one specific numeric type), _String, and _Bool.

Anyway, directly matching on a `Value` is not the suggested way to decode information from JSON in aeson. Instead, you should use a *JSON parser*. The interface to that `Parser` is similar to the one in `attoparsec`; in particular, it also uses the `Applicative` functions. The main difference is the set of basic blocks for parsers. In aeson, you use (.:), which extracts a value with a given key. The most common way to convert from JSON to `Person` is as follows:

```
import Data.Aeson.Types
import Control.Applicative

jsonToPerson :: Value -> Parser Person
```

```
jsonToPerson (Object o) = Person <$> o .: "first" <*> o .: "last"
jsonToPerson _           = Control.Applicative.empty
```

The functions for converting JSON back and forth are not usually defined alone but rather as part of the ToJSON and FromJSON type classes that aeson provides. Let's add them to the code for the Person type.

```
instance ToJSON Person where
  toJSON = personToJSON

instance FromJSON Person where
  parseJSON = jsonToPerson
```

The great benefit of using ToJSON and FromJSON is that aeson includes a bunch of predefined instances for many types. For example, once you write it for Person, you can also serialize into JSON lists of people, objects containing Persons, and so on. In particular, let's use the just-defined instance for defining the parser for Client and the corresponding instances of ToJSON and FromJSON. Notice that FromJSON allows you to be more general in the types you accept as identifiers.

```
{-# LANGUAGE FlexibleInstances #-}

jsonToClient :: FromJSON i => Value -> Parser (Client i)
jsonToClient (Object o) =
  case M.lookup "type" o of
    Just (String "govorg")     -> GovOrg <$> o .: "id" <*> o .: "name"
    Just (String "company")    -> Company <$> o .: "id" <*> o .: "name"
                                          <*> o .: "person"
                                          <*> o .: "duty"
    Just (String "individual") -> Individual <$> o .: "id"
                                             <*> o .: "person"
    _                          -> Control.Applicative.empty
jsonToClient _ = Control.Applicative.empty

instance ToJSON (Client Integer) where
  toJSON = clientToJSON

instance FromJSON i => FromJSON (Client i) where
  parseJSON = jsonToClient
```

Using the interpreter, you can see how the conversion to JSON works correctly.[3]

```
*> :{
*| toJSON $ Company (1 :: Integer) "Black Hole Inc."
*|                  (Person "John" "Smith") "Traveller"
*| :}
Object fromList [("name",String "Black Hole Inc.")
               ,("duty",String "Traveller")
               ,("person",Object fromList [("last",String "Smith")
                                          ,("first",String "John")])
               ,("id",Number 1.0),("type",String "company")]
```

To make the converse operation, you need to call fromJSON, which runs the Parser with a given Value and produces a Result that may be either Success or Error. Notice that the code uses an explicit signature to tell the interpreter which FromJSON instance it needs to use.

```
*> :{
*| fromJSON $ toJSON $
*|   Company (1 :: Integer) "Black Hole Inc."
*|           (Person "John" "Smith") "Traveller" :: Result (Client Integer)
*| :}
Success (Company { clientId = 1, clientName = "Black Hole Inc."
                 , person = Person {firstName = "John", lastName = "Smith"}
                 , duty = "Traveller" })
```

Once you know how to convert from and to aeson Value, the next step is to convert those Values into actual textual representations. For generating the text, you just need to use encode, which returns a ByteString. In the case of moving from text to JSON, you have several possibilities:

- decode takes a ByteString, parses the text to produce an aeson Value, and then converts that Value into some other type using FromJSON. The result is wrapped on a Maybe to signal failure.

- eitherDecode performs the same task, but in the case of failure, the error message is returned in the Left constructor of an Either.

---

[3] The order of the fields in the object may differ. The order of keys is irrelevant for JSON.

- You can perform the two steps separately. First, aeson provides json, an attoparsec Parser from ByteString into Value. Then, you can call fromJSON to generate the final value.

One small tidbit is that encoding and decoding in aeson work on lazy ByteStrings. We have seen that other libraries, such as conduit, use strict ByteStrings instead. In those cases, you need to perform a conversion, as shown in the following code:

```
import Data.Conduit
import qualified Data.Conduit.Binary as B
import qualified Data.Conduit.List as L
import qualified Data.ByteString.Lazy as LB

saveClients :: FilePath -> [Client Integer] -> IO ()
saveClients fPath clients = runConduitRes $
  yield (toJSON clients) .| L.map (LB.toStrict . encode)
                         .| B.sinkFile fPath
```

Exercise 10-3 asks you to use JSON to save and load products and purchases in a file.

EXERCISE 10-3. JSON FOR PRODUCTS AND PURCHASES

Write ToJSON and FromJSON instances of the Product and Purchase data types that were introduced in Exercise 10-1. Then, using aeson and conduit, create an application that reads a list of Products represented in JSON and shows the average price.

ToJSON and FromJSON instances always follow the same pattern: ToJSON writes each of the fields of a constructor in key-value pairs in JSON, with an additional field for knowing the constructor if the data type has more than one (like type in the Client example). FromJSON just tries to read each of these keys. Haskell tries to avoid boilerplate code as much as possible, and this is a clear case of it. In case you don't need any special behavior, aeson can write the instances for you.

To do so, you need to enable the DeriveGeneric extension in GHC and add Generic to the list of instances in the deriving clause, as we have done in the previous chapter for Binary and CSV. A Generic instance contains information about the constructors and fields in a data type. Then, you just need to write empty instances of ToJSON and

FromJSON, and using that Generic information, aeson will do the rest. Here's the code for the Client version:

```
{-# LANGUAGE DeriveGeneric #-}

import GHC.Generics

data Client i = ... deriving (Show, Generic)
data Person = ... deriving (Show, Read, Generic)

instance ToJSON   i => ToJSON   (Client i)
instance FromJSON i => FromJSON (Client i)
instance ToJSON   Person
instance FromJSON Person
```

These automatically derived instances will use as keys the name of the fields declared in the constructors. For that reason, it works only on data declarations using record syntax. If your type has more than one constructor, the key that will be used to distinguish them is called tag.

PARSING COMMAND-LINE ARGUMENTS

Every time you find some operation that involves parsing in some way or another, you will most likely find an Applicative interface to it. In addition to JSON decoding via aeson, one other useful package is optparse-applicative, which helps describe and organize the set of command-line arguments to an application.

For example, this is how you would define the arguments to an application that expects one file name containing a list of clients and another argument specifying whether the information is kept in JSON format or not:

```
import Options.Applicative

data Args = Args String Bool  -- data type holding the arguments

args :: Parser Args           -- read the arguments
args = Args <$> strOption (long "file" <> help "Database of clients to load")
            <*> switch (long "json" <> help "Whether the database uses JSON")
```

```
argsInfo :: ParserInfo Args    -- define arguments + help text
argsInfo = info args fullDesc

main :: IO ()
main = do Args fPath json <- execParser argsInfo
          ...
```

The great benefit of `Applicative` is that it provides a common interface to tasks that are not necessarily related at first sight. It's becoming widely used, and nowadays `Applicative` is seen as a fundamental type class in Haskell, like `Functor` and `Monad`.

Summary

In this chapter, you learned how to deal with text in a variety of situations in Haskell.

- You saw the differences between the `String`, `ByteString`, and `Text` types, as well as the purpose of each of them.

- Both `text` and `bytestring` provide `Builder` types that allow you to efficiently generate textual data.

- You were introduced to the converse operation, parsing, via the `attoparsec` package. That library uses the combinator approach to generate modular and easy-to-read parsers.

- You were introduced to the `Applicative` type class, which lies between `Functor` and `Monad` in strength. You also learned about the `Alternative` and `Traversable` type classes.

- Finally, I discussed the conversion of JSON back and forth using the `aeson` library.

Safe Database Access

In the previous two chapters, you saw how to access the file system to read and save information in a durable way. You've been given all the tools for dealing with either a custom file format or a treelike information representation such as JSON.

However, in most production system applications, you aren't working with files. Instead, a *database management system* (DBMS) is used to store the application's information and keep it safe. Furthermore, most DBMSs provide functionalities such as transactions, logging, and recovery and replication, which are quite useful for maintenance, protection against errors, and scalability. This chapter will provide you a bird's-eye view of the many possibilities of database access in the Haskell ecosystem, in particular those that enable you to access relational DBMSs based on SQL.

In this chapter, I cover two specific libraries: *Persistent* and *Esqueleto*. These libraries are not tied to any specific DBMS but provide an abstraction layer over whatever DBMS you might choose to use. The main advantage of using Persistent is that it allows interaction with the database using user-defined Haskell abstract data types, which are converted from and to database format without further intervention (similar to object-relational mappers in the object-oriented world). This ensures a high degree of type safety when working with database code. Esqueleto is the companion library to Persistent, which focuses on specifics for SQL-based DBMSs.

Database Access Landscape

You can see that Haskell has a strong ecosystem of database access libraries just by going to the Hackage website and seeing the number of libraries listed under the "Database" tag (more than 400 at the moment of writing). Broadly speaking, those libraries can be categorized in three groups:

1. Native implementations of a database in Haskell. The main example of this group is `acid-state`, which allows you to save

A. Serrano Mena, *Practical Haskell*, https://doi.org/10.1007/978-1-4842-8581-7_11

Haskell data types directly on disk. The main downside of this approach is that interoperability with other systems and languages is harmed.

2. Libraries for accessing a particular DBMS, such as `sqlite-simple`, `mysql-simple`, `pgsql-simple` (for some of the best-known relational ones), or `MongoDB`. These libraries are easy to understand for users of the corresponding DBMS but are also tied to a specific choice of system, making it difficult to migrate.

3. Abstraction layers over several DBMSs, which provide a common interface for several systems (usually along with specific connectors for each of them). The range of DBMSs covered by each library is different; some focus only on the relational, SQL-based one, while others try to include nonrelational ones. The main advantage of these libraries is that the choice of DBMS can be reviewed while keeping intact almost all the database access code in the application. This goes well with Haskell's philosophy of reusability.

Abstracting Over Several DBMSs

In Hackage, you will find a group of packages that focus on the SQL world, which is the biggest one among database users. From these, HDBC (from Haskell Database Connectivity) and `hsql` hide the specific details of each DBMS but otherwise expose the SQL model (tables, rows, and columns) as is, without any further abstraction. You just need to plug in the package corresponding to the specific DBMS you want to use (such as `hsql-mysql` or `HDBC-postgresql`). This gives you as the developer the full power of those systems, allowing the use of prepared statements or controlling the transaction boundaries. However, when using any of these libraries, you need to write the SQL statements by hand, which is usually a source of errors, and you need to marshal the results afterward (which are given using a specific data type for SQL values) into your own data type. Because of these problems, these packages are not often used directly but rather as a dependent of a higher-level one.

Tip   The libraries that provide a common layer over different database systems are the most interesting to study. By learning just one, you get access to a big range of databases.

On that higher level, you will find HaskellDB. The idea from its developers was to expose the abstraction that the SQL databases are built upon: the relational algebra. Thus, you work with basic operations such as projection or restriction that can describe all the queries you can pose to the database. Furthermore, the schema for the tables is also embedded in the Haskell code, so you can guarantee the safety of all your queries (you won't be accessing a nonexistent column, and you won't be comparing columns of different types). The main drawback of HaskellDB is that it exposes an abstraction that is not as well known as SQL queries, so to use it you have to relearn how to express some concepts.

Introducing Persistent and Esqueleto

Persistent, available in Hackage and Stackage under the package name `persistent`, supports both relational and nonrelational DBMSs, which eases the transition between those two worlds in case it's needed for enhancing the scalability of the application. When using Persistent, you still use your Haskell data types (i.e., you don't need to marshal from and to your `Client` type), and the library generates all the glue code automatically (by using a Template Haskell). This gives you real type checking of your database statements, preventing a great range of application errors coming from this fact.

If you're from an object-oriented programming background, you may recognize in this description the concept of an object-relational mapping (ORM), which also takes care of gluing a class with a specific table in a database. However, because it's implemented in a functional language that embodies purity, Persistent doesn't save automatically any change you do to the value holding the information about one of your rows. Rather, you need to explicitly ask for insertions, updates, and deletions.

One disadvantage of Persistent is that it supports only those operations common to every database it allows you to connect to. Since this includes both relational and nonrelational DBMSs, the common ground is sometimes limited. For example, you cannot easily express a join of two tables (in the SQL sense), since DBMSs such as

MongoDB don't have this concept. For that matter, some libraries have been developed that extend Persistent in one direction while restricting the applicable databases. This is the case of *Esqueleto*, a domain-specific language for expressing SQL queries inside Haskell using Persistent models.

Persistent itself encompasses a lot of related functionality in three areas: describing the *schema* of a database in such a way that can be used to work with usual Haskell data types, creating and adapting the schema of an existing database into a new one and adding or deleting columns (this is called the *migration* functionality), and performing actual work with the information in the database (insertions, updates, deletions, and queries).

Connection

The DBMS is the software performing the actual work of storing and retrieving information from a database. The flow of work is quite simple: you send a statement to the DBMS, and it does some work, returning some values or information about the success of the operation. But before sending statements, you need to know how to establish the initial connection to the DBMS.

If you look around, you will see that along with the basic `persistent` package, there are many others with a name that comes from joining `persistent-` with the name of a DBMS (e.g., `persistent-sqlite`). Each of these packages provides a *back end* for a specific system, that is, the code that is needed to communicate with it and make sense of the results it returns.

Caution   In Hackage, there are other packages starting with `persistent-` (like `persistent-map`). Usually, only those with the "Database" tag are related to Persistent.

Each back end provides two ways to communicate with the corresponding system: via a single connection or by creating a pool of connections (a set of open connections that are reused by different operations to increase the ability to share resources and thus enhance performance). For the first case, each back end has a `withDBMSConn` function that generates a connection given the parameters needed for each specific system. This connection can be used then as a parameter to the `runSqlPersistM` function, which executes a set of database actions. For example, here's the code needed to insert a Client (which holds a first name, a last name, an address, a country, and an age) inside an SQLite database saved in the example.db file. Notice that at this point the code won't compile because you haven't provided the definitions for the entities in the database yet. You'll learn how to do so in the next pages.

```
{-# LANGUAGE OverloadedStrings, TypeApplications #-}

import Database.Persist.Sqlite  -- from persistent-sqlite
import Control.Monad.Logger     -- from monad-logger

exampleConn = runNoLoggingT $
  withSqliteConn @(NoLoggingT IO) "example.db" $ \conn ->
    liftIO $ flip runSqlPersistM conn $ do
      spain    <- insert $ Country "Spain"
      _client1 <- insert $ Client "Alejandro" "Serrano"
                                  "Home Town, 1" spain 30
      return ()
```

The preceding code uses some fancy GHC extensions. First, the withSqliteConn function expects a Text value with the path to the database. So, I've used the OverloadedStrings GHC extension in order to write that value in the code using string literal syntax. Another extension, TypeApplications, is needed to specify the withSqliteConn in which monad we are operating. In older versions of GHC, you would use type annotations, but in modern ones types can be specified directly using the @T syntax. In this case, we choose an IO monad wrapper with a dummy logging interface, namely, NoLoggingT. That logging interface comes from the monad-logger package, which is heavily used by persistent.

Since opening a connection and running some action in the database is so common, many of the back ends provide a special runDBMS convenience function for those simple cases. For example, the previous code can be written more concisely using runSqlite. Doing so frees you from passing the conn value yourself through several functions, as you can see in the following example. Also, the dummy logging interface is selected, so you don't need a call to runNoLoggingT. In every other aspect, the two pieces of code are interchangeable.

```
exampleConn = runSqlite @IO "example.db" $ do
  spain     <- insert $ Country "Spain"
  _client1  <- insert $ Client "Alejandro" "Serrano"
                                  "Home Town, 1" spain 30
  return ()
```

Creating a pool is usually as easy as creating a single connection. Instead of withDBMSConn, you use the corresponding withDBMSPool function, which takes as input the information to contact the database and the maximum number of connections to keep open. Then, you use the runSqlPersistMPool function with the actions to execute. Here's the same example for SQLite but using a pool of ten connections (it doesn't make much sense to use a pool in this little example; rather, you would share the pool between different actions). Notice how similar the code is to the example with a single connection.

```
examplePool = runNoLoggingT $
  withSqlitePool @(NoLoggingT IO) "example.db" 10 $ \pool ->
    liftIO $ flip runSqlPersistMPool pool $ do
      spain     <- insert $ Country "Spain"
      _client1  <- insert $ Client "Alejandro" "Serrano"
                                      "Home Town, 1" spain 30
      return ()
```

There is a large disparity of connection methods between DBMSs. Table 11-1 includes a brief explanation of the parameters for each of the more commonly encountered systems.

Table 11-1. *Connection Parameters for Persistent Back Ends*

DBMS	Single Connection	Connection Pool	Parameters
Sqlite	`withSqliteConn`	`withSqlitePool`	Just the path to the file, or `":memory:"` to create a temporary in-memory database.
PostgreSQL	`withPostgresqlConn`	`withPostgreSqlPool`	A connection string of the form `"host=h port=p user=u password=p dbname=db"`.
MySQL	`withMySQLConn`	`withMySQLPool`	A value of the type `ConnectionInfo`. A `defaultConnectionInfo` value is provided, which connects to database `test` in `localhost`, whose fields `connectHost`, `connectUser`, and so on, can be then modified to your needs.
MongoDB	`withMongoDBConn`	`withMongoDBPool`	A set of different parameters for the database including host, port, authentication, and idle time. Note: The pooled version needs two extra parameters for the number of stripes and connections per stripe.

Schemas and Migrations

As mentioned in the introduction, Persistent needs a description of the database schema you will be working with to ensure type safety. In addition, it also needs information about the mapping between this schema and the actual Haskell data types you will use to represent the data. To bring all of this together, Persistent uses quite complex types to encode all the invariants and relations. Right now in the book, many of the techniques used in those types haven't been introduced yet. Chapter 13 will be providing all that information.

The good news is that you don't have to care about all of this because Persistent comes with a package, `persistent-template`, which is able to generate all the necessary code (Haskell data types, instances for some type classes, glue code for the marshaling) from a single description of the database schema. For the rest of the chapter, I assume that your project has both `persistent` and `persistent-template` listed as dependencies, in addition to the SQLite back end.

Note   `persistent-template` uses Template Haskell to generate all its code. You were introduced to Template Haskell in Chapter 6. As a small reminder, Template Haskell is the metaprogramming facility of GHC, which means that at compile time a function can generate new or manipulate existing code.

Describing the Entities

I'll start with a simple example for the time machine store: describing a database for holding the information of the clients. To make things easier, let's assume that the clients are always individuals, whose information is composed by first and last names, an address, and an age. The following code defines a database entity for holding this information. This definition will be used later to communicate with the correct tables or documents in the database.

```
{-# LANGUAGE TemplateHaskell, QuasiQuotes, OverloadedStrings,
             DataKinds, TypeFamilies, EmptyDataDecls,
             MultiParamTypeClasses, FlexibleContexts, UndecidableInsatnces,
             GADTs, DerivingStrategies, GeneralizedNewtypeDeriving #-}

import Database.Persist.TH

mkPersist sqlSettings [persistLowerCase|
Client
  firstName String
  lastName  String
  address   String
  age       Int
  deriving Show
|]
```

After several language extensions that you need to enable, which are listed inside the {-# LANGUAGE #-} pragma (and routinely change between Persistent versions), there's a call to mkPersist. This function needs settings for generating the code and the description of the database. In this case, the code is telling the code generation to follow SQL standard conventions by giving sqlSettings as first parameter.[1] The latter parameter is not given using usual Haskell syntax but rather using *quasiquotation*: the code between [, |, and |] won't be parsed by the Haskell compiler but rather by a custom reader (in this case, persistLowerCase). Thus, the important thing to know is how to express the database schema for this quasiquoter.

Caution   Be aware that inside a quasiquoter you're no longer writing Haskell code but some custom Persistent syntax. The need to learn an additional (albeit small) language is seen by some people as a drawback of the persistent-template library.

As you can see, there's a block for each kind of entity you want to store. In this case, you have only one, namely, Client. Then, you can find all the fields that make that entity, first the name and then the type. Finally, you can include a deriving clause like you would do with the definition of any other Haskell data type. These are the most basic constructs; you will see more as the chapter progresses.

Tip   If you write json next to the entity name in the quasiquotation (e.g., Client json), Persistent will derive instances of aeson's ToJSON and FromJSON automatically. This will be handy in the next chapter, where you'll learn how to create a web application using Haskell.

Since the code uses persistLowerCase as a quasiquoter, each entity will be mapped to a table and each field to a column, whose name will consist of converting from camel case (each word in an identifier starts with capital letter) to underscore case (different

---

[1] This does not imply that you cannot use this definition in nonrelational DBMSs. It's just that the choices that will be made for representing the information (such as using integers for holding primary keys) are more suited to a SQL database than others.

words in an identifier are separated by underscores). In this example, the data will be saved in a client table with the columns first_name, last_name, address, and age. If you want to retain the names using camel case, you need to use persistUpperCase instead of persistLowerCase.

In addition to the glue code for contacting the database, mkPersist will also generate data type constructors representing each of the fields in the entity. These constructors' names are created by juxtaposing the name of the entity with the name of each of the fields, in camel case. In this case, you would obtain ClientFirstName, ClientLastName, and so on. In particular, this means you can use the same field name in different entities (e.g., using a field name for both individual and company entities) since the prefix will take them apart. This is different from Haskell records, which cannot share field names.

You may have noticed that so far there hasn't been any description of an *identifier*, that is, no indication of what the table's primary key might be. The primary key is a piece of information that uniquely determines a row in a table, and it's commonly used in SQL environments. Persistent developers found this idea of an identifier interesting too, and that's why a schema always defines an implicit id field for each entity. In conclusion, in addition to all the explicitly declared fields, you have a ClientId field representing the unique identifier of each row.

This identifier field is used, in addition to performance considerations, to refer to an entity from another or to embed an entity inside another. For example, let's add information about the country of residence of each client. A simple solution would be to add another String field for the country name. However, as database theory shows, this is not a good idea because you waste a lot of space with repeated information, and even worse, you may have problems when the same country is not written the same everywhere (e.g., "United States" vs. "US" vs. "USA"). The correct solution is to create a new entity that will hold information about countries and refer to it in Client (this is called *normalization* in database jargon). This is perfect for an identifier field. The new schema declaration looks like this:

```
mkPersist sqlSettings [persistLowerCase|
Country
  name String
  deriving Show
Client
  firstName String
  lastName  String
```

```
address    String
country    CountryId
age        Int
deriving Show
|]
```

With this schema definition, the insertions shown in the previous section are correct Haskell code. Notice that Persistent has created a data type for each entity. This data type can be thought of as being defined as a record whose only constructor shares its name with the entity being defined. Thus, in the example, the constructors Country and Client have been generated. Another remark is that insert returns the identifier of the new entity in the database, and the code uses that for referring to the country "Spain" in the client.

IDENTIFIERS ARE SPECIAL

In most databases, the identifier column is just another column, with the special qualities of being unique among the rows and usually being autoincremental. However, you have seen that Persistent treats those fields in a special way. Why is that the case?

The main reason is that by having special data types for each identifier of each entity, it's not possible to mix identifiers of different entities. In this example, ClientId will be a different type from CountryId, so you cannot pass a value of the latter when an element of the former is requested.

A second reason is that by hiding the details of how the identifier is represented, Persistent goes further into supporting different databases; it can choose the representation depending on the final DBMS. For example, MongoDB has a special type called ObjectId that is developed specifically for identifying an object. This is different from the path taken by SQL databases.

I have discussed how Persistent always generates a special identifier field per entity. However, in other cases, there are other *uniqueness constraints*, which are a set of fields that uniquely identifies a value in the database. Since the combined value of those fields must appear only once in the database, it must be protected by the DBMS for duplicates. In that way, the database can protect data for a whole class of incorrect values.

Furthermore, the extra work in inserting and updating is often surpassed by the increase in performance that can be achieved when the uniqueness is guaranteed.

A uniqueness constraint is declared inside the entity it refers to by giving it a name, which must start with a capital letter (in the following examples, all the constraints are prefixed with Unique, but this is not a requirement), and then listing the fields that are included in the constraint. For example, you can consider that the combination of first and last names, an address, and a country uniquely identifies a client in a database, so it makes sense to add a uniqueness constraint to it. Furthermore, countries are also uniquely identified by their name (no two countries share a name). The following is the code for doing this, where some other entities and fields have been omitted:

```
mkPersist sqlSettings [persistLowerCase|
Country
  ...
  UniqueCountryName name
  deriving Show
Client
  ...
  UniqueClient firstName lastName address country
  deriving Show
|]
```

For data mining purposes, it's helpful to save the age of each client. However, not all clients would be happy giving that piece of information, so it's better to make it optional. This corresponds to the notion of a *nullable* column in SQL and of a value wrapped on Maybe in Haskell. Indeed, that last word is the one chosen by Persistent to indicate that a field is optional for a value. If you want to make age optional, change its declaration from age Int to age Int Maybe.

In addition to the age, it's also useful to save information about the gender of the clients. Near the beginning of the book, I discussed how using a Boolean value is not the right choice for representing the gender in Haskell. Rather, you should use a data type specific to that task. This increases type safety and removes the errors because of inconsistent mappings (is True equal to male or female?).

The same arguments are relevant to Persistent. When you want to save a value in a field from a set of them, don't use a Boolean or an integer. You have already seen how to overcome this problem when the set of values is big and can change with time (as countries do). For a small fixed list of values, the best option is to use an enumeration written in Haskell and use its type inside the declaration of the entity (in this example, creating a Gender data type and including a gender Gender field declaration in the Client entity). The only stone in the path is that you need to include some extra code to make a new data type available to Persistent, and because of limitations in Template Haskell, you must do so in a separate file. In this case, start by writing this code in a new Chapter11.Gender module:

```
{-# LANGUAGE TemplateHaskell #-}

module Chapter11.Gender where

import Database.Persist.TH

data Gender = Male | Female
    deriving (Show, Read, Eq)
derivePersistField "Gender"
```

The important part is the call to derivePersistField. Now, in the file with the schema declaration, import this new module and add a gender Gender Maybe line to it (making the gender information optional is also a good choice). Now a Client value looks like this:

```
Client "Alejandro" "Serrano" "Home Town, 1" spain (Just 25) (Just Male)
```

The previous information makes up the basics of the schema language, but many more features are available. For that reason, I strongly recommend you survey the Persistent documentation[2] or the Book of Yesod[3] before declaring your entities.

Creating the Database

Let's now look at the converse scenario. Say you try to run some code similar to the code in the chapter introduction for adding a country and a client to a completely empty database. Here's an example:

```
runSqlite @IO "example.db" $ do
  spain     <- insert $ Country "Spain"
```

---

[2] Available at https://github.com/yesodweb/persistent/tree/master/docs.
[3] Available at www.yesodweb.com/book/persistent.

```
_client1  <- insert $ Client "Alejandro" "Serrano"
                             "Home Town, 1" spain
                             (Just 30) (Just Male)
return ()
```

When you execute this, either via an executable or via GHCi, you will receive an error message like this:

```
chapter11: user error (SQLite3 returned ErrorError while attempting to
perform prepare "INSERT INTO \"country\"(\"name\") VALUES(?)": no such
table: country)
```

The source of this error is simple. You have declared how to map entities to a database, but none of the tables referenced in that code exists yet. The good news is that, as I mentioned in the introduction of this chapter, Persistent includes functionality to automatically create or adapt a database to the format expected by a schema. This adaptation process is called the *migration* of the database.

Performing a migration in Persistent consists of two steps. First, you need to tell Persistent to generate the code that will migrate the database. For that task, the library uses Template Haskell once again, and you would need to add the schema declaration all over again. Since using the same schema for creating the mappings and the migration is common, you can use the convenience function share to pass the quasiquoted code to both functions. In concrete words, this means you only need to change the call to mkPersist to read instead.

share [mkPersist sqlSettings, **mkMigrate "migrateAll"**] [persistLowerCase|

The second step is to execute the migration by calling runMigration with a single argument that is the name given to mkMigrate. For example, you can generate the tables in an SQLite database using this:

```
runSqlite @IO "example.db" $ runMigration migrateAll
```

If you include that line of code before the two insertions in the database, you will see a log of the migration being output to your screen. That log should be similar to the following. You can see in the output how all the fields and constraints in the entities are translated quite naturally in tables in the SQL world.

```
Migrating: CREATE TABLE "country"("id" INTEGER PRIMARY KEY,"name" VARCHAR
NOT NULL,CONSTRAINT "unique_country_name" UNIQUE ("name"))
Migrating: CREATE TABLE "client"("id" INTEGER PRIMARY KEY,"first_name"
VARCHAR NOT NULL,"last_name" VARCHAR NOT NULL,"address" VARCHAR NOT
NULL,"country" INTEGER NOT NULL REFERENCES "country","age" INTEGER
NULL,"gender" VARCHAR NULL,CONSTRAINT "unique_client" UNIQUE ("first_
name","last_name","address","country"))
```

It's important to notice that migrations can only add and delete columns; there's no way for the code to know when a field name has been changed into another one. However, the simple case of adding a new field poses a question: Which value should be written for those rows that were already there? The solution comes in the form of a new attribute that can be added to a field, namely, `default`, which defines this value to write in the case of a migration.

Caution   The `default` attribute applies only to migrations. It doesn't have any effect on your actual Haskell code, and it doesn't allow you to leave the value of that field undefined.

As an example, let's add a `canWeSend` field to the `Country` entity expressing whether the time machines and accessories can be shipped to that specific country. Since you have already created the tables and added some values, the migration procedure needs information of the values to write in that field. If you consider that the best choice is `True` (shipments can be made to all countries already in the database), the schema definition must be changed to read as follows:

```
share [mkPersist sqlSettings, mkMigrate "migrateAll"] [persistLowerCase|
Country
  name       String
  canWeSend Bool default=True
  UniqueCountryName name
  deriving Show
Client
  ...
|]
```

The sidebar "Using an Existing Database" shows how to deal with legacy databases having table names and column names not matching your entities and fields. Then, Exercise 11-1 guides you in defining the entity that will be used throughout this chapter for products.

USING AN EXISTING DATABASE

You've seen how to use migration to create or adapt an existing database to the table schema that Persistent expects. However, a quite common scenario involves an already existing database that you want to access.

In those cases, you can specify `sql` attributes to change the names of the tables that entities and fields are mapped to. Furthermore, you can specify the `id` attribute on an entity to declare the column in the table containing the identifier. The following is an example for `Country`:

```
Country sql=my_country_table id=the_country_identifier
    name        String
    canWeSend Bool default=True sql=send_there_is_possible
    UniqueCountryName name
    deriving Show
```

The table name will be `my_country_table`. The column named `the_country_identifier` will be treated as the ID column.

EXERCISE 11-1. DEFINING PRODUCTS

Add the definition of a `Product` entity to the database. That entity must include the name and description of each product, its price as a `Double` value, and the number of elements in stock.

Be aware that Persistent does not allow using `Integer` values in fields. Rather, you should use `Int64`, which represents those integer values that fit in 64 bits.

Finally, let's add a simple definition for purchases in the store. A purchase will be a collection of a client, a single product for which the client may have ordered more than one unit, and the total amount that was paid (there's an implicit assumption that each purchase contains only one type of product). The entity Purchase in this case will relate a Client and a Product, so you need to use their identifiers, as the following code shows:

```
share [mkPersist sqlSettings, mkMigrate "migrateAll"] [persistLowerCase|
...
Client
  ...
Product
  ...
Purchase
  client  ClientId
  product ProductId
  number  Int
  amount  Double
  deriving Show
|]
```

Queries

Querying is one of the most basic operations you can perform with a database. A good knowledge of the different options for selecting data from your sources is instrumental for obtaining the performance that applications require. As you will see in this section, Persistent provides several ways to query for data, and Esqueleto extends that feature even more with SQL-only operators such as joins.

Note   In the rest of examples in the chapter, I will show only the statements. If you want to execute any of those statements, wrap them inside a runSqlite call (or the corresponding version for other databases), as done in the migration examples. The code won't show all signature, because some of them contain type system features that will be introduced later (in Chapter 13). GHC correctly infers the signatures in the missing cases, so you can still copy and paste the examples as they appear in the book.

Queries by Identifier or Uniqueness

Since every entity in the database is embellished by Persistent with a unique identifier, the simplest way to query a database is indeed to ask for a value with a given identifier. This is done using the function get, which returns its value wrapped in a Maybe. It may be the case that for a given identifier there's no associated value. For example, you have defined the client field in the Purchase entity to hold a ClientId; that identifier can be used afterward to retrieve all the information about a client. The following code performs that task:

```
import Database.Persist.Sql

getPurchaseClient p = get (purchaseClient p)  -- returns Maybe Client
```

If you have the identifier but have not obtained it from a previous query and thus it is wrapped in the appropriate constructor for identifier, you can still look for the object using the Key corresponding to that type. Although better to be avoided, this option may be needed, for example, if you are obtaining the identifier from the route in a web application (the URL looks like /clients/5, where 5 is the client identifier). For example, the code for asking for a Client by identifier is as follows:

```
getClientById n = get $ ClientKey n
```

Another way of identifying a value was discussed before: uniqueness constraints. For each of these constraints, Persistent generates a constructor that takes as parameters a value for all the fields in its definition. Then, you can use the getBy function to query the database using that combination of data. For example, you defined previously a UniqueClient constraint on the entity Client, so you can query with one of them as follows:

```
getClientByInfo :: MonadIO m
                => String -> String -> String -> String
                -> SqlPersistT m (Maybe Client)
getClientByInfo fName lName addr cnName = do
    cn <- getBy $ UniqueCountryName cnName
    case cn of
      Just (Entity cId _) ->
        do cl <- getBy $ UniqueClient fName lName addr cId
```

```
case cl of
  Just (Entity _ client) -> return $ Just client
  Nothing                -> return Nothing
Nothing -> return Nothing
```

It's important to notice that the result of getBy is not just the value you asked for but rather a combination of the identifier associated with the value and the value itself, provided inside the Entity data type. In the previous example, you can find two different usages of getBy: one for finding the identifier of the country given its name (check how in the Entity pattern matching only the identifier is actually bound to a variable) and another one for finding a client with given personal attributes and belonging to that country.

Selecting Several Entities

The full power of a database is unleashed when you perform queries not only via identifiers but also based on other fields within entities. Furthermore, the languages in which queries are posed are usually quite expressive. For example, you could be asking for all those clients coming from the United States who have bought at least two products in the last few years to create a better campaign for clients in that part of the world.

Those queries are usually not guaranteed to return only one or no results but can produce a set of values that fulfill the requirements of the query. You can ask Persistent to represent that set using two different approaches: either as a Source from the conduit library or as a plain list. You can also choose to just return the first value of the set wrapped on a Maybe. You may then get Nothing back if the query selects an empty set.

On an orthogonal axis, you can ask Persistent to show the entire set of fields of each value matched by the query (i.e., all the fields belonging to the entities) or just return their identifiers. In the first case, the information from the fields is wrapped inside an Entity constructor (as done with getBy), which contains both the entity and its identifier. Five out of the six possible combinations have a corresponding function in Persistent, as Table 11-2 shows.

Table 11-2. *Query Functions in Persistent*

	As a Source	**As a List**	**Only First Result in a Maybe**
Identifier and value	selectSource	selectList	selectFirst
Only identifier	selectKeys	selectKeysList	Not available

All the functions listed in Table 11-2 have the same parameters and are used in the same way, so in the examples I'll use selectList because it's the one that shows output simply while still letting you form an idea about what's going on in the database.

The first of the two parameters is a list of *filters*. Each filter constrains the value of one or more fields to satisfy a specified condition. For example, you might require the age of a Client to be greater than 18. The way in which you write those filters is by using one of the constructors that Persistent has created for each of the fields in an entity and a set of built-in operators. The age filter, for example, is represented as ClientAge >=. Just 18 (you need to include Just because age was an optional field, so its values are wrapped in Maybe).

In addition to the simple equality and ordering operators (==.) and (!=.) – notice that "not equals" is written using C-like syntax, not as (/=.)[4] – (>.), (>=.), (<.), and (<=.) – Persistent supports an operator for a field having a value from a set of wanted ones, namely, (<-.) and read as "in" and its negation (/<-.) "not in." In the following example, I ask for all those Clients coming from Spain or Germany older than 18, using that operator. Notice how I need to get the identifiers of those countries prior to creating the actual query.

```
getAdultsOfSpainAndGermany :: MonadIO m => SqlPersistT m [Entity Client]
getAdultsOfSpainAndGermany = do
  es <- getBy $ UniqueCountryName "Spain"
  de <- getBy $ UniqueCountryName "Germany"
  let countries = map entityKey (catMaybes [es, de])
  selectList [ ClientCountry <-. countries, ClientAge >=. Just 18 ] []
```

In case you want to know only the number of clients that fulfill those conditions, you may be tempted to just apply length to the resulting list. However, this is not very efficient since you'll be bringing a lot of data from the database only to discard it

---

[4] (/=.) is used on update queries, as shown in the next section.

afterward. Instead, you should use the count function, which just returns the numbers of values satisfying the query. Here's an example:

```
countAdultsOfSpainAndGermany :: MonadIO m => SqlPersistT m Int
countAdultsOfSpainAndGermany = do
  es <- getBy $ UniqueCountryName "Spain"
  de <- getBy $ UniqueCountryName "Germany"
  let countries = map entityKey (catMaybes [es, de])
  count [ ClientCountry <-. countries, ClientAge >=. Just 18 ]
```

Sometimes, the operators introduced up to this point are not enough or are not convenient for expressing disjunctive queries. In those cases, you can use the "or" operator, (||.), for merging two lists of filters into a single query. For example, say you want to obtain the clients from Spain and the United States who are at or above the legal age at which alcohol may be purchased. However, that age is not the same in both countries. In Spain, it's 18, whereas in the United States, it is 21. Thus, the query must reflect that fact: get clients from Spain older than 18 or from the United States older than 21, as the code shows:

```
getAdultsOfSpainAndUS :: MonadIO m => SqlPersistT m [Entity Client]
getAdultsOfSpainAndUS = do
  Just (Entity esId _) <- getBy $ UniqueCountryName "Spain"
  Just (Entity usId _) <- getBy $ UniqueCountryName
                                    "United States of America"
  selectList (  [ ClientCountry ==. esId, ClientAge >=. Just 18 ]
            ||. [ ClientCountry ==. usId, ClientAge >=. Just 21 ] )
            []
```

I've been silently adding an empty list as a second parameter to . selectList. That list represents the *options* to the query, which do not affect the results themselves but rather the way the results are presented. One typical option involves sorting by one or more fields. In the previous example, if you want to return the clients from the oldest to the youngest one, you must change the list of options to [Desc ClientAge]. As you can see, the way to indicate the ordering is by using one of the constructors Asc or Desc and the constructor corresponding to the field.

Other options are used to extract just one subset of the results. If you think of the entire set of results as an ordered list, OffsetBy allows you to discard some elements at the beginning and return only those from one point to the end, and LimitTo limits the number of returned values to those smaller than a certain amount, ignoring the elements past that amount. Those options are useful to paginate information in a web application. For example, in the store you may decide to show the products in pages of 10. Therefore, page *n* (starting at 1) would show ten products starting from the element *(n-1)*10* (the results from Persistent are zero-indexed). The corresponding query to obtain those products follows:

```
getProductsPage n   -- returns [Entity Product]
  = selectList [ ] [ Asc ProductPrice, LimitTo 10, OffsetBy ((n-1)*10) ]
```

SQL Queries with Esqueleto

Using only get, getBy, selectList, and count (a version not previously introduced that returns only the number of results), let's try to obtain the countries of all those clients that bought more than three products. The following implementation does it in several steps. It first gets all the possible buyers, then counts the number of purchases of each of them, filters those with more than three, and finally gets all the countries that are left. Notice how the code is quite intricate and performs several round-trips to the database.

```
getCountriesWithBigBuyers :: MonadIO m => SqlPersistT m [Country]
getCountriesWithBigBuyers = do
  buyers <- selectKeysList [ ] [ ]
  buyersPurchases <- mapM (\b -> count [ PurchaseClient ==. b ]
                      >>= \c -> return (b,c)) buyers
  let buyersPurchases' = filter (\(_,c) -> c > 3) buyersPurchases
  mapM (\(b,_) -> do Just cl <- get b
                     Just cn <- get $ clientCountry cl
                     return cn)
        buyersPurchases'
```

If you are used to relational databases, there's a feature from its queries that would come to your mind to solve this problem: *joins*. However, Persistent aims to support also nonrelational databases, making the ability to join unavailable to you.

Note   To be completely honest, there's support in Persistent for sending a raw query to the database. But that means that there's no type checking and automatic marshaling, so you've lost all the benefits of using the library.

As I have already introduced, the solution to this problem is using another library, namely, Esqueleto. The esqueleto package provides support for writing SQL queries that are type checked. Furthermore, it reuses the schema definitions from Persistent, making the former a great companion to the latter.

As in the previous case, you can return the results in two different data structures. The select function shows the queried values as a list, whereas selectSource wraps them into a conduit source. Both take as an argument a SqlQuery, so you need to focus on how to construct values of that type. That single argument must be of a certain monadic type, so it's fairly common to use a do block at that point. Inside that monad, several special functions can be called to specify a query.

The first thing to do is to select which entities you'll query. To do that, you use from. In its most simple incarnation, we provide a table as argument, which includes the type of entities being queried; but as we'll see shortly, we can also use it to query several types of entities by providing a join. The result of from is a reference or sequence of references to entities in the database. We can then use where_ (notice the final _, which prevents collision with the where keyword) to specify restrictions over the fields of those entities, inside an expression that may contain the following:

- Access to a field of an entity using (^.).

- Constant values wrapped using val or lists of them wrapped using valList.

- Comparisons with (==.), (!=.), and the rest of operators used in Persistent, remarking that (<-.) takes the name in_ and (/<-.) is called notIn.

- Grouping of several constraints with (&&.) (for "and") and (||.) (for "or"). Notice that this is different from plain Persistent because in that case there is no conjunctive operator; the set of filters in the list is implicitly conjoined.

Another possible function is orderBy, which takes a list of expressions of the form asc (entity ^. field) or desc (entity ^. field), representing ascending and descending order over those fields. As a simple example, let's just return all the clients older than 25 years, ordered by last and first names. Note that we have imported Database.Esqueleto qualified, since several names conflict with Persistent. However, in most cases, you replace the latter entirely by the former, so there is no conflict.

```
import Database.Esqueleto.Experimental ((^.), (?.))
import qualified Database.Esqueleto.Experimental as E

getPeopleOver25 :: MonadIO m => SqlPersistT m [Entity Client]
getPeopleOver25 =
  E.select $ do
  client <- E.from $ E.table @Client
  E.where_ $ client ^. ClientAge E.>. E.just (E.val 25)
  E.orderBy [ E.asc (client ^. ClientLastName),
             E.asc (client ^. ClientFirstName) ]
  return client
```

The code makes explicit that ClientAge has a Maybe value. The constant value the field is compared to must be wrapped first with val and then with just.

Note   At the moment of writing, the functions used in this chapter live in an Experimental module. However, this is planned to become the main Esqueleto module in the short term.

The return value of the monad may not be all the entities that are queried; only a subset of the information may be relevant to the next steps, and the rest could be discarded. For example, let's try to get the information about all the clients from Spain or Germany older than 25. As you can see in the following code, I select both Client and Country as entities to query, make sure that both entities are linked correctly (the Country in Client is the same as the Country identifier), and perform restrictions over the country name and the client age. Finally, I just return the client information, not the country name.

```
getPeopleOver25FromSpainOrGermany
  :: MonadIO m => SqlPersistT m [Entity Client]
```

```
getPeopleOver25FromSpainOrGermany =
  E.select $ do
  client <- E.from $ E.table @Client
  country <- E.from $ E.table @Country
  E.where_ $
    (client ^. ClientAge E.>. E.just (E.val 25))
    E.&&. (country ^. CountryName `E.in_` E.valList [ "Spain", "Germany" ])
    E.&&. (client ^. ClientCountry E.==. country ^. CountryId)
    E.orderBy [ E.asc (client ^. ClientLastName)
              , E.asc (client ^. ClientFirstName) ]
  return client
```

Here, you've actually seen an example of a join that was implicit in the link between the country from a client and the entity representing the country itself. Esqueleto allows you to be a bit more explicit, using the InnerJoin constructor as an argument to from. Then, with the on function, you specify the conditions for the join of the entities. The previous example could be rephrased as follows:

```
getPeopleOver25FromSpainOrGermanyJoin
  :: MonadIO m => SqlPersistT m [Entity Client]
getPeopleOver25FromSpainOrGermanyJoin =
  E.select $ do
  client E.:& country <- E.from $
    E.table @Client `E.innerJoin` E.table @Country
    `E.on` \(client E.:& country) ->
      client ^. ClientCountry E.==. country ^. CountryId
  E.where_ $
    (client ^. ClientAge E.>. E.just (E.val 25))
    E.&&. (country ^. CountryName `E.in_` E.valList [ "Spain", "Germany" ])
    E.orderBy [ E.asc (client ^. ClientLastName)
              , E.asc (client ^. ClientFirstName) ]
  return client
```

In addition to inner joins, Esqueleto supports speaking about outer joins, which are useful in many situations.

To wrap up this fast introduction to Esqueleto, now you need to learn a bit about expressing *grouping* like you do in SQL. The grouping itself is done via the groupBy function, which takes as an argument a field to make the grouping. Then, you can use *aggregation* operators such as sum_, min_, max_, avg_, or countRows over other fields to perform that operation over all values of each group. Explaining in detail how these operations work would take a long time, and that is a task better suited to a book on SQL, from which Esqueleto takes its concepts.

As an example of grouping, let's try to compute the amount of money spent by each client in their purchases. To do so, the idea is to group the information of all Purchase entities by the Client identifier and then use the sum_ aggregator. Notice how a left outer join is needed to aggregate also over those clients that haven't yet purchased any product.

```
getMoneyByClient
  :: MonadIO m => SqlPersistT m [(Entity Client, E.Value (Maybe Double))]
getMoneyByClient =
  E.select $ do
  client E.:& purchase <- E.from $
    E.table @Client `E.leftJoin` E.table @Purchase
    `E.on` \(client E.:& purchase) ->
      E.just (client ^. ClientId) E.==. purchase ?. PurchaseClient
  E.groupBy (client ^.ClientId)
  let s = E.sum_ (purchase ?. PurchaseAmount)
  return (client, s)
```

The language supported by Esqueleto is indeed expressive and allows you to express queries far beyond what has been explained here. My recommendation for those moments when you need to perform powerful queries against a relational database is to read its documentation in more detail to discover the full generality of its constructions.

Insertions, Updates, and Deletions

At the beginning of the chapter, you were introduced to the way of inserting new values in the database, via insert. That function returns the identifier that was assigned to the new value that was saved on the database, which comes in handy when referring to it on other database values. However, in some cases, the value won't be inserted because of collisions on the uniqueness constraints. If this happens, it's recommended that you use instead insertUnique, which returns a Maybe value, which will be Nothing if the value could not be inserted.

I mentioned that Persistent embraces the pure functional paradigm, so all changes made to a database value must be explicit. The easiest way to modify a value is by using replace. That function takes an identifier and a value of one of your entities and replaces whatever value was saved before in the database with the mentioned identifier with the new value. For example, a quite slow but simple way to make sure that all the names in the database start with a capital letter would be as follows:

```
import Data.Char

capitalizeNamesSlow :: MonadIO m => SqlPersistT m ()
capitalizeNamesSlow = do
  clients <- selectList [] []
  mapM_ (\(Entity ident client) ->
            let c:rest  = clientFirstName client
              in replace ident
                    $ client { clientFirstName = (toUpper c):rest })
        clients
```

This solution is slow because it needs to bring all the data from the database to the program and then send back all the information for each client. In simple cases, the same task can be performed right on the database side, without any information being sent back and forth. Persistent includes support for doing such an *in-place update* when the operation either is assignment to a constant or involves only numerical data present in the value. The function that performs such an operation is updateWhere; all it takes as a parameter are a list of filters to specify which elements in the database will be affected by the changes and a list of in-place updates. Each update is represented using a field name, one of the update operators ((=.) for direct assignment and -, (+=.), (-=.), (*=.), or (/=.) for applying a numerical operation), and a constant value that is the argument in the update.

For example, let's decide to provide a 10 percent discount. However, you don't want to provide such a big discount to all the products because in the case of expensive ones, that discount is too high. The solution is to provide only a 3 percent discount on all products whose price is higher than 10,000. The following code uses 10,000 as the dividing line and applies either a 3 percent or a 10 percent discount as appropriate:

```
discount :: MonadIO m => SqlPersistT m ()
discount = do
  updateWhere [ ProductPrice <=. 10000 ] [ ProductPrice *=. 0.9 ]
  updateWhere [ ProductPrice >. 10000 ] [ ProductPrice *=. 0.97 ]
```

As with the queries, Persistent is not powerful enough to represent some of the conditions for updating in just one expression. Thus, you have to resort either to multiple queries and updates or to using a more powerful language such as Esqueleto. In the second instance, you need to change the call to select and from into a call to update. That function takes as a parameter another function, whose type will inform Esqueleto about which entities are affected by the change. To perform queries inside an update block, you can use subSelectUnsafe, which works in a similar way to select but it's allowed to return only one result.

When using update instead of select, you are allowed to use one extra function inside the monad: set. This function is the one describing the changes to perform in the database. It takes as a first argument the value to modify and then a list of in-place updates as in Persistent. As an example, let's say you decide to use a better policy for discounts. You apply them only to those products that don't sell well. The way you define a low amount of sales is via the total amount of purchases being less than 10. You can perform the query and the update at once with the following code:

```
betterDiscount :: MonadIO m => SqlPersistT m ()
betterDiscount = E.update $ \product -> do
  let totalAmount = E.subSelectUnsafe $ do
                      purchase <- E.from $ E.table @Purchase
                      E.where_ $ product ^. ProductId
                                         E.==. purchase ^. PurchaseProduct
                      E.groupBy (purchase ^. PurchaseProduct)
                      return $ E.sum_ (purchase ^. PurchaseAmount)
  E.where_ $ E.isNothing totalAmount
           E.||. totalAmount E.<. E.just (E.val (10 :: Double))
  E.set product [ ProductPrice E.*=. E.val 0.9]
```

And now you come to the most difficult point for any database. After some time, it may be necessary to delete some of the information that you stored for either space or efficiency reasons. Doing so is easy if you know a way to uniquely identify the value to delete in the database, either via its identifier or via a set of fields with a uniqueness constraint. In the first case, you can use the delete function, and for the second case, the deleteBy function is provided.

However, there are cases where you want to delete a set of values that satisfy certain conditions. Using the functions you already know, that would mean obtaining the value identifiers, maybe via selectKeysList, and then mapping over all of them with delete. But considering everything you've learned in this chapter, you may be expecting a function that performs this task without any round-trip of data between the database and your application. And it exists: it's called deleteWhere (similarly to updateWhere).

For example, as a way to clean the database, you may want to delete all the products in the database that are no longer in stock. The corresponding Persistent call is as follows, assuming that the stock never gets to negative values:

```
cleanProductStock :: MonadIO m => SqlPersistT m ()
cleanProductStock = deleteWhere [ ProductInStock ==. 0 ]
```

However, after careful thought, you can find that this code, even completely correct, would be dangerous to your database. If a client purchased one of the products that was no longer in stock, that line would make the reference to the product identifier incorrect because the product would no longer be in the database. A possible way to correct this problem is to create a better query that checks that there's no Purchase entity with that product. Once again, Persistent itself doesn't allow you to express that code; you need to use Esqueleto and its delete function, which works like update but deletes the resulting values. Notice in the following code how the notExists function performs the check for a corresponding purchase:

```
cleanProductStock' :: MonadIO m => SqlPersistT m ()
cleanProductStock' = E.delete $ do
  product <- E.from $ E.table @Product
  E.where_ $
    (product ^. ProductInStock E.==. E.val 0)
    E.&&. (E.notExists $ do
            purchase <- E.from $ E.table @Purchase
            E.where_ (purchase ^. PurchaseProduct
                        E.==. product ^. ProductId))
```

As you can see, performing updates and deletions in database values is easy using both Persistent and Esqueleto. The bulk of the learning process is to understand how to create good constraints for the values that will be affected by those operations. This shows one advantage of using high-level programming languages such as Haskell; you can express the concepts of your domain in a simple way and concentrate on the rules of your application.

Summary

In this chapter, you learned how Haskell allows you to interface with a DBMS in a type-safe manner.

- You saw the landscape of database access libraries in Hackage, and the focus moved to those that provide abstractions over several databases.

- In particular, the choice of libraries was Persistent and Esqueleto, which allow you to access both relational and nonrelational databases and to work with them in a type-safe way, making it harder to write illegal queries, something that is easy when working with raw database statements.

- You learned how to connect to databases both with and without a pool of connections.

- You were exposed to the language for specifying the database schema, with the idea that using that information combined with Template Haskell will create a bunch of data types and glue code for talking with the DBMS and will migrate the database.

- Much of the chapter was devoted to queries, either via identifiers, by a set of fields uniquely constrained, or in general by any field. For those cases where Persistent was not enough (like joins), Esqueleto was introduced.

- Finally, you read about performing insertions, updates, and deletions with those libraries.

CHAPTER 12

Web Applications

Throughout the book, you've been preparing for this moment: you know how to save information about clients and products, and you know a couple of algorithms to mine that data for interesting patterns. Now it's time to create an interface for clients to make purchases. This data will be the input to K-means and Apriori.

The most interoperable and arguably the most widely used way to create an interface for such an application is to write a web application. Your clients will be expecting to just enter a web address in the browser and get the list of products, put them in a virtual cart, and pay at the end. For that reason, this chapter will focus on building web applications using Haskell.

The development of such an application is divided into two parts. In the first part is the back end, which includes a server that will listen for HTTP requests and return and update information about clients, products, and purchases. For this task, you will reuse much of the knowledge from previous chapters and also learn about WAI, the underlying technology for web applications in Haskell, and `digestive-functors`, a library for handling forms using applicative style.

Then, the focus will turn to the front end, that is, the code that ultimately runs in the browsers of your clients, making the correct requests to the back end. Usually, this part would be written in JavaScript; but, as you will see, it's possible to reuse most of your Haskell knowledge if you use a language such as Elm. This will lead to consider how to manage a graphical stateful application in functional style.

Haskell Web Ecosystem

Web applications are becoming the standard way to interact with users. The benefits of this approach are many; you don't have to create a different executable for each system from which your client may access your application (although you still need to consider interoperability issues between browsers), and you don't need users to download or execute any binary code. Everything runs smoothly inside the browser.

409

© Alejandro Serrano Mena 2022
A. Serrano Mena, *Practical Haskell*, https://doi.org/10.1007/978-1-4842-8581-7_12

If you look at Hackage, you can see an increasing number of packages that deal with web applications. These packages range from being traditional, using patterns similar to frameworks in other languages, to experimental ways of composing an application (in this last group, Functional Reactive Programming [FRP] libraries are becoming popular).

Given the number of possibilities, I will give you an overview of the most important libraries you can use for developing a web application, as I did for accessing a database management system. Of course, this chapter cannot possibly cover everything related to web applications in Haskell. It will focus on a handful of libraries: WAI, `blaze-html`, Hamlet, and `digestive-functors` are the chosen ones for the back end. For the front end, I'll introduce a language different from Haskell but based on it: Elm.

Web Applications

In other language ecosystems, one usually goes for a *web framework* to develop a web application. Such a framework is usually a monolithic library that provides everything in one place. However, Haskell developers usually strive for more modularity, and the most common pattern in Hackage is a set of packages that are developed together that share part of their name (e.g., all the packages starting with `yesod`) but do not require each other in order to be fully functional. This means you can build your web application by pulling different pieces from different projects, without the resulting code turning messy at all. Indeed, the Time Machine Store presented in this chapter will use routing, templating, and form-handling libraries from different projects all at once.

The Haskell community has set a basis for all web frameworks in the form of the *Web Application Interface (WAI)*.[1] In principle, you could use any server that understands this interface to run your code (as you can use many servlet engines to run Java web applications). But in practice, only the Warp server is used in production. WAI is quite simple, and in fact we are going to interface with it directly in this chapter, instead of pulling a bigger framework. Still, if you need to build a production web application in Haskell, it is quite useful to know the most common frameworks in use. Since this is an ever-changing process, an updated list of Haskell web frameworks (including the ones mentioned as follows) and pointers to their websites can be consulted at `wiki.haskell.org/Web/Frameworks`.

---

[1] In the previous edition of this book, the Spock and Scotty frameworks were introduced, instead of interfacing directly with WAI. The community, however, has moved more into the extreme directions of using WAI or going for a complete framework.

Happstack is one of the most veteran frameworks in the wild. One of the most prominent uses of Happstack is `clckwrks`, a content management system. The main package, `happstack-server`, provides access to almost all the information about HTTP requests and responses, including compression, cookies, or authentication. On top of that, a Happstack user would usually add `happstack-foundation` as a dependency, which adds a lot of packages that work together well in a Happstack environment. Most often, data gets handled via the `acid-state` package, routing is done with the `web-routes` package, and form handling takes place via `reform`. There's no preferred templating engine although HSP (Haskell Server Pages), Heist, and Hamlet are listed in the documentation. The ideas behind HSP are similar to other templating languages such as JavaServer Pages (JSP): you write the HTML you want to be generated, decorated with small chunks of code written in Haskell.

Snap is another popular framework built upon WAI. There are two main features in the design of Snap. The first one is the focus on giving the developers tools for writing modular components that are later composed (called *snaplets*), instead of aiming for monolithic applications. The second one is the use of Heist as their choice of templating library, which uses plain HTML in combination with special tags to request information from other layers of the application.

A third choice is *Yesod*. The main goal of Yesod developers is to make everything as type-safe as possible. The Persistent library that has already been discussed is developed as part of this framework. If you remember, Persistent schemas were described using a small language that was parsed using quasiquotation and Template Haskell. Yesod brings the same ideas to other parts of the web application; routing and templating are specified using those blocks. For templating, the *Shakespeare* library can output each common language on the Web with the use of several quasiquoters: *Hamlet* for HTML documents (which will be discussed in this chapter), Cassius and Lucius for style sheets, and Julius for JavaScript code.

Servant is younger than the other frameworks, but it is regarded nowadays as the best way to develop web applications in Haskell. Its goal is also to make Haskell type-safety guarantees work for us, but with an approach completely different to Yesod's. Most parts of the application are described using a type, and this type is later used to automatically generate routing, templating, or marshaling to JSON. Due to the more complex nature of the type-level part of a Servant application, to use it proficiently you need to master the techniques described in the next chapter.

Compilation to JavaScript

Up to now, the frameworks I have discussed deal with the back end (also known as the *server side*) of the application. They allow you to generate HTML pages that will be the part that the user will ultimately see. Unfortunately, HTML itself is not able to describe all kinds of behaviors that are expected in a dynamic web page, and developers need to resort to JavaScript. Every modern browser includes a JavaScript interpreter that exposes an enormous amount of functionality to the user and allows for creating sophisticated applications (think of the various web pages that show interactive maps).

The problem is that you may not want to code your entire front end (or client side) in JavaScript. JavaScript is a mixed imperative and prototype-oriented language. Even though it integrates some features from the functional paradigm, its syntax and, more importantly, its concepts are very different from Haskell's. Using the same language for both the back end and the front end reduces the mental effort you need to make when working on both parts at the same time, and it increases the possibilities of sharing code between the parts.

However, making the browsers support a new language is just an illusion. JavaScript is the language where all the efforts are focused. For that reason, many compilers have included the option to generate JavaScript as output apart from binary code. Then, you can use your preferred programming language to write dynamic web pages and still retain the ubiquity of support that JavaScript has on browsers. Furthermore, these days, the speed and quality of JavaScript implementations are quite impressive. The functional community as a whole has worked in that direction, and there are several Haskell-inspired languages that can be compiled into JavaScript.

Some projects such as *GHCJS*, *WebGHC*, and *Haste* modify the GHC compiler itself to output this alternative representation. These projects have different areas of focus, from allowing seamless execution of any application that can be compiled by GHC into a web environment, replicating the entire runtime, to trying to balance full compatibility with GHC and better interoperability with other JavaScript codes. Unfortunately, it seems that these projects have not caught upon Haskell practitioners, and at the moment of writing, using and developing with them is not as simple as using GHC.

An alternative approach is to create a completely new language, but strongly based on the syntax and concepts of Haskell. There are two main projects in this area. *PureScript* is the closest language to Haskell and shares with it a powerful type system. The main difference is that code is not executed lazily, it uses the most common execution model inherited from JavaScript instead. The other side of the spectrum is covered by *Elm*, which removes some Haskell's features (like type classes) in order to provide a simpler language. But we still have higher-order functions, pattern matching, and many of the defining features of Haskell. Elm is the focus of our section about front end.

Like in the case of web frameworks, many other languages and packages provide support for compiling into JavaScript. You can get an up-to-date list with pointers on documentation at `wiki.haskell.org/The_JavaScript_Problem`.

RESTful Structure

Before starting with the coding, I will introduce some of the general patterns in the design of the application, which are based on the Representational State Transfer (REST) principles. Many of these concepts are visible in many other web frameworks, both inside and outside the Haskell world.

The core idea is that the web application provides access to a set of *resources*, which can be queried or modified. The information of a client or a product is an example of resources in the Time Machine Store. Each of these resources is accessed through a unique identifier, which in a web application is a URL. For example, `/clients` could be the identifier of the list of all clients, and `/product/3` may identify the information of the product whose identifier in the database is the number 3.

Given that URLs are central to knowing which data must be queried or affected by a request, the web framework of choice should include good support for specifying URL patterns and point to the right code to execute. Each of these patterns is called a *route*. For example, you can describe the route for products as `/product/<number>`, meaning that when any URL starting with `/product/` is found followed by a number, some handling code is executed.

For each resource, an application can have several *request methods*, each of them being a particular action over the resource. For web applications, which are the focus of this chapter, the most used request methods are `GET`, which retrieves a particular object or lists the elements in a collection; `POST`, which is used to create a new element inside a specific resource; `PUT`, which replaces the information of an entire resource with new information coming with the request; and `DELETE`, which erases the resource from the system. The REST architecture style imposes several constraints on how each method should behave (e.g., `GET` should not modify the resource at all). You can read about it in many books about this topic, so I won't delve into details here.

Finally, for each supported combination of resource identifier and request method, the application should give a response using standard formats. When using REST over HTTP, this means using HTTP status codes (e.g., returning a 404 error when some resource is not found) and encoding the queried information using HTML, XML, or JSON. Furthermore, the consumer can specify a list of supported response types, and the server should try to satisfy that requirement.

Back End with WAI

In this section, you will develop the back end of the Time Machine Store. Because of space constraints, I will focus primarily on querying and updating information about products. Support for clients and purchases is left as a good exercise to put together much of the knowledge you've acquired up to this point.

Simple Skeleton

The first thing to do is to set up a project with an executable stanza that will start the server, adding wai, warp, and http-types as dependencies. You've already gone through these steps in the first four chapters. Now repeat them in Exercise 12-1 to create the basis for the store. Remember that exercise solutions are included with this book's example download from the Apress.com catalog page.

EXERCISE 12-1. SETTING UP THE PROJECT

Create a new Cabal package, either using Cabal or Stack, named chapter12. This package should contain a stanza that will generate the time-machine-store executable. Add wai, warp, and http-types as dependencies of the executable.

Now you're ready to start building your web application. The following shows a simple application that responds the same literal content regardless of the request:

```
{-# LANGUAGE OverloadedStrings #-}

import Network.HTTP.Types
import Network.Wai
import Network.Wai.Handler.Warp

main :: IO ()
main = run 3000 $ \request respond ->
  respond $ responseLBS ok200 [] $
    mconcat [ "<html><body>"
            , "  <h1>Hello Practical Haskell!</h1>"
            , "</body></html>"]
```

The entry point of the application, the `main` function, starts your web application at port 3000 by means of the `run` function. The beauty of the WAI is how simple and functionally an application is defined: it is literally a *function* which receives the request as argument. This beauty is a bit lost, however, in how you return your response: instead of being merely the result of the function, you need to explicitly call the given `respond` function with the response.[2] HTTP responses require at least a status code, like `ok200` earlier, which comes from the `http-types` package, and some content. WAI handles natively a wide range of sources; here, we use a `ByteString`, but you may also use a file path directly if you are sending some static resource.

Note   In the preceding code block, we use the `OverloadedStrings` extension to write literal `ByteStrings` as string literals. In fact, most code in this chapter uses it, since routes and HTML templates both use string-like types different from `String`.

---

[2] In older versions of WAI, the response was actually defined in that way, as the result of the function. Alas, that made deterministic resource handling challenging, because the moment in which the content was sent was not clear. The current version avoids these problems; you can safely close your database handles after calling the respond function, since at that point your response is guaranteed to be handled by the web server.

You can check that your web application works by building the package at the command line and calling it. Then point your browser to http://localhost:3000/ to run the application and show the result on your screen.

The previous web application was so simple that it never checked the *request* from the user. There is a wide range of information available in the request parameter, like the *method* (whether you have a GET or a POST) and the *path* or *route* that was requested. The pattern of extracting this information and matching over it gives a nice declarative feeling to your web application.

```
main :: IO ()
main = run 3000 app

app :: Application
app request respond =
  case (parseMethod (requestMethod request), pathInfo request) of
    (Right GET, ["about"]) ->
      respond $ responseHtml ok200 $
        mconcat [ "<html><body>"
                , "  <h1>Hello Practical Haskell!</h1>"
                , "</body></html>"]
    _ ->
      respond $ responseHtml notFound404
        "<h1>Not found :(</h1>"
```

Since now we only return our "Hello Practical Haskell!" content in the /about route, it is a good idiom to handle every other request by returning the well-known 404 HTTP status code. Note how the exhaustiveness checks within the Haskell compiler help us in this case to ensure that routes other than /about are also handled.

Another change introduced in the previous example is the separation from the web application itself into an app function, which is then executed via the run function in the entry point main. Once again, we stress how the building blocks of WAI are very modular, and you are thus free to refactor or extract parts of the code without further problems. Exercise 12-2 asks you to do so for our small sample application.

EXERCISE 12-2. REFACTORING THE APPLICATION

Extract each of the handlers, the one for /about and the generic "not found" one, into their own definitions.

Showing Products from the Database

Now let's move on to the main task in this section: showing information about products. The access to that data will be via the Persistent library (thus, you should include persistent, persistent-template, and persistent-sqlite as dependencies) using the same schema from Chapter 11. In the examples, I will assume that the database schema is described in the module Chapter12.Database.

There are two changes to be done to the main function to make the database available to the application. First, you should make sure the schema described via Persistent coincides with the actual database schema. As you know, this is achieved via a migration, which should be the first thing to appear in main.

Each time we access the database, we could, in principle, start a new connection using runSqlite and execute the actions there, since any WAI application can run any IO action. However, it's more performant to create a pool of connections, for which we use the facilities provided by the resource-pool package.

```
import Data.Pool
import qualified Database.Persist.Sqlite as Db
import Control.Monad.Logger
import Control.Monad.Trans
import Control.Monad.IO.Class

mainDb :: IO ()
mainDb = do
  Db.runSqlite "example.db" $ Db.runMigration migrateAll
  runNoLoggingT $ Db.withSqlitePool "example.db" 10 $ \pool ->
    liftIO $ run 3000 (app pool)

app :: Pool SqlBackend -> Application
app pool request respond = ...
```

The creation of the connection pool is done with the usual withSqlitePool function. Note that we do not use the pool yet, but we pass a reference to it to our app function. By using the runSqlPersistMPool function, we can execute some database action in one of the connections handled by that pool, only at the moment in which it is needed.

Coming back to our products, each product will be available through a URL such as /product/n, where *n* is the unique identifier given by the DBMS to that product. That means that our paths must consist of two components, the first one being the literal product string. Moreover, we must ensure that the second component is a real decimal number; the text package contains a specific Data.Text.Read module to detect simple patterns which is quite handy in this case.

```
{-# LANGUAGE RecordWildCards #-}

import qualified Data.Text.Read as Read

app :: Pool SqlBackend -> Application
app pool request respond =
  case (parseMethod (requestMethod request), pathInfo request) of
    (Right GET, ["product", productIdParam])
      | Right (productId, "") <- Read.decimal productIdParam -> do
      product <- flip runSqlPersistMPool pool $
        Db.get $ ProductKey productId
      case product of
        Just Product { .. } -> respond $ responseHtml ok200 $
          mconcat [ "<html><body>"
                  , "  <h1>Hello Practical Haskell!</h1>"
                  , "</body></html>"]
        Nothing -> respond $ responseHtml notFound404
          "<h1>Product not found :(</h1>"
    _ ->
      respond $ responseHtml notFound404
        "<h1>Not found :(</h1>"
```

The rest of the code is a straightforward access to the database as explained in Chapter 11 for accessing a value via its identifier and composing the returned HTML value. The code uses record wildcards to bind variables from the Product record easily. When a product identifier is not found, the status code of the response is set to 404 using the same approach as for "not found" route in the previous section.

In the code shown previously, we've spared you from the ugly code required to construct the resulting HTML page via simple string concatenation. After seeing how many checks a Haskell compiler can do for you in so many realms, you should ask whether there's some tool for helping in writing HTML code, making sure you close all tags, using indentation to discern the document structure, and so on. The answer is positive: I'm going to show you two different libraries that take different paths for this task.

The first option is the `blaze-html` package. The idea is that each HTML element is represented by a function whose final parameter is a monadic value representing all those tags nested inside. This way, you can write nested do blocks to simulate the document structure in your Haskell code. The other main combinator is (!), which allows you to include HTML attributes for each element.

Since there are several versions of the (X)HTML standard, `blaze-html` provides different packages defining the accepted tags and attributes for each. In the following code, I've rewritten the handler for products to use `blaze-html` instead of string concatenation. Notice how you need to call `toHtml` to convert a string into a value that can be consumed by `blaze-html` and to convert from a `blaze-html` value into `Text` that can be returned as part of the handler via `renderHtml`.

```
import qualified Text.Blaze.Html5 as H
import qualified Text.Blaze.Html5.Attributes as A
import Text.Blaze.Html.Renderer.Text (renderHtml)

app pool request respond =
  case (parseMethod (requestMethod request), pathInfo request) of
    (Right GET, ["product", productIdParam])
      ...
      case product of
        Just Product { .. } -> respond $ responseHtml ok200 $
          renderHtml $
            H.html $ do
              H.head $
                H.title "Time Machine Store"
              H.body $ do
                H.h1 $ H.toHtml productName
                H.p H.! A.id "descr" $ H.toHtml productDescription
```

```
          Nothing -> ...
```

A second choice for embedding HTML values in a type-safe way is to use the templating system called *Shakespeare*. The distinctive characteristic of this package is its use of quasiquotation to provide different syntax modes closer to the ones used on the Web. The one we shall explore here is *Hamlet*, which returns well-formatted HTML.

```
{-# LANGUAGE QuasiQuotes, TemplateHaskell #-}

import Text.Hamlet

app pool request respond =
  case (parseMethod (requestMethod request), pathInfo request) of
    (Right GET, ["product", productIdParam])
      ...
      case product of
        Just Product { .. } -> respond $ responseHtml ok200 $
          renderHtml [shamlet|
            <html>
              <head>
                <title>Time Machine Store
              <body>
                <h1>#{productName}
                <p id=descr>#{productDescription}
          |]
        Nothing -> ...
```

Hamlet templates use opening tags in the same way as HTML. However, indentation is the syntactic element marking the nesting structure, so closing tags are not needed, as you can see in the previous example. At any moment, you can "escape" to the Haskell world via #{ }, and the result of the expression inside the brackets will be printed safely at that point.

In this simple web application, the shamlet function is used for parsing the HTML block. This is a simple function that just returns an Html value, which can be rendered using renderHtml (the same as was presented for blaze-html). But Shakespeare provides other quasiquoters that are much more powerful than this:

- The hamlet function allows you to use *type-safe URLs*. The idea is to define all possible routes in your web application using an ADT. Each of the constructors will describe a URL pattern along with the set of parameters. Then, instead of building your HTML links by hand, you specify one of these constructors every time you need a link. The web-routes generates most of the boilerplate code needed to use this feature.

- The ihamlet function adds *internationalization* support to the mix. You can create a general document structure for your templates and then include different messages for each language that your web application supports.

Finally, for each of these functions, Hamlet provides a corresponding function ending in File (shamletFile, hamletFile, ihamletFile) that reads the template for an external file. In that way, you can separate the view of your data from the logic in the server.

Hamlet includes not only tags and brackets for variables but also control structures for simple cases that are common when building an HTML page. For example, the following code uses $forall to iterate through all the products in the database, writing a row in a table for each of them:

```
app pool request respond =
  case (parseMethod (requestMethod request), pathInfo request) of
    ...
    (Right GET, ["products"]) -> do
      products <- flip runSqlPersistMPool pool $ Db.selectList [] []
      respond $ responseHtml ok200 $
        renderHtml [shamlet|
          <html>
            <head>
              <title>Time Machine Store
            <body>
              <h1>Products
              <table>
                <tr>
                  <th>Name
                  <th>Description
                $forall Db.Entity _ p <- products
```

```
        <tr>
          <td>#{productName p}
          <td>#{productDescription p}
  |]
```

Exercise 12-3 asks you to implement the same functionality as you've done for products, but now you can do this for clients of the Time Machine Store.

EXERCISE 12-3. QUERYING ABOUT CLIENTS

Include the new routes /clients and /client/:clientId that return information about all clients and a particular client in HTML format. Use any of the presented templating systems for generating the HTML output.

Inserting New Products Using Forms

Right now, you have tools only for writing routes that use information from the URL to respond. But when a user is expected to give some data interactively, the interface should present a form, and the web application should take as input the information from that form. How to do this in an elegant and composable way will be the main topic of this section.

There is a lot of (boring) work related to forms in web applications: information may come from different sources (query parameters and HTML forms, to mention some), you need to manually convert from Text to the required format, and deal with erroneous input. You should aim instead to have a centralized description of each form in your web application that can be reused between different handlers (e.g., your product form may be used both for creating a new one and for updating the information of an existing one).

The package you will use in this web application for form handling is called digestive-functors. One interesting feature of this library is its use of the applicative style, which gives forms the same flavor as JSON handling with aeson, which has been already discussed in this book. The digestive-functors package also separates the description of the data and validation for building a value from the way in which that form should be visualized, giving a modular approach to form handling.

Each form you build with this library must build a value of a specific type, which would usually be one of the types you use in your database schema. In addition, the Form type (the one describing each form in the page) needs a type variable describing the format in which errors will be presented. For each argument in the constructor of that type, you must specify which field in your form will handle its value, one of the basic kinds of fields you can have in an HTML form, the initial value for an empty form, and any extra validation required. For example, this is a form for the Country type, which needs a string and a Boolean value and shows the errors as strings. Notice how the field is specified using the string or bool function, and the initial value is specified wrapped in Maybe.

```
import Text.Digestive
```

```
countryForm :: Monad m => Form String m Country
countryForm = Country <$> "name" .: string Nothing
                      <*> "send" .: bool (Just True)
```

Caution   Both aeson and digestive-functors contain a function called (.:). Be aware of this fact; you will need to qualify at least one of them if you're using the two modules in the same source file.

For further validation, you must wrap one of those simple specifications inside validate or check. The difference between them is that validate may also parse the value into a new one (maybe of another type), whereas check is only a Boolean predicate that leaves the value as is. Both functions need as extra input the error message that should be provided to the user when the value does not fulfill the requirements. The following code implements a form for Product values; it uses validate to convert from strings to numbers and uses check to constrain the possible items in stock to be larger or equal to zero:

```
import Text.Digestive.Util
```

```
productForm :: Monad m => Form String m Product
productForm
  = Product <$> "name"        .: string Nothing
            <*> "description" .: string Nothing
```

```
          <*> "price"        .: validate isANumber (string Nothing)
          <*> "inStock"      .: check "Must be >= 0" (>= 0)
                                   (validate isANumber (string Nothing))
isANumber :: (Num a, Read a) => String -> Result String a
isANumber = maybe (Error "Not a number") Success . readMaybe
```

Once you have the description of your form, it's time to define how it will be *seen* by the user. The code you need to create should take a *view* of the form (in other words, a definition of the form plus values for each of the fields) and return the HTML output. There are packages for integrating forms with almost any of the templating systems I introduced at the beginning of the chapter. In this section, I will use blaze-html as an example, so you need to add digestive-functors-blaze as a dependency.

Note   You might need to relax the dependency solver constraints to install digestive-functors in newer GHC versions. You can use --allow-newer in Cabal or add allow-newer: true to your stack.yaml file to make the project compile. You will definitely run into this issue during your Haskell journey, as it tends to take some time until the community "catches up" with each new GHC version.

The module Text.Digestive.Blaze.Html5 includes functions for all the types of inputs that the HTML standard supports. Each of the functions takes as parameters at least the name of the field it refers to and the view it handles. In addition to input controls, this package can also generate code for input labels and for the errors that concern each field. As an example, here's a possible way to show the information of a form for a product. Notice the inclusion of inputSubmit for creating a Submit button.

```
import qualified Text.Blaze.Html5 as H   -- from previous examples
import Text.Digestive.Blaze.Html5

productView :: View H.Html -> H.Html
productView view = do
  form view "/new-product" $ do
    label     "name"    view "Name:"
    inputText "name"    view
    H.br
```

```
inputTextArea Nothing Nothing "description" view
H.br
label      "price"   view "Price:"
inputText "price"    view
errorList "price"    view
label      "inStock" view "# in Stock:"
inputText "inStock" view
errorList "inStock" view
H.br
inputSubmit "Submit"
```

Now let's create the form that will be shown when the user of the web application wants to add a new product. Since there's no information about that new product, you should show the form with the initial data defined in productForm. This is done by creating an empty view using getForm. You can integrate that view's form in a larger web page by invoking productView, as the following code shows:

```
app pool request respond =
  case (parseMethod (requestMethod request), pathInfo request) of
    ...
    (Right GET, ["new-product"]) -> do
      view <- getForm "product" productForm
      respond $ responseHtml ok200 $ renderHtml $
        H.html $ do
          H.head $ H.title "Time Machine Store"
          H.body $ productView (fmap H.toHtml view)
```

Note   getForm returns a View String value (since the definition of productForm had type Form String m Product), whereas productView needs a View H.Html value. You can move from the former to the latter by mapping H.toHtml on every field using fmap, as the previous code does. The idea behind this conversion is that you should map the errors in the form from the String type to an HTML representation.

When the form is sent by the browser back to the web application, the POST request method is used instead of GET. Thus, in that case, you have to read the values sent by the user and then either write the new product on the database if the values are correct or return the same form with error messages. The key point is the change from getForm to postForm, which doesn't use the initial data but rather a dictionary of fields and values from the request. Except for this change, the code for this request is straightforward. If the input data is valid (postForm returns a Just value), contact the database and redirect to the page for the product; in the other case, return the same form (the productView function will take care of showing the errors). Note that the post function lives in a different package, namely, wai-digestive-functors, which you should include as dependency.

```
import Network.Wai.Digestive

app pool request respond =
  case (parseMethod (requestMethod request), pathInfo request) of
    ...
    (Right POST, ["new-product"]) -> do
      (view, product) <- postForm "product" productForm
                                  (\_ -> bodyFormEnv undefined request)
        case product of
          Just p -> do
            ProductKey newId <- flip runSqlPersistMPool pool $ Db.insert p
            respond $ redirect $ "/product/" <> show newId
          Nothing -> respond $ responseHtml ok200 $ renderHtml $
            H.html $ do
              H.head $ H.title "Time Machine Store"
              H.body $ productView (fmap H.toHtml view)
```

This section serves as a good introduction to building REST web applications in Haskell using WAI. To fix the concepts in your mind, you should try to complete the back end of the application as Exercise 12-4 suggests. Afterward, if you are interested in web applications in Haskell, you can dive more deeply into WAI (e.g., how to deal with sessions or cookies), especially by checking the documentation of both wai and wai-extra packages, or learn about any of the other frameworks that were mentioned earlier.

EXERCISE 12-4. REGISTERING CLIENTS

Create a new handler for registering clients at route /register. As in the case of products, you need to add handlers for both the GET and POST request methods.

Hint: You may want to read the documentation of the choice combinator in digestive-functors to learn how to build a drop-down list with possible countries in your HTML form.

Front End with Elm

This section is devoted to creating a rich front end for the Time Machine Store web application using Elm. As in the previous section, space constraints limit the discussion to a shallow introduction to the Elm ecosystem and its use to show some products using the back end described earlier.

GETTING ELM IN YOUR SYSTEM

The Elm website, located at elm-lang.org, has at the moment of writing a big Install button in its main page. In Windows and Mac, it is recommended to use the installer, which also sets up the correct paths in the system; in Linux, this setup needs to be done manually.

In this section, we are going to use one of Elm's facilities for rapid application development: elm reactor. Usually, in order to use one of these JavaScript-based languages, you need to create an accompanying web page, compile the code to JavaScript, and then call it from the page. Each step is easy, but it creates quite some overhead for a few simple examples. In contrast, using reactor you just need to initialize a folder as a project and then point your browser directly to an Elm source file. The code is then compiled and executed, without any further configuration.

As I have just mentioned, the first step is setting up a folder as a project. To do so, simply move to that folder in a command line and run elm init. A new elm.json file and a src folder should have been created. The former file describes where the code is located and which are the packages the project depends on:

```
{
    "type": "application",
    "source-directories": [ "src" ],
    "elm-version": "0.19.1",
    "dependencies": {
        "direct": { ... },
        "indirect": { ... }
    },
    ...
}
```

Let us begin with a very simple Elm application, which just greets a person. The name of that person will not be subject to change, you just can change it by setting the right variable in the code. Nevertheless, this small application already contains most components of the so-called Elm Architecture.

```
import Browser
import Html exposing (..)

main = Browser.sandbox { init = init
                       , update = \_ model -> model
                       , view = view }

type alias Model = { currentName : String }

init : Model
init = { currentName = "Alejandro" }

view : Model -> Html ()
view model = div [] [ text "Hello, ", text model.currentName, text "!"]
```

Before explaining how the application works, let me point out how to use elm reactor to run the application. In the same terminal in which you created the project, run elm reactor.

```
$ elm reactor
Go to <http://localhost:8000> to see your project dashboard.
```

Now open a browser and go to the specified website. You will see a list of files. Navigate to the src folder, in which source files should reside, and then click the file corresponding to your application. If everything has gone well, you should see a big *"Hello, Alejandro!"* in your screen. Otherwise, the output of the compiler is shown directly in the browser window, which is a very helpful way to diagnose why your application does not work.

The simplest version of the Elm Architecture, depicted in Figure 12-1, requires us to provide three components: the model, which is the data our application saves; the update function, which describes how the model is updated in response to events such as user input; and the view, which specifies how to render the data in the model as HTML. In turn, the model is defined in two parts: first of all, you need to declare a data type which defines all the possible states of the application, and in addition you have to specify the initial state.

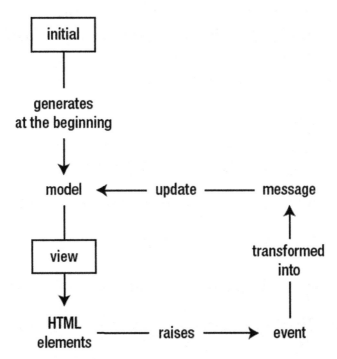

Figure 12-1. *Simple Elm Architecture*

In this case, the model is simply a string. In the code, though, we use a kind of types which is not available in Haskell's type system, namely, *records* or *row*. Our Model type is made up of one single piece of data, which is available under the identifier currentName. If you look closely at the following view function, you can see that we use model.currentName to access the information. These types, inherited from JavaScript, provide a simple way to gather information without the overhead of using constructors everywhere. The init function specifies the initial value for this field; feel free to use your own name there.

The view function describes how to turn a value of the Model type into an HTML document. There is nothing surprising: Elm's approach to markup follows similar ideas as the blaze-html package we have discussed earlier.

Using Browser.sandbox, we put together the initial state of the model and the view. This function also requires an update function, but for now this function never changes the model. It is not very important here, though, because we have not set up in moment in the application in which an event is raised, and thus the update function shall be called. Let us look at a new version of the application in which you can change the person to be greeted:

```
import Browser
import Html exposing (..)
import Html.Attributes exposing (..)
import Html.Events exposing (onInput, onClick)

main = Browser.sandbox { init = init, update = update, view = view }

type alias Model = { currentName : String, textboxName : String }

init : Model
init = { currentName = "Alejandro", textboxName = "Alejandro" }

type Msg = TextboxChanged String
         | MakeCurrent

update : Msg -> Model -> Model
update msg model = case msg of
  TextboxChanged nm -> { model | textboxName = nm }
  MakeCurrent       -> { model | currentName = model.textboxName }
```

```
view : Model -> Html Msg
view model
  = div []
       [ div [] [ text "Hello, ", text model.currentName, text "!"]
       , input [ placeholder "Write your name here"
               , value model.textboxName
               , onInput TextboxChanged ] []
       , button [ onClick MakeCurrent ] [ text "Greet me!" ]
       ]
```

The first thing I have done is enlarging the model to incorporate both the current name and the information which is currently saved in a textbox. One possibility would have been to keep the greeting completely in sync with the value of the textbox, but in this example, the user must click a *Greet me!* button explicitly. This way, we look at a bit more complex workflow.

The next place to look at is the definition of view. In addition to the previous line of text, we now have an input element (corresponding to the textbox) and a button element. In both cases, we set up handlers for possible events: in the case of the textbox when the text changes and in the case of the button whenever it is clicked. In contrast to many graphical interface toolkits, these handlers do not specify functions to run, but rather *messages* to be sent.

This leads us to the definition of the Msg type, which declares all possible messages that the application can handle. In our case, they correspond closely to the user interface elements, but in general, they might describe any possible event in the application, like a change in the data. The update function is responsible for taking each of the messages and specifying how they affect the underlying model of the application. In this case, the TextboxChanged messages updated the corresponding field in the model, and the MakeCurrent message moves the name from the temporary to definite storage. In turn, this causes the view function to run, leading to visible output for the user.

The right way to think about the Elm Architecture is like a state machine. Each constructor in the Model type defines one state in the application, along with any additional data that it might need. Messages move the application to different states. Apart from this core, we need a way to reflect the changes in the data to the outside; this is the role of the view function. This architecture is a very common way to define user interfaces in the functional world,[3] and it has been slowly gaining traction out of this niche. Popular projects like React use very similar ideas.

Retrieving Products

The architecture composed of a model, an update function, and a view works well if your application is self-sufficient, that is, if all the data is contained in the initial state or a product of the user input. But this is not true for many (or even almost all) web applications: the data is not present at the beginning of the application but obtained later by making calls to remote servers (usually your application back end). This behavior requires an extension to the Elm Architecture.

The core idea to model operations which are out of the control of the application, and might be asynchronous, is to use *commands*. A command represents any operation that we want to request from the outside world – what exactly depends on the library you are using. Once the command finishes working, and has a final value, a message is sent to the application. This message is handled in the same fashion that any user input: by calling the update function which performs any required changes to the model and then updating the view.

In the following example, we are going to request the information about a product given its identifier. We assume the back end gives us back JSON, which is the easiest format to parse in Elm. For both tasks, we need to add a couple of dependencies to our project. Instead of changing the elm.json file by hand, Elm provides built-in commands to request them:

```
$ elm install elm/json
I found it in your elm.json file, but in the "indirect" dependencies.
Should I move it into "direct" dependencies for more general use? [Y/n]: y
Success!
$ elm install elm/http
Here is my plan:
...
Success!
```

---

[3] The gloss library uses the same concepts but oriented to 2-D games in Haskell.

Before I dive in the application itself, let us have a look at the way in which Elm handles JSON decoding. As we discussed earlier, Elm does not feature type classes nor automatic derivation via `Generic`, so we need to write them by hand. However, these decoders look very similar to the handwritten `FromJSON` instances you wrote in Chapter 10. The `(.:)` function, which looked for a named field in an object, is now simply called `field`; and the decoding of basic types is performed by a set of basic decoders such as `string` or `int`.

```
import Json.Decode exposing (Decoder, map2, field, string)

type alias Product = { name : String, description : String }

productDecoder : Decoder Product
productDecoder = map2 Product (field "name"        string)
                              (field "description" string)
```

Our model becomes more complex with the introduction of the HTTP call. As in the case of the greeter, we need a piece of data to hold the current input in the textbox, which we can later query. The rest of our `Model` describes the status of the HTTP call: no request may have been issued yet (because the application `JustStarted`), the request may be in progress (`LoadingProduct`), or it might have been either with an error or successfully. In the latter case, we also save the result of the request as a `Product`.

```
type alias Model = { productId : String, productStatus : ProductStatus }

type ProductStatus = JustStarted
                   | LoadingProduct
                   | Error
                   | ProductData Product
```

The set of messages we handle is also quite like our previous application. We have messages coming from changes in the textbox input and clicking the button. To those we add a third one which represents that the HTTP call has finished, so we can look at the result.

```
import Http

type Msg = TextboxChanged String | Load
         | ReceivedInfo (Result Http.Error Product)
```

This means that there is one more case to handle in the update function:

```
import Browser

update : Msg -> Model -> (Model, Cmd Msg)
update msg model = case msg of
  TextboxChanged pid -> ({ model | productId = pid }, Cmd.none)
  Load -> ( { model | productStatus = LoadingProduct }
          , Http.get
              { url = "http://practical.haskell/product/" ++ model.productId
              , expect = Http.expectJson ReceivedInfo productDecoder
              } )
  ReceivedInfo result -> case result of
    Ok p  -> ({ model | productStatus = ProductData p }, Cmd.none)
    Err _ -> ({ model | productStatus = Error },         Cmd.none)
```

This is not the only change to the function. In this revised version of the Architecture, updates may also issue the commands we have been talking about previously. As a result, the function returns a pair of the model and the list of commands to request. In this case, most updates do not issue a command, which is represented by Cmd.none. In the case of a Load message, we want to make an HTTP call, and if the request is successful, apply the productDecoder and then send the ReceivedInfo message. The init function is also allowed to issue some commands at the beginning of the web application.

```
init : () -> (Model, Cmd Msg)
init _ = ( { productId = "", productStatus = JustStarted } , Cmd.none )
```

We still need to put these pieces together. The aforementioned Browser.sandbox is no longer enough when we introduce commands, so we need to change to the more powerful Browser.element.

```
main = Browser.element { init = init
                       , update = update
                       , subscriptions = \_ -> Sub.none
                       , view = view
                       }
```

In the preceding code, you can see that `Browser.element` requires `subscriptions` in addition to the three components I have discussed throughout this chapter. By subscribing, you can get a *stream* of events in your application, in contrast to a command, which gives you back only *one* message. The archetypal example of a subscription is time: you can request to get a tick every *n* seconds, and the system sends the corresponding message every time the wait is over. In this example, we do not want to subscribe to anything, so we initialize the corresponding field to a function which always returns `Sub.none`, in the same way that our initial style requests no command using `Cmd.none`.

The missing piece is the view function to turn the model into HTML elements. Exercise 12-5 asks you to implement this function.

EXERCISE 12-5. A VIEW FOR PRODUCTS

Implement the missing view function in the preceding application. Remember that you need to have at least one textbox whose changes lead to `TextboxChanged` messages and a button that raises a `Load` message when clicked.

Elm is a very productive language, even though some Haskell features are missing from the language. In fact, its designers argue that a simpler language makes it easier to introduce functional programming in an area of programming – web applications – where only JavaScript has been traditionally used.

SAME ORIGIN POLICY

If you're executing all these examples in a local environment, your web page may not work at all. In that case, you'll have been surely bitten by the Same Origin Policy. This policy, implemented in every browser in the wild, forbids a page in a domain to obtain information from other domains. In this case, a local page may not send information to a web application in `localhost:3000`, which we have used for our back end.

The easiest solution is to add a header to allow communication from any domain in the code. This can be done easily using the `wai-cors` package and wrapping your app to become `simpleCors app`. In this way, you notify your browser that the server admits calls from everywhere.

Having said that, it's obvious that you shouldn't add that header in every web application you create because you may be exposing information to other domains. The best solution is to sever both the back end and front end from the same domain. Alternatively, you can include a restrictive list of allowed clients by defining a `CorsResourcePolicy` from the package mentioned earlier.

Summary

This chapter served as an introduction to web application building in Haskell.

- You learned about the many libraries that the Haskell ecosystem provides for each feature required in a web application: routing, templating, form handling, and so on.

- The chapter focused on the development of the Time Machine Store following the principles of the *REST* architectural style and using the WAI package.

- Two *templating systems* were discussed: `blaze-html`, which provides a set of combinators for composing HTML documents, and Hamlet, which uses quasiquotation to embed a markup language inside Haskell code.

- For handling input from the user, you learned about the `digestive-functors` library.

- Finally, Elm was introduced as a way to program rich front-end web pages using a Haskell-inspired language, and you saw a small demo for obtaining remote information.

PART IV

Domain-Specific Languages

Strong Types for Describing Offers

You've already finished two of the main tasks in this book: implementing some data mining algorithms for analyzing clients and their purchases and looking at several ways to save the information about purchases in a durable container. This chapter is the starting point of the last task: creating a *domain-specific language* (DSL) for expressing offers to be applied in the Time Machine Store. You will provide a set of combinators to create the offers, which are initially basic offers.

Not all offers expressible in this language will be valid. The interesting part is that you can use the type system to help avoid many of the wrong offers, and this chapter will teach you the features needed to do that.

I will introduce you first to *generalized algebraic data types* (GADTs), which are a way to create more concrete constructors for your data types. Then, you will see how to encode other invariants using different techniques. In particular, this chapter discusses both *functional dependencies* (FDs) and *type families* (TFs), along with *singletons*.

Once you've read this chapter, you'll have a thorough grasp of the complete Haskell type system. You will be able to understand code that uses the advanced features described here, and you also will be able to use them in your own code.

Domain-Specific Languages

A *domain-specific language* (DSL) refers usually to a language not intended for expressing any computer program but rather data or computations about a *specific problem* space. For example, SQL can be seen as a DSL for expressing database queries. Haskell is not a DSL, but rather a general-purpose language, because it's not tied to any particular application domain.

© Alejandro Serrano Mena 2022
A. Serrano Mena, *Practical Haskell*, https://doi.org/10.1007/978-1-4842-8581-7_13

The existence of DSLs is not new in computer science. Many of the programs you use contain one or several DSLs at their core. For example, CSS is a DSL for expressing presentation attributes of markup elements, regular expressions are a DSL for expressing patterns over a string, hardware designers use specific languages for designing circuits, and so on.

Again, a DSL is not intended to express just any domain but rather a specific one. This means a DSL is tightly linked to the things you intend to express, allowing you to communicate those concepts using exactly the abstractions you need for that domain. This gives you two advantages:

- You no longer need developers to write the business rules in your program. If your DSL really expresses the rules using the usual abstractions for the intended domain, the experts on that specific domain can be the ones writing the rules. This decreases the mismatch between domain experts and programmers.

- You need to implement only a core DSL, which is usually quite small, and then use the new abstractions to build the rest of the system. This makes the programs easier to write, easier to understand, and easier to maintain because the abstraction of the domain is not scattered between different moving parts.

These advantages are important in the software engineering process. As a result, the concept of DSLs has risen in importance, and many problems are now tackled by means of a custom language for a domain. In fact, many tools are geared toward designing DSLs, and this chapter will make the case that Haskell is one of best in this field.

Embedding Your Language in Haskell

Any DSL you design will ultimately be integrated inside a larger application. That larger application will be written in a general-purpose language, like Haskell. Thus, it's important to consider the ways in which the DSL can hook into that other language, usually called the *host*.

One possibility is to make the DSL completely independent of the host language. In that case, you need to develop a full set of tools for this language. At the very least, you need to write a parser for the language. Thus, you get a lot of freedom in the design, but you need to put a lot of effort into its implementation. This way of integrating your language, called *external* or *stand-alone*, is useful when the DSL forms the core of your application and you want to provide extra tools (such as debuggers and IDE integration). Think of HTML as a perfect example of this kind of DSL.

In contrast, you can also develop an *embedded* or *internal* DSL, where your language is expressed using some of the constructs of the host language. The main advantage of this approach is that you don't need to write as many of the tools, and the host language can help you in designing the DSL in such a way that you don't need extra passes to detect those values of your DSL that are illegal. Furthermore, you are not tied to using only one DSL at once; you can embed several of them in your application. The main disadvantage is that you're limited by the host language. In particular, the internals of your DSL may be exposed in the case of an error. Haskell has several features that make it a good host language for embedded DSLs:

- Its powerful type system allows you to express invariants that valid values in your DSL must satisfy. This means the extra safety Haskell provides is also in your language.

- Haskell syntax is terse, so it doesn't introduce many strange symbols in your DSL. Using operators and the mixfix application, you can make the values in your new language resemble a natural language description.

- Type classes, especially applicatives, monads, and do notation, provide a convenient framework for expressing the abstractions that are part of a DSL. This means Haskell developers can use a well-known notation for many concepts.

Many of the libraries I've talked about in this book are actually embedded DSLs: parser combinators like `attoparsec` for describing grammars only need to use special functions, a query language such as Esqueleto uses a combination of type classes and custom data types, and `digestive-functors` expresses forms using applicative style and a set of basic ways to treat a form value. As you can see, the features of Haskell are used differently by each DSL, depending on how convenient the features are.

There are two main trends in how embedded DSLs express their behavior in Haskell. A *shallow embedding* encodes the values in your language directly by their meaning inside Haskell (this meaning is called the language's *interpretation*). For example, say you create a DSL for stack operations; its shallow embedding would represent each operation with a Haskell function, as this code shows:

```haskell
pop :: [a] -> [a]
pop (x:xs) = xs
pop _       = error "empty stack"
push :: a -> [a] -> [a]
push x xs = x:xs
-- A value in our language: its interpretation directly works on a stack
v :: [Int] -> [Int]
v = push 1 . pop . pop . push 2
```

A *deep embedding* separates the use of the language into two parts. First, you create a representation of the value in your language as a syntax tree, using Haskell data types. The previous example would be deeply embedded as follows:

```haskell
data StackOps a = Pop (StackOps a) | Push a (StackOps a) | End
-- The same value represented as a syntax tree
v :: StackOps Int
v = Push 1 $ Pop $ Pop $ Push 2 $ End
```

Next, you give an *interpretation* of the syntax tree that converts it to its meaning inside Haskell. The advantage is that now you can add some extra optimizations as you go; for example, Pop after Push is like performing no operation at all.

```haskell
interpret :: StackOps a -> [a] -> [a]
interpret (Pop (Push _ ops)) stack = interpret ops stack
interpret (Pop ops)          stack = tail $ interpret ops stack
interpret (Push e ops)       stack = e : interpret ops stack
interpret End                stack = stack
```

You've seen the two advantages of using deep instead of shallow embedding. First, you can give more than one interpretation; that is, you can treat the values of your embedded DSL in different ways depending on the situation. Additionally, you can inspect the syntax tree before creating the meaning and implementing optimizations or statistics about your value.

In this chapter, I will show how to design a deep embedding of the offers language inside Haskell. The next chapter will explain a conceptual tool, attribute grammars, and a concrete implementation of those ideas, UUAGC, which help you express the behavior of one of the offers applied to a basket of products.

The Offers Language

Let's create a DSL for expressing the offers in the Time Machine Store. In addition to empowering managers to directly encode the offers for your application (so you don't need to manually implement them each time), implementing the language will be a good way to learn more Haskell. You don't need a big language for the second objective, so I will keep the core DSL small. As a general guide, you should always try to make your DSL as small as possible because it is easier to work with a small core. For complex needs, you can write functions that generate compound expressions out of the simple language you have created.

The first things the offers language needs to provide are the basic offers that the Store may use. In this case, you have three of them: giving something as a present, discounting some percentage of the price, and discounting some absolute value from the price. From these basic offers, you will be able to generate values in the DSL by combining offers and extra pieces of data. In this case, the combinations can be split into three groups:

1. The language may restrict the offer to be valid only on a set of products.

2. By default, all the offers are valid for an indefinite period of time. The language will provide ways to constrain the starting and ending dates of the offer to extend the offer for a longer time.

3. The language will allow you to make an offer be the union of two offers (e.g., give a free balloon and a 10 percent discount), be just the best out of two (e.g., either give a 10 percent or give a $5 discount), or be conditional upon satisfying some property in the purchase (such as applying an offer only when the client purchases more than $100 worth of products).

From this description, the data declaration for the syntax tree is straightforward to obtain.

```
data Offer a = Present a
             | PercentDiscount  Float
             | AbsoluteDiscount Float
             | Restrict [a] (Offer a)
             -- product restriction (1)
             | From Integer (Offer a)
             -- time restriction (2)
             | Until Integer (Offer a)
             | Extend Integer (Offer a)
             | Both (Offer a) (Offer a)
             -- offer combinators (3)
             | BetterOf (Offer a) (Offer a)
             | If (Expr a) (Offer a) (Offer a)
             deriving Show
```

In some cases when using conditional expressions, you may need to express that no offer is given if some condition is not satisfied. For those cases, you would need a "no offer" value. One approach would be to include an extra constructor in the data type. However, you can see that an absolute discount of $0 is equivalent to no offer. Thus, you can keep the core as is and define this offer in terms of the others.

```
noOffer :: Offer a
noOffer = AbsoluteDiscount 0
```

The missing part from the code of the Offer type is the declaration of the Expr data type that will encode the expressions that may appear as conditions over the purchase. This should include the amount and prices of several of the items in the shopping basket, comparisons between those quantities, and Boolean combinations of conditions (and, or, and not). Notice in the following code how you need to lift basic integer and floating-point values into the language via the IVal and FVal constructors:

```
data Expr a
  = AmountOf a | PriceOf a
  -- information about the cart
  | TotalNumberProducts | TotalPrice
```

```
-- lifting numerical values
| IVal Integer | FVal Float
-- arithmetic
| (Expr a) :+: (Expr a) | (Expr a) :*: (Expr a)
-- comparison
| (Expr a) :<: (Expr a) | (Expr a) :<=: (Expr a)
| (Expr a) :>: (Expr a) | (Expr a) :>=: (Expr a)
-- boolean operations
| (Expr a) :&&: (Expr a) | (Expr a) :||: (Expr a) | Not (Expr a)
deriving Show
```

For example, let's express the offer "for the next 30 days, you will get the best of these two details: either getting a discount of $10 off your final bill and getting a balloon as a present or, if you buy more than $100 of products, a 5 percent discount." The value for this offer is as follows:

```
v :: Offer String
v = Until 30 $ BetterOf (AbsoluteDiscount 10.0)
                        (Both (Present "balloon")
                              (If (TotalPrice :>: IVal 100)
                                  (PercentDiscount 5.0)
                                  noOffer))
```

These data types are the core of our DSL. But as Exercise 13-1 shows, you can add some helper functions to make it easier to describe offers that follow the same pattern often.

EXERCISE 13-1. OFFER PATTERNS

You've seen how noOffer could be defined in terms of more basic constructors, keeping the core language simple. Following the same idea, write definitions for the following patterns of offers:

- period f d o will constrain the offer o for the following d days starting from day f. Remember that From and Until have as arguments specific points in time, not lengths.

- allOf os should be the conjunction with all the offers in the list os.

> Then, express the following offer: "From the third day and for five days hence, you will get a free balloon, a free chocolate muffin, and a 10 percent discount in the Time Machine Store." Check whether your expression corresponds to the correct offer expressed using the core DSL.

In addition to constraining the kind of basic offers that you can express, there are two further requirements that all values in your DSL must satisfy. The first one is the *Presents Rule*: at some time during the year, the number of presents that will be given for free with a purchase is limited. Thus, the system should check that constraint. The second one is the *Duration Rule*: you don't want to allow offers if they violate a time restriction. You'll learn how to enforce these two rules in the language later in this chapter.

Adding Safety to the Expression Language

I emphasized in the introduction to the chapter that Haskell's strong type system helps you to forbid incorrect values in your DSL. In the first implementation I showed previously, you can create such incorrect values without much problem. Take the following example, which creates an Expr value by taking the disjunction of the price and some other expression. But a price alone is not a Boolean value, so you wouldn't be able to give any meaning to it.

```
incorrectExpression :: Expr Char
incorrectExpression = TotalPrice :||: (TotalNumberProducts :<: PriceOf 'a')
```

The remedy, which is common to all the examples, is to add a tag to the types involved in the DSL and constrain the ways in which the values of different types can be combined between them:

- Amounts, prices of items, and constant values (those created through the FVal or IVal constructors) should be tagged as numbers.

- Comparisons will take as arguments only values tagged as numbers and will produce a value tagged as a Boolean.

- Boolean operators will combine only those expressions tagged as Booleans.

- The final expression in an offer must be tagged as a Boolean.

The perfect way to add this tag to expressions is by adding a new type parameter to the Expr data type. In that case, Expr a t will be an expression over products of type a tagged with type t. Now, if each combinator that makes up an expression is a regular function instead of a constructor, you could enforce the constraints by restricting the signature of the function. Here's an example, but you would have a similar function for each combinator:

```
(:||:) :: Expr a Bool -> Expr a Bool -> Expr a Bool
```

The problem is that plain data declarations do not allow you to return different types depending on the constructor of a value. All constructors *uniformly* construct values of the type expressed after the data keyword. *Generalized algebraic data types* (GADTs) lift that restriction; now each of the constructors of the data type can return a different set of type parameters to the type being defined. That is, in the definition of Expr a t, you can return Expr a Bool, Expr Int Int, and so on, but not Offer Char.

The syntax starts with the same keyword, data, followed by the name and type variables of the type to define. But instead of equal signs, you need to write where and list the constructors via its signatures. Your expression data type written as a GADT becomes the following:

```
{-# LANGUAGE GADTs #-}
data Expr a r where
  AmountOf           :: a -> Expr a Integer
  PriceOf            :: a -> Expr a Float
  TotalNumberProducts :: Expr a Integer
  TotalPrice         :: Expr a Float
  IVal               :: Integer -> Expr a Integer
  FVal               :: Float -> Expr a Float
  (:+:)              :: Num n => Expr a n -> Expr a n -> Expr a n
  (:*:)              :: Num n => Expr a n -> Expr a n -> Expr a n
  (:<:)              :: Num n => Expr a n -> Expr a n -> Expr a Bool
  (:<=:)             :: Num n => Expr a n -> Expr a n -> Expr a Bool
  (:>:)              :: Num n => Expr a n -> Expr a n -> Expr a Bool
  (:>=:)             :: Num n => Expr a n -> Expr a n -> Expr a Bool
  (:&&:)             :: Expr a Bool -> Expr a Bool -> Expr a Bool
  (:||:)             :: Expr a Bool -> Expr a Bool -> Expr a Bool
  Not                :: Expr a Bool -> Expr a Bool
```

Since the arithmetic and comparison operators need to work on both Integer and Float values, we cannot use a type there directly. Instead, we use a Num constraint, since both types are instances of that type class.

447

Now if you try to build some code with the incorrect expression that started this section, you will get a compile error because the expression will not type check. This is the first example of using the strong type system to constrain the kind of values that the DSL can express.

GADTs solve another problem that will appear in one way or another later. Suppose you want to interpret one expression using the original Expr data type. This interpretation will be a function that, given a list of products as *(name, price)* pairs, returns the result of applying the expression to it. Since the result of the expression can be either an Integer, a Float, or a Bool, you need a sum type as a return value. Here's a small excerpt of the interpretation for the (:||:) case; notice how you need to take care of type mismatches explicitly in the code:

```
data ExprR = EInt Integer | EFloat Float | EBool Bool
interpretExpr :: Expr a -> [(a,Float)] -> ExprR
interpretExpr (e1 :||: e2) list =
  case (interpretExpr e1 list, interpretExpr e2 list) of
    (EBool b1, EBool b2) -> EBool (b1 || b2)
    _                        -> error "type error"
interpretExpr ...            = ...
```

But if you use your GADT, you no longer need to create a special data type for the return value of the expression because the resulting value can depend on the tag in the Expr type. This gives you a new way of achieving polymorphism. Before, you could return a value of a subpart of your input type, and now, thanks to GADTs, that type doesn't have to be uniform over all constructors, thus making the function return values from different types. Check how this is the case in the interpretation function for the (:||:) and (:+:) cases, as shown here:

```
interpretExpr :: Eq a => Expr a t -> [(a,Float)] -> t
interpretExpr (e1 :+: e2)  list
  = interpretExpr e1 list + interpretExpr e2 list
interpretExpr (e1 :||: e2) list
  = interpretExpr e1 list || interpretExpr e2 list
interpretExpr ... = ...
```

This interpretation function still needs some love. Exercise 13-2 asks you to complete the work.

EXERCISE 13-2. COMPLETE INTERPRETATION FOR EXPRESSIONS

Write the missing code of the `interpretExpr` function for the cases of `Expr` being defined by a regular ADT and by a GADT. In the case of `PriceOf`, you should take into account that the same product may appear more than once in the purchase list.

Even though here you're tagging types using built-in types from the `Prelude` module, nothing stops you from using any other type here. Actually, it may be the case that you create new data types *only* for tagging other types. In that case, you don't even need any constructors in the declaration since you will never use them. You can create empty `data` declarations if you enable the `EmptyDataDecls` extension.

I'll show an example of how this could be useful. In the Time Machine Store, there will be many users. But not all of them will have the same role in the store; some will be administrators or store managers (who are able to change everything), some will be store people (who are allowed only to update products in the database), and some will be regular users (who are the ones making the purchases). You can tag the level of access to the store using a set of empty data types.

```
{-# LANGUAGE EmptyDataDecls, GADTs #-}
data AllowEverything
data AllowProducts
data AllowPurchases
data Person = Person :: { firstName :: String, lastName :: String }
data User r where
  Admin        :: Person -> User AllowEverything
  StoreManager :: Person -> User AllowEverything
  StorePerson  :: Person -> User AllowProducts
  Client       :: Person -> User AllowPurchases
```

Now a function that should be called only by people with access to everything can be defined to require the value tagged with the correct type.

```
changePurchaseFinalPrice
  :: User AllowEverything -> Purchase -> Float -> Purchase
changePurchaseFinalPrice = ...
```

Time traveling is a tiresome task, so users of your time machines need to eat snacks from time to time. However, people have constraints on the food they can take, such as vegetarian, no pork, low salt, and so on. Exercise 13-3 asks you to build a GADT that represents those snacks tagged with constraints.

EXERCISE 13-3. SNACKS FOR TIME TRAVELERS

Create a GADT representing a set of possible snacks for the Time Machine Store. The snacks must be tagged with a type defining whether it's OK for vegetarians and whether it contains pork. Use empty data types as shown in this section.

Type-Level Programming

It seems that this idea of tagging types with extra information is quite successful, at least for expressions. However, the way in which you can do it is quite limited because you can use only other types and only as constants or variables that you don't inspect.

One way to have a more powerful type system is by allowing values, in addition to types, to take part in other types. For example, you might be interested in tagging lists with their length and expressing things such as "the length of append l1 l2 is the sum of the lengths of l1 and l2." As you can see, in this case, the tag is not another type, but rather a number (or a *value* in the world of Haskell). *Dependent type systems* open the last barrier that Haskell imposes between values and types and allow you to create types depending on values, as the list tagged with its length that was being discussed.

Haskell is *not* a dependently typed language, though; it imposes a clear separation between the world of terms or expressions and the world of types. In Haskell, values are only allowed to depend on other values (via regular function parameters) or on types (via parametric or ad hoc polymorphism), whereas types are allowed to depend only on other types (via type variables). On the other hand, it's forbidden to use terms as parameters to types. When working with GADTs, you used some empty data types as tags. This approach mimics partly dependent typing but allows tagging only with constant values, not performing any operation on the types. The rest of the chapter is devoted to showing different ways in which you could describe operations that work on types. All these methods are known collectively as *type-level programming* techniques.

DEPENDENTLY TYPED LANGUAGES

Dependent typing is an extensive area of knowledge. It is expected that Haskell gets more and more of these features as time progresses. If you want to learn more about dependent types, you can read *Type-Drive Development with Idris* and *Programming in Idris: A Tutorial* both by Edwin Brady,[1] "Dependently Typed Programming in Agda" by Ulf Norell and James Chapman,[2] *Certified Programming with Dependent Types* by Adam Chlipala,[3] or *Software Foundations* by Benjamin C. Pierce et al.[4] (the latter two using Coq).

The programming techniques that will be presented in the rest of the chapter are usually categorized as *advanced* Haskell features. You don't need to understand every detail of functional dependencies and type families to be a proficient Haskell programmer. Indeed, these features are recent additions to the Haskell language, so their use is not widespread yet.

However, type-level programming is becoming an increasingly important technique. More recent libraries, such as Persistent and Yesod, make heavy use of them. Even though you may skip some of this material in a first reading, you should come back to it in the future. It will help you understand many of the error messages and design decisions of those libraries, and it will also help you build better applications.

Two Styles of Programming

Type-level programming in Haskell generates many of its ideas from enhancements in ad hoc polymorphism. There are two different ways you can simulate parts of dependent typing in Haskell:

- *Functional dependencies* (FDs) allow you to constrain the parameters of type classes. Given the correct constraints, the Haskell compiler can infer a unique type, which can be seen as the result of a type-level function.

---

[1] Available at the Idris website, www.idris-lang.org/documentation/.

[2] Available at the Agda website, http://wiki.portal.chalmers.se/agda/.

[3] Available at http://adam.chlipala.net/cpdt/.

[4] Available at www.cis.upenn.edu/~bcpierce/sf/.

- *Type families* (TFs) let you create functions that assign a type given a set of other types. Recent versions of GHC include two kinds of type families. *Closed type families* are the closest to the intuitive notion of type function, and *open type families* are like type classes in the sense that you may add a new rule to an open type family at any point, like you may add an instance to a type class.

Both ways are equally powerful, so in principle it doesn't matter which one you choose to encode your invariants. However, in some cases, it's easier to use FDs, and in other cases, it's better to use TFs. As a rule of thumb, start using TFs (because the type-level concepts they expose are closer to the simple Haskell level) and use FDs if you need more expressiveness in the relations between types.

Caution   Although they have the same power, mixing FDs and TFs in the same code can become challenging. Thus, if you depend on a library that exposes FDs or TFs, you should use the same technique to avoid further problems. The situation, however, may improve in newer versions of the GHC compiler.

Representing Natural Numbers

Since the tags that will be used to check the Presents Rule are natural numbers, you must know how they are encoded as values previous to using FDs or TFs to represent them at the type level. This section tries to give a fast-paced introduction to natural numbers. Feel free to skip it if you already know the standard data type for natural numbers and how addition, maximum, and minimum are coded using them.

The most common way to represent natural numbers as a data type is based on the axioms stated by the 19th-century mathematician Giuseppe Peano. In particular, he gave two rules for constructing numbers:

- *Zero* is a natural number.

- For every natural number n, there exists a *successor of n*, which is also a natural number.

You can encode those axioms in a Haskell data declaration like so:

```
data Number = Zero | Succ Number deriving Show
```

The number 1, for example, is the successor of 0; the number 2 is the successor of 1; and so on.

```
one :: Number
one = Succ Zero
two :: Number
two = Succ one  -- Succ (Succ Zero)
```

Note   You can think of this encoding of natural numbers as lists in which you don't care about elements. Then, addition would be concatenation of lists, taking the minimum would be returning the list with the smallest number of elements, and so on.

Now let's move to the operations. The first one you will need to use is addition. Like with most Haskell data types, the best way to design a function over Number is to handle each constructor and use recursion for nested values. In this case, you have two different constructors:

- If you add 0 to any natural number y, the result is y.

- If you add the successor of x to y, this is equal to the successor of the addition of x and y. Since the successor is equivalent to (+1), you can see this as encoding the algebraic law that reads $(x + 1) + y = (x + y) + 1$.

In Haskell syntax, the branches of the plus' function are written as follows:

```
plus' :: Number -> Number -> Number
plus' Zero     y = y
plus' (Succ x) y = Succ (plus' x y)
```

You can test whether the function works correctly by summing up 1 and 2, for example.

```
*Chapter13.Numbers> plus' one two
Succ (Succ (Succ Zero))
```

The result is the number 3 represented in this way, as you can see in the output.

For the maximum, there are also two cases to consider. First, any of the numbers can be 0, in which case you know for sure that the other number is greater than or equal to 0.

The other case is when both numbers are successors, for example, $x + 1$ and $y + 1$. In this case, the maximum can be computed by recursively computing the maximum of x and y and then adding 1.

```
max' :: Number -> Number -> Number
max' Zero y = y
max' x Zero = x
max' (Succ x) (Succ y) = Succ (max' x y)
```

The minimum function has a similar skeleton. Exercise 13-4 asks you to write the full code.

EXERCISE 13-4. MINIMUM OF NATURAL NUMBERS

Write a function `min'` of type Number -> Number -> Number that computes the minimum value of the two natural numbers given as arguments.

Functional Dependencies

As stated in the previous section, *functional dependencies* represent one of the ways in which you can encode type-level operations in Haskell. However, the original intention of FDs was to enhance the type class mechanism by constraining the set of types that can be related via a multiparameter type class. In this section, I'll start looking at this original aim and then move on to encoding the Presents Rule via FDs.

Categories of Products with FDs

Let's diverge for a moment from the offers language and focus on a completely different problem. Until now, all the products in the Time Machine Store were represented using the same data type, `Product`. However, the information for describing a time machine is not the same as that needed to describe a book or a costume. Thus, it may be interesting to make `Product` a type class and make data types represent different categories of products.

In addition to different fields to describe them, you use different products in different ways. For example, you travel with a time machine, but you read a book. It would be interesting to specify, for each category of products, which operations are available to perform upon them. Then, you could include specific instructions on how to perform each operation and a specification of which operation should be used to test the product.

From this discussion, the task is to create a `Product` type class with two parameters, one defining the category of products and the other one the operations that the category supports. The following code includes as operations the price of a product and the operation functions discussed earlier:

```
class Product p op where
  price :: p -> Float
  perform :: p -> op -> String
  testOperation :: p -> op
```

Note   Remember that you need to enable the `MultiParamTypeClasses` extension for GHC to accept this code.

Given a simple data type for representing time machines and their operations, writing its instance declaration is straightforward. The following code shows a possible way in which you could do this:

```
data TimeMachine = TimeMachine { model :: String }
                   deriving Show
data TimeMachineOps = Travel Integer | Park deriving Show
instance Product TimeMachine TimeMachineOps where
  price _ = 1000.0
  perform (TimeMachine m) (Travel y)
     = "Travelling to " ++ show y ++ " with " ++ m
  perform (TimeMachine m) Park
     = "Parking time machine " ++ m
  testOperation _ = Travel 0
```

Of course, the main aim for creating a type class is to write a function that works on any kind of `Product`. For example, a function could get the total price of a list of products of the same category, and another one performs the test operation on a concrete product. The definitions are as follows:

```
totalAmount :: Product p op => [p] -> Float
totalAmount = foldr (+) 0.0 . map price
performTest :: Product p op => p -> String
performTest p = perform p $ testOperation p
```

The problem is that this code will not compile. Instead, you will get several errors similar to the following:

```
src/Chapter13/CategoriesFnDeps.hs:
    Could not deduce (Product p op0) arising from a use of `price'
    from the context (Product p op)
      bound by the type signature for
                  totalAmount :: Product p op => [p] -> Float
      at src/Chapter13/CategoriesFnDeps.hs:
    The type variable `op0' is ambiguous
    Possible fix: add a type signature that fixes these type variable(s)
    Note: there is a potential instance available:
      instance Product TimeMachine TimeMachineOps
        -- Defined at src/Chapter13/CategoriesFnDeps.hs:18:10
```

The error message tells you that there's not enough information to infer which operation type corresponds to each product category. But the intent of the code is clear. For TimeMachine, the corresponding operation type is TimeMachineOps, and only that one. Somehow, the compiler should infer that when you're using a TimeMachine, the operations will always belong to TimeMachineOps.

The problem is that the type class declaration, as it stands, does not declare this intention in any way. Any two types p and op could be related via Product. For example, you can add an instance that uses TimeMachine as the category, but book operations are as follows:

```
data Book = Book { title :: String, author :: String, rating :: Integer }
            deriving Show
data BookOps = Read | Highlight | WriteCritique deriving Show
instance Product TimeMachine BookOps where
```

```
price _            = 500.0
perform _ _        = "What?!"
testOperation _    = Read   -- ??
```

The compiler won't complain because the code is perfectly fine. But now you can see why the definitions of totalAmount or testOperation were ambiguous. Potentially, there is another instance where a declaration different from Product TimeMachine TimeMachineOps may be applicable.

The solution is to add a constraint to the type class declaration that exactly expresses that given a specific category of products, only one possibility is available for the set of operations. This is done via a *functional dependency*, a concept from database theory that describes exactly these scenarios. Functional dependencies are written in the head of the class declaration, separated from the name and type variables by the | sign, and with commas between each of them. Each functional dependency, in turn, follows the same schema, $x_1 \ldots x_n \rightarrow y_1 \ldots y_m$, expressing that for each unique substitution of the types x_1 to x_n, there's only one possible compound value of y_1 to y_m. Note that you need to enable the FunctionalDependencies extension to use this syntax in your own type classes.

In this case, categories constrain the operations, so the functional dependency to add is p -> op. The refined head of the definition of the type class should be changed to the following:

```
class Product p op | p -> op where
```

Once you do this, the compiler will complain about two different Product instances given for a TimeMachine.

```
src/Chapter13/CategoriesFnDeps.hs:
    Functional dependencies conflict between instance declarations:
      instance Product TimeMachine TimeMachineOps
        -- Defined at src/Chapter13/CategoriesFnDeps.hs
      instance Product TimeMachine BookOps
        -- Defined at src/Chapter13/CategoriesFnDeps.hs
```

Now the compiler allows the definition of totalPrice and performTest because it knows that given a category for products, only one possible set of operations will be available, so it can select them.

Functional dependencies are helpful once you understand when they are needed in a type class declaration. The "Functional Dependencies in Monad Classes" sidebar describes their use in monad classes. Then Exercise 13-5 proposes a task for helping you understand these ideas.

FUNCTIONAL DEPENDENCIES IN MONAD CLASSES

When the type classes supporting the lifting of the basic operation in each monad transformer (MonadState, MonadReader, MonadWriter, etc.) were discussed in Chapter 7, functional dependencies appeared in the class declarations but weren't explained.

The crux of a type class such as MonadState is that it declares both the monad that performs the operations and the type of elements saved in the state because they are both needed in the signatures of some operations. The functional dependency states that given a specific monad, the type of the state values is automatically known. Think of the State Int monad, for example. From its signature, you already know that only Int can be the type of elements saved in the state.

EXERCISE 13-5. PRODUCTS AND BAGS

In the store, two kinds of bags are available: big and small. Create new data types called BigBag and SmallBag for representing each kind of bag. Then, add a new parameter to the Product type class for stating which bag you should use for each category of products. In principle, time machines should go on big bags, whereas books need only small ones. Think carefully about extra functional dependencies.

Vectors Using FDs

At first sight, it seems that functional dependencies have nothing to do with type-level operations in Haskell. However, a second look will show how you can encode type-level functions in this way.

To begin with, let's create the representation of natural numbers at type level. Once again, the best way is to use empty data types. For each constructor in the original declaration, an empty data type is needed. In the case of numbers, two of them will be used: one for representing the zero tag and one for successors.

```
{-# LANGUAGE EmptyDataDecls #-}
data Zero
data Succ n
```

Caution   Notice that in almost every example in this section, the code will use more and more GHC extensions. These will be shown using the LANGUAGE pragma. Most of the extensions are needed only for enabling certain syntactic constructs, and the compiler will tell you to enable them if you forget, so you don't need to worry too much about them.

With only the data types just given, you can represent lists tagged with their length. Following the usual convention in dependently typed languages, lists tagged with numbers will be called Vects.

```
{-# LANGUAGE GADTs #-}
data Vect n a where
  VNil  :: Vect Zero a
  VCons :: a -> Vect n a -> Vect (Succ n) a
```

To check that our vectors record their length correctly, let's ask the interpreter for the type of a list having three elements:

```
*Chapter12.VecFnDeps> :t VCons 'a' (VCons 'b' (VCons 'c' VNil))
VCons 'a' (VCons 'b' (VCons 'c' VNil))
  :: Vect (Succ (Succ (Succ Zero))) Char
```

You can see that the first argument of Vect is the representation of the number 3 using the Peano encoding. An immediate use for this additional information is to create a completely type-safe head which only works with vectors of at least one element:

```
headVect :: Vect (Succ n) a -> a
headVect (VCons x _) = x
```

In fact, if you try to pattern match with VNil, the compiler rejects such declaration, because an empty vector cannot have a length of the form (Succ n).

Now it's time to use the type class system in your favor. Each type-level operation will be encoded as a type class that will have as variables the input arguments to the type-level operation and an extra one that represents the result of the operation. For example, class Plus x y z represents "the result of the addition of *x* and *y* is *z*," or in other terms $x + y = z$. But in order to be a function, you must explicitly say that for any pair of values *x* and *y*, there's only one possible result *z*. Specifying that is a perfect job for a functional dependency. Thus, the entire type class declaration representing type-level addition is as follows:

```
{-# LANGUAGE MultiParamTypeClasses, FunctionalDependencies #-}
class Plus x y z | x y -> z
```

Note   Since the Plus type class is used only for its results at type level, it's not necessary to include any function in its body. In that case, Haskell allows you to omit the where keyword from the declaration.

The type class declaration is just describing the number of arguments to the type-level function. For expressing the rules that make the operation, you need to write different instances. Usually, these instances correspond to each of the cases in a function definition. Let's see how they look for addition.

```
{-# LANGUAGE FlexibleInstances, UndecidableInstances #-}
instance Plus Zero x x
instance Plus x y z => Plus (Succ x) y (Succ z)
```

This is expressing the same logic for Peano addition but in a backward style of reasoning. The first instance encodes the rule of adding 0 to a number, whose result is the same as the second argument. The second rule is a bit subtler; it's expressing that if you know that $x + y = z$, you can infer the addition $(x + 1) + y$, which will be exactly $z + 1$. In some sense, the declaration is reversing the way in which you write the pattern matching on the arguments and handling the recursion via a call to a smaller instance.

To understand how this encoding works, Exercise 13-6 asks you to define binary tree tagged with height, in a similar fashion to vectors.

EXERCISE 13-6. BINARY TREES TAGGED WITH HEIGHT

Create a `BinaryTree` data type with two constructors: `Leafs`, which contain only one element, and `Nodes`, which contain an element and two subtrees. The type must be tagged with the height of the tree. Hint: Implement the `max'` function for Peano numbers using a type class `Max` and functional dependencies.

Enforcing the Presents Rule with FDs

The next step is to use these new data types and type class inside the declaration of `Offer`. The first step is adding a variable to the type. We shall use this additional argument to tag the offer with the maximum number of presents inside it.

```
data Offer a p where
```

The basic constructor `Present` should reflect that one present is given with it. On the other hand, neither a percentage discount nor an absolute discount adds any present to the offer, so their tags should be zero. Remember that instead of plain numbers, you need to use Peano numerals.

```
Present          :: a -> Offer a (Succ Zero)
PercentDiscount  :: Float -> Offer a Zero
AbsoluteDiscount :: Float -> Offer a Zero
```

The combination of several offers is straightforward: when two offers are applied at the same time, you get the presents of both.

```
Both :: Plus p q r => Offer a p -> Offer a q -> Offer a r
```

As you can see, the code includes a context with the `Plus` type class. This is expressing that if $p + q = r$, then the union of an offer with p presents and another one with q presents is an offer with r presents. If you check in the interpreter for the type of a test present, the compiler will follow the rules for the `Plus` type class to get a final type. Here's one example of its output:

```
*> :t let p = Present 'a' in Both p (BetterOf p (Both p p))
let p = Present 'a' in Both p (BetterOf p (Both p p))
  :: Offer Char (Succ (Succ (Succ (Succ Zero))))
```

The other combinator for offers is `BetterOf`. Since you don't know in advance which of the branches will be taken, you cannot compute the exact amount of presents for that offer. But you can still get some bounds: you always get at most the larger amount from any of the two suboffers. Here, we use the `Max` type class you have been asked to define in Exercise 13-6.

```
BetterOf :: Max p q r => Offer a p -> Offer a q -> Offer a r
```

Another interesting constructor is the restriction one, which should take the minimum between the number of elements in a list and the number of presents. Let's again follow the same steps to use functional dependencies for encoding this type-level operation. Declare the type class with an extra argument for the result and specify that the last argument functionally depends on all the rest.

```
class Min x y z | x y -> z
```

For each rule in the function definition, you must include an instance declaration. Remember that the style of programming must be backward; in other words, you must specify the recurring conditions before the full result.

```
instance Min Zero      y     Zero
instance Min (Succ x) Zero Zero
instance Min x y z => Min (Succ x) (Succ y) (Succ z)
```

The final part is to use the type class in the declaration of the constructor. Since we need to know the number of elements in the list, we change from using a simple list `[a]` to a list tagged with its length `Vect n a`. Furthermore, we restrict ourselves to nonempty lists.

```
{-# LANGUAGE FlexibleContexts #-}
  Restrict :: Min (Succ n) p r => Vect (Succ n) a -> Offer a p -> Offer a r
```

There are still some constructors left for the full offers language. Exercise 13-7 asks you to write the rest of them, encoding the type-level functions needed as functional dependencies.

EXERCISE 13-7. OFFERS WITH FUNCTIONAL DEPENDENCIES

Include the constructors for the remaining offers language: From, Until, Extend, and If. Write them following the same technique from this section. In the case of conditionals, the same considerations as BetterOf should be taken: you cannot always compute the exact value, but you can approximate it.

A LOGIC TYPE-LEVEL LANGUAGE

If you've ever used a logic programming language, such as Prolog or Datalog, you may find some resemblance between the way you encode type-level functions using instance declarations and the way you write predicates on these languages. This relation is indeed true: programming with functional dependencies exposes a logic programming style in a Haskell type system.

This extra paradigm brought into Haskell is the main criticism with functional dependencies. The programmer should not change programming styles when moving from term-level to type-level coding. Type families, as you will see later, have a more functional style in their declaration.

Type Families

You've already seen how functional dependencies can empower you to construct a stronger type system. This section will show you how to express the same kind of invariants but using the language of *type families* (TFs). In short, a type family is a function at the type level. It gives you a type given some other types as parameters, but in an ad hoc way and in contrast to parametric polymorphism. The type family may appear in the top level of your module or inside a type class. You will see the purpose of each of them in this section.

Vectors Using TFs

The definition of a type family is usually quite simple given a corresponding definition at the term level. In the example you've been dealing with, the first type-level function that you need is addition, so I will show you that one first. The same data types that were used for encoding natural numbers earlier with FDs will be used with type families.

```
{-# LANGUAGE EmptyDataDecls #-}
data Zero
data Succ n
```

The Vect data type will also be reused.

```
{-# LANGUAGE GADTs #-}
data Vect n a where
  VNil  :: Vect Zero a
  VCons :: a -> Vect n a -> Vect (Succ n) a
```

A TF starts with the type family keywords, followed by the declaration of its name and arguments and the where keyword. This first line defines the signature of the type-level function. After the signature, the type family is defined using pattern matching on its arguments. There are two small syntactic differences between TFs and regular functions. Whereas term-level functions must start with a lowercase letter, type family names must start with an uppercase one. In this case, the code will refer to addition at the type level with the name Plus. The other difference is that all the rules for a TF must be indented, in contrast to regular functions where rules appeared at the same indentation level of signatures. This is the definition of addition using TFs:

```
{-# LANGUAGE TypeFamilies #-}
type family Plus x y where
  Plus Zero     x = x
  Plus (Succ x) y = Succ (Plus x y)
```

As you can see, the type instances completely mimic the definition of the (+) function on regular, term-level, natural numbers. This similarity makes it easier to port code from term level to type level if you use type families.

One function which can be defined using Plus is the append of two vectors. If you have a vector of length n and another of length m, the resulting vector has length $n+m$. The compiler is able to check that fact in the following code:

```
append :: Vect x a -> Vect y a -> Vect (Plus x y) a
append VNil          ys = ys
append (VCons x xs) ys = VCons x (append xs ys)
```

Caution   The previous code uses closed TFs, an extension available only since version 7.8.1 of the GHC compiler. You can always use open TFs for maximum backward compatibility, which are described in the next section.

Enforcing the Presents Rule with TFs

The next step is to use Plus inside the definition of the Offer data type. As in the case of FDs, the basic constructors use the representation of the numbers 0 and 1 using the Peano data type.

```
data Offer a p where
  Present          :: a -> Offer a (Succ Zero)
  PercentDiscount  :: Float -> Offer a Zero
  AbsoluteDiscount :: Float -> Offer a Zero
```

The place where the Plus TF is expected to be used is in the Both constructor. When using TFs, you don't need to use the type context part of the signature; you can just use an applied TF in the place where a type is expected. For example, in this constructor, Plus p q is used in lieu of a type:

```
Both :: Offer a p -> Offer a q -> Offer a (Plus p q)
```

To reinforce the steps you need to follow to use a TF for encoding a type-level function, let's use the same process for restriction. Looking at the previous sections, you can see that in that case you need to define a type-level minimum function. The following code does so with a TF Min:

```
type family Min x y where
  Min Zero      y          = Zero
  Min x         Zero       = Zero
  Min (Succ x) (Succ y) = Succ (Min x y)
```

The corresponding Restrict constructor is easily updated from FDs to TFs:

```
Restrict :: Vect (Succ n) a -> Offer a p -> Offer a (Min (Succ n) p)
```

As in the previous case, it's your task (in Exercise 13-8) to write the rest of the cases of the data type.

EXERCISE 13-8. OFFERS WITH TYPE FAMILIES

Include the constructors for the rest of the offers language: From, Until, Extend, BetterOf, and If. At this point, you'll know that you'll need a type-level function that encodes the maximum of two natural numbers in the last two cases. Define it using type families.

Categories of Products with TFs

The introduction to type-level programming in Haskell stated that functional dependencies and type families had the same power of expressiveness. You've already seen how both can encode type-level functions, but there's still the question of how to use type families to solve the problem with categories of products.

One possibility is to define a TF that assigns the type of operations to each type of product. Following the instructions from the previous section, an Operation function would resemble the following:

```
type family Operation x where
  Operation TimeMachine = TimeMachineOps
  Operation Book        = BookOps
```

This is not a satisfactory solution, though. When you used a type class along with an FD, you had the option of adding a new product along with its sets of operations at any moment, via a new instance declaration. However, if you follow the approach I've just shown, with the previous definition of a TF, you need to add both an instance to the Product type class and a new equation to the Operation type family. This makes the type class and the type family tightly coupled and thus less maintainable.

The problem in this case does not lie in the use of type families but rather in the fact that the type family is defined as a *closed* one. GHC supports two kinds of type families. The closed ones, which I've already introduced, cannot be enlarged with more rules after its definition. In contrast, *open type families* define a partial function that can be refined or enlarged in other parts of the code.

To define a type family as open, drop the final where keyword from its declaration.

```
type family Operation x
```

Each time you want to add a new rule to the type family, you have to include it after the type instance keywords. For example, the previous two relations between products and operations would read as follows:

```
type instance Operation TimeMachine = TimeMachineOps
type instance Operation Book        = BookOps
```

Notice that in this case the instance declarations appear at the same level of the signature, since they may be defined in completely different modules.

TYPE INSTANCES MUST NOT OVERLAP

There's an important difference between closed and open type families. Closed type families follow the usual evaluation model. The first rule is tried; if it doesn't match, the second rule is tried, and so on, until a match is ultimately found. This can be done because rules from a closed type family have a *defined order*. However, rules from an open type family come from different, unrelated places and have no order. If the compiler found that two patterns match, it wouldn't be able to know which choice to take. Thus, GHC forces type instance declarations to not overlap.

Take as an example the definition of the Min TF shown earlier. If the compiler had to compute the result of Min Zero Zero, both the first and second rules would match. It knows that it should use the first one because the TF is closed. But if you were to define Min as an open TF (e.g., because your version of GHC is earlier than 7.8.1), you would need to refine the declaration to make type instances not overlap. You could achieve it by making the second rule fire only when the first argument is larger than zero.

```
type instance Min Zero      y        = Zero
type instance Min (Succ x) Zero      = Zero
type instance Min (Succ x) (Succ y) = Succ (Min x y)
```

Now each application of the open TF Min has one and only one rule to apply.

In many of the cases where functional dependencies are used, you want to create a type-level function but also enforce each implementer of the type class to add a new rule to that type-level function. Or from another point of view, you want to add a type-level function inside the type class. When you enable the TypeFamilies extension, type class declarations are allowed to contain both term-level and type-level function signatures, as desired. The type-level signatures inside a type class are known as *associated types*.

Note   Remember that types have a simple kind system (the only possible kinds are * and function-like kinds such as * -> *) that checks whether the application of type constructors is correct. If you don't remember all the details, you can refer to Part 1 of the book, where I introduced the kind system.

Let's see how you would rework[5] the Product type class to use associated types instead of functional dependencies. If you remember the original definition, there was a p variable representing the category of products and an op variable for the operations for that category. The latter was functionally dependent on the former, so it's a perfect candidate for being changed into an associated type. Thus, the new code drops the op parameter and adds a type-level function called Operation, as follows:

```
class Product p where
  type Operation p :: *
  price :: p -> Float
  perform :: p -> Operation p -> String
  testOperation :: p -> Operation p
```

---

[5] The following code works on a different module from the Operation type family introduced earlier. If you try to define Operation inside a type class at the same time of the Operation type family, there will be a name collision, and the compiler won't be able to continue.

As you can see, any appearance of op in the old declaration is now replaced with Operation p, which gives back the type corresponding to the operations. An implementation of Operation must also appear in every instantiation of the Product type class, like the following one for TimeMachine:

```
instance Product TimeMachine where
  type Operation TimeMachine = TimeMachineOps
  price _ = 1000.0
  perform (TimeMachine m) (Travel y)
    = "Travelling to " ++ show y ++ " with " ++ m
  perform (TimeMachine m) Park
    = "Parking time machine " ++ m
  testOperation _ = Travel 0
```

Like in the previous section, the type of bag that each category of products needs should be encoded at the type level. Exercise 13-9 asks you to do so, now using associated types.

EXERCISE 13-9. PRODUCTS AND BAGS, REDUX

Using the previously defined data types BigBag and SmallBag, represent the kind of bag each category of product needs. To do this, add a new associated type to the Product type class. Finally, include the instances that express that time machines should go on big bags, whereas books need only small ones.

For the simple scenario of one of the types being completely dependent on the rest of the variables in the type class (like operations and bags in this section), associated types usually make more explicit that only one possibility can be chosen in each instance. However, functional dependencies shouldn't be overlooked, because they allow richer expression of dependence.

There's one last addition to the type system brought by type families. Consider the following function, performTestFromOther, which executes the test operation of a product on a completely different product:

```
performTestFromOther p q = perform p $ testOperation q
```

The task now is to give a type signature that is as abstract as possible to allow the function to be used in the largest variety of situations. A first approximation is to require p and q to be of the same type, which should implement the Product type class. Indeed, if you try to add the following type signature to the function, the compiler will accept the definition:

```
performTestFromOther :: Product p => p -> p -> String
```

But this signature is overly restrictive. You don't need both arguments to have the same type. The only thing you need is for them to support the same operations, that is, for their Operation associated type to coincide. This kind of requisite can be expressed in Haskell using an *equality constraint* x ~ y, which states that x and y must be syntactically equal after all type families have been resolved. The most general constraint for this case is then as follows:

```
performTestFromOther :: (Product p, Product q, Operation p ~ Operation q)
                     => p -> q -> String
```

Actually, if you try to compile the code without giving an explicit type signature, GHC will give you this more general type as a hint. You could directly copy that signature in your code, removing the initial forall part that is implicit for every free variable in the signature. Here's an example:

```
Warning: Top-level binding with no type signature:
      performTestFromOther
         :: forall p p1.
            (Product p, Product p1, Operation p ~ Operation p1) =>
            p -> p1 -> String
```

Equality constraints are not often seen in handwritten code, but they are essential to understanding GHC error messages. In most of the instances where the type families do not coincide, the compiler will warn you about an equality constraint (one with ~) not being respected.

DATA FAMILIES

Being completely correct, the previous sections didn't introduce type families but a subclass of them called *type synonym families.* When using this subclass, you need to use it in both parameters and return expression types that were already defined elsewhere.

There is another kind of TF, called a *data family*, where you directly list the constructors for each instance of the family instead of using another type. For example, the `Product` type class and its `TimeMachine` instance could also be defined as follows:

```
class Product p where
  data Operation p
  price :: p -> Float
  perform :: p -> Operation2 p -> String
  testOperation :: p -> Operation2 p
instance Product TimeMachine where
  data Operation TimeMachine = Travel Integer | Park
  price _ = 1000.0
  perform (TimeMachine m) (Travel y) = "Travelling to " ++ show y ++ "
with " ++ m
  perform (TimeMachine m) Park        = "Parking time machine " ++ m
  testOperation _ = Travel 0
```

Type synonym and data families are not interchangeable, though, because they have different properties (e.g., data families can be partially applied, while type synonym families can't).

Many of the techniques in this chapter are applied in libraries in Hackage to make stronger guarantees about the code that is executed. You've already used associated types, although you didn't know it back then, when writing the schema description in Persistent.[6] Another interesting package that uses type-level programming is HList, which allows you to create lists whose elements have different types.

---

[6] You can check the definitions that are created by running GHC with the `-ddump-splices` option.

Data Type Promotion and Singletons

From version 7.4.1 on, GHC includes an extension called *data type promotion*. When enabled, for each data type at the term level, a new set of types is created at the type level (the type is *promoted*). Furthermore, a new kind is associated to each of these promoted data types, leading to safer type-level programming. In this section, you'll see how to take advantage of this feature and how to promote functions in addition to data types using the singletons package.

A Further Refinement to the Presents Rule

Let's start from scratch with the implementation of the Presents Rule (if you're writing the code as you read, start a new empty module). But now instead of creating empty data types for representing 0 and successors, the code will use a regular data declaration and turn on the DataKinds extension – which enables data type *promotion*. The code is similar to the following:

```
{-# LANGUAGE DataKinds #-}
data Nat = Zero | Succ Nat
```

If on the same file you include the declaration of lists tagged with their length from the section on functional dependencies, the code will compile just fine. As a reminder, here's the definition of the Vect data type:

```
{-# LANGUAGE GADTs #-}
data Vect n a where
  VNil  :: Vect Zero a
  VCons :: a -> Vect n a -> Vect (Succ n) a
```

It seems that you've used the data type from the term level inside a type, as you would do in a dependently typed language! However, this would defy the strict separation between types and terms in the Haskell language. The truth is that when the DataKinds extension is enabled, the compiler creates a *copy* of the data type in the type level. Conceptually and for now, you can think of the source file with DataKinds as being equivalent to the following:

```
data Nat = Zero | Succ Nat
data Zero
data Succ nat
```

The compiler can distinguish between constructors and type names because they live in separate worlds. In the rare event in which the compiler could not make that distinction, you can use the syntax `'Identifier` to refer explicitly to the `Identifier` at the type level. For example, you may write the definition of Vect as more explicit about Zero and Succ being promoted types.

```
data Vect n a where
  VNil  :: Vect 'Zero a
  VCons :: a -> Vect n a -> Vect ('Succ n) a
```

The next step for porting the code to this new file is to declare a type family Plus, which will encode addition. You can copy the code from the previous section (including the TypeFamilies pragma). If you now ask for the kind of Plus, you get

```
*> :kind Plus
Plus :: Nat -> Nat -> Nat
```

The compiler has inferred the right kinds.[7] Following the same idea of being explicit as adding type signatures to every definition, we can add kind annotations to our Plus type family to indicate the kind of arguments and the result kind:

```
type family Plus (x :: Nat) (y :: Nat) :: Nat where
```

Note   Remember that kinds are used to categorize types, like types do for values. In Haskell, without data type promotion, all the fully applied data types have kind *. However, this extension opens the door to user-defined kinds, as the example shows.

The next step is to use this new approach to your advantage. For example, right now I haven't explicitly forbidden writing a type such as Vect Int Char. But this makes no sense. The only possible values for the first variable in Vect should be those from the kind Nat (which are the one representing numbers). You can write it explicitly in the type declaration.

```
data Vect (n :: Nat) a where
```

---

[7] In older versions of GHC, kinds always defaulted to *, and you had to be more explicit.

> **Note**   In this case, the annotation is not needed because the compiler is able to infer that the kind of n must be Nat. But it's still interesting to make it explicit, at least for documentation purposes and to ensure that a change in your code doesn't make the compiler infer a different type.

This same idea should be applied to Offer, which has a type parameter that should take values only from type-level natural numbers. The corresponding refinement of this data type should be declared as follows:

```
data Offer a (p :: Nat) where
```

As you can see, the DataKinds extension brings to type-level programming most of the safety that types give to the Haskell programs at the term level. Furthermore, the automatic promotion makes it easier to declare the types that will be used for programming at the type level. However, the kind system is not as powerful as the type system (e.g., you don't have anything like *kind classes*), but for most of the type-level programming, this extension should be more than enough.

Cooking with Singletons

The DataKinds extension is really useful, but it doesn't give you the full package. Your data types can be promoted to the type level seamlessly, but you still need to define your type-level functions using either FDs or TFs. If you are using some functionality that was already available at the term level, this means that you need to duplicate code and to do so in different styles of programming, hurting the readability and maintainability of the code.

The singletons package provides a pragmatic solution to this problem. Using the metaprogramming facilities of Template Haskell, it creates type-level versions of the term-level functions you ask for. Although the two worlds are still separated, this library creates the illusion that the same constructors and functions are used in both levels seamlessly.

To start using the package, you must add it as a dependency of your project and import the Data.Singletons.TH module in your source file. The expansion of Template Haskell blocks user type families and data type promotion, so in addition to the metaprogramming extensions, you need to enable them in your source file, or the code will refuse to compile.

The module provides a lot of functionality, but the most interesting one for your needs here is promote. Using it, you can create type-level versions of both data types and functions. The functions will be encoded at the type level using TFs, with a name resulting in changing the first letter of the function name into uppercase. For example, here's how you could promote natural number operations that have been guiding you in the chapter:

```
{-# LANGUAGE GADTs, DataKinds, TypeFamilies, UndecidableInstances #-}
{-# LANGUAGE TemplateHaskell #-}
import Data.Singletons.TH hiding (Min)
$(promote [d|
  data Nat = Zero | Succ Nat
           deriving (Show, Eq)
  plus :: Nat -> Nat -> Nat
  plus Zero      y = y
  plus (Succ x) y = Succ (plus x y)
  min :: Nat -> Nat -> Nat
  min Zero        _        = Zero
  min _           Zero     = Zero
  min (Succ x) (Succ y) = Succ (min x y)
  |])
```

Caution   The code inside the block starting from [d| to |] must be indented to work correctly. Double-check this fact when working with singletons.

THE SINGLETONS PRELUDE

In this section, we are defining our own version of promoted natural numbers and several operations over them. This is not needed, though, since the singletons package contains a quite complete copy of Haskell's Prelude in the type level. You can find it in the Data.Singletons.Prelude module.

Enforcing the Duration Rule

Since now you're able to reuse most of your regular Haskell knowledge in the type level via promotion, you may think about encoding a more complicated invariant: the Duration Rule. To do so, let's create a data type for ranges of time. Three cases must be handled: a range that is open only at the end, which means that the offer is applicable from a specific point in time (e.g., an infinite range would be an open range starting at 0); a closed range with start and end points; and an empty range, which is the one to be forbidden. As a further example, let's define a type-level Infinite range using promotion. This code uses the promoted Nat functionality from the previous section:

```
$(promote [d|
  data Range = Empty | Open Nat | Closed Nat Nat
  infinite :: Range
  infinite = Open Zero
  |])
```

Now let's create the TFs that will be ultimately called when applying the From and Until constructors of the Offer data type. For the first case, the function will be restrictFrom and should take as arguments the range of days that the offer is available for before the restriction and the new point in time for the initial day of the offer. The code is a bit long but should be straightforward to understand.

```
$(promote [d|
  data Comparison = Less' | Equal' | Greater'
  compare' :: Nat -> Nat -> Comparison
  compare' Zero     Zero     = Equal'
  compare' Zero     (Succ _) = Less'
  compare' (Succ _) Zero     = Greater'
  compare' (Succ x) (Succ y) = compare' x y
  restrictFrom :: Nat -> Range -> Range
  restrictFrom _ Empty = Empty
  restrictFrom n (Open f)
    = restrictFrom1 n f (compare' n f)
  restrictFrom n (Closed f t)
    = restrictFrom2 n f t (compare' n f) (compare' n t)
  restrictFrom1 :: Nat -> Nat -> Comparison -> Range
```

```
restrictFrom1 n _ Greater' = Open n
restrictFrom1 _ f Equal'   = Open f
restrictFrom1 _ f Less'    = Open f
restrictFrom2 :: Nat -> Nat -> Nat -> Comparison -> Comparison -> Range
restrictFrom2 _ _ _ Greater' Greater' = Empty
restrictFrom2 _ _ _ Greater' Equal'   = Empty
restrictFrom2 n _ t Greater' Less'    = Closed n t
restrictFrom2 _ f t Equal'   _        = Closed f t
restrictFrom2 _ f t Less'    _        = Closed f t
 |])
```

Caution   I am adding ticks to the end of some names to disambiguate them from the ones in the singletons' Prelude.

Almost any use of singletons leads to the UndecidableInstances extension. This is because the compiler cannot prove that the TFs you've created will always terminate their execution when you have nested TFs. This nesting appears in the promoted TFs because of the call to compare inside restrictFrom. However, if you know that the function you wrote will terminate, it's safe to unveil that restriction and tell the compiler to accept that function without further termination checks.

The first step for tagging your offers with duration information is to enlarge the initial type with a new type variable of kind Range, which was promoted previously. To keep the examples concise, I will use the original Offer data type, instead of the one tagged with a number of presents. The declaration of the GADT reads as follows:

```
data Offer a (r :: Range) where
```

The basic combinators for offers (presents and discounts) have an infinite duration by default. To write them down, you can use the Infinite TF that was created in the previous promotion.

```
Present          :: a -> Offer a Infinite
PercentDiscount  :: Float -> Offer a Infinite
AbsoluteDiscount :: Float -> Offer a Infinite
```

As a first approximation, you could write the time restriction From as follows:

```
From :: (n :: Nat) -> Offer a d -> Offer a (RestrictFrom n d)
```

However, this will make the compiler quite unhappy and will make it show the following type error:

```
src/Chapter13/CheckDurationPromotion.hs:
    Expected a type, but `(n :: Nat)' has kind `Nat'
    In the type `(n :: Nat)'
    In the definition of data constructor `From'
    In the data declaration for `Offer'
```

The problem is that you cannot use promoted kinds in a constructor; only types of kind * are allowed. In particular, using Nat is forbidden.

Fortunately, there's a construction that helps you overcome this difficulty. The idea is to create a regular data type that carries as a tag the type-level number you need. In that way, you have a value that you can use at runtime, and the tag gives the type-level information. This data type will have only one possible value for each possible tag. For that reason, they are called *singleton data types*. For example, a singleton type SNat corresponding to the Nat promoted kind would read as follows:

```
data SNat (n :: Nat) where
  SZero :: SNat Zero
  SSucc :: SNat n -> SNat (Succ n)
```

By the way in which this type is constructed, given a type of kind Nat, only one value of SNat is possible. For example, the only inhabitant of SNat (Succ (Succ Zero)) is SSucc (SSucc SZero). So, you've reflected the type corresponding to 2 as a runtime value, as desired. If you look at the output from GHCi, you can spot the explicit reference to promoted constructors, which are shown with the ' sign in front of them.

```
*Chapter13.CheckDurationPromotion> :t SSucc (SSucc SZero)
SSucc (SSucc SZero)
  :: SNat ('Succ ('Succ 'Zero))
```

The next step is to use this singleton type in the constructor From that uses as runtime arguments only values of kind *. Notice how you have access to the type-level number n from the argument to SNat.

```
From :: SNat n -> Offer a d -> Offer a (RestrictFrom n d)
```

Another easy construction involves moving from the SNat singleton data type back to the initial Nat data type before its promotion. Once the conversion is done, you have a runtime value that you may use in regular functions. The following piece of code defines that conversion and uses it to print an offer restriction:

```
toNat :: SNat n -> Nat
toNat SZero     = Zero
toNat (SSucc n) = Succ (toNat n)
printDateRestriction :: Offer a r -> String
printDateRestriction (From n _)  = "From " ++ show (toNat n)
printDateRestriction (Until n _) = "Until" ++ show (toNat n)
printDateRestriction _           = "No date restriction"
```

Once again, the creation of a singleton type given a data type that is promoted is just boilerplate. The singletons library includes another function of singletons that supersedes promote and that generates singleton types along with promoting data types and functions. For example, if you want to generate SNat automatically, you can include in your source file the following:

```
{-# LANGUAGE ScopedTypeVariables #-}
{-# LANGUAGE EmptyCase #-}
{-# LANGUAGE InstanceSigs #-}
$(singletons [d|
  data Nat = Zero | Succ Nat
           deriving (Show, Eq)
  |])
```

In addition, the singletons library includes a SingI type class with only one function, sing. The purpose of this function is to create the unique value of a singleton type given its corresponding promoted data type. In this way, you don't have to write the constructors as you did before with SNat. For example, the inhabitants corresponding to the first four natural numbers at the type level can be written like so:

```
zero :: SNat Zero
zero = sing    -- results in SZero
one :: SNat (Succ Zero)
one = sing     -- results in SSucc SZero
two :: SNat (Succ (Succ Zero))
```

```
two = sing      -- results in SSucc (SSucc SZero)
three :: SNat (Succ (Succ (Succ Zero)))
three = sing  -- results in SSucc (SSucc (SSucc SZero))
```

The singletons package also provides a type class for converting from a singleton type to the regular data type. It's called SingE and has a single function fromSing. Instead of the homemade toNat function, you could use that function to turn the singleton three into a term-level Nat.

```
*Chapter13.CheckDurationPromotion> fromSing three
Succ (Succ (Succ Zero))
```

There are some constructors left for the full Offer data type. Exercise 13-10 asks you to finish the job.

EXERCISE 13-10. OFFERS WITH SINGLETONS

Add the rest of constructors to the Offer GADT: Restrict should keep its duration; Until should change the duration in a similar way to From; Both, BetterOf, and If must compute the smallest duration range that includes those of both arguments (i.e., the intersection). At this point, you can use Offer to build a complete offer and compute its range.

```
*> let one = SSucc SZero                    -- build the singleton 1
*> let three = SSucc (SSucc (SSucc SZero))  -- build the singleton 3
*> :t let p = Present 'a' in Both (From one p) (BetterOf p (Until three p))
let p = Present 'a' in Both (From one p) (BetterOf p (Until three p))
  :: Offer Char ('Closed ('Succ 'Zero) ('Succ ('Succ ('Succ 'Zero))))
```

TYPE-LEVEL LITERALS

GHC provides extra features for tagging types with either natural numbers or strings. If you enable the TypeOperators extension and import the GHC.TypeLits module, you can use numbers and string literals at those places where you need a type of kind Nat (for natural numbers) or Symbol (for strings).

Using these literals, the Vect data type could have been declared as follows:

```
data Vect n a where
  VNil  :: Vect 0 a
  VCons :: a -> Vect n a -> Vect (n + 1) a
```

Note that this module provides only a small set of operations on natural numbers, namely, addition, product, and exponentiation, as well as a type class that encodes whether two type-level numbers are related as being less or equal.

Singleton types put an end to the bird's-eye view on type-level programming in Haskell. The relation between term-level data types and functions, their corresponding promoted types and kinds, and the singleton types is subtle, but each one serves a purpose:

- data and function declarations express how to create values that Haskell can use to compute at runtime.

- Promoted data types and kinds and type-level functions expressed as either FDs or TFs are evaluated at compile time and allow you to tag values with stronger types that introduce extra invariants.

- Singleton types are the bridge between the worlds. When you need a type-level value that should also be reflected at runtime, you should use them.

Exercise 13-11 provides an exercise on a different domain to help you better understand these relations.

EXERCISE 13-11. RECTANGLES AND BOUNDING BOXES

For this exercise, you will use the following data type, which represents images built from rectangles. The Rect constructor represents a single rectangle, and then you can combine images (with Union), take just the common part (with Intersection), or put together several copies in a row (using Replicate).

```
data Rectangle = R { topLeft :: (Nat, Nat), bottomRight :: (Nat, Nat) }
data Image = Rect Rectangle
           | Union Image Image
```

```
| Intersection Image Image
| Replicate Nat Image
```

You must tag images with their bounding box, that is, the smallest rectangle that contains the whole of the image. For example, if you have the union of the rectangles from (1,0) to (5,4) and from (0,1) to (3,2), the bounding box is (0,0) to (5,4). You can draw them on paper to convince yourself about that.

The type-level calculations should be developed using the techniques from the `singletons` package. Think carefully about which places need singleton types.

Summary

In this chapter, you explored many of the advanced features of the Haskell type system while designing a domain-specific language for expressing offers for the Time Machine Store.

- This chapter introduced the concepts of external/stand-alone and internal/embedded *domain-specific languages* and the difference between deep and shallow embedding.

- *Generalized algebraic data types* allow constructors of a data type to build values with different types; you used that extra functionality to create type-safe expressions.

- You were introduced to the idea of *tagging* a type with some extra information, which allows you to check stronger invariants at compile time.

- You explored several possibilities for doing *type-level programming* in Haskell, including *functional dependencies, type families,* and *data type promotion.* The main characteristic of Haskell in this aspect is the separation between the term and type worlds.

- Functional dependencies and *associated types* refine the type class mechanism in Haskell and were covered in this chapter.

- *Data type promotion* and the `singletons` library make it possible for you to move declarations from the term level to the type level. Furthermore, it extends the *kind system* to provide safer type-level programming in Haskell.

Interpreting Offers with Attributes

This chapter continues the work of the previous one in creating a DSL for expressing offers for the Time Machine Store. As you may remember, deep embedding was chosen as the way to model the offers language in Haskell. A deeply embedded language is divided between its *syntax*, expressed as a set of Haskell data types, and its *interpretation*, which is responsible for assigning a meaning to each value in the language. In this example, the interpretation of an offer could be a function that, given a list of products and prices, applies the offers and discounts and returns the new price.

In principle, the interpretations could be defined as plain Haskell functions over the DSL values. However, almost every interpretation you can give follows a set of patterns. Thus, it's interesting to consider those patterns and build a conceptual model that better defines the interpretations. This is what *attribute grammars* do for you. Then, you can use a tool to generate the Haskell code that corresponds to an attribute grammar, saving you from having to write a lot of boilerplate code. In particular, this chapter will devote most of its time to the topic of programming with the Utrecht University Attribute Grammar Compiler (UUAGC).

In addition to plain programming, in this chapter you will also consider the relations between attribute grammars and other Haskell concepts, such as monads. You will revisit the ideas of *origami programming* from Chapter 3 and will apply them to general data types (not only lists). Finally, I shall introduce the idea of *data type–generic programming*, which allows us to create algorithms which work on many different data types in a uniform manner.

© Alejandro Serrano Mena 2022
A. Serrano Mena, *Practical Haskell*, https://doi.org/10.1007/978-1-4842-8581-7_14

Interpretations and Attribute Grammars

In this section, you'll learn about attribute grammars. To help, a simple language is given an interpretation in Haskell. That language is then reworked using attributes.

A Simple Interpretation

Let's consider a simple language that contains only three combinators for building its expressions. Say you have a basic AmountOf with a character as a parameter and then the addition and product of two expressions. Let's express the language in a simple Haskell data type.

```
data Expr = Plus  Expr Expr
          | Times Expr Expr
          | AmountOf Char
```

The desired interpretation of this data type is parameterized by a string and gives a number as a result. When AmountOf is found, the number of characters of a given type is counted. The other two combinators just perform the sum or multiplication of the numbers in their subexpressions. The corresponding Haskell code for this interpretation is straightforward to write.

```
meaning :: Expr -> [Char] -> Int
meaning (Plus  l r)  p = meaning l p + meaning r p
meaning (Times l r)  p = meaning l p * meaning r p
meaning (AmountOf c) p = length $ filter (== c) p
```

Introducing Attribute Grammars

The previous section's interpretation is quite simple. Still, it contains a lot of boilerplate code. The recursive nature of this definition is explicit by calling meaning on the subexpressions, and the p list must be explicitly threaded throughout the entire function. *Attribute grammars* provide a higher-level model for writing interpretations (and, as you will see later, many other kinds of functions), focusing on the data being used and produced, saving you from thinking about all the small details related to information flow. As a result, your code becomes much more maintainable.

In addition, attribute grammars contribute to the modularity of the code. You can separate your interpretation into several parts (and even in several files) and then ask the attribute grammar system to join them together to compute all the information you need from your data type in the smallest number of passes.

The main disadvantage of attribute grammars is that they have a different computational model than plain Haskell, even though the integration is tight. As you will see in this chapter, it's easy to understand attribute grammars in Haskell terms, so this disadvantage shouldn't block you from using them.

Let's return to the expression example. If instead of plain Haskell you were using attribute grammars, you would be thinking about this interpretation in different terms. From the attribute grammar point of view, your data type is a *tree* whose nodes keep some *attributes* within them. In this example, the attributes would be the string that you're exploring and the result of the interpretation.

When looking closer, you can see that those pieces of information are different. On one hand, the string to explore is passed from each expression to its subexpressions as a parameter. You say that this attribute is flowing *top-down* from the expression. On the other hand, the numeric results at each point in the expression are built considering the results of its subexpressions and combining them in some way. Thus, the flow is *bottom-up* in this case. Figure 14-1 shows the flow of information.

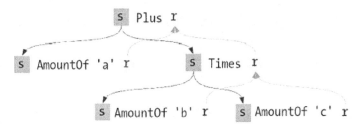

Figure 14-1. *Tree and attributes for* AmountOf 'a' `Plus` (AmountOf 'b' `Times` AmountOf 'c')

In the attribute grammar jargon, the numeric result is a *synthesized attribute*, whereas the string to explore is an *inherited attribute*. The names roughly reflect the different flow direction, which is the important difference between both. To define this interpretation as an attribute grammar, you would need the following three pieces of information, as the example shows:

1. Which are the possible nodes in your tree. This is done via the definition of a set of data types in which every constructor represents a kind of node.

2. The attributes to be computed and whether they are inherited or synthesized.

3. How to pass the information from parent to children nodes in the case of the inherited attributes and how to compute the value of synthesized attributes from their children.

The purpose of an *attribute grammar system* is to take all that information and generate the necessary code for computing the final value of the attributes at each node. Here, you can see the main advantage of using an attribute grammar vs. writing the interpretation directly in Haskell, because the attribute grammar system would take care of the following automatically:

- When an attribute needs to be transported in a more complex fashion than just top-down or bottom-up (e.g., between sibling nodes), the Haskell code can become quite complex. But with an attribute grammar, this behavior is expressed declaratively, and the system takes care of keeping track of it.

- Sometimes, the value of an attribute depends on another one. This means attributes must be ordered in some way for the whole computation to proceed, maybe doing more than one traversal of the same tree. Attribute grammar systems perform this ordering automatically (and in many cases, in an optimal way), so you don't need to think about it.

Hackage includes several implementations of attribute grammars in its package repository. One option is to use *Happy*, the parser generator included in the Haskell Platform and that has support for attributes in its grammars. Happy is an external tool that preprocesses a grammar description and generates the Haskell code needed for parsing it.

AspectAG is a library for embedding attribute grammars inside Haskell. So, you don't need an extra step of building prior to compilation. It's an interesting option for working with attribute grammars inside Haskell but has the downside of needing a lot of type-level programming to make it work.

The tool that will be presented in this chapter is the *Utrecht University Attribute Grammar Compiler* (UUAGC). Like with Happy, it's a preprocessor that generates Haskell code from the description of the grammar. In contrast to Happy, UUAGC is focused specifically on defining attribute grammars. Thus, the connection between the attribute grammar formalism and UUAGC code is much more explicit in this case, making it a better choice for learning about these grammars.

INSTALLING UUAGC

UUAGC is available in Hackage, so you just need to execute the usual command to get it on your system.

```
$ cabal install uuagc
```

By following these instructions, you also install integration with Cabal, which is found in the uuagc-cabal package. You'll be using uuagc-cabal to build the attribute grammars in the upcoming sections.

Unfortunately, by the time of writing, UUAGC doesn't work on the latest GHC 9.x series, so you might need to add --with-compiler=ghc-8.10.7 in the Cabal command to use an earlier version. The code produced by the tool, however, works on every version.

Your First Attribute Grammar

Now let's create the attribute grammar corresponding to the simple numeric expressions introduced in the previous section. For the source file, you have two conventions to follow: UUAGC source files end with .ag, and files must be found inside a folder structure that follows the module name. The conventions follow Haskell's. In this case, the module will be Chapter14.Simple, so the file should be found in src/Chapter14/Simple.ag.

Synthesizing the Result

In the previous section, the three pieces of information required to define an attribute grammar were presented. When programming with UUAGC, each of these pieces is declared separately. The first one is the declaration of the data type that attributes will refer to. The syntax is quite similar to Haskell's `data`, but it has two differences:

1. No equal sign should appear after the name of the data type. Instead, each constructor declaration must begin with a vertical bar: |.

2. All the arguments to a constructor must be named, as happens with records in Haskell. However, no brackets should be used around the fields.

Furthermore, when using type variables or compound types, they must be placed inside { and }. This tells UUAGC to parse the content of the brackets as regular Haskell code instead of as an attribute grammar. Taking into account all these differences, the data type for expressions looks like the following:

```
data Expr
  | Plus  left :: Expr right :: Expr
  | Times left :: Expr right :: Expr
  | AmountOf c :: Char
```

Note   UUAGC supports two kinds of syntax. The one used in the examples of this chapter is dubbed "Haskell syntax" because of its resemblance to that language. The "classical syntax" is quite different from Haskell's; you can spot it in UUAGC code because all the keywords are written in capitals.

The next step is to declare the attributes that each node will have. In UUAGC, all nodes representing constructors of the same data type contain the same attributes. The syntax for specifying this is the `attr` keyword, followed by the names of the data types you want to add the attributes to. Then, you must include a line per attribute, which starts with `inh` or `syn`, depending on whether you want to create an inherited or synthesized attribute, respectively, the name of the attribute and its type. The attributes in this example have a String flowing top-down and a numeric result being synthesized:

```
attr Expr
  inh string :: String
  syn result :: Int
```

Finally, you need to specify the way attributes are computed based on other attributes and on the parameters inside the constructors. This is called the semantics of the attributes and is specified via a sem block in the UUAGC source file. This block starts with the name of the data type and then a block per constructor to be described. Each of those blocks contains the code related to defining each of the attributes of that node. The right side for each constructor follows plain Haskell syntax, with three syntactical modifications:

1. The value of an attribute at a child node is accessed via the syntax node.attribute. The special name lhs is reserved for referring to the *parent* of the current node. The idea of a parent is not found in Haskell code, so let's clarify it using an example. Say you have a value of the following form Plus (AmountOf 'a') (AmountOf 'b'), that is, a parent Plus node with two AmountOf children nodes. At each node, both a string and a result attribute will be handled. From the point of view of AmountOf 'a', lhs.string refers to the attribute in the parent node, that is, the value of the string attribute in the Plus node.

2. At the right side of the declaration of each attribute, the references to other attributes or parameters of the constructor must be preceded by the @ sign.

3. UUAGC uses indentation to delimit blocks. However, you can ask the preprocessor to keep a piece of code exactly as it appears in the source file, wrapping it between { and }.

In particular, this convention implies that the declaration of a synthesized attribute must be similar to lhs.attribute = ... because you're defining the value of such an attribute in the parent node. In this case, the meaning function can be translated into the following sem block:

```
sem Expr
  | Plus      lhs.result = @left.result + @right.result
  | Times     lhs.result = @left.result * @right.result
  | AmountOf lhs.result = { length $ filter (== @c) @lhs.string }
```

Integrating UUAGC in Your Package

As mentioned earlier, UUAGC is not a library but a preprocessor for Haskell code. This means the attribute grammars you write cannot be directly compiled by GHC or any other Haskell compiler; rather, they need to be converted into Haskell source by UUAGC. You can do the translation yourself each time your attribute grammar changes, but it's better to tell Cabal that you're using UUAGC and let the tool take care of preprocessing files that have changes while it takes care of which files need to be recompiled.

To start, create a new package with an executable stanza. Following the convention in the previous chapters, I'll call the package chapter14, and the executable will be named uuagc-examples. The Cabal stanza corresponding to that executable reads as follows:

```
executable uuagc-examples
  hs-source-dirs:    src
  build-depends:     base >= 4
  ghc-options:       -Wall
  other-modules:     Chapter14.Simple
  main-is:           Main.hs
  default-language: Haskell2010
```

The next step is to tell Cabal to call the preprocessor before compilation. This is done by using Cabal's ability to customize the build with hooks. To do so, create a new file named Setup.hs at the root of your project with the following content:

```
import Distribution.Simple
import Distribution.Simple.UUAGC (uuagcLibUserHook)
import UU.UUAGC (uuagc)

main = defaultMainWithHooks (uuagcLibUserHook uuagc)
```

In addition, you have to indicate Cabal how to build this Setup.hs file, in particular, what the build-time dependencies are. This is done by adding another stanza to the chapter14.cabal file:

```
custom-setup
  setup-depends:
base, Cabal, uuagc, uuagc-cabal
```

The final step is to tell UUAGC which files must be handled by it and which compilation options it should apply. To do this, create a uuagc_options file in the root of your project (next to the .cabal and Setup.hs files) with the following contents:

```
file : "src/Chapter14/Simple.ag"
options : data, semfuns, catas, pretty, wrappers, rename,
          module "Chapter14.Simple", haskellsyntax, signatures
```

Notice that you need to include both the path to the attribute grammar (in the file field) and the name of the module that will be created (in this case, Chapter14.Simple). Furthermore, if you want to use "Haskell syntax" as presented in the examples of this chapter, you should remember to always include the haskellsyntax option.

After all this preparation, you can run Cabal to build your project. The output will be a bit different than usual because you're using a custom setup script and UUAGC is preprocessing your files. The following is a sample of the output, but it may be a bit different on your system depending on the versions installed:

```
$ cabal configure
Resolving dependencies...
[1 of 1] Compiling Main                ( Setup.hs, dist/setup/Main.o )
Linking ./dist/setup/setup ...
Configuring chapter14-0.1...
$ cabal build
Building chapter14-0.1...
Preprocessing executable 'uuagc-examples' for chapter14-0.1...
Building executable 'uuagc-examples' for chapter14-0.1...
...
Linking dist/build/uuagc-examples/uuagc-examples ...
```

For each new attribute grammar that you need to compile, you must include a new pair of lines defining it in the uuagc_options file. The advantage of this methodology is that Cabal takes care of rebuilding only the parts that have changed and doesn't call the preprocessor if it's not strictly needed.

UUAGC CODE GENERATION

By default, UUAGC takes advantage of lazy evaluation for executing attribute grammars. But you can also instruct it to optimize the code. In that case, a specific sequence of visits through the tree will be scheduled, resulting in stricter code.

This chapter focuses on the use of UUAGC with Haskell. But the preprocessor can generate code for other functional languages, including OCaml and Clean. In those cases, the right sides should be written in the corresponding back-end language instead of in Haskell.

Executing the Attribute Grammar

Of course, writing and compiling the attribute grammar isn't useful at all if you cannot call it in your own Haskell code. Depending on the options given to UUAGC,[1] the preprocessor generates several functions and data types that you should use when taking advantage of attribute grammars:

- The data declaration in a grammar is transformed to a data declaration in Haskell, but with the constructors prefixed with the name of the data type, in this case Expr. If you want constructors to appear as written in the grammar, don't use the rename option in UUAGC. However, in that case, you have to take care that constructor names do not collide.

- The data types Inh_Expr and Syn_Expr represent the inherited and synthesized attributes at each node of the Expr data type. Both are declared as records, with the field names including also the names of the attributes and the type of record they are in. In this example, the names boil down to string_Inh_Expr and result_Syn_Expr.

---

[1] You will learn how to specify those options in the next section.

- A function sem_Expr converts a value of the data type into a function that takes as parameters the initial inherited attributes and returns a tuple of synthesized attributes. However, the function that you get may have the attributes in any order, so it's customary to use the wrap_Expr function, which takes attribute records as parameters.

For example, a function that would execute the computational actions of the attribute grammar to get the synthesized values in the root of the tree for the Expr data type would read as follows. Note that this function should be found in a *different file* from the attribute grammar definition itself, so you need to import the module generated by UUAGC.

```
import Chapter14.Simple

executeExpr :: Expr -> String -> Int
executeExpr e s =
  let syn = wrap_Expr (sem_Expr e) (Inh_Expr s)   -- returns Syn_Expr
  in result_Syn_Expr syn
```

And now you can use that function to test your attribute grammar.

```
*Chapter14.Simple> :{
*Chapter14.Simple| let e = Expr_Times (Expr_AmountOf 'e')
*Chapter14.Simple|                    (Expr_Plus (Expr_AmountOf 'a')
*Chapter14.Simple|                               (Expr_AmountOf 'o'))
*Chapter14.Simple| in executeExpr e "hello"
*Chapter14.Simple| :}
1
```

Expression Interpretation

Let's move now to a larger attribute grammar. In this case, the focus would be conditional expressions inside an offer. The aim is to obtain a function that, given an expression and a list of products, returns the result of applying the expression to that list.

Using an Attribute Grammar

You've seen in the example for simple numeric expressions how UUAGC separates the three pieces of information needed to define a whole attribute grammar. The first block defines the base data type into which attributes will be computed. The following code is a straightforward translation of the Expr data type found in the previous chapter. Notice that in order to keep the code a bit shorter, only one kind of Boolean comparison between numbers is included.

```
data Expr a
  | AmountOf product :: {a}
  | PriceOf  product :: {a}
  | TotalNumberOfProducts
  | TotalPrice
  | IVal val :: Int
  | FVal val :: Float
  | Plus  right :: (Expr {a})  left :: (Expr {a})
  | Times right :: (Expr {a})  left :: (Expr {a})
  | LessThan right :: (Expr {a})  left :: (Expr {a})
  | Or  right :: (Expr {a})  left :: (Expr {a})
  | And right :: (Expr {a})  left :: (Expr {a})
  | Not inner :: (Expr {a})
```

Note   To compile this attribute grammar, you need to enable the ScopedTypeVariables extension for GHC. The easiest way to do this is to add a line similar to extensions: ScopedTypeVariables to the Cabal stanza.

In this case, I'll return to the simple modeling of expression results. Three different attributes will hold the result of the expression as integer, float, or Boolean. At any point, only one of the components will hold a Just value, whereas the others will be Nothing. As you know from the previous chapter, you could refine the definition of Expr using GADTs to make this tupling unnecessary. However, the focus in this chapter is on attribute grammars, so let's try to keep the types as simple as possible. The result of an expression depends on the subexpressions, so this attribute should be a synthesized one.

In addition to computing the result, you need to thread the list of products among subexpressions because the constructors AmountOf, PriceOf, TotalAmountOfProduct, and TotalPrice need that information. In an attribute grammar setting, that information would be represented via an inherited attribute. The declaration of the set of attributes for Expr is as follows:

```
attr Expr
  inh products  :: {[(a, Float)]}
  syn intValue  :: {Maybe Int}
  syn fltValue  :: {Maybe Float}
  syn boolValue :: {Maybe Bool}
```

Note   Remember that compound types such as [(a, Float)] or Maybe Bool must be written inside brackets to stop UUAGC from parsing them as special attribute grammar syntax.

Following the example in this section, let's write the sem block for Expr. The initial declaration is a bit more complex in this case because you need to declare that the elements in the expression are instances of the Eq type class to be able to define the operations. Thus, the declaration reads as follows:

```
sem Eq {a} => Expr
```

One simple constructor is the TotalNumberOfProducts. In this case, the only attribute with a concrete value should be the integer one; the rest should be given a Nothing value. Since nodes of that kind don't have any children, you don't need to include any code for the inherited products attribute. The full code in this case is as follows:

```
| TotalNumberOfProducts lhs.intValue  = Just $ length @lhs.products
                         lhs.fltValue  = Nothing
                         lhs.boolValue = Nothing
```

A more complex example is the Plus one. In this case, the integer and floating values should be updated, but each of them should take a Just value only if both subexpressions also take this value. You can achieve this concisely using the Applicative instance of Maybe. The following code defines the synthesized attributes of the Plus constructor. The code for inherited ones is also straightforward because it copies only the value of products from the node to their children.

```
| Plus   lhs.intValue    = {(+) <$> @right.intValue <*> @left.intValue }
        lhs.fltValue    = {(+) <$> @right.fltValue <*> @left.fltValue }
        lhs.boolValue   = Nothing
        right.products = @lhs.products
        left.products   = @lhs.products
```

Given these examples, the rest of the cases should be easy to write. Exercise 14-1 asks you to do so.

EXERCISE 14-1. FULL EXPRESSION ATTRIBUTE GRAMMAR

Complete the remaining cases of the sem block of Expr. Hint: Use the previous examples as templates, either performing some computation over the products list or combining the value of subexpressions using Applicative syntax.

For example, a function that would execute the computational actions of the attribute grammar to get the synthesized values in the root of the tree for the Expr data type would read as follows:

```
executeExpr :: Ord a => Expr a -> [(a,Float)]
           -> (Maybe Int, Maybe Float, Maybe Bool)
executeExpr e products =
  let syn = wrap_Expr (sem_Expr e) (Inh_Expr products)   -- returns Syn_Expr
  in ( intValue_Syn_Expr  syn
     , fltValue_Syn_Expr  syn
     , boolValue_Syn_Expr syn )
```

And you can use that function to test your attribute grammar.

```
*Chapter14.Expr> :{
*Chapter14.Expr| let e = Expr_And
*Chapter14.Expr|                (Expr_AmountOf 'a' `Expr_LessThan` Expr_IVal 2)
*Chapter14.Expr|                (Expr_FVal 300.0 `Expr_LessThan` Expr_TotalPrice)
*Chapter14.Expr|      p = [('a',15.0), ('b',400.0)]
```

```
*Chapter14.Expr| in executeExpr e p
*Chapter14.Expr| :}
(Nothing,Nothing,Just True)
```

Precomputing Some Values

The attribute grammar for Expr works fine but could be enhanced in terms of performance. In the preceding code, each time a TotalNumberOfProducts or TotalPrice constructor is found, the full product list has to be traversed. Since it's quite common to find those basic combinators in the expressions, it's useful to cache the results to be reused each time they are needed. Let's see how to implement that caching in the attribute grammar.

The most common way to cope with this situation is by adding a new data type with only one constructor that wraps the entire expression tree. This data type is usually called Root. The following is its definition plus an indication to derive a Show type class instance, since it will be interesting to inspect those trees:

```
data Root a
  | Root expr :: (Expr {a})
deriving Root Expr : Show
```

Note   Adding an extra Root data type is merely a convention used for initializing inherited attributes. In many cases, it's not needed, and, of course, you can use a name different from Root.

The precomputed values will be stored in the numberOfProducts and totalPrice attributes. Those attributes must be passed top-down from the root of the tree. Thus, they must be inherited attributes of the Expr data type. Furthermore, if you want to get back the result of the computation from Root, you have to include the same synthesized attributes that Expr had. The attr part of the grammar should be changed to the following:

```
attr Root Expr
  inh products  :: {[(a, Float)]}
  syn intValue  :: {Maybe Int}
```

```
syn fltValue  :: {Maybe Float}
syn boolValue :: {Maybe Bool}
```

```
attr Expr
  inh numberOfProducts :: Int
  inh totalPrice       :: Float
```

Notice how UUAGC allows you to include in the same declaration several data types that share attributes. To use that functionality, just include all the data types after the `attr` keyword. In this example, the products, intValue, fltValue, and boolValue attributes are declared for both the Root and Expr data types.

Finally, you need to add the computation rules. The ones for computing the new inherited attributes of an Expr from a Root are straightforward given the grammar of the previous section.

```
sem Eq {a} => Root
  | Root expr.numberOfProducts = length @lhs.products
         expr.totalPrice       = foldr (\(_,p) x -> p + x) 0.0 @lhs.
products
```

Now you might expect extra declarations for threading the new inherited attributes inside Expr and taking the synthesized attributes from Expr to save it into Root. The good news is that they are not needed at all. UUAGC has some built-in rules that fire in case you haven't specified how to compute some attribute. For inherited attributes, the computation proceeds by copying the value from the parent to its children. For synthesized attributes, the result is taken from a child. (If you need to combine information from several children, there are other kinds of rules; you'll get in touch with them in the next section.) These rules are collectively known as *copy rules* because they take care of the simple case of attributes being copied. The flow of the inherited products attribute in the previous grammar didn't have to be specified; this rule would take care of it.

One thing that should be changed is the computation of the synthesized attributes in those constructors that were to be enhanced. Instead of computing the result each time, they should use the precomputed values from the Root. For example, TotalNumberOfProducts should be changed to the following:

```
| TotalNumberOfProducts lhs.intValue  = Just @lhs.numberOfProducts
                         lhs.fltValue  = Nothing
                         lhs.boolValue = Nothing
```

The core of the idea is that each time you need to initialize some values for the rest of the computation of the attributes, it's useful to wrap the entire tree inside a data type with only one constructor, which includes that initialization in its sem block.

A Different (Monadic) View

When learning about a new concept, it's useful to relate it to concepts you're already familiar with. You've already seen how attribute grammars come into existence when trying to declaratively define the flow of information. In the first simple interpretation, the parameters to functions became inherited attributes, and the tuple of results corresponded to the synthesized attributes. In Chapters 6 and 7, another different concept was used to thread information in that way: the Reader and Writer monads. Indeed, you can express the attribute grammar developed in this section using the monadic setting. I'll show how to do that. Note that the code from this section is independent of the attribute grammar and should be written in a different file, which should contain the definition of the Expr data type from the previous chapter.

First, you need to overcome a little technicality: the type used in the Writer must be a monoid. However, the interest here lies only in the last value output by the function, so you can "fake" this behavior by providing a Monoid instance that does this, as shown here:

```
import Data.Monoid

newtype Result = Result (Maybe Int, Maybe Float, Maybe Bool) deriving Show

instance Semigroup Result where
  _ <> r2 = r2

instance Monoid Result where
  _ `mappend` r2 = r2
  mempty         = Result (Nothing, Nothing, Nothing)
```

The Semigroup instance is only required in GHC version 8.4 or newer. The reason is that from that version on, Semigroup is a superclass of Monoid, and thus any instance of the latter must also be an instance of the former. In fact, some versions of GHC have a specific warning about types missing Semigroup instances.

Caution   Although type correct, this instance doesn't express a true monoid. The problem is that x `mappend` mempty = mempty, which is not what is necessary. A correct solution for this problem would be to save a list of output results and get the last one at the end of the attribute computation.

As mentioned, the behavior of inherited attributes can be seen as wrapped in a Reader monad, and the synthesized attributes can be seen as wrapped in a Writer one. Thus, the type signature of the function to write is as follows:

```
sem :: Eq a => Expr a -> ReaderT [(a,Float)] (Writer Result) ()
```

The corresponding code that calls the function passing the initial values would be as follows:

```
import Control.Monad.Reader
import Control.Monad.Writer

executeExpr :: Eq a => Expr a -> [(a, Float)] -> Result
executeExpr e p = execWriter (runReaderT (sem e) p)
```

Let's see how the computation of two of the constructors is expressed in this setting. First, you have TotalNumberProducts, which takes the inherited attribute (which is now the information in the Reader monad) and produces a new synthesized attribute with the length of the list.

```
sem TotalNumberProducts = do products <- ask
                             tell $ Result ( Just (length products)
                                           , Nothing, Nothing )
```

A second combinator to look at is the addition of two numbers. In this case, you need to compute the synthesized attributes locally and get those results to create the new synthesized attributes. The first part can be achieved using listen, the counterpart of Reader's function local for the Writer monad.

```
sem (e1 :+: e2) = do (_, Result (i1, f1, _)) <- listen (sem e1)
                     (_, Result (i2, f2, _)) <- listen (sem e2)
                     tell $ Result ( (+) <$> i1 <*> i2
                                   , (+) <$> f1 <*> f2, Nothing )
```

As you can see, attribute grammars express the concepts behind the `Reader` and `Writer` monads in a new setting. The main advantage is that you can refer to attributes by name, instead of stacking several monad transformers and having to access each of them by a different amount of `lift`. The intuitive idea that `Reader` and `Writer` monads can be combined easily and in any order to yield a new monad is made explicit by the fact that you can combine attribute grammars just by merging their attributes.

Offer Interpretations

It's time to move forward from conditional expressions to full values of type `Offer`, which represent the possible discounts in the Time Machine Store. As in the previous section, the examples will revolve around the initial definition of this data type, prior to adding extra type safety, in order to keep the code clean and concise.

Checking the Presents Rule

You've already seen several ways in which the Presents Rule of the offers (remember, the number of free presents in an offer may be limited) can be checked. Using strong typing, you looked at a way to count the maximum number of presents, but the implementation gives no clue about what presents are inside. The task in this section is to create a small attribute grammar that computes the largest possible set of presents that a single customer can get for free.

As in the previous section, the main data type is a straightforward translation from Haskell into the UUAGC syntax. The `data` declaration that will be used, and that contains the names given to the fields of each constructor, reads as follows:

```
data Offer a
  | Present  present :: {a}
  | PercentDiscount  discount :: Float
  | AbsoluteDiscount discount :: Float
  | Restrict products :: {[a]} inner :: (Offer {a})
  | From    from  :: Int inner :: (Offer {a})
  | Until   until :: Int inner :: (Offer {a})
  | Extend times :: Int inner :: (Offer {a})
  | Both     left :: (Offer {a}) right :: (Offer {a})
```

```
    | BetterOf left :: (Offer {a}) right :: (Offer {a})
    | If cond :: (Root {a}) then :: (Offer {a}) else :: (Offer {a})
```

```
deriving Offer : Show
```

The list of presents is something that is computed bottom-up, so it should be a synthesized attribute. In the code example, the attribute will be called `presents`. Here's the `attr` part of the grammar:

```
attr Offer
  syn presents :: {[a]}
```

The next step is to write the `sem` block that tells the preprocessor how to compute the value of that attribute. In most cases of the data type, presents are just accumulated from all the suboffers. However, there are two special cases to consider:

1. When you find a `Present` constructor, you know that the number of presents returned by that offer is a singleton list including the value in its parameter.

2. When a `Restrict` constructor is found, you must delete from the present list all those products that are not inside the restriction list.

In terms of code, this corresponds to the following `sem` block. Remember that any code written inside brackets will be copied unchanged into the generated Haskell code. The case of imports is treated specially by UUAGC; you should write `imports` before the block to ensure that the imports are treated according to Haskell rules. In this example, we bring the module `Data.List` into scope.

```
imports
{
import Data.List
}
```

```
sem Eq {a} => Offer
    | Present  lhs.presents = [@present]
    | Restrict lhs.presents = { @products `intersect` @inner.presents }
```

Now it is time to write the computation for the rest of the cases, which is the concatenation of the lists for those constructors with suboffers and the empty list for other basic combinators such as discounts. Luckily, UUAGC acknowledges that this is a common pattern and provides special syntax for that case, extending the built-in copy rule mechanism for synthesized attributes. With this syntax, you need to provide a function that merges the attribute from the children and a base case for those nodes with no children at all. In this case, the `attr` part of the grammar can be decorated with (++) as the function to merge and [ ] as the initial value, so it reads as follows:

```
attr Offer
  syn presents use {++} {[]} :: {[a]}
```

If you don't specify how to compute the value of the `presents` attribute, the rule that just copies it will no longer be applied. Instead, the preprocessor will use the operations in the `use` declaration.

If you look a bit closer at the operations specified, you'll notice that they are indeed the `Monoid` instance for lists. Remember the previous discussion about the relation between attribute grammars and monads? When using a synthesized attribute with `use`, you can see it being a `Writer`, where the `Monoid` instance of the attribute type is exactly defined by the operations in `use` (instead of the operation that just forgets about the first argument of `mappend`).

The Duration Rule could also be checked using an attribute grammar. Exercise 14-2 asks you to do so.

EXERCISE 14-2. THE DURATION RULE

Compute the maximum duration of an offer using an attribute grammar. The rules for doing so should be the same as in Chapter 13. Decorate your attributes with `use`, as shown in this section, to specify the common behavior of joining offers.

Showing an HTML Description

The last example for attribute grammars will show a description of an offer as HTML. This is an interesting example of how a grammar can be used not only to consume information but also to show that information in a new way. Furthermore, this grammar will show some subtleties related to attribute handling.

The generated HTML should have three parts:

1. A list of all the presents that you may get via the offer. This is done by reusing the presents attribute from the previous section.

2. A small table of contents that should show a small description of the first and second levels of the offer tree, in which item is a link to the full description.

3. Finally, the full description of the offer as a series of nested lists.

The markup for the full description will be stored in an html attribute and will be encoded using the blaze-html library presented in Chapter 12. Thus, to follow this section, you need to add blaze-html as a dependency. To obtain the final markup that comprises the three parts, the code will use the trick of adding an extra root data type, which will be called HtmlRoot. In the following code block, the imports related to blaze-html are gathered here:

```
imports
{
import Data.List
import Data.String
import qualified Text.Blaze.Html5 as H
import qualified Text.Blaze.Html5.Attributes as A
}

data HtmlRoot a
  | HtmlRoot root :: (Offer {a})
```

In addition, each node will keep its title and the list of titles of the children immediately below. In that way, the uppermost node will have the information needed for the table of contents. The main issue with building the table is generating links to the full description. For that, you need to assign a unique identifier to each node. However, this identifier behaves both as an inherited attribute and a synthesized attribute. This has the effect of *threading* the attribute *among siblings* of the same node in addition to going up and down. Figure 14-2 shows the flow of information of such an identifier through a basic offer.

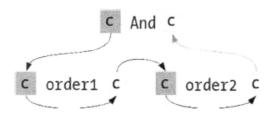

Figure 14-2. *Attribute c threaded through siblings of an And node*

These kinds of attributes that are both inherited and synthesized are known in the field of attribute grammars as *chained*. If you want to relate the behavior of chained attributes to a monad, it would be the State one in this case. The attribute can be seen as a value that changes throughout the exploration of the whole tree.

The declaration of such an attribute inside a UUAGC source file can be done by writing the same attribute named both as inh and syn. But to stress that an attribute is chained, UUAGC uses chn as its identifier. Following the general pattern in computer science for naming a source of unique numbers, this attribute will be called counter. The definition of all these attributes reads as follows:

```
attr Offer
  chn counter    :: Int
  syn title      :: String
  syn subtitles :: {[(String,Int)]}
  syn presents use {++} {[]} :: {[a]}  -- from previous section

attr HtmlRoot Offer
  syn html         :: {H.Html}
```

Obviously, now the attribute grammar should be executed starting on an HtmlRoot value. The corresponding describeOffer function reads as follows:

```
describeOffer :: (Eq a, Show a) => Offer a -> H.Html
describeOffer o
  = html_Syn_HtmlRoot $ wrap_HtmlRoot (sem_HtmlRoot $ HtmlRoot_HtmlRoot o)
                                      Inh_HtmlRoot
```

Let's first consider the computation of the counter attribute. At each node, the final value should be different from all their children and the value from its parent. You can achieve this by adding 1 to the value of the last child. For example, the value for basic combinators is just the one from the parent plus 1 and is expressed as follows:

```
sem Eq {a}, Show {a} => Offer
  | Present PercentDiscount AbsoluteDiscount  -- applies to all these
      lhs.counter = @lhs.counter + 1
```

Since `counter` is both an inherited attribute and a synthesized attribute, `lhs.counter` is referring to different attributes on each side. On the right side, `@lhs.counter` is the value that comes from the parent. On the left side, `lhs.counter` is the value that will be given back as an identifier for this node.

This code is not completely correct, though. If inside another attribute (e.g., when creating the HTML markup for that node) you refer to `lhs.counter`, you'll be referring to the value from the parent. But this is not what you need. Two children of the same parent would get the same `counter` value since they share the same parent. The solution is to save the new value in a *local* attribute, which works as a local variable inside a node. In that way, each node would retain its `ident` value, notwithstanding any change in its parent. You don't need to declare local attributes; use them only in a node, prefixing them by the `loc` keyword. In the example, I'm using a local attribute called `ident` to thread the value of the counter to other nodes while making a unique identifier available for other attributes:

```
  | Present PercentDiscount AbsoluteDiscount
      loc.ident   = @lhs.counter + 1
      lhs.counter = @loc.ident
```

For a constructor with more than one child, you should thread the attribute from one to the other. In this example, the `Both` and `BetterOf` constructors do so through their `left` and `right` children.

```
  | Both BetterOf
      left.counter  = @lhs.counter
      right.counter = @left.counter
      loc.ident     = @right.counter + 1
      lhs.counter   = @loc.ident
```

Think carefully about the rest of the threading for Exercise 14-3.

EXERCISE 14-3. THREADING THE COUNTER

Complete the computation of the counter and ident attributes for the Restrict, From, Until, Extend, and If constructors.

Using local attributes can help you write more concise code for computing the HTML markup. For example, you can divide the markup of each node into two parts: the HTML corresponding to the description of the constructor (htmlText) and the HTML corresponding to their children (htmlChild). Then, both attributes are joined in a single Html value, as shown here:

```
| Present PercentDiscount AbsoluteDiscount Restrict
  From Until Extend Both BetterOf If
    lhs.html = { do H.a H.! A.name
                            (fromString ("elt" ++ show @loc.ident))
                   $ H.toHtml @loc.htmlText
              @loc.htmlChild }
```

Note   You can write all the rules as they are shown, one below the other. UUAGC will take care of merging all the attribute computations for each constructor.

Now each of the constructors must give the value of those local attributes to build their HTML markup. This code is quite straightforward. As an example, the code that does so for the PercentDiscount and BetterOf constructors follows:

```
| PercentDiscount
    loc.htmlText  = show @discount ++ "% discount"
    loc.htmlChild = H.toHtml ""
| BetterOf
    loc.htmlText  = "Better of"
    loc.htmlChild = { H.ul $ do H.li @left.html
                                H.li @right.html }
```

I mentioned that each of the nodes should save the title and subtitle attributes for the final table of contents. The first one will be a simple String value, whereas the other should collect the titles and identifiers of each of the immediate children. For the constructors that are being tackled, it reads as follows:

```
| PercentDiscount
    lhs.title     = { "DISCOUNT: " ++ show @discount ++ "%" }
    lhs.subtitles = []
| BetterOf
    lhs.title     = { "BETTER OF" }
    lhs.subtitles = [ (@left.title,  @left.counter)
                    , (@right.title, @right.counter) ]
```

The rest of the constructors are left as an exercise to the reader, specifically as Exercise 14-4.

EXERCISE 14-4. BUILDING DESCRIPTIONS

Complete the computation of the htmlText, htmlChild, title, and subtitle attributes for the Present, AbsoluteDiscount, Restrict, From, Until, Extend, Both, and If constructors.

The final touch is to take all that information and build the whole Html value representing the description. The following code takes advantage of the encoding as a monad of blaze-html, using mapM_ to generate lists of elements. For the rest, the code is just generating the markup from the inner elements.

```
sem Eq {a}, Show {a} => HtmlRoot
  | HtmlRoot root.counter = 1
              lhs.html = {
                do H.h1 $ H.toHtml "Description of an offer"
                   H.h2 $ H.toHtml "Possible presents:"
                   H.ul $ mapM_ (\e -> H.li $ H.toHtml (show e)) @root.
                   presents
                   H.h2 $ H.toHtml "Main offer"
                   H.a H.! A.href (fromString ("#elt" ++ show @root.counter))
                         $ H.toHtml @root.title
                   H.ul $ mapM_ (\(s, e) -> H.li $ H.a H.! A.href
```

```
                              (fromString ("#elt" ++
                                 show e))
                           $ H.toHtml st)
                 @root.subtitles
        H.h2 $ H.toHtml "Complete offer"
        @root.html }
```

One important advantage of describing the generation of the markup as an attribute grammar is that you didn't have to take care of *ordering* the computation. UUAGC is able to find a sorting of the attributes, in the way that each of them needs only the previous ones to be computed. If this cannot be done, the preprocessor will emit a warning telling you that your attribute grammar is *circular*.

Programming with Data Types

Attribute grammars provide us a common language to describe operations performed over any data type. Any Haskell value can be seen as a tree and can be decorated using attributes which flow either top-down or bottom-up. But this is not the only way to look at data types in a uniform manner: *folds* provide a similar generalization. In fact, Haskell has powerful features to describe operations based on the shape of a data type; this is what we call *data type–generic* programming.

Origami Programming over Any Data Type

In Chapter 3, you saw how folds can be a powerful tool for understanding code on lists. The basic idea of a fold was to replace the (:) constructor with some function f and [] with some initial value i, as Figure 14-3 shows.

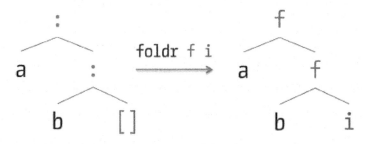

Figure 14-3. *Reminder of the behavior of foldr*

Interestingly, the notion of a fold can be defined for every Haskell data type. For each constructor, you supply a function that will "replace" it and then evaluate the resulting tree. In addition, the fold should call itself recursively in those places where the definition of the data type is also recursive. These generalized folds are also called *catamorphisms.*

For example, consider the simple language in the first section of this chapter, where the hard-coded Char parameter to AmountOf has been generalized to a type variable in the Expr type.

```
data Expr a = Plus  (Expr a) (Expr a)
            | Times (Expr a) (Expr a)
            | AmountOf a
```

In this case, a fold would have as parameters a function for Plus, other for Times, and finally another for AmountOf. As I stated before, the implementation should call each of those functions depending on the constructor of the value and have recursive calls in the places where the definition of Expr has Expr again as argument. With those ideas, the full code reads as follows:

```
foldExpr plusFn timesFn amountFn e =
  let f = foldExpr plusFn timesFn amountFn
  in case e of
       Plus  e1 e2 -> plusFn  (f e1) (f e2)
       Times e1 e2 -> timesFn (f e1) (f e2)
       AmountOf x  -> amountFn x
```

The interpretation shown in the first section can now be reworked as a fold like in the following code:

```
meaning :: Eq a => [a] -> Expr a -> Int
meaning s = foldExpr (+) (*) (\x -> length $ filter (==x) s)
```

The types of the parameters can be recovered from the data type definition. A specific fold will produce an element of some type b for each value. Thus, for each place where you may get a value from a recursive place, b must appear in its type. You have

510

also additional parameters for the information encoded in each constructor. With these guidelines, these types read as follows:

```
plusFn   :: b -> b -> b
timesFn  :: b -> b -> b
amountFn :: a -> b
```

When reading about folds or catamorphisms, you'll sometimes find the term *algebra*. A D-*algebra* for a data type D is just a tuple that contains all the functions required to perform a fold over that data structure. You can create a newtype for an algebra for Expr.

```
newtype ExprAlgebra a b = ExprAlgebra (b -> b -> b, b -> b -> b, a -> b)
```

Thus, a fold over a data type D can be seen as a function taking a D-algebra and a value of D and returning the appropriate value. Let's express the fold over Expr using algebra terms.

```
foldExpr' :: ExprAlgebra a b -> Expr a -> b
foldExpr' a@(ExprAlgebra (plusFn,timesFn,amountFn)) e =
  case e of
    Plus  e1 e2 -> plusFn  (foldExpr' a e1) (foldExpr' a e2)
    Times e1 e2 -> timesFn (foldExpr' a e1) (foldExpr' a e2)
    AmountOf x  -> amountFn x
```

You can practice those ideas by adding new constructors in Exercise 14-5.

EXERCISE 14-5. LARGER EXPRESSIONS

Extend the Expr data type with the constructors Minus and DividedBy and complete the corresponding fold functions for those new constructors.

Folds are closely related to attribute grammars. What you're doing with an attribute grammar is defining a specific algebra for your data type, an algebra that computes the value of the attributes. If you look at the generated Haskell code by UUAGC, you'll notice that there are some parts labeled as cata. These are the functions starting with sem_ that you used previously. What this function does is fold over the structure while expecting the initial inherited values you give with the function starting with wrap_.

Once you feel comfortable with these ideas, you can dive into other ways data types can be constructed and consumed in a generic fashion. For example, the notion of unfold (also called *anamorphism*) can also be generalized, and combinations of folds and unfold give rise to other interesting functions. A good library to look at is `recursion-schemes` by Edward A. Kmett. Knowing these patterns will help you when reusing a lot of code that is already written and that follows the same structure on different data types.

In addition to libraries, there's also a lot of information about how you can use this idea of folding over any data type to create more elegant code. "Origami programming" by Jeremy Gibbons was already mentioned in Chapter 3. "Functional Programming with Bananas, Lenses, Envelopes and Barbed Wire" by Erik Meijer, Maarten Fokkinga, and Ross Paterson discusses all these generalizations of folds and unfolds and shows how to use equational reasoning as you saw in Chapter 3 for lists, but over any data type.

Data Type–Generic Programming

You've already seen two kinds of polymorphism in Haskell. Parametric polymorphism treats values as black boxes, with no inspection of the content. Ad hoc polymorphism, on the other hand, allows you to treat each case separately.

But there's a third kind of polymorphism available in GHC, namely, *data type–generic programming* (or simply *generics*). In this setting, your functions must work for any data type, but you may depend on the structure of your `data` declaration. There are several libraries of doing this kind of programming available in Hackage. GHC integrates its own in the compiler in the `GHC.Generics` module, and this is the one I am going to discuss.

Data type–generic programming works in Haskell because data types are only made of three different building blocks:

- Fields, which contain one value of a certain type.

- Products, which put together several fields into a constructor. We use the symbol (`:*:`) to express products.

- Choice of constructors, for those data types which have more than one. In this case, we use the symbol (`:+:`).

Besides those, we need a way to describe constructors which have no data associated with them. One example of such a constructor is the empty list [ ]. In fact, let's look at the description of the type of lists of Booleans:

```
*> import GHC.Generics
*> :kind! Rep [Bool]
Rep [Bool] :: * -> *
= D1 ('MetaData "[]" "GHC.Types" "ghc-prim" 'False)
      (C1 ('MetaCons "[]" 'PrefixI 'False) U1
    :+: C1 ('MetaCons ":" ('InfixI 'LeftAssociative 9) 'False)
          (    S1 ('MetaSel 'Nothing ...) (Rec0 Bool)
          :*: S1 ('MetaSel 'Nothing ...) (Rec0 [Bool]))))
```

Apart from the building blocks mentioned earlier, this description – which has been automatically generated by GHC – also mentions *metadata*, like the name of the constructors. Those are visible with names D1, C1, and S1. If we strip those out, we obtain the core of the description of a list of Booleans, namely:

```
U1 :+: (Rec0 Bool) :*: (Rec0 [Bool])
```

You should read this as "you have two constructors, one with no fields, and one with two fields, the first one of type Bool and the second one of type [Bool]." For most data type–generic programming tasks, the name of the data type and the constructors is not used at all.

In order to work with the generic version of a data type, you need to convert it to its description, which is nothing else than the Rep t type family discussed earlier. There is one type class, Generic, which takes care of this:

```
instance Generic [a] where
  type Rep [a] = -- shown above
  from []      = L1 U1
  from (x:xs) = R1 (K1 x :*: K1 xs)
  to (L1 U1)              = []
  to (R1 (K1 x :*: K1 xs)) = x:xs
```

Note that the appearance of a choice of constructors results in the use of L1 and R1 to choose which constructor to take. The rest of the building blocks, (:*:), U1, and Rec0, have only one constructor, whose name coincides with that of the type, except for Rec0 which uses K1.

The question is: How can we define a generic operation by taking advantage of this uniform description of data types? The procedure is always similar: we have to define two type classes. The first one represents the operation itself, whereas the second one is used to disassemble the building blocks and derive the implementation. Furthermore, in the first type class, we specify how to derive a function automatically using the second one.

Because code is worth a thousand words, let's define one operation in a generic fashion. A call to getall with a given type should return the values of all the fields of that type in the data structure. For example:

```
* GHC.Generics> getall (Proxy :: Proxy Int) (Maybe 3 :: Maybe Int)
[3]
```

Note   A proxy is a dummy value whose only purpose is to fix a type for the compiler. They are defined in the Data.Proxy module.

The first step, as discussed earlier, is to introduce a type class for the operation and another for the building blocks:

```
{-# LANGUAGE KindSignatures #-}
{-# LANGUAGE MultiParamTypeClasses #-}

class GetAll t a where
  getall :: Proxy t -> a -> [t]

class GGetAll t (f :: * -> *) where
  ggetall :: Proxy t -> f x -> [t]
```

As you can see, they look fairly similar, except for the *kind* of the second argument. In the GHC.Generics module, all the building blocks have a kind * -> *. As a result, the second argument to ggetall must be given an additional type argument, so it reads f x instead of simply f.

Now the next step is to define how the ggetall function is implemented for each of the building blocks of a data type. In most cases, these instances call each other recursively, until they get to U1 or Rec0, where we need to do the real work. In our case, the choice of constructors simply recurs to the chosen branch, products concatenate the values from their components, and fieldless constructors U1 add no values to the mix.

```
{-# LANGUAGE FlexibleInstances #-}
{-# LANGUAGE TypeOperators #-}

instance (GGetAll t f, GGetAll t g) => GGetAll t (f :+: g) where
  ggetall p (L1 x) = ggetall p x
  ggetall p (R1 y) = ggetall p y

instance (GGetAll t f, GGetAll t g) => GGetAll t (f :*: g) where
  ggetall p (x :*: y) = ggetall p x ++ ggetall p y

instance GGetAll t U1 where
  ggetall p U1 = []
```

The case of fields follows a similar pattern in all data type–generic constructors. We always call the nongeneric version of the type class, GetAll in this case, from the generic version applied to Rec0. This is not enough in this case, because without further information we would never reach any real field. For that reason, we add two instances for the nongeneric type class. The first one says that each type t contains exactly one value of type t. The other one says that if the types are different, by default there are no values of the chosen type. This instance is marked as *overlappable*, because it just works as a catch-all instance; in some cases like obtaining the Ints from an [Int], we shall override that default.

```
instance (GetAll t s) => GGetAll t (Rec0 s) where
  ggetall p (K1 x) = getall p x
instance {-# OVERLAPS #-} GetAll t t where
  getall p x = [x]
instance {-# OVERLAPPABLE #-} GetAll t s where
  getall p x = []
```

Since the representations also contain metadata about the names of the data type, constructors, and fields, we have one last case to handle. Metadata is represented uniformly via the M1 building block; we do not need three different instances. It is quite common to not do anything interesting in these instances, apart from calling the generic operation recursively.

```
instance (GGetAll t f) => GGetAll t (M1 v i f) where
  ggetall p (M1 x) = ggetall p x
```

The last step is to declare how to obtain the implementation of the nongeneric type class from the building blocks of the generic one. This is done via a *default signature*. These are like default implementations, but with a constraint over the way in which the code can be derived. The pattern is once again very similar for every generic operation: you always require a Generic instance and an instance of the generic type class for the description of the type.

```
{-# LANGUAGE DefaultSignatures #-}

class GetAll t a where
  getall :: Proxy t -> a -> [t]
  default getall :: (Generic a, GGetAll t (Rep a)) => Proxy t -> a -> [t]
  getall p = ggetall p . from
```

If you have a type for which you want to implement getall, you don't need to write the code any more. Just derive its Generic instance, which is done automatically by the compiler, and ask it to implement the GetAll type class:

```
{-# LANGUAGE DeriveGeneric #-}

data Tree a = Node a | Branch (Tree a) (Tree a)
            deriving (Show, Eq, Generic)

instance GetAll a (Tree a)   -- look ma, no code!
```

This was a very fast-paced introduction to data type–generic programming, with the aim for you to taste its flavor. If you want to dive into it, I recommend looking at the lecture notes called "Applying Type-Level and Generic Programming in Haskell" by Andres Löh.

Summary

This chapter introduced attribute grammars as a way to give interpretations to a DSL encoded as a Haskell data type.

- You delved into the general idea of *attributing* a tree whose nodes are the constructors of a specific Haskell data type.

- Three kinds of *attributes* were distinguished: *synthesized* (bottom-up), *inherited* (top-down), and *chained* (threaded among siblings).

- Monads are related to attribute grammars: `Reader` corresponds to inherited attributes, `Writer` to synthesized attributes, and `State` to chained attributes.

- You learned how to configure and use the *Utrecht University Attribute Grammar Compiler* to preprocess your attribute grammars into Haskell code.

- UUAGC provides many facilities for writing concise attribute grammars. In this chapter, you became familiar with use *declarations* and *local attributes*.

- The idea of *fold* (or *catamorphism*) was generalized from lists to any possible Haskell data type.

- Finally, you have seen how to define operations which depend on the structure of the data type using `GHC.Generics`.

PART V

Engineering the Store

CHAPTER 15

Documenting, Testing, and Verifying

At this point, you know many of the features and intricacies of the Haskell language and many of its libraries. This chapter won't teach you any more about the language but rather will focus on some tools that help you in the process of coding libraries and applications. These tools support good engineering practices within Haskell.

An important and often overlooked practice as you program is to write *good documentation* for the source. Even though Haskell is a high-level language, there's always room for documenting the purpose of each data type and function in your modules. *Haddock* is bundled with the Haskell Platform, and it creates beautiful documentation pages from special comments in your code.

The main set of tools I will cover is related to *testing*. Automatically testing your code ensures that any change in the code does not affect the behavior that it should have. Programmers today see unit testing as an essential activity, and you will learn how to create unit tests in Haskell with *HUnit*.

Haskell was the first language to support *randomized testing* in addition to unit testing, with its *QuickCheck* library. This form of testing generates random calls to your functions and ensures that certain properties of the output are satisfied, freeing the tester from the task of writing hundreds of test cases. Another tool called *SmallCheck* builds on this idea but performs *exhaustive testing*. This means a certain piece of code is called not with random inputs but with all possible inputs up to a size limit.

Testing can show that a bug exists in your implementation but testing along does not give you complete assurance of their absence. The next step is to *formally verify* that the implementation satisfies the properties that are requested. You'll get a glimpse of how this can be done using *LiquidHaskell*, an extension of Haskell with refinement types.

© Alejandro Serrano Mena 2022
A. Serrano Mena, *Practical Haskell*, https://doi.org/10.1007/978-1-4842-8581-7_15

Documenting Binary Trees with Haddock

Binary trees, like those in Chapter 4, are going to be the working example throughout this chapter. As a reminder, the following is the definition of the `BinaryTree` data type. The constructors refer either to a leaf or to a node that handles some inner information on it. In addition, there are a couple of tree functions.

```
data BinaryTree a = Leaf
                  | Node a (BinaryTree a) (BinaryTree a)
                  deriving (Show, Eq)

treeInsert :: Ord a => a -> BinaryTree a -> BinaryTree a
treeInsert x Leaf = Node x Leaf Leaf
treeInsert x (Node y l r) | x <= y      = Node y (treeInsert x l) r
                          | otherwise = Node y l (treeInsert x r)

treeMerge :: Ord a => BinaryTree a -> BinaryTree a -> BinaryTree a
treeMerge t Leaf        = t
treeMerge t (Node x l r) = treeInsert x $ treeMerge (treeMerge t l) r
```

Even without any extra comments, you can generate a summary of the modules in the package by running `cabal haddock` or `stack haddock` in the root of your project. A set of HTML pages will be created in the `dist/doc/html` folder in your package if using Cabal or `.stack-work/install` if using Stack. If you open them, you'll see the documentation in the same format in which the documentation from Hackage is presented. However, the information there is rough: only a list of modules and, inside each module, a list of all the definitions. It would be nice to incorporate comments and examples into each of the functions, data types, and type classes.

The way you can convey extra information to be included in those HTML pages is via *documentation comments*. Documentation comments are written in the same file where the code is written, which helps you keep both code and documentation in sync. They follow the same syntax as regular comments, but they start with a special marker. This idea is found in other documentation systems such as Javadoc and Doxygen.

The marker in the comment changes depending on whether you want to include the documentation of an element before or after the declaration. If you want to write the documentation and then the element, you will mark that documentation with |; if instead you want to include the documentation after the element, start your comment with ^. Comments beginning with | are used normally for documenting data types, functions, and type classes, whereas ^ is more often found while discussing constructors and function arguments. As an example, you can document the BinaryTree type as follows:

```
-- | A typical binary tree
data BinaryTree a = Node a (BinaryTree a) (BinaryTree a) -- ^Inner nodes
                  | Leaf                                  -- ^Leaves
                  deriving (Eq, Show)
```

Figure 15-1 shows how the comments here manifest themselves in the HTML page created by the Haddock tool.

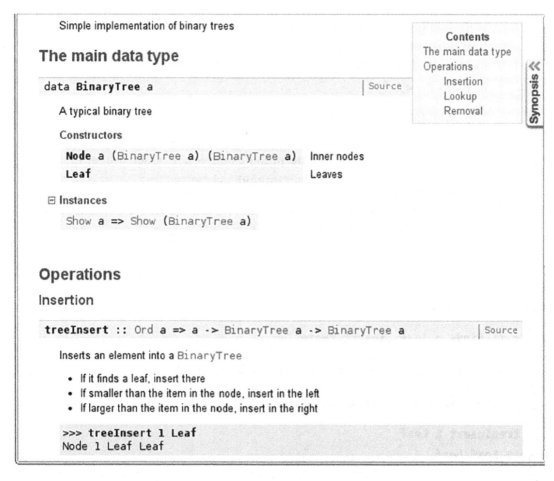

Figure 15-1. *BinaryTree documentation generated by Haddock*

Caution   Haskell single-line comments start with - - followed by a space. You should respect this syntax in documentation comments and use a space between - - and either | or ^, as the example shows.

Haddock has a rich syntax for writing the documentation:

- If you refer to other declarations by writing it in single quotes, Haddock will generate a link to that place. This functionality is also available for linking to modules; in that case, you need to write its name in double quotes.

- Unnumbered lists are declared by prefixing each of the items by *. In the case of numbered lists, you can choose between writing n. or (n) for the nth element. Be aware that each item should be surrounded by blank lines.

- You can introduce pieces of code by prefixing each line with >. Additionally, Haddock supports the declaration of properties, which are prefixed by prop>, and of interpreter examples, in which the input is written after >>> and the output immediately after.

Here, you can see an example of documentation for the treeInsert function. Notice that the comments are written in multiple-line style. Again, you can see the effect of these comments in Figure 15-1.

```
{-|
Inserts an element into a 'BinaryTree'

 * If it finds a leaf, insert there

 * If smaller than the item in the node, insert in the left

 * If larger than the item in the node, insert in the right

>>> treeInsert 1 Leaf
Node 1 Leaf Leaf
-}
treeInsert :: Ord a => a -> BinaryTree a -> BinaryTree a
```

```
treeInsert x Leaf = Node x Leaf Leaf
treeInsert x (Node y l r) | x <= y      = Node y (treeInsert x l) r
                          | otherwise = Node y l (treeInsert x r)
```

Another interesting feature of Haddock is the ability to organize the declarations in your code and to show its documentation divided into sections. The only requirement is that you must use an explicit export list. This is a good programming practice anyway, so it shouldn't put any extra burden on you. In the list of exports, you can include a documentation comment starting with * to indicate that a new section starts at that point, or you can use ** for a subsection. Here's a possible declaration list for a full-blown binary tree implementation:

```
-- | Simple implementation of binary trees
module Chapter15.BinaryTree (
  -- * The main data type
  BinaryTree(..),
  -- * Operations
  -- ** Insertion
  treeInsert, treeMerge,
  -- ** Lookup
  treeFind, treeFindMin,
  -- ** Removal
  treeDelete
) where
```

If you look carefully at Figure 15-1, you will notice some hyperlinks labeled as Source. The target of each of those links is the definition of that element in a colored version of your source. You can get them in your own documentation by running cabal haddock --hyperlink-source instead of plain cabal haddock. Notice that you need to have the package hscolour in your system for this feature to work.

HLINT

A Haskell compiler checks whether your source code complies with the syntax and semantics of the language. However, there are cases where your code is correct but it's not easy to read or contains some fragment that is usually seen as confusing and may lead to errors in the future. *HLint* is a tool that suggests changes to Haskell source in order to make the code much clearer.

You can get HLint onto your system by the usual procedure of running `cabal install hlint` on the command line. Then you can run `hlint <source file>` and get a list of suggestions. For example, say you change the third line of `treeInsert` to read as follows:

```
treeInsert x (Node y l r) | (x <= y) = Node y (treeInsert x l) r
```

If you run HLint, the following change will be suggested:

```
src/Chapter15/BinaryTree.hs:39:29: Warning: Redundant bracket
Found:
  (x <= y)
Why not:
  x <= y
```

HLint covers many style issues in code. HLint is also aware of laziness, so it ensures that your code never evaluates more – which could have a negative performance impact – when suggesting a change. Furthermore, HLint can apply the suggestions directly to your code.

Unit Testing with HUnit

Unit testing is a methodology for checking that your functions perform their work as intended. Following these methods, the programmer writes a set of test cases, with each of them executing a piece of code and describing the expected result. These tests can be run at the developer's discretion or can be used to check automatically that code that was working fine doesn't break after changes (this is called *regression testing*).

To provide a unified interface to the various testing methods available, the Haskell community has created several *test frameworks*. In this section, I'll introduce the Tasty library, but many others are available. HTF, `test-framework`, and Hspec are other interesting options. The good news is that any of these test frameworks can be integrated into your Cabal project and run through the same command-line option.

Declaring Tests in Cabal

In principle, you could create the application that runs your tests as a mere executable in your package. However, Cabal embodies the idea of tests in its core and has special support for them. In this section, you'll learn how to add a test executable to your Cabal project.

Inside a Cabal file, a test is defined in its own stanza, like library and executable parts were. Thus, the declaration of a test inside the project file is headed by test-suite followed by the name of the test suite. The key field to include in that stanza is the type one. Cabal has extensible support for different kinds of test providers that can run the tests in the project in different ways.

The focus in this section will be on type being equal to exitcode-stdio-1.0, which is the best-supported option at the moment of writing. By specifying that test provider, you declare to Cabal that your tests should be compiled as an executable file. The file will run to execute the tests and will tell Cabal whether the tests were successful via its exit code. The good news is that all the test frameworks in Hackage are knowledgeable about this way of running them and make it easy to integrate them as a Cabal test.

The rest of the test-suite stanza, when type is exitcode-stdio-1.0, is equal to the definition of a regular executable. As an example, here's the stanza corresponding to the tests of the current chapter, which has the Tasty framework as a dependency, along with the packages needed to run tests from HUnit, QuickCheck, and SmallCheck within Tasty:

```
test-suite Tasty
  type:              exitcode-stdio-1.0
  build-depends:     base >= 4, tasty, tasty-hunit,
                     tasty-quickcheck, tasty-smallcheck
  hs-source-dirs:    test
  main-is:           Tasty.hs
  default-language:  Haskell2010
```

Notice that I've declared that the source files for my tests will reside in the test directory. It's a good practice to keep source code and tests in different folders to make it easier to find the place where you include new functionality or new checks of behavior.

There's one final quirk to consider. Often, you'll need to access the functions declared in your library stanza inside a test-suite one. One possibility is to reference the source folder also in your test-suite stanza. However, this causes double compiles (the same file has to be compiled in both the library and test-suite stanzas) and doesn't delimit the responsibility of this stanza. Instead, Cabal supports having a test suite or executable in a Cabal project depend on its library part. To declare this dependency, just add the name of the package in the corresponding build-depends list. For example, in the previous case, you'll get the following:

```
build-depends:    base >= 4, tasty, tasty-hunit,
                  tasty-quickcheck, tasty-smallcheck,
                  chapter15
```

Now you're ready to run the tests that you'll declare in the next section through the cabal or stack command-line tools. This functionality is quite useful because it centralizes all the project information in a single place.

Writing Unit Tests

First, you need to create the test/Tasty.hs file that the stanza specifies as the main file. This file should contain a module named Main. The main executable file of a stanza is the only exception to the rule of naming both the file and the module with the same identifier, making it easier to create projects with more than one executable or test. The examples will use the Tasty test framework and the HUnit tool, so you should import the corresponding modules. The following skeleton will be the base for the rest of the section:

```
module Main where

import Test.Tasty
import Test.Tasty.HUnit as HU
```

A test suite in Tasty is composed of basic *test cases* that you can later group to get a hierarchical organization. Test cases are different depending on the testing tool you would like to use (HUnit, QuickCheck, or SmallCheck). In the case of HUnit, a test case is defined by the testCase function, which takes as arguments a name and an *assertion*, which encodes the specific functionality to be checked. For example, the following test case checks that the result equality of inserting 1 into an empty tree is the expected one using the HUnit combinatory assertEqual.

```
import Chapter15.BinaryTree

hunitTestInsertOnLeaf :: TestTree
hunitTestInsertOnLeaf = HU.testCase "Insert 'a' on empty tree" $
  assertEqual "Insertion is wrong"
              (treeInsert 'a' Leaf) (Node 'a' Leaf Leaf)
```

Note   TestTree is one of the types used in the Tasty framework. It's not related to the binary trees you've been using as examples throughout the chapter.

As discussed, Tasty allows a hierarchical organization of the test cases into test groups. A test group is defined via the testGroup function, which needs to be given a name for the group and a list of elements. Those elements can be nested groups or basic test cases. Here's an example of an organization of tests:

```
allTests :: TestTree
allTests = testGroup "Tasty Tests" [
    testGroup "HUnit Tests" [ hunitTestInsertOnLeaf ]
  ]
```

In this case, there's a top-level group called "Tasty Tests" that has another group called "HUnit Tests" inside. This nested group is where the code puts the test case defined previously.

There's one last step before being able to run the tests. Since you declared that an executable will be responsible for automatically executing them, you need to provide a main entry point. The good news is that Tasty includes a simple function for this task, which you can include in all your tests. You just need to specify the test case or test group that will be run to defaultMain, as follows:

```
main :: IO ()
main = defaultMain allTests
```

It's time to execute this first test. It is as easy as running cabal test or stack test, depending on your choice of build tool. In either case, the test suite will be executed, and the main results are shown on the screen.

```
$ cabal test
```

```
Running 1 test suites...
Test suite Tasty: RUNNING...
Test suite Tasty: PASS
Test suite logged to: dist/test/chapter15-0.1-Tasty.log
1 of 1 test suites (1 of 1 test cases) passed.
```

If you now go to the log file shown in the message, you can see a more detailed explanation of the test suite run.

```
Tasty Tests
  HUnit Tests
    Insert 1 on empty tree: OK
```

As you can see, the file shows the hierarchical structure declared in the source file.

In addition to "long" combinators such as assertEqual, HUnit includes infix combinators that allow a more concise expression of expected equality. These are (@?=) and (@=?). Both operators check whether the elements at each side are equal. The difference is in where one writes the value to check and where the value is known to be correct. The rule of thumb is that the former should be written next to the ? sign, and the latter (the expected value) should be written next to the = sign. Thus, the previous example could have also been written in the following two forms. Remember that the expression with treeInsert is the one to check, so it should be near the ? sign.

```
hunitTestInsertOnLeaf' = HU.testCase "Insert 'a' on empty tree" $
  treeInsert 'a' Leaf HU.@?= Node 'a' Leaf Leaf
hunitTestInsertOnLeaf" = HU.testCase "Insert 'a' on empty tree" $
  Node 'a' Leaf Leaf HU.@=? treeInsert 'a' Leaf
```

Equality is the most common check in unit tests, but HUnit also allows you to check a Boolean property on the result. For example, you could check that after inserting an item in the tree, that item can be found. In this case, let's create a template for several unit tests by creating a function that returns a test case given an original tree and the item to insert.

```
import Data.Maybe

hunitTestInsertFind :: Ord a => a -> BinaryTree a -> TestTree
hunitTestInsertFind e t = HU.testCase "Insert can be found" $
  assertBool "Cannot find element" (isJust $ treeFind e $ treeInsert e t)
```

As in the previous case, HUnit has a more concise version of the `assertBool` combinator, namely, (@?).

```
hunitTestInsertFind' e t = HU.testCase "Insert can be found" $
  (isJust $ treeFind e $ treeInsert e t) HU.@? "Cannot find element"
```

Now you can add several unit tests to your list by providing different parameters to this template.

```
allTests = testGroup "Tasty Tests" [
    testGroup "HUnit Tests" [
      hunitTestInsertOnLeaf
    , hunitTestInsertFind 'b' Leaf
    , hunitTestInsertFind 'c' (Node 'd' Leaf Leaf)
    ]
  ]
```

HUnit is a small library, but it embodies the most common uses of unit testing. In Exercise 15-1, you will write some extra tests to check the implementation of binary trees. Following the exercise, you will learn a little about a framework named Hspec.

EXERCISE 15-1. UNIT TESTING BINARY TREES

Write test cases to check that once you add an element to a binary tree, the size (the number of internal nodes) is increased by 1. Additionally, write test cases to check that deleting an element indeed removes it from the binary tree.

HSPEC

In this chapter, the test framework used to integrate all the tests is Tasty. However, as mentioned earlier, several other test frameworks are available in Hackage. Hspec is one of them and is targeted at teams that use the Behavior-Driven Development (BDD) methodology. Here's an example of the usage:

```
import Data.Maybe
import Test.Hspec
import Test.HUnit
```

```
main = hspec $ do
  describe "Insertion in binary tree" $ do
    it "Inserts correctly 1 in empty tree" $
      treeInsert 1 Leaf @?= Node 1 Leaf Leaf
    it "Finds 1 after inserting it on a tree" $
      isJust $ treeFind 1 $ treeInsert 1 (Node 2 Leaf Leaf)
    it "Gets the minimum correctly" $
      pendingWith "Needs to be implemented"
```

As you can see, Hspec embodies a more textual style for describing tests. The aim is to be closer to the language used in the specification phase, making it easier to write the tests that check that a further implementation is correct.

Randomized Testing with QuickCheck

Unit testing is the most common approach to checking that your implementation satisfies the requirements. However, unit testing imposes quite a big load of work. For each requirement, you need to create several test cases, which you must ensure cover a big enough number of possible scenarios. Typically, you include test cases for extreme values, empty collections, invalid data, and so on.

Instead of having to think about all this by yourself, it would be great if you could express your specifications at a higher level and then test whether those properties hold for your program. Haskell's usage of higher-order functions makes it easy to express those properties. For example, the property "reversing a list twice is the same as leaving it as is" can be written as reverse . reverse = id. The bad news is that doing so automatically is a task that's impossible to achieve for every single property in the wild (but you'll see in the next section how formal verification can help you in those cases where an entire proof of correctness is possible).

QuickCheck tries to bring these two worlds together. Using this library, you express how your program should behave in the form of high-level properties. Then, the tool creates a lot of random values that your program is tested against. If you use a sufficiently large set of tests (hundreds or thousands), your confidence in that property holding is increased. Furthermore, QuickCheck includes a *shrinking* component that is used when a value that doesn't satisfy your specification is found. Its task is trying to make that value as small as possible, helping you in reproducing and tracking the source of the bug.

Testing List Properties

Let's start by testing some simple properties of list functions. In particular, let's focus on the reverse function, which builds a list in the opposite order. The initial implementation will include a small error so you can see how Tasty shows the problems of a failing QuickCheck test.

```
reverse' :: [a] -> [a]
reverse' []      = []
reverse' [x]     = [x, x]
reverse' (x:xs) = reverse' xs ++ [x]
```

For the first property, you may want to check that the length of a list is respected by reversing it (of course, this is false in this example). Here's the corresponding definition for that QuickCheck property:

```
{-# LANGUAGE ScopedTypeVariables #-}

import Test.Tasty.QuickCheck as QC

reverseTests :: TestTree
reverseTests = testGroup "Tests over reverse"
  [ QC.testProperty "reverse respects length" $
     \(lst :: [Integer]) -> length (reverse' lst) == length lst ]
```

As you can see, the definition starts similarly to an HUnit test. You call the testProperty function and give a name to the property. Then, you define the body of the property as a function, which should hold for every possible value of the arguments of that function. In other words, you can think of the property as having "for all" before each of the arguments to the body function.

Note   In some cases, you will need to restrict the types of the arguments to QuickCheck properties. The reason is that it's not possible to create random values for every possible type in Haskell. For example, you cannot generate a list of functions. Thus, in the example, the code works only for lists of integers, even though the reverse' function is applicable to any kind of list.

If you add reverseTest to the list of Tasty tests that was called allTests and then build and run the new set of tests, you should get an error message.

```
Test suite Tasty: RUNNING...
Tasty Tests
  Tests over reverse
    reverse respects length: FAIL
      *** Failed! Falsifiable (after 3 tests and 3 shrinks):
    [0]
```

The message is telling you that after trying three times, it was able to find an example where the property does not hold (although given that QuickCheck tests in a random fashion, the number in the counterexample may be different in your case). Then, it shrank the list until it made the example small. Indeed, a singleton list is the smallest example where the reverse' function fails.

Test your understanding of QuickCheck by doing Exercise 15-2.

EXERCISE 15-2. QUICKCHECKING REVERSE

Add more QuickCheck properties on the reverse' function that was defined at the beginning of the section. For example, applying it twice returns the original result (reverse' . reverse' == id), or the head of the list is the last element of the reversed list.

After checking that the properties do not hold for the initial implementation, change the code to be correct. Does the new version pass all the tests?

Testing Binary Tree Properties

Testing lists is interesting, but in most of the cases, you are going to be creating tests of your own data types. To create such tests on a given type, you must provide QuickCheck with a *generator* of random values of that type. You do so by creating an instance of the Gen type class, which you do by implementing the arbitrary function. You can use several tools to generate random values of binary trees:

- You can generate values of other data types by calling their corresponding Gen instance. In the case of binary trees, this should be done for the elements in the nodes.

- You can make a random choice between several generators via the oneof function, which takes a list of them and at runtime gives back one of the specified generators. A more refined version of oneof is frequency, which in addition to the possible outcomes includes a relative frequency in which each generator should appear. You'll see how to use this latter function to decide at each point whether to generate a node or a leaf of the tree.

- If you need your values to satisfy a certain condition, you can add a call to suchThat. This function will make sure that the given predicate holds for the random values.

One of the most important properties of a random generator is that it should *stop* and produce a value at some point. QuickCheck refines that idea and asks the generators to give back values of a certain *maximum size*. Think of the size as some intrinsic measure of "how big" a value is. The length of a list, the number of leaves in a tree, and the absolute value of an integer are some examples of these sizes. If your data type admits this idea, you can get the information of the wanted size via the sized QuickCheck function.

For the working example, the idea of size makes sense: it's the maximum number of levels that the tree may have. The strategy for generating random trees to satisfy this property is to choose between creating a leaf or a node with a decreasing probability for the second of those choices. If the generation reaches the point in which the size of the tree must be 0, it just returns a Leaf. Here's the translation of this idea into code:

```
instance Arbitrary a => Arbitrary (BinaryTree a) where
  arbitrary = sized $ \n ->
    if (n == 0)
       then return Leaf
       else frequency [(1, return Leaf),
                        (n, resize (n-1) arbitrary)]
```

If you look at the Gen type class, you'll notice another function, which has the responsibility of shrinking a value into smaller parts. For a given value, shrink should return the list of those smaller pieces that should be checked. In the case of binary trees, the natural choices are the subtrees of a given tree, as this code shows:

```
shrink Leaf          = []
shrink (Node _ l r) = [l, r]
```

Armed with this instance, you can test properties of binary trees. After inserting an item, let's check that it can be found in the tree. The declaration of that test is the following:

```
qcTestInsert :: TestTree
qcTestInsert = QC.testProperty "insert => you will find it" $
  \(n :: Int) t -> treeFind n (treeInsert n t) == Just n
```

Another possible test is checking that if you insert and delete an element from a tree, you can no longer find that element. Here, it is in QuickCheck terms:

```
qcTestDelete = QC.testProperty "delete => not find it" $
  \(n :: Int) t -> (treeFind n $ treeDelete n $ treeInsert n t) == Nothing
```

However, if you think about it, this is not a correct property to check. It may be the case that the tree t did have a copy of the element n, so inserting and deleting the item will leave that initial copy. Thus, the result of treeFind will not be Nothing, but Just n.

The solution is telling QuickCheck that the random items to test need to fulfill some precondition (in this case, that it doesn't contain the number n initially). This is done via the (==>) combinator, which takes as arguments the Boolean condition to satisfy and the actual property body. Here's an example:

```
qcTestDelete = QC.testProperty "delete => not find it" $
  \(n :: Int) t ->
     (treeFind n t == Nothing) QC.==>
     (treeFind n $ treeDelete n $ treeInsert n t) == Nothing
```

These examples show how QuickCheck allows you to get a higher-level view on the tests. Instead of focusing on single test cases, you declare properties, which are closer to the original specification.

SMALLCHECK

QuickCheck uses random data to test properties of your code. SmallCheck follows a similar spirit, but instead of creating random values, it tests properties with every possible value from a set. For example, you could check the `reverse . reverse == id` property on every list up to a certain length.

The public interface of SmallCheck is almost the same as that of QuickCheck. It's also integrated in almost every Haskell test framework, including Tasty and Hspec.

Formal Verification with LiquidHaskell

Testing is a very useful tool to gain confidence about your code performing correctly. But even when using randomized testing, your code only runs on a *subset* of all possible inputs. There are other techniques which give you full guarantees over your code; these are collectively known as *formal verification*. Although these techniques differ in many conceptual and technical aspects, in all cases the workflow consists on describing the intention of your code in some formal language and then running some tool (maybe completely automatic, maybe with some human intervention) to verify that the code complies with that specification.

The type system in Haskell can be seen as a form of formal verification, in which types are the formal language and the compiler automatically checks for compliance. Stronger type systems, like dependent types, allow for more invariants to be expressed and checked. In this section, we are going to introduce *LiquidHaskell*, which extends regular Haskell with *refinement types*. In a nutshell, a refinement type is the combination of a type (in the usual sense) with a predicate over the values. For example, "integers which are greater than 0" combines the type "integer" with the predicate "greater than 0." The main selling point of LiquidHaskell is that you do not need to learn other languages to implement your code, only a refined version of types to describe your specification.

INSTALLING Z3

To perform its duty, LiquidHaskell requires Z3, a so-called SMT solver, which is used internally to verify the assertions. At the moment of writing, you can get binaries for Z3 at `https://github.com/Z3Prover/z3/releases`. Regardless of the operating system, `z3` needs to be on your PATH.

LiquidHaskell readily integrates with the plug-in system in GHC, which means that you only need to slightly change the stanza where you want verification to happen. In particular, you need to replace base with `liquid-base` in your dependencies, add the tool and Prelude packages, and indicate that you want to use the LiquidHaskell plug-in.

```
build-depends: liquidhaskell, liquid-base, liquid-prelude
ghc-options:   -fplugin=LiquidHaskell
```

As an example of usage of LiquidHaskell, we are going to verify some properties of the BinaryTree type introduced in the Haddock section (which I assume you have imported or copied verbatim from that section). Let's start with a simple treeSize function, which gives you the number of nodes in the tree. The code is straightforward; the interesting part is the annotations between {-@ and @-}. Those annotations, in addition to your code, are the input to LiquidHaskell. The most important one is the second one, which *refines* the type signature of treeSize. In particular, it states that the output of the function is not any integer, but an integer greater or equal to 0. The refined type Nat is defined in LiquidHaskell's standard library.

```
{-@ LIQUID "--no-termination" @-}

import Language.Haskell.Liquid.Prelude

{-@ treeSize :: BinaryTree a -> Nat @-}
treeSize :: BinaryTree a -> Int
treeSize Leaf         = 0
treeSize (Node _ l r) = 1 + treeSize l + treeSize r
```

Since you've configured the plug-in, building this project now also calls LiquidHaskell. If everything is fine, a nice SAFE message is reported. You can try to break this invariant and see how LiquidHaskell no longer accepts the code.

Note   The other annotation instructs LiquidHaskell for not checking whether your functions terminate for all inputs. This is another of the interesting features of LiquidHaskell (in fact, very few of your functions should loop indefinitely), but we shall not focus on it.

Now that `treeSize` has been accepted by LiquidHaskell, we can use it to describe a certain property of binary trees, namely, their size. To instruct the verifier to do so, we need to declare it as a *measure*. Not every function can be used as a measure, but when that is possible the workflow becomes easier. For the rest of the cases, LiquidHaskell supports *reflection* of functions.

```
{-@ measure treeSize @-}
```

Going back to our example in the Haddock section, here is an annotation for the `treeInsert` function we defined back there, along with an incorrect implementation. The annotation declares that if you insert a value x on a binary tree v, the size of the resulting tree w is one more than that of v. As you can see here, the general syntax of a refinement type is {name: Type | predicate}.

```
{-@ treeInsert :: x: a -> v: BinaryTree a
               -> {w: BinaryTree a | treeSize w = treeSize v + 1} @-}
treeInsert :: Ord a => a -> BinaryTree a -> BinaryTree a
treeInsert x Leaf = Node x Leaf Leaf
treeInsert x (Node y l r) | x <= y    = Node y l r
                          | otherwise = Node y l (treeInsert y r)
```

If you run LiquidHaskell over this code, you get the following error message:

```
error: Liquid Type Mismatch

    The inferred type
      VV : {v : (BinaryTree a) | treeSize v == (1 + treeSize l) + treeSize r
                              && treeSize v >= 0}

    is not a subtype of the required type
      VV : {VV : (BinaryTree a) | treeSize VV == treeSize ?a + 1}

24 |    | x <= y    = Node y l r
           ^^^^^^^^^^
```

This error message tells you that the second branch of the function does not obey its specification. Indeed, the size of the tree is not increased in that case.

Caution   One of the weak points of LiquidHaskell is the poor explanations given whenever the specification is not followed. In most cases, you just get a pair of expected vs. actual refinement types, but no indication of why the latter is not good enough.

That bug is not the only one present in the code (can you find it before I tell you where it is?). However, the second bug does not relate to the size of the binary trees, but about the elements which are present. To keep track of that property, we define a new function treeElements and declare it as an additional measure.

```
import Data.Set

{-@ measure treeElements @-}
treeElements :: (Ord a) => Tree a -> Set a
treeElements Empty        = empty
treeElements (Node x l r) = singleton x `union`
                              treeElements l `union` treeElements r
```

The second step is to refine the signature to introduce a new property that the function must obey. If you insert a value x in the tree v, regardless of what happens, the value x should be present in the output tree w.

```
{-@ treeInsert :: x: a -> v: BinaryTree a
                -> {w: BinaryTree a | treeSize w = treeSize v + 1
                                    && member x (treeElements w) } @-}
```

The error message has been left out for conciseness, but it points directly toward the third equation in treeInsert. Indeed, if you read instead Node y (treeInsert x l) r, in the original version the value x is lost if it is greater than y.

Describing Binary Search Trees

In the previous section, we have been treating binary trees as binary *search* trees in an implicit way. By using treeInsert, you always get a tree in which all values at the left of a node are less than or equal to the value in that node, and conversely the ones in the right subtree are greater than the value. This invariant is not present in the Haskell definition of SearchTree (which is just a copy of BinaryTree with renamed constructors), but we can make LiquidHaskell aware of it using an annotation.

```
data SearchTree a = EmptyS | NodeS a (SearchTree a) (SearchTree a)
                deriving (Show, Eq, Ord)

{-@ data SearchTree a = EmptyS
                    | NodeS { x:: a
                            , left  :: SearchTree {v: a | v <= x}
                            , right :: SearchTree {v: a | v >  x} }
@-}
```

To understand the annotation, it is important to realize that by writing SearchTree {v: a | predicate} we are refining the *elements* of that search tree, not the structure of the search tree itself. Here is an example of a function which does not obey the invariant: we create a node without checking that the elements in t1 are smaller than the value x, not t2 greater than x.

```
wrong :: a -> SearchTree a -> SearchTree a -> SearchTree a
wrong x t1 t2 = NodeS x t1 t2

error: Liquid Type Mismatch

   The inferred type
     VV : a

   is not a subtype of the equired type
     VV : {VV : a | VV <= x}

   in the Context
     x : a

 69 | wrong x t1 t2 = NodeS x t1 t2
                      ^^^^^^^^^^
```

As a final example, we can copy treeInsert and make it work on our new SearchTree type. The previous properties based on size and element were enough to detect some errors, but not to find this bug in which x and y are mixed:

```
treeInsertS :: Ord a => a -> SearchTree a -> SearchTree a
treeInsertS x EmptyS = NodeS x EmptyS EmptyS
treeInsertS x (NodeS y l r)
  | x <= y    = NodeS x (treeInsertS y l) r
  | otherwise = NodeS y l (treeInsertS x r)
```

To check that you understand how LiquidHaskell works, Exercise 15-3 asks you to implement some more functions over trees.

EXERCISE 15-3. VERIFYING BINARY TREES

Try to write a merge function, on both binary trees and search trees. The signature for this function should be

```
mergeTree :: Tree a -> Tree a -> Tree a
```

This function should combine both trees into a single one with all the elements. Think about properties such as: how does the elements and size look like?

This was just a brief introduction to LiquidHaskell. Some details we have left without treatment are LiquidHaskell's ability to check termination (you never go into an infinite loop) and totality (you cover all possible cases) of your functions. Also, the properties we checked upon trees were quite simple, but there is much more you can do. One important subset is dependent properties, in which the refinement of an argument depends on the value of the previous one. Finally, LiquidHaskell gives you the power to not only automatically check for compliance with respect to a specification but also to prove manually properties about your program in an equational reasoning style.

Summary

The focus of this chapter was on tools that help with the testing and maintainability of Haskell code bases.

- *Haddock* is the preferred tool for associating pieces of documentation to Haskell declarations and creating beautiful visualizations for it.

- Cabal has support for including tests in packages. You learned how to declare a `test-suite` *stanza* and got familiar with several Haskell *test frameworks*: Tasty and Hspec.

- The *HUnit* library for unit testing was introduced.

- You read about the benefits of *randomized testing* and learned how to create these kinds of tests using the *QuickCheck* library.

- As a final touch, you saw examples of how to *formally verify* your code by annotating it and running it through LiquidHaskell.

CHAPTER 16

Architecting Your Application

In a programming book, you usually learn a new language via brief examples. Alas, real applications are usually much bigger than 10 or 20 lines and need further work in designing, maintaining, and refactoring their code. This chapter tries to bridge the gap between those two worlds by offering a set of guidelines. Of course, this advice is not carved in stone, but it can give you a good idea of how to use functional programming.

I've introduced many different tools for Haskell programming throughout the book: test frameworks, profiling tools, and so on. In this chapter, you'll see a summary of all of them and get some suggestions concerning other good programs that couldn't be covered in depth here.

Then I'll compare how design patterns are applied in object-oriented programming and how you can use them in the functional realm. As you'll see, the gap is not so wide, and many of the concepts translate into functional equivalents but with a different implementation.

One concept which is very specific of Haskell is that of monad. Although you can define them in any language, Haskell gives you libraries and notation to use them more succinctly. At the end of the chapter, I'll describe some design patterns related to monads and review the most commonly found ones.

Tools

During the course of this book, I have presented many tools. In this section, I will recap all of them and introduce some others. Because of a lack of space, I am not able to cover every possible tool, but all of them have good and complete documentation on the Internet.

© Alejandro Serrano Mena 2022
A. Serrano Mena, *Practical Haskell*, https://doi.org/10.1007/978-1-4842-8581-7_16

Project and Dependency Management

Cabal and *Stack* are the tools for managing projects in the Haskell world. As you have seen throughout the book, they share a declarative way to specify which kind of software artifacts should be built, the dependencies you need, and options for compilation. Each artifact is defined in a so-called *stanza*.

Most of the power of Haskell comes from the great repository of libraries called *Hackage*. This repository is managed by the Haskell community, which uploads its latest work to make it available to the outer world. Using the `cabal install` command, you can automatically get a copy of a package and compile it. For those cases in which stability is preferred over novelty, *Stackage* provides a curated subset of Hackage which is known to compile together.

Note   Pay attention to licensing when using code from repositories such as Hackage. Each Cabal file should list the license, so it's easy to check that a specific package license is suitable for your use case.

Code Style

You need to write code that satisfies the constraints of the compiler to produce some library or executable. However, code that is accepted may not necessarily be easily maintainable, or it may follow a pattern whose behavior is usually confusing for later readers.

One piece of advice I strongly suggest you follow is to always enable the `-Wall` flag of the compiler. Setting this flag causes the compiler not only to look for errors but also to issue *warnings* for your code. The *HLint* tool is also useful in generating warnings, helping you find poorly written sections of code that may prove troublesome later.

In many cases, you also want your code to follow some style guidelines, that is, a set of recommendations on indentation, newlines, whether to use anonymous functions or define them in `let` blocks, and so on. *Stylish Haskell* is a tool that can help you with guidelines. It reads your code and produces a new version following some configurable options. Furthermore, it's possible to integrate it into Visual Studio Code, Emacs, `vi`, and many other editors, so you can make it part of your daily development experience.

Documentation

In the previous chapter, I discussed the importance of good and up-to-date documentation. As you now know, *Haddock* is the recommended tool for maintaining that documentation. The main benefit of using Haddock is that the information about an element appears near the element itself. Haddock is also the tool used to produce the massive amount of help documents in Hackage. Finally, Haddock's output shows the documentation coverage, so you can quickly see whether you've forgotten to document any of the functions within your code.

Searching a large number of packages for functions and data types can be a time-consuming task. *Hoogle* was introduced earlier in the book as a way to search Haskell declarations not only by name or description but also by taking into account the types that are involved in a function's signature.

Test and Verification

One big part of Chapter 15 has been devoted to testing using *HUnit*, *QuickCheck*, and *SmallCheck*. I can't stress enough how important testing is for a successful development project. The great benefit of property-based testing tools, such as QuickCheck or SmallCheck, is that you indicate how your program should behave at a higher level. Then, it generates small unit tests for a variety of scenarios. In that way, the coverage is much higher than using traditional tools.

Type-level programming in Haskell opens the door to formally verifying some properties of your data types and algorithms directly inside the language. If this is not enough, you can complement strong types with refinement types as targeted by *LiquidHaskell*. While formal verification consumes more time than basic testing, it's the only technique that can guarantee a complete absence of bugs.

Benchmarking

Functional correctness is an important consideration for a piece of code. In many cases, though, an application should run with a certain performance. The *Criterion* tool helps you define test cases and get statistics on the time of execution. The tool runs the test enough times to make the computed time statistically significant and evaluates the result completely (in other cases, some part of the computation wouldn't be measured because of laziness).

Profiling

Chapter 5 introduced the *GHC profiler*, which allows you to gather information about the time and memory consumption of your applications. Because of the lazy nature of Haskell, memory profiling becomes much more important than in other languages. Used wisely, it can shorten the investigation process for performance problems and guide you toward those places you should spend more time optimizing.

The main disadvantage of the profiler is that it's not designed for applications with several threads, such as those you can write with the libraries presented in Chapter 8. For those cases, it's interesting to consider *ThreadScope*, a graphic tool for reading GHC event logs. These event logs include information about when different threads are created and terminated, along with the activity of each of them.

Coverage

When you design tests, it's important to ensure that every possible path of execution is covered. That is, make sure that you've covered all possible branches of conditionals, all possible patterns for a data type and match, and so on. The hpc tool, included with GHC, gathers important statistics about the code used in a certain execution. This information can be used to produce a report with the different kinds of coverage and the achieved percentage.

Remote Monitoring

In many cases, applications are not processes with a limited life but are server-like in nature. One example of this kind is web applications. The ekg package enables you to get statistics of the performance and behavior of an application while executing. In addition, it does so via a web interface, so its management is quite simple. When using ekg, you're not restricted to the information it gives by default; you can include your own counters. For example, for a web application you might be interested in knowing how many pages are served by the minute or how many database connections are kept open through time.

Design Patterns and Functional Programming

You may have heard that functional programming makes design patterns completely irrelevant. This is quite a strong statement. Of course, many of the object-oriented design patterns won't be directly applicable, because you're working in a different programming paradigm. But this doesn't mean that a software project developed using Haskell wouldn't need a careful analysis and design prior to the start of coding. Furthermore, common and reusable ways of solving problems (called *patterns*) also appear in functional code.

In many cases, the statement about design patterns being irrelevant refers to those design patterns I call *code templates*. Think of the Singleton[1] design pattern for keeping just one instance of a specific class in memory. When you need to apply it, you know exactly what to write, and it always looks the same. The code is just boilerplate; that's the reason why languages like Scala offer specific syntax just for this case. In those scenarios, a Haskell solution would usually abstract the pattern at a high level, usually in a type class or in a higher-order function.

In some other cases, the language features allow a specific pattern to integrate seamlessly into the language. One example is the Strategy design pattern. It's used to define a computation with some moving parts that depend on later considerations, such as changing the code that shows the total amount, depending on the currency you're using. In an object-oriented setting, you would define an abstract class or interface, and derived classes would have the code for each currency. Within Haskell, you would instead use a higher-order function, which takes as parameters all those parts of the computation that may change.

From a conceptual point of view, some patterns are still there. In any software system, whether it's developed in procedural, object-oriented, or functional style, you have the problem of incompatible interfaces between components. In the object-oriented world, you would define a common interface and create wrapper classes to access the functionality of each component (this is known as the Adapter pattern). In Haskell, you would use type classes instead and make each component an instance of that class. In that way, you have a common method to communicate with all of them. In this case, the problem (communicating with incompatible systems) and the idea of the solution (defining a common protocol and making the systems adapt to it) remain; the change is just in the implementation.

---

[1] In the following pages, I'll refer to several object-oriented design patterns covered in the book *Design Patterns: Elements of Reusable Object-Oriented Software*.

Inside the base libraries, you can find functors, foldables, applicatives, monads, and many other type classes, which are at a high level of abstraction. In those cases, applying a design pattern is equivalent to instantiating a type class. Some of these type classes actually make the pattern more general. An iterator in object-oriented languages only allows operating on values from the beginning to the end of a collection. But in Haskell you have a whole range of operations of collections: applying a function inside a container via `Functor`, applying a function repeatedly to obtain a result via `Foldable`, or iterating while maintaining the structure via `Traversable`.

You've seen that some patterns are subsumed by language features or higher-level abstraction. Of course, many others remain in their original incarnation. One example is the Pool design pattern, which provides a way to efficiently manage a set of resources. You can find many packages that use this pattern. One example is how the Persistent database access layer uses a pool to manage database connections.

Of course, some Haskell features, such as immutability of values, higher-order functions, and laziness, affect the way in which you design your application. Think of concurrency: in an imperative setting, you have to use locks, semaphores, or rendezvous mechanisms to control access to shared resources. In many cases, the reason why you need those low-level operations is the possibility of side effects in any part of the code. Haskell, on the other hand, provides clear separation between pure code and the possible side effects. Thus, you can use a more elegant solution to that problem. When dealing with concurrency in Haskell, you use Software Transactional Memory, which embodies the concept of transactions.

Finally, I would like to point out that the Haskell philosophy and features get on well with the iterative and agile development methodologies. Being able to test functions directly in the interpreter helps you to test your code as you write it. And with QuickCheck, you can generate many more tests than you would if you had to write all of them by hand. In addition to that, Haskell is amenable to refactoring. Higher-order functions allow you to get the skeleton of an algorithm and then obtain variants by function application, and strong types guarantee that your code doesn't change in unexpected ways.

Many other benefits of a language like Haskell, such as strong typing or strict separation between pure code and code with side effects, were already discussed in Chapter 1. In general, Haskell gives you another perspective on your software design, which will greatly benefit your daily programming.

Medium-Level Guidelines

In this section, I'm not going to mention micro-optimizations or code templates for Haskell code. Instead, I will introduce some general guidelines that will make your code much more readable and maintainable.

Use Higher-Order Combinators

Using functions such as `map`, `filter`, and `fold` will make the purpose of your code more apparent to a future reader of it. You saw in Chapters 3 and 14 how recursion over a data type can usually be turned into a series of calls to these functions, so you should keep its use to a minimum.

Refactor

In the previous section, I discussed how Haskell goes quite well with agile programming methodologies. The ability to pass functions as parameters can help you to build functions that encapsulate the common parts of many algorithms. Many classes of problems can be divided in a general skeleton and then instantiated to each case by introducing the small parts that are missing.

The benefits of higher-order refactoring are twofold. First, you reduce the amount of code you have to maintain, and thus you have fewer possibilities of introducing new bugs because your code will have been much better tested. Furthermore, when you abstract a common pattern in your code, the correctness or the corner cases of your approach become more obvious.

Use Type Classes Wisely

Type classes are a powerful tool for abstracting the common idioms of several data types. The Haskell libraries are full of type classes, and almost every important programming concept is implemented as a type class. Try to follow the steps of those libraries and implement your concepts as type classes.

At this point, I'll give you one word of warning: sometimes, type classes are overused, and the code becomes much more difficult to read. The resolution mechanism of type class instances happens in the compiler, and the specific instance being chosen may not be directly apparent. Thus, a more direct approach like abstract data types or higher-order functions may be desirable. In particular, be aware of these two scenarios:

1. If all your type classes have only one instance, it may be the case that you don't really need to abstract those specific concepts.

2. Don't directly map object-oriented classes or interfaces to type classes.

Enforce Invariants via the Type System

Chapter 13 discussed many ways in which you can enforce invariants in your values via strong types. Using those techniques in your code will benefit you in the short term because more errors will be caught by the compiler; you will also benefit in the long term because modifications that would break your invariants will be denied.

The type system can help you catch many errors even if you don't follow all these techniques. One good example is newtype. You can separate different concepts (such as money, a record identifier, or distance) even if they have the same computer representation (which in that case would be an integer).

Stay (As) Pure and Polymorphic (As Possible)

If you write your functions by separating side effects from the rest of your computation, you'll have a much easier time testing your code. One useful pattern is to create a core of pure functions that work on your core data types, apply a lot of QuickCheck tests and even formal verification, and build from there.

In case you need to work with monadic contexts, try to use monad classes (such as MonadState, MonadError, etc.) to specify exactly what functionality you need from a monad stack. The solution of specifying the complete monad stack you're using from the beginning is not maintainable because usually you need to add layers for extra functionality. Furthermore, keeping your code polymorphic will enable you to use it in different ways. For example, you may be interested in testing your Persistent code against a list instead of a database, something that would be possible if instead of SqlPersistT (the actual transformer) you specify PersistQuery (the monad class) in your signature.

The essence of this advice is that polymorphism opens the door to reusability. If instead of a function using a list of integers you write a function that works on any Traversable whose elements are Nums, you will be able to change both the representation of the container (tree instead of lists) and the type of number (Integers instead of Ints) without any further change.

Tip   You can find many more guidelines in the "Hoogle Overview" article by Neil Mitchell in issue 12 of *The Monad.Reader* (the community-managed Haskell magazine), as well as several talks and StackOverflow answers by Don Stewart.

Patterns with Monads

Almost any developer which comes to hear about Haskell also hears about monads. Although monads are a very general concept, which underlies ideas present in other languages such as list comprehensions, promises, or continue-if-not-null operators, Haskell is one of the few languages which makes this concept so central. In this last section of the book, we review and introduce many of the most common monads and discuss two design patterns related to them.

Summary of Monads

Table 16-1 shows the most important monad classes and which monads (shown in italics) or monad transformers (shown in regular face) are instances of each class, along with the most important operations that each class embodies. There are more monads explained in this table than there are throughout the entire book. In particular, two kinds of additions are found:

- In some cases, the specific monad has been introduced, but not the monad class that abstracts the pattern. This is the case of the Par monad, which implements the ParFuture and ParIVar type classes, or the MonadRandom class.

- Other monads are completely new, but I think they deserve to be listed. MonadSupply, which is used to having a source of new values (which you can use as unique identifiers, for example), fits in this case.

Table 16-1.   *Common and Useful Monad Classes*

Class	Available	Package	Description	Operations
	IdentityT	mtl	Function application: no extra effect	None
MonadPlus	MaybeT ListT	mtl mtl	Choice and failure	mzero: Represents failure mplus: Offers choice between two results guard: Checks a Boolean condition
MonadLogic	LogicT	logict	Backtracking and fair interleaving	interleave: Fair disjunction (>>-): Fair conjunction ifte: Conditional check with cut once: Commits to first answer and prunes
MonadZip	ListT	mtl	Parallel comprehension	mzip: Converts two lists into a list of pairs munzip: Converts a list of pairs into two lists
MonadReader	ReaderT r Monoid w => RWST r w s	mtl mtl	Adds a context with a read-only value	ask: Gets the value from the context local: Executes some computation with a new context
MonadWriter	Monoid w => WriterT w Monoid w => RWST r w s	mtl mtl	Produces a write-only output by appending several values	tell: Appends a new value listen: Obtains the output of a subcomputation

(continued)

Table 16-1. (*continued*)

Class	Available	Package	Description	Operations
MonadState	StateT s Monoid w => RWST r w s	mtl mtl	Keeps an internal state that can be both read and modified	get: Obtains the current value of state put: Gives a new value to the state modify: Applies a function to the state
	ST	base	Restricted mutable variables	Creation and modification of IORef values
MonadSupply	Monoid s => SupplyT s	monad- supply	Consumes values from a supply	supply: Gets the next value
MonadError	*IO* MaybeT ExcepT e	base mtl mtl	Failure with some extra information: depending on the monad, the failure is represented as pure errors or as extensible exceptions	throwError: Signals failure catchError: Recovers from error
MonadCatch	*IO* CatchT == ExceptT SomeException	base exceptions	Throwing and catching extensible exceptions	throwM: Throws an exception catch, handle: Recover from one exception type catches, handles: Recover from several exception types bracket: Resource acquisition and disposal

(*continued*)

Table 16-1. (*continued*)

Class	Available	Package	Description	Operations
MonadIO	*IO* *ParIO*	base monad-par	Performs unrestricted side effects, such as reading and writing files or communicating through network	liftIO: Moves a computation in the IO monad into the current monad stack
MonadRandom	*IO* RandT	base MonadRandom	Generates random values	getRandom, randomIO: Get unbounded random value getRandomR, randomRIO: Random value within bounds
ParFuture	*Par* *ParIO*	monad-par	Parallelism based on promises	spawn, spawnP: Asynchronously execute a function and return an IVar that will give its result get: Obtains the result inside an IVar, blocking if needed
ParIVar	*Par* *ParIO*	monad-par	Dataflow parallelism, where dependencies are given via IVars	fork: Starts a computation in parallel new: Creates a new IVar for holding a value put: Writes a value inside an IVar

(continued)

Table 16-1. (*continued*)

Class	Available	Package	Description	Operations
	Eval	`parallel`	Deterministic parallelism based on strategies for evaluating lazy types	`rseq, rdeepseq`: Evaluate its argument sequentially `rpar`: Evaluates its argument in parallel
	STM	`stm`	Atomic transactions	`atomically`: Executes a transaction in an atomic way `retry`: Rolls back the current transaction and tries to execute it again when the circumstances had changed `orElse`: Executes a transaction in some other fails Creation and modification of TVars, TQueues, and others
MonadResource	ResourceT	`resourcet`	Safe allocation and release of resources	`allocate`: Performs some resource acquisition and registers the action needed for releasing at the end `release`: Deallocates a resource prematurely

(*continued*)

Table 16-1. (*continued*)

Class	Available	Package	Description	Operations
	`ConduitT i o`	`conduit`	Streaming data	`await`: Consumes the next element from the input stream `leftover`: Puts back an element in the input stream `yield`: Generates an element in the output stream
	Parser	`attoparsec`	Matches a list of characters against a predefined pattern	`Parser` more often used via its `Applicative` interface
`PersistStore`	`SqlPersistT`	`persistent`	Obtains and manages records in a database using its key	`get`: Obtains the record with a given key `insert`: Creates a new record in the database `repsert`: Replaces a record with new information or creates a new one if that key didn't exist `delete`: Deletes a record with a given key

(continued)

Table 16-1. (*continued*)

Class	Available	Package	Description	Operations
PersistUnique			Obtains and manages records in a database using unique constraints	getBy: Obtains the record with a given unique constraint insertUnique: Inserts checking uniqueness constraints deleteBy: Deletes the record with a given constraint
PersistQuery			Obtains and manages records in a database via queries	selectSource, selectList: Obtain the record that satisfies a given set of conditions update: Modifies information of a given record updateWhere: Modifies all records from a query deleteWhere: Deletes all records from a query
MonadCont	ContT	mtl	Computations that can be interrupted and resumed	callCC: Calls a function with its current continuation
MonadFree	FreeT f	free	Free monad over a functor	
MonadTrans	All monad transformers	mtl	Type class that all monad transformers instantiate	lift: Moves a computation one layer up in the stack

Restrictive Monad Classes

Looking at the previous table, you may notice that some monads provide a very restricted set of operations – for example, ReaderT just offers the ability to obtain a single value – while others open the door to many different effects; think of IO or the monads from the persistent package. The latter case goes at odds with Haskell's philosophy of making types describe your functions: if your signature mentions IO, nothing really could be said about its behavior. Here, I describe a small pattern to restrict the operations while keeping a good performance.

To understand this pattern, we need to look back at the monad classes introduced in Chapter 7. At that point, the problem was different: we had just introduced monad transformers, and we wanted to have a common interface for any stack which contained a given layer, regardless of where that layer was found. That is, we wanted to keep using the ask function for any stack which contained a ReaderT transformer.

Imagine now that we want to use file operations in a function. If we throw an IO monad in the signature, we could also do network operations or create threads. Or even worse, if we want to write a combinator – a function which takes another as parameter – and we allow IO there, we can never be sure about what that function will do. This is the perfect scenario to restrict the set of operations allowed by IO to the file system subset.

The solution is to introduce a new *monad class* with only the desired set of operations. In this case, let's call that monad MonadFS, to follow the convention from the mtl package:

```
class Monad m => MonadFS m where
  readFile  :: FilePath -> m ByteString
  writeFile :: FilePath -> ByteString -> m ()
```

Now you can guarantee that a function only uses those operations, and not any from IO, by requiring a MonadFS constructor. For example:

```
copyFile :: MonadFS m => FilePath -> FilePath -> m ()
copyFile inFile outFile = do contents <- readFile inFile
                             writeFile outFile contents
```

Being able to specify very tightly the requirements of copyFile is great, but quite useless if you cannot execute the code. The trick is to create an instance of the restrictive monad class for the monad you wanted to restrict. In this case, this boils down to a MonadFS instance for IO:

```
instance MonadFS IO where ...
```

The consequence is that now you can use `copyFile` anywhere a function which operates on `IO` is expected. Furthermore, the cost of this abstraction is almost negligible, since GHC specializes functions like `copyFile` when they are used with a single type class.

Roll Your Own Monad

Monads appear everywhere in Haskell code. The special `do` notation provides a convenient syntax for sequencing and composing actions, and there are many libraries and functions operating on monadic code. Thus, writing a monad appears as an obvious choice for developing a domain-specific language for your actions.

In Hackage, there are several packages that ease the creation of those monads, like `operational` or `free`. The latter will be focused on in this section. In any case, all these packages encompass a similar abstraction, which is the "sequence of actions": each monadic value is a list of primitive operations. To create the full monad, you need to provide two sets of data:

1. The primitive operations that you may take and the building blocks of your monad

2. How each operation affects the related context and which value provides to the next computation in the list

As a running example, let's consider a small DSL that allows you to manage a database of clients. The basic operations will be adding a new client, querying the client by its identifier, and replacing the information about a client. So, in some sense, it's a restricted version of Persistent. The data types used to define `Clients` are as follows:

```
newtype ClientId = ClientId Integer            deriving Show
data Client = Client { clientName :: String } deriving Show
```

When using the `free` package, each operation is encoded as a constructor in a regular data type. This is called the *syntax* of the monad. For each operation, you need to first write the parameters to the operation in question. For example, writing a new client in the database takes that client as the parameter. Then, you need to define how the result of the operation gets threaded to the next step in the computation. This is done by requiring a function from the result type to a yet-unknown data type that will refer to a list of computations. In the example of new clients, the result is a ClientId, which must be threaded to the next computation, r. The code for all operations reads as follows:

```
data AdminOp r = GetClient  ClientId          (Client   -> r)
               | SaveClient ClientId Client r
               | NewClient  Client            (ClientId -> r)
```

Notice that the SaveClient operation doesn't return any value, so the next operation doesn't take any parameter. Thus, you only need to specify r in the data constructor.

The free package mandates that every operation data type follows this schema and that the type is an instance of Functor. The good news is that once again you can use the deriving functionality in GHC and automatically generate such an instance. It now reads as follows:

```
{-# LANGUAGE DeriveFunctor #-}
data AdminOp r = ...
               deriving Functor
```

Your monad will now be the *free monad* over that Functor in question. You could refer each time to the Free type parametrized by your operations, but usually you define a type synonym, as follows:

```
import Control.Monad.Free
type Admin = Free AdminOp
```

Still, you cannot use your data type directly inside a do block. You first need to lift your operations to the free monad. For this matter, you should use the liftF function from Control.Monad.Free. The only item left is what to provide as the last parameter in each operation. As a rule of thumb, you should provide id if the next list of operation must be given a parameter and provide () elsewhere. In this case, it means the following:

```
getClient :: ClientId -> Admin Client
getClient i = liftF $ GetClient i id
saveClient :: ClientId -> Client -> Admin ()
saveClient i c = liftF $ SaveClient i c ()
newClient :: Client -> Admin ClientId
newClient c = liftF $ NewClient c id
```

Finally, you have a monad! It can even be used within the do notation.

```
import Data.Char
exampleAdmin :: String -> Admin String
exampleAdmin s = do i <- newClient $ Client s
                    n <- fmap clientName $ getClient i
                    return $ map toUpper n
```

However, exampleAdmin won't have any effect by itself. At this point, this is only a description of the computation that should happen. The free package represents the list of operations using two constructors: one operation followed by a list of other operations uses Free, whereas the end of a computation is marked using Pure. This means that the previous example is equivalent to writing this:

```
Free (NewClient (Client s) (\i ->
  Free (fmap clientName (GetClient i (\n ->
    Pure $ map toUpper n)))))
```

The final step is giving an *interpretation* of each operation. The following example interprets the operations as working on an association list of identifiers and clients. As you can see, the interface is like other run functions on other monads.

```
import Data.List
runAdmin :: Admin a -> ([(Integer,Client)],a)
runAdmin m = runAdmin' m []
  where runAdmin' (Free (GetClient  (ClientId i) n))   l =
          let Just c = lookup i l in runAdmin' (n c) l
        runAdmin' (Free (SaveClient (ClientId i) c n)) l =
          let l' = deleteBy (\(j,_) (k,_) -> j == k) (i, c) l
            in runAdmin' n $ (i,c):l'
        runAdmin' (Free (NewClient c n)) [] =
          runAdmin' (n $ ClientId 1) [(1,c)]
        runAdmin' (Free (NewClient c n)) l =
          let (i',_) = maximumBy (\(j,_) (k,_) -> compare j k) l
            in runAdmin' (n $ ClientId (i' + 1)) $ (i' + 1,c):l
        runAdmin' (Pure c)                      l = (l, c)
```

In this case, this interpretation could be used for testing purposes, and another interpretation would provide real access to a database. You may check that your monad indeed works on the interpreter.

```
*Chapter16.FreeMonads> runAdmin $ exampleAdmin "Alejandro"
([(1,Client {clientName = "Alejandro"})], "ALEJANDRO")
```

The `free` package provides many more features for rolling your own monads. For example, you may decide to create a monad transformer instead of a plain monad, just by using `FreeT` instead of `Free`. If your application will revolve around a custom monad, it's useful to read the documentation of the `Control.Monad.Free.Church` module, which can enhance the performance in the long term. Finally, `free` provides not only free monads but also free `Applicatives`, `Alternatives`, and `MonadPlus`.

Summary

In this chapter, you got a bird's-eye view of design using Haskell and functional patterns.

- I walked you through many of the tools that the Haskell Platform and Hackage provide for documentation, testing, profiling, and project management.

- I discussed the relation between functional design and more traditional object-oriented patterns. Some patterns are kept, others change the way in which they are implemented, and still others are not needed anymore.

- I explained some specific design patterns related to monads. You can find a summary of useful monad classes in Table 16-1. Furthermore, you have learned how to restrict monads using type classes and how to roll your own monad.

CHAPTER 17

Looking Further

Congratulations for arriving at this point. Thus far in the book, you've learned many of the features that Haskell provides in terms of language and libraries. The notions of functor, monad, and GADT should not be alien to you anymore. You've also seen how to design large applications in Haskell and how to manage databases and web applications. And above all, you've seen how a strong type system encourages a more systematic way of writing software and helps in reducing time spent in coding and maintenance.

As with any other language, a book cannot contain every single use of Haskell. Hackage and Stackage provide an enormous amount of functionality already packaged and should be your entry point for discovering the vast field of Haskell libraries. The book has just skimmed the surface of parallel and concurrent code libraries or web frameworks, to mention two examples of places where you may deepen your knowledge.

The Haskell language also has more surprises built into its compiler. In the previous chapter, I mentioned data type generic programming, and along with type-level programming, it can reduce even more boilerplate code for validation while increasing safety. The metaprogramming facility Template Haskell has been used extensively in the book, but how to create your own quasiquoters is beyond the scope of the book. Another place where you may expect new techniques to appear is in kind-level programming.

In conclusion, I hope this book doesn't put an end to your journey in Haskell and functional programming but encourages you to use this language in your daily or hobby projects and to look at many of the available resources that are online. Thanks for reading!

Projects

In the previous chapter, I have discussed application and library design in Haskell. In this section, I'll describe some projects to put that advice in practice, along with the design considerations you might look at. From those considerations, you can infer patterns to apply in your own designs.

© Alejandro Serrano Mena 2022
A. Serrano Mena, *Practical Haskell*, https://doi.org/10.1007/978-1-4842-8581-7_17

In addition, you can see these projects as extra, more comprehensive exercises for practicing your Haskell skills. In each of these cases, the solution is more open-ended than for the tasks suggested in the rest of the book. One hint for all the cases is to search libraries in Hackage or Stackage that may help solve the problem at hand.

Data Mining Library

Part 2 of the book was devoted to developing two data mining algorithms: K-means for clustering and Apriori for association rule learning. This first project entails turning the code you already have into a full-fledged data mining library, with support for different algorithms for each problem.

Even if you consider only one problem, such as clustering, it's interesting to look at the *commonalities* of each algorithm solving that task. For example, data can come from different sources (a list, a conduit source, a database query), but you should provide a common interface to all of them to make the algorithms independent of that choice. In Haskell, this level of abstraction is obtained via *type classes*. Here, you may create a `ClusteringDataSource` one.

A good library includes not only data types, functions, and type classes but also an exploration of the laws and properties that the user should count on. For data types, it's useful to consider whether a given type is an instance of one of the common abstractions in the Haskell Platform. Here are some examples:

- Many data types are composed in a way that allows you to generate a new value from the other two. The `Monoid` type class handles this case. Making your type a monoid can guide you into thinking whether a neutral element would be useful in your case.

- Other types fit more into the container-like intuition. In those cases, try to instantiate the `Functor`, `Foldable`, and `Traversable` type classes.

- Those data types that entail some kind of computational context, or in some way a description of a set of actions to take, fit well into the `Applicative` and `Monad` abstractions. Additionally, if your type allows choice, `Alternative` and `MonadPlus` may help.

Figure 17-1 shows most of these type classes, along with their parent-child relation. `Alternative` is not nominally a superclass of `MonadPlus` (it does not appear in its declaration), but this is more of a historical accident than an explicit design choice in the base libraries.

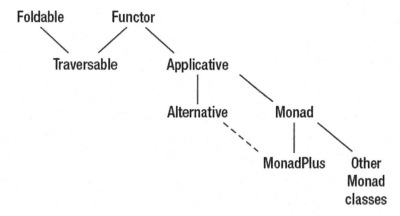

Figure 17-1. *Important type classes in the Haskell Platform*

When writing instances of these well-known abstractions, you should abide by the rules they come with, even though those rules are not checked by the compiler. Users of your library would be surprised to find an instance of `Functor` that doesn't satisfy that `fmap id = id`, for example. The general guideline is the *no-surprises rule*, sometimes referred to as the *principle of least astonishment*: make your library do what users expect from it or otherwise document the behavior prominently. For help in ensuring that rules are always kept correct, you may use formal verification or QuickCheck.

One extra consideration you should make is for performance. Be aware that your previous ideas about code optimization may not be useful in Haskell, where code is evaluated lazily. I've already discussed the GHC profiler and the Criterion package, which are valuable in spotting performance deficiencies and finding the cause. If you're interested in complexity analysis of Haskell code, you should read the book *Purely Functional Data Structures* by Chris Okasaki (Cambridge University Press, 1999).

WRITE APPLICATIONS AS LIBRARIES

Your software design can greatly benefit from thinking of your application as a core library that is later consumed by a front-end application. Cabal embodies this strategy by allowing a stanza for the library part and referring to it in an executable.

The reason for this advice is this: knowing that another developer may consume your code, one is usually more careful when refining the abstractions that will be exposed. Also, it makes it easier to refactor and reuse the core parts of your project, instead of entangling them with the interaction-specific code.

Store Network Client

In the Store internal network, you need to create a server and clients that can be used by workers. This kind of application uses a variety of functionality: keeping an internal consistent state, communicating through a network, logging problematic scenarios, and so on. As you saw in Chapter 7, such functionality is a perfect task for a monad stack, which brings together the features you need from different pieces. In this case, a possible choice of monad transformers may be as follows:

- IO and ConduitM for managing the network connections, or Process if you prefer to use the actor model.

- SqlPersistT for database access, via the Persistent network.

- STM can be used to keep the internal state consistent against concurrent modifications. If you follow the actor model, a simpler StateT transformer can keep the state.

- ReaderT could keep track of different configuration options, like the port you're using for communication or the database connection options.

- The logging functionality can be implemented via WriterT.

However, you shouldn't just create a big monad stack and pass it everywhere. As discussed earlier, you should try to keep your code as polymorphic as possible. If instead of ReaderT r (SqlPersistT IO) you program against MonadReader, you can grow or shrink your monad stack at will during the development of your application. It is not uncommon for you to decide to add a new layer during the development of the application. One function that queries the database and logs some information should have a signature like this:

```
getClientInformation :: (PersistQuery m, MonadWriter String m)
                     => ClientId -> m [Client]
```

instead of the more specific one shown here:

```
getClientInformation :: ClientId -> WriterT String (SqlPersistM [Client])
```

Developing against monad classes also helps in separating the different concerns of your application. In this sense, monad classes resemble *aspect-oriented programming*, where you define each part of your application dealing with some different feature separately and then mix them together. The signature, via the list of monad classes needed to implement some function, defines exactly which functionality is needed from the context. Giving a specific incarnation via a monad stack is the equivalent of choosing the implementation.

Administration Interface and Tetris

An administration interface for the Store is a way to manage products and stock in the system and to modify and decline purchases from clients. Tetris, on the other hand, is the perfect game for entertaining time travelers while the time machines operate their magic. What those two applications have in common is that the set of actions you can perform on them are limited. In the administration interface, you can access only certain functionality depending on your security level; in Tetris, you can move the current piece in only three directions or rotate it.

In different parts of the book, I have discussed how a domain-specific language (DSL) can help you constrain the value that can be represented by a data type. In that case, the aim was to restrict the data that can be expressed and processed by the application. But you can follow the same idea and create a *domain-specific language* for the *actions* that your application is able to take. There are several examples of this pattern: Esqueleto embodies a SQL-like language for expressing database queries, `attoparsec` has a language based on the Applicative interface for describing parsers, and Spock uses its own DSL to specify routes in your web application. The DSL approach has two main advantages:

1. It restricts what you can do in a certain context. It's not the same to have a signature using the IO type, which may use unrestricted side effects, as it is to have a specific monad for your application that allows only network and database connections. The type system can be used to ensure many more invariants.

2. If you use a deep embedding for your actions, you can provide several interpretations for the same DSL. This can be useful in testing. For example, if your DSL is used for network communication, you can provide an interpretation that fakes a network conversation between two peers.

Within Haskell libraries and applications, you can find two different ways in which domain-specific languages for actions are implemented. You have seen examples of both throughout the book.

1. One possibility is developing a *combinator library*. In this case, you specify a set of basic constructs and a series of functions that combines those basic blocks. This is the approach taken by the `attoparsec` library for building parsers.

2. The other option is *rolling your own monad*, as described in the previous chapter. A successful example of building an application around a monad is XMonad, a window manager written in Haskell; but you can also find this pattern in Spock, which defines the `ActionT` monad transformer, and Esqueleto, where queries are expressed as values of the `SqlQuery` monad.

One important consideration is whether you need to inspect the structure of your computation before executing it. For example, you might want to perform optimizations in the monadic code. In that case, rolling your own monad in the form of a free or operational monad usually gives you more hooks to perform that work, in comparison to combinator libraries.

Additional Haskell Resources

Haskell has an active community on the Internet, as the enormous database of packages and the level of activity in forums and mailing lists acknowledges. The places where you can look for more information include the following:

- Haskell's main page, at `www.haskell.org`, contains pointers to many tutorials and resources. It's built as a wiki, and its users are always adding new information that may be interesting for Haskell developers.

- *The Monad.Reader* was a regular magazine with articles practical or enlightening to developers. Unfortunately, there are no new issues since 2015, but you can still check all the published issues at `themonadreader.wordpress.com`.

- If you want to look at examples of elegant and instructive functional code, you should look at the *"Functional Pearls"* section on Haskell's wiki, at `wiki.haskell.org/Research_papers/Functional_pearls`.

- To stay tuned with the latest news of Haskell, GHC, and Hackage, you can subscribe to the Planet Haskell feed aggregator at `planet.haskell.org`. You'll see that there are quite a number of bloggers speaking about Haskell.

- Another way to keep yourself updated is the Haskell subreddit at `www.reddit.com/r/haskell/`. Reddit allows you to comment about articles; many interesting discussions start in this way.

- The Haskell community maintains a mailing list called Café, at `mail.haskell.org/mailman/listinfo/haskell-cafe`, which is a space where many discussions about the language and libraries take place. If you look at the archives, you'll notice that the list welcomes both newcomers and experienced developers. If you have a question, just ask, and you'll get a gentle response.

- There is another mailing list more focused on beginners at `mail.haskell.org/mailman/listinfo/beginners`.

- If you prefer more direct communication, you can use IRC. The `#haskell` channel at `irc.freenode.net` is usually filled with people talking about the language.

Other Functional Languages

Most of the concepts and ideas in this book are applicable to many other programming languages. One of the closest set of languages is the ML family, which includes OCaml and F# (this language integrates into Microsoft's .NET Framework, allowing easy interoperability with software written in C#). The main difference with Haskell is the use of strictness instead of laziness. Languages from the Lisp family, like Racket or Clojure, also embody functional concepts. Some languages mix functional concepts with other paradigms. One interesting example is Scala, which puts under the same umbrella functional and object-oriented programming inside the Java platform. Newer languages, such as Swift (for the iOS platform) and Kotlin (for the Java platform), also embody many functional ideas.

In this book, I've mentioned several places where Haskell abstractions are directly applicable in other languages. The monad concept lies behind the LINQ libraries in C#, the for expressions in Scala, and the computation expressions in F#. Libraries for Software Transactional Memory have been put into many other languages. Parser combinators are becoming increasingly used for treating text data. As you can see, the intuition gained from working on Haskell can be reused in many other scenarios.

FUNCTIONAL LIBRARIES IN OTHER LANGUAGES

Not many languages are so focused on functional programming as Haskell is. For that reason, their base libraries may lack some types and functions that you take for granted in Haskell. Fortunately, there are many open source libraries filling those gaps:

- Scalaz and Cats (typelevel.org) are two ecosystems for functional and category theory–oriented programming in Scala. Both define monoids, functors, monads, and many other type classes (traits in Scala's lingo).

- Arrow (arrow-kt.io) describes itself as a "functional companion to Kotlin's standard library." Bow (bow-swift.io) is a similar library but for Swift.

Time Travelling with Haskell

Now that you've come to this point, it's time to tell you one secret that only Haskellers are allowed to know: our code can travel in time! To do so, you need to kindly ask the Doctor[1] for his TARDIS Time Machine. Gratefully, the machine has a Haskell form: it can be converted into a monad.

The `Tardis` monad is provided by the `tardis` package in Hackage. The interface is similar to a `State` monad, but you can work with state that travels in the normal way, from the current step of execution forward in time, and with state that works backward in time. For each of those states you have a pair of functions.

- You move the state forward in time by updating it using `sendFuture`, and you are able to get it at other point in the execution via `getPast`.

- The state that travels backward is updated via `sendPast` and obtained via `getFuture`.

In both cases, it's important to understand that you can obtain only the last version of each state. For example, if you call `sendFuture` twice, any call to `getPast` will retrieve the second version of `sendFuture`.

It's time to play the trick. Let's code a function that, given a list of numbers, builds a new list of tuples, with each tuple showing the current sum up to that point from the beginning of the list, and the same but from the end of the list. You can see the result as two states traveling in opposite directions in time: the sum from the beginning goes forward, and the sum from the end travels backward. Figure A-1 shows this graphically.

---

[1] The Doctor is the name of the main character of the BBC series *Doctor Who*, a Time Lord who travels space and time in his Time And Relative Dimension In Space (TARDIS) machine.

© Alejandro Serrano Mena 2022
A. Serrano Mena, *Practical Haskell*, https://doi.org/10.1007/978-1-4842-8581-7

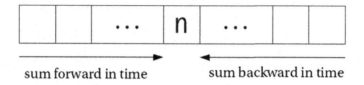

sum forward in time   sum backward in time

Figure A-1. *Forward and backward states in Tardis*

The corresponding Haskell code follows:

```haskell
{-# LANGUAGE RecursiveDo #-}

import Control.Monad.Tardis

sumListTardis :: [Int] -> [(Int,Int)]
sumListTardis lst = evalTardis (sumListTardis' lst) (0, 0)

sumListTardis' :: [Int] -> Tardis Int Int [(Int,Int)]
sumListTardis' (x:xs) = do
  sumFw <- getPast
  let newFw = sumFw + x
  sendFuture $ newFw
  rec let newBw = sumBw + x
      sendPast $ newBw
      sumBw <- getFuture
  rest <- sumListTardis' xs
  return $ (newFw, newBw):rest
sumListTardis' [] = return []
```

The forward state handling is straightforward. At each step, you just take the previous state from the past and send to the future a new value that sums the current number to the forward state.

The backward state is much more mysterious. As you can see, the information is sent to the past and then brought from the future. This way of working is needed because if you first send to the past and then try to bring from the future, you would try to get the value of the last call to getPast, which is the present moment. This is impossible because the state would depend on itself in a direct way. Instead, the code asks to create a *recursive* do block, which starts with the rec keyword and allows you to refer to a later value.

Note   Not all monads support the rec keyword. To use it, the monad you're working on must be an instance of the MonadFix type class.

You can run the Tardis over some list and check that everything works:

```
*> sumListTardis [1,2,3,4]
[(1,10),(3,9),(6,7),(10,4)]
```

While Tardis seems like very weird stuff, with no real applications, there are cases in real life where a computation receives feedback from itself. The archetypical example is in circuits, where an output cable may be connected to an input port again. As in the previous case, in circuits you need to be careful not to create a dependence of a value on itself; you usually add some delay to make the input depend on the output in some previous moment. Another example is bowling, where the points scored after a strike or spare depends on the score in later rounds.[2]

If only you had known that you could travel into the future! Instead of moving step-by-step through examples and exercises, you could have traveled and asked your future self to give you all your Haskell knowledge. But such is the mystery of laziness, of type classes, and of higher-order functions. It's now time to have fun and explore the rest of the Haskell universe!

---

[2] You can read more about bowling and Tardis in an article by Dan Burton, available at http://unknownparallel.wordpress.com/2012/11/05/bowling-on-a-tardis/.

Index

A

Abstraction layers, 380–381

ActionT monad, 570

Actual integer value, 354

Ad hoc polymorphism
    built-in type classes, 135–140
    declaring classes and
        instances, 130–135

Administration interface, 569–570

Aggregation, 83, 86, 185, 201, 202, 239

Aggregation function, 85

Aggregation operator, 86, 404

Algebraic data types (ADTs), 15, 39–43, 61,
    66, 78, 80, 321, 420, 449

Alternative type class, 366–367

AMQP, 271
    in Haskell, 293–297
    message queues, 291–293

amqp-worker, 271, 293, 295–297

Anamorphism, 512

Anonymous functions, 70–73, 106, 212,
    258, 546

app function, 416, 418

Applicative type class, 211, 361–370, 373, 378

Apriori algorithm, 229, 235,
    241–246, 277–279

Arbitrary function, 534

Arrow syntax, 16

Artificial intelligence, 186

AspectAG, 487

Aspect-oriented programming, 569

Associated values, 119, 121, 396

Association rules, 186, 229, 237, 238, 241,
    243, 245, 246, 566

Association rules learning
    apriori algorithm, 241–246
    flattening values into
        transactions, 238–240
    items and rules, 238
    transactions, 237

Associative binary operation, 146

Atomic transactions, 270, 283–287

Attoparsec library, 343, 353–360, 365, 373,
    441, 558, 569, 570

attr keyword, 488, 498

Attributes
    chained, 505
    executing, 492–493
    expression, 485
    grammar system, 486
    higher-level model, 484
    inh and syn, 505
    integrating UUAGC, 490–492
    modularity, 485
    synthesizing, 488–490
    top-down, 485
    tree and, 485
    usage, 494–497

Authentication system, 325

AvlTree, 124

A. Serrano Mena, *Practical Haskell*, https://doi.org/10.1007/978-1-4842-8581-7

B

C

E

G

H

T

Printed in the United States
by Baker & Taylor Publisher Services